MW01421095

Hidden Interests
in Credit and Finance

Hidden Interests in Credit and Finance

Power, Ethics, and Social Capital across the Last Millennium

James B. Greenberg and Thomas K. Park

LEXINGTON BOOKS
Lanham • Boulder • New York • London

Cover image: St. Peter holding the keys to heaven and the rock (Peter) on which the Church was metaphorically built, late fifteenth century. Wood.

Published by Lexington Books
An imprint of The Rowman & Littlefield Publishing Group, Inc.
4501 Forbes Boulevard, Suite 200, Lanham, Maryland 20706
www.rowman.com

Unit A, Whitacre Mews, 26-34 Stannary Street, London SE11 4AB

Copyright © 2017 by Lexington Books

All rights reserved. No part of this book may be reproduced in any form or by any electronic or mechanical means, including information storage and retrieval systems, without written permission from the publisher, except by a reviewer who may quote passages in a review.

British Library Cataloguing in Publication Information Available

Library of Congress Cataloging-in-Publication Data

Includes bibliographic references and index.
ISBN: 978-1-4985-4578-5 (cloth : alk. paper)
ISBN: 978-1-4985-4579-2 (electronic)

∞™ The paper used in this publication meets the minimum requirements of American National Standard for Information Sciences—Permanence of Paper for Printed Library Materials, ANSI/NISO Z39.48-1992.

Printed in the United States of America

Contents

Introduction		vii
1	Finance in the Middle Ages and the Scholastic Tradition	1
2	Credit and Faith in Medieval Iberia: The Road Not Taken	27
3	Early European Finance 1050–1650	57
4	Transcending Feudal Finance in Western Europe	83
5	Mercantile Credit and the Atlantic Slave Trade	115
6	Chayanov, Marx, and Hidden Interests in Rural Morocco	145
7	Ethnicity and Social Capital in 1970s Sefrou	167
8	Problematizing Modern Consumer Credit	189
9	An Anthropology of the 2008 Credit Crisis	213
Conclusion: Hidden Interests and the Development of Finance		241
References		265
Index		285
About the Author		313

Introduction

In an earlier book, *The Roots of Western Finance*,[1] we followed the evolution of five core aspects of finance: the technical components of the activities financed, the multidimensional milieux in which financial activities took place, the parties to financial ventures, the ways in which differential advantage was attained in credit transactions, and the purposes to which finance was harnessed. Our story began in Mesopotamia in the fourth millennium BC, and in due course examined finance in dynastic Egypt, the Republic of Rome, Attic Greece, the Judeo-Christian tradition, and the Islamic world to 1100 AD.

We saw slow development of more equitable financial instruments balancing profit, liability and risk in Mesopotamia, then the gradual application of more sophisticated ethical principles to finance: in Egypt, investment in the gods and the afterlife, charity for the poor, truth and fairness in legal justice, and faith in the judgment of the gods; in Athens, virtue, character (*ēthikē*), service to others (charis), and friendship (philia); and in the Roman Republic, honor (*benignitas*) trust (*fides*), generosity (*liberalitas*), *benignitas*, benevolence (*beneuolentia*), and gratefulness (*gratia*). The early Judeo-Christian tradition focused, along with the promotion of core virtues such as charity and justice, on a critique of exploitation in lending (viewed as usury) and ethical attention to the purpose to which loans were put, but it was the Islamic tradition that most explicitly tackled justice in lending by insisting on transparency about the contributions of each party to a contract as well as attention to a just division of profit, liability, and risk among the parties.

While there are a plethora of reasons, a *conjoncture* if ever there was one, why industrial capitalism developed where and when it did, the financial apparatus fundamental to its development has, as we have argued, much greater historical and multicultural depth than is generally appreciated. What makes the capitalist economy distinctive is the gradual transformation of the price structure for key factors of production (e.g., land, labor, and capital) from prices largely tied to institutionalized inequalities into prices that more accurately reflect their productive value. Although Marx famously declared, "Accumulate, accumulate! This is the sacred law of the capitalist economy." Braudel argued, "one could just as well say the sacred law is 'Borrow, borrow!'"[2]

As we will see in the following chapters, this financial turn transformed competition into a force that stimulates production in a much more direct way. Where modern economies do resemble earlier economies is that there remain age-old benefits from business trust and institutionalized justice in lending. Transparency in lending, despite not being particularly emphasized in Western finance has long since motivated the assessment of liability, profit, and risk over the expected time frame of the loan and such assessments have also generally recognized the significance of trust and honor in business. Given that both trust and honor are relative, social networking and the establishment of trustworthiness has been a key to profitability recognized since ancient times.

Jack Goody, observed, "What is common among most western historians, including those like Weber and Braudel who study the problem comparatively, is that even after considering data from different societies, all end up where they started, seeing Europe as the 'real' home of capitalism."[3] In our view, a financial history should recognize both continuity and change and Goody's insights into the deep roots of the "Western" financial system are correct. The present economy depends as much on social capital or networking and justice in lending as did earlier economies because humans remain social beings. Yet, transformations in system variables introduce, over time, new factors affecting the financial sector and its governance. As Foucault once said in response to the question of whether the present should be seen as a rupture with the past, "No it is a day like any other, or rather it is a day which is never quite like the others."[4] Part of our misunderstanding of the past is due to misunderstanding of the present though this is only half of the problem. Memory is selective and tends to serve particular interests in the present even though richer historical insight enables a better understanding of reality.

In this book, we will focus on countries around the Mediterranean beginning in the eleventh century as merchants outside of Iberia once again began to flourish on the northern coast. Major fairs across Europe gradually give way to finance centered in urban areas. A more complete European financial history than we can provide, would incorporate much more detail on geopolitical processes, but the reader can easily consult the many historical works documenting national, political, and economic transformations, the gradual domination of Mediterranean shipping by Christians, and the rise of global commerce.

We do feel an obligation to look at the imbrication of merchant power and Vatican corruption in the rehabilitation of "interest,"[5] and the myriad complexities of local political and economic processes that provided *fora* for the exercise of financial expertise. It has long been noted that the great European fairs of Champagne, Besançon, and Lyon, and later bourses of Antwerp, Amsterdam, and London became incubators for financial expertise and the exemplars of a modern market in formation but they owed their existence quite obviously to the conjuncture of many other processes as well.

Much has been written about these late appearing concentrators of exchange but their main innovations can be easily summarized. By virtue of concentrating commerce or finance in one place throughout the year at a propitious time in history they greatly empowered market financing, information clearing, and market evaluation of credit worthiness. If other factors of production were not yet priced in a remotely efficient sense at least capital was beginning to be. None of this would have been possible without the pre-established financial techniques built by Italians on the basis of earlier traditions from outside Europe.

It has sometimes been assumed that Church advocacy of charity and humility combined with constraints on greed and injustice, miraculously maintained in an era of extraordinary secular and Papal corruption, had a uniquely negative impact on the development of a modern financial system. Our analysis suggests, to the contrary, that systems of ethics were not only important to earlier financial systems but have continued to be so even for today's financial systems. Likewise, social capital and financial networking have continued to be indispensable as a fundamental assurance of credit worthiness. Although the great bourses introduced a viable market assessment of credit worthiness this involved no more than the summing up of information from social networks and thus was merely a reworking of an ancient idea. The notion that Europeans could have produced a prosperous capitalist economy, without millennia of ethical and legal thought, the evolution of financial instruments, or the development of appropriate social capital, is less than persuasive. Both were long multicultural projects that are, for the most part, little appreciated today.

Our decision to focus on the origin and development of the most critical components of modern finance in a broad comparative and non-Eurocentric perspective has determined the choice of chapters in this second book as well as in our earlier one.

In our initial chapter, we consider the Byzantine and Ottoman governments' surprisingly flexible adaptations of traditional views on finance that gradually came to dominate the Mediterranean. By the twelfth century, commercial practice as moderated by governments in the Eastern Mediterranean along with new scholastic thinking in Italy stimulated a European focus on finance that led to the establishment of innovative institutions. These innovations facilitated the growth in scale of capitalistic finance even as they obscured key aspects of trade from investor scrutiny. The development of new perspectives on usury by Catholic theologians pushed Europe in many new directions. Together these technical and ethical innovations promoted a widening gap between European / Christian ways of finance and Muslim approaches toward finance and lending. In retrospect, this has had both positive and negative consequences that continue to shape our current world. These changes have many implications for any anthropology of credit.[6]

If there was a baton of European financial insight to pass, it went from Byzantium to Italy to Bruges, Lyon, Antwerp, Amsterdam, and London. By the seventeenth century, flexible financial instruments prone to favor the lender had spread widely and the accumulation of unprecedented wealth was buttressed by access to both financing and power. The idea of a just sharing of risk, liability or profit no longer seemed rational to those with the upper hand. Repression of peasant and urban revolts in the thirteenth to sixteenth centuries raised few general qualms in Europe before it arrived on the verge of the Industrial Revolution. As the excessive corruption of the Church faded in the face of the Reformation its secular influence, not surprisingly, dissipated. Schumpeter has suggested that the economic insights of the scholastics, including the notion of opportunity cost defining a just rate of interest or the tie between business profit and interest, were several centuries ahead of their time.[7] The infrastructure to implement such ideas felicitously was, unfortunately, centuries away and the powers in the world were initially little motivated to construct such infrastructure.

During the Middle Ages, Iberia was made and remade by struggles between Muslims and Christians that ultimately changed both trade patterns across the Mediterranean and Iberia's place within international patterns of trade. Under Islamic rule, Christians, Muslims, and Jews commonly did business with one another, and by the tenth century had developed a thriving financial infrastructure and international trade with the Middle East and beyond that had made Córdoba the most populous and prosperous city in Western Europe. The Christian reconquest of Iberia stimulated the growth of urbanism outside of Iberia but increasingly strained ties between Muslims, Christians, and Jews. As Christian kingdoms reconquered Iberia, Iberian knowledge of the classics impacted the rest of Europe but the Islamic financial concerns with the transparency of transactions, and fair division of profits and losses, and risks and liabilities were rejected in favor of Roman law and its concept of *caveat emptor*.

Other financial insights derived from the rich Islamic tradition traveled primarily in the fifteenth century, and in diluted form, via the School of Salamanca's influence on the scholastic tradition. The financial contributions of the School of Salamanca to an ethical rehabilitation of interest were not negligible but they came late and long after the Italians with their own connections to the Near East had found other ways to innovate. Europe was set on its own course, one staked out in the Agora of Athens and the center of financial expertise passed at least for a time to Europe.

Our chapter on Iberia explores why this occurred, how the financing of trade changed, how capital mobility and trade relations were affected, how intellectual ideas changed, and why the development of capitalism after the Reconquest seems to have taken a very different path from that followed in Islamic Iberia, one only marginally influenced by Islamic ethics of trade, finance and credit, or its sophisticated system of commercial law. The flows of precious metals to Spain failed to alleviate or may even have aggravated the pattern of financial and social irresponsibility in the Iberian Peninsula which increasingly relied on expertise from Italy. Even the goods brought back from the Americas were frequently sold on credit, and used to finance elite lifestyles and warfare rather than investment in broader productive activities.

In an age of internationalization, as in the subsequent age of globalization, competition among European powers militarized trade. European powers not only had to fortify their trading outposts, but had as well to provide merchant ships with armed escorts, against rival companies, privateers, and pirates. The costs of protection and the risks of trade/warfare were so great that only the best-financed companies could survive. We argue that competition among European powers for colonies and trade significantly increased both the cost of trade and the demand for capital, and was a significant factor in the formation of public banks and stock companies.

Our chapter on Early European Finance focuses on the mutual influence of state finance and the private banking sector as old ways of financing the state become untenable once large portions of the economy escaped easy scrutiny within the private international banking system. Once funds could be transferred internationally via overlapping bank accounts, goods in one place could be exchanged for goods in another without recourse to physical transfers of the sort that states could traditionally monitor. Similarly, once the bulk of wealth was spread within multiple accounts in several countries sovereigns found it harder to tax or confiscate private wealth. Even the Vatican could transfer tithes across Europe without actually transporting funds. Cities and governments of all kinds gradually had increasing recourse to the sale of annuities and monopolies to supplement their declining revenues from traditional sources. This new world of international finance has had myriad consequences.

The chapter, *Transcending Feudal Finance in Western Europe*, traces the rise of trade in northwestern Europe during the Middle Ages. Using England as an example of a feudal society, this chapter lays out the economic logic of feudal society, and then examines the variety of forces that led to the rebirth of trade across Europe that began during the twelfth and thirteenth centuries. Part of this story is the rediscovery of ancient techniques of handling money and credit that led to the creation of financial infrastructure needed not just to handle money, credit, bookkeeping, shipping, and information, but also to enforce contracts, collect debts, and settle disputes. The implementation of these techniques provided the framework for the development of large scale trade. The chapter details how trade transformed feudal society.

We argue that, in contrast to early medieval kings who stood at the apex of social and political hierarchies in which all wealth and privilege seemed to flow from their favor, by the fourteenth century, trade caused wealth to flow through market channels, creating new social hierarchies very different in nature from the top-down feudal order. Nevertheless, while commercial hierarchies grew organically from the bottom up, because they continued to depend on the state and its courts for sanctions, relationships developed that were not necessarily less exploitative, but were more subtle and more apt to be enfolded and hidden in the legal details of the transaction. States such as England also had long enduring incentives to innovate financially and this culminated in the major role as a financial center gradually assumed by the City of London in both its on-shore and off-shore financial incarnations.

We specifically argue in this chapter that at the end of the seventeenth century, a revolution in finance was in progress that created the institutional and legal frameworks needed to support modern credit. This transformation saw the creation of an institutional matrix—national banks, joint-stock companies, stock exchanges, commercial law, and court enforcement of contracts) that allowed debts not just to circulate outside of personal ties or social networks but also to be bought and sold as if it were a true commodity.[8] Transforming debt and credit contracts into fully tradable assets greatly enhanced the ramifications of financial instruments.

The spread of banking in England, we argue, went hand and hand with the rise of industrial capitalism. As land, labor, and capital as factors of production came under the logic of the market its disciplines gave rise to new rationalities, new levels of abstraction and quantification that required standardization and uniformity that increasingly became the subject of accounting that transformed how investments were seen and managed. Here we argue that the rise of capitalism was accompanied by a process of discretization, a term we take from the mathematics of the era, where it refers to reducing geometries to discrete numbers to render proofs more calculable.

Capitalism has pursued an analogous path, using abstractions of two sorts. The first sort translated physical things into financial instruments where for example a house comes to be symbolically represented by a title, which can be used to secure a loan, and so free the capital physically embodied in the house for other purposes. The second attached numbers to things—putting prices to disparate and non-comparable things, allowing them to be categorized and assembled into spreadsheets, accounts rendered, and decisions made. Where once enterprises were constituted by men and women doing concrete things in particular places, under this logic they cease to be treated as individuals and became an entry of labor costs. As the elements of enterprise become discretely calculable, the rates of return may be compared across a wide range of alternatives both within a firm or just as easily between investments in firms, industries, sectors, and nations. In recent years, mortgage futures have benefitted from discretization: since the interest is usually paid off first, contracts on the future value of the equity and the interest obligation benefit from differential discounting.

Our chapter on the slave trade examines the dynamics of mercantile trade from the fourteenth to eighteenth centuries, and explores how mercantilism differed from capitalism. While the period in which slave labor was the key to productive profit was finite in duration, it became a crucible for some of the new financial technologies. It is clear this was an institution centered trade, not one involving a free consumer market, much less an efficient capitalist market. Here we specifically look at how credit was used at each step of the Atlantic triangular trade, from obtaining royal licenses, to raising the capital needed to build boats, stock them with trade goods, and pay sailors. To an extraordinary degree, ethical considerations were overridden by the search for profit. Credit played a central role in the barter for slaves between Africans and Europeans. The internal trade in Africa that brought slaves to markets likewise depended on credit. In the Americas, where coinage was in chronic short supply, slaves were also often sold on credit.

Our next chapter turns to examine credit in Islamic Morocco. During the nineteenth century, European powers throughout the Islamic world gradually imposed what has been called a system of capitulations on Islamic states. In this system, which began in the Ottoman city of Izmir and eventually spread to Morocco, foreign merchants among other provisions were given special legal status that included the right to have their financial disputes with local merchants handled by consular courts. The capitulations system provided strong incentives for Muslim, or indigenous Jewish, merchants to enter into partnerships with foreign merchants. The system created an elaborate network of credit contracts covering investments in commodities and land. Our chapter contrasting a Chayanovian and a Marxist perspective on this process looks at the consequences of this credit system in Morocco on the eve of the French protectorate and argues that credit insidiously undermined indigenous governance. The chapter goes on to examine the significant misunderstandings of Islamic finance held by foreign consuls and merchants and the consequences of such misunderstandings.

While we have regularly alluded to social capital, it is only in more recent periods that data to illustrate its importance has been available. In the chapter "Ethnicity and Social Capital in 1970s Sefrou," we measure the dominance of particular ethnic groups within a set of "annuities" providing leasehold over urban shops. A real test of the significance of social capital benefits from a close examination of its imbrication in the urban market. We reanalyze data collected by Clifford Geertz to look at the influence of ethnicity within the urban market. Geertz provided an analysis that can be shown to be faulty but a mathematically correct analysis demonstrates that ethnic networks dominate most trades in the market to a significant degree. They dominate higher value traditional trades more than they do low value trades or trades of recent origin. While comparable data is not available for most historical contexts, this chapter demonstrates both the potential and probable influence of social capital within well-functioning, if less than ideally efficient, market systems in the Islamic world. The Sefrou system appears to reflect traditional values known to prevail in Islamic urban markets, characterized by a version of an urban annuity in which *waqf* institutions auction leaseholds for their urban shops. This is a practice that has prevailed in the Islamic world for more than a millennium.

The penultimate chapter suggests that modern consumer credit, in a non-embryonic form, had to await the capitalist economy and the arrival of modern consumers. It explores the historical roots of modern consumer credit from the nineteenth century and argues that modern consumer credit, in contrast to earlier forms, is increasingly institutionalized and impersonal and so requires vast regulatory scaffolds. The chapter begins by looking at credit among London's urban poor in the nineteenth century, and considers English practices of debt collection—debtor's prisons and poor houses, as well as the rise of voluntary associations and friendly societies, penny banks, postal savings, and savings banks. It then moves on to consider the first steps toward modern consumer credit—installment savings, finance companies, and the rise of credit bureaus. Finally, we take up the topic of investment hedging, credit cards for a broad portfolio of consumers, and how such risk based lending prepared the ground for predatory lending and corporate concealment of both profit and risk.

The credit crisis of 2008 could be said to illustrate a large proportion of the faults possible due to an ignorance of history and a lack of concern for ethics. At its epicenter were the mortgage markets where banks and mortgage brokers began lending to the large pool of high risk buyers with low credit ratings, the so-called subprime market. Banks and mortgage companies knew perfectly well the risks involved but believed that such risks were insurable. While blaming individuals may satisfy some deep-seated need to hold someone accountable, this is not particularly satisfying as an explanation. Our chapter on the crisis explores other kinds of explanation, beginning with a critique of popular off-the-shelf explanations for the causes of "bubbles," and the underlying classical model of markets as trending naturally toward equilibrium. We consider the Keynesian view that markets are fundamentally unstable and explore Marxist suggestions that locate market instability within basic contradictions between capitalist expansion and labor impoverishment.

In that chapter's conclusions, we suggest that credit is best viewed as a social force with a direction and scale causing multidimensional impacts. We argue that the financial crisis in 2008 was in many ways a perfect storm to which multiple systemic problems contributed: the complex architecture of financial markets, regulatory failure, imperfect information, strategies of risk management including risk concealment facilitated by the rapid discretization of capital, and above all the failure to recognize the significance of transparency, ethics, and trust in financial success. Financial forces were allowed to run amuck.

The concluding chapter of this book focuses primarily on bringing all the strands of both books together into a properly anthropological theory of credit. We return to our paradigmatic claim that such a theory must scrutinize credit technology, the context in which it is implemented, the players who lend and borrow, the empowerments operative in creating the financial inequalities in play, and the explicit and implicit motivations driving the financial markets. We argue that financial contracts are best seen not as real commodities but as forces with instrumental causality and a multitude of societal and economic impacts.

NOTES

1. Park and Greenberg, *The Roots of Western Finance* (Lanham, MD: Lexington Books, 2017).

2. Braudel, *Civilisation matérielle, Economie et Capitalisme,* vol. 2, 339: "Accumulez, accumulez! c'est la loi et les prophètes!" pour une économie capitaliste. On pourrait tout aussi bien dire : "Empruntez, empruntez! c'est la loi et les prophètes!" For the admonishment to accumulate Braudel cites Marx, *Oeuvres*, édition La Pléiade I:1099. By accumulate Marx meant the transformation of surplus-value into productive capital—a key to capitalist growth he attributes to earlier economists. In Chapter 32 of Capital Vol 3, Marx emphasizes, among other things, the need to consider

the rate of turnover of loan capital to estimate its equivalence in productive capital. Braudel does not bother with this distinction. The citation from Marx (Capital Vol.1 Chapter 24.3) has been literally translated by Ben Fowkes. Capital Volume 1:742 as "Accumulate. Accumulate! That is Moses and the prophets!" The German is "Akkumuliert, Akkumuliert! Das ist Moses und die Propheten."

3. Goody, *The Theft of History,* 216.

4. Foucault, *Dits et Ecrits, 1954–1988, Tome* II: 1267. On postmodernism. Foucault takes the position that there is no modernism nor therefor such a thing as postmodernism since there are no real ruptures in history.

5. Steinmetz, *The Richest Man Who Ever Lived,* provides a readable account of Jacob Fuller's influence on Vatican and Hapsburg policies in the early sixteenth century.

6. While we accept use of the word capitalism to point to general phenomena, like Wolf, *Europe and the People without History,* Roseberry, "Anthropology, History, and Modes of Production," and Braudel, *Civilisations matérielle, Economie et Capitalism* we prefer to view capitalist economies as ones where there is a significant degree of efficiency in the price structure of the factors of production. An argument we make in part derived from this perspective is that particular insights into the diverse history of capitalism may be had by examining credit—as it at once delineates economic, political, and social relations, shaped in specific cultural traditions. *See also* Greenberg, "Medio Milenio de Credito entre los Mixes de Oaxaca," and "Capital, Ritual, and the Boundaries of the Closed Corporate Community."

7. Schumpeter, *History of Economic Analysis*, 103–06.

8. We follow Marx in viewing true commodities in a capitalist economy as products fully alienated from their producer by socioeconomic processes. Obviously, this is not the case for a credit relationship which by definition involves a lasting tie between lender and borrower. While the entire contract can be, and has been, commoditized and traded this does not lead to an internal creditor-debtor relationship similar to that between producer and their alienated product. Glossing over this significant difference inhibits analysis and obscures the impacts and ethical components of credit.

Chapter 1

Finance in the Middle Ages and the Scholastic Tradition

This chapter focuses on financial thinking in the Mediterranean from the era of the Byzantine Empire and the early florescence of the Italian city states to the work of the scholastics (primarily from the eleventh century to the early seventeenth century). Although trade in this period clearly drove intellectual change, here we examine core intellectual accomplishments rather than the specific practices of merchants which form the focus of most later chapters. The financial ideas developed in this period in turn facilitated trade in the Mediterranean as well as throughout Western Europe. Both the Byzantines and Ottomans developed new economic roles for the state even as the Italians contributed influential innovations in state-private sector finance. Within the Catholic Church, the scholastics gradually reformed financial instruments and invented perspectives that rehabilitated lending at (reasonable) rates of interest in cases where loans did not cause clear harm to the recipient or the lender. Schumpeter in fact claims that: analysis reveals that the fundamental factor that raises interest above zero is the prevalence of business profit—all the other facts that may produce the same results are not necessarily inherent in the capitalist process. This proposition constitutes the main positive contribution of scholastic interest analysis. Adumbrated before, it was first clearly stated by St. Antonine, who explained that though the circulating coin might be sterile, money capital is not so because command of it is a condition for embarking upon business.[1]

These changes were rooted both in ethical discourse and in a felt need by authorities to address practical realities but were much troubled by legacy arguments against usury.

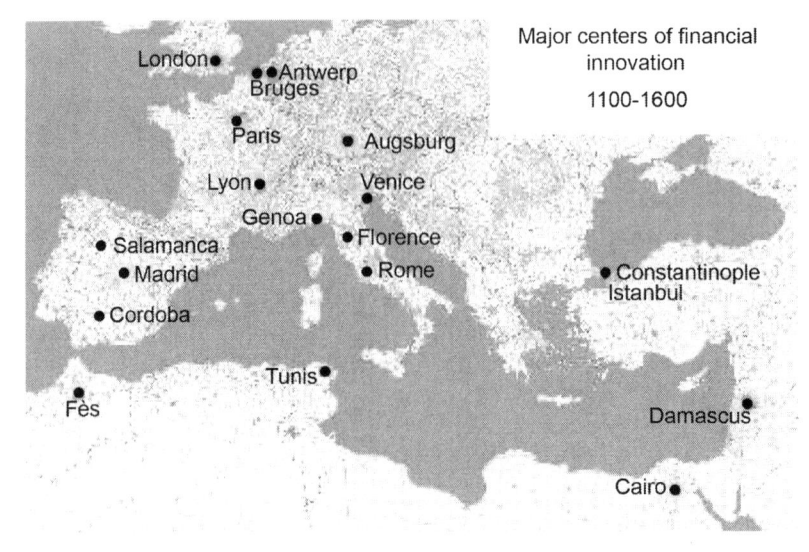

Figure 1.1 Major centers of financial innovation in Europe and Near East, AD 1100–1600. *Source*: Map drawn by Thomas K. Park.

HISTORICAL CONTEXT

The expansion of Italian city states (e.g., Venice, Genoa, Pisa, Florence, and Amalfi) from the eleventh century together with the efforts of the Byzantine Empire led to the gradual domination of Christian powers over maritime trade in the Mediterranean. The city states as well as Western European powers such as Roger, the Norman Count of Sicily, also contributed during the eleventh century to transforming the Mediterranean into a sea dominated by Christians through systematic participation in piracy against unallied merchant ships. This made the northern coasts with their many havens much safer than the southern coasts with their far fewer ports of call. Thus, despite the continued power of Muslim states around the Mediterranean, Christian states increasingly dominated long distance maritime trade by the twelfth century.[2]

This change in trade patterns stimulated finance and forced Europeans to think critically about prohibitions on lending at interest. It also brought to the fore a whole set of issues related to just profits, prices, and returns to trade. Scholars also believe major changes in property law developed along with growing literacy in the eleventh and twelfth centuries that led to increasing consistency of rules and the gradual acceptance of ingenious rationalizations for the grants of property, in return for services or payments, viewed as usufruct or something close to modern ownership.[3] Merchants from Venice and Genoa quickly focused their own activities on the traditional Byzantine trade space. The crusades, begun in the twelfth century, also reoriented Western Europe toward the eastern end of the Mediterranean.

A key financial concern for each of these states was how to meld their traditional financial and ethical approaches with the needs of a rapidly changing financial and political landscape. The Christian states as well as the Ottoman state had inherited financial practices heavily imbued by the ideas of classical Greece. During the Greco-Roman period, there were several ways of financing long-term commercial ventures. In the Republic of Rome one type of partnership was the *societas* created to harness capital from each member and share profits proportionately from *societas* activities, but liability was not shared (i.e. not unlimited) so a grievance could only be brought against the individual partner and could not be generalized to the capital of the partnership or its other partners.

The later and much more popular *commenda*, used by Muslims, Jews, and Christians throughout the Byzantine and Ottoman periods as well as in medieval Italy and Spain complemented partnerships of this type primarily in being more suited to long distance trade by having a financier, or sitting partner, and a mobile partner who put the funds to work as well as an explicit sharing of profits and investment (money versus labor). Almost as important, it had liability protections for the mobile partner both from others and from the sitting partner—provided the activities were reasonable, legal, and prudently profit oriented. Because the partnership itself had unlimited liability, it was more accountable from the perspective of those who dealt with it even as it provided incentives for young and energetic people to work with the funds of older merchants.

Nevertheless, the *commenda*, termed the *chreokoinonia*[4] in the Byzantine world, due to its unlimited liability had no advantages when it came to the question of attracting expanded investment into a given partnership. In this regard, it had in common with many types of partnerships, including the *societas*, difficulty in expanding its capital base. The *commenda* imposed significant risks because of its general (unlimited) liability, so potential participants who had no time to actively participate or knew little about crucial aspects of the business would be extremely reluctant to invest. The *societas*, in which only the personal assets of the partner who engaged in a transaction at risk, could at least attract investors who were confident about their evaluation of the potential returns. A key issue of the time due to the expanding European economy was the perceived advantage of larger-scale enterprises, state or private, and the need to address issues of liability without throwing out the ethical considerations which had begun to dominate finance. Later chapters address finance by banks and the invention of the *compagnia*, and its corporate descendants, which came to key European arrangements for limited liability.

THE BYZANTINE EMPIRE

The notion of harnessing wider sources of capital was stimulated by the development of state financing of individual merchants through the extensive use of tax farming in the Byzantine Empire beginning in the eleventh century;[5] a practice assiduously copied in the Ottoman period. Initially, the state claimed major resources such as mines, and encouraged elites to exploit these resources in a continuous fashion in return for a fixed payment to the Byzantine state. Potential revenues to the tax farmer were enormous, and there was a strong incentive to exploit the resource in a long-term fashion; concessions could be renewed and regularly were even assumed by the tax farmer's heirs.[6] From the eleventh century, the state granted other resources such as *klasmatic* (undeveloped) lands, in large blocks to individuals and monasteries in the hopes that they would thereby be developed and would improve the economy. These were nominally gifts but could be taken back and so might be seen as loans conditional on performance benefitting society and the economy.[7] Building and managing the economy through loans was an integral part of Byzantine finance from the eleventh century.

The early medieval church, both Catholic and Byzantine conceived of the facilitation of a just price as a state obligation. Both Byzantine and Catholic scholars defined this as historically and socially produced and tended to imagine the fair interactions among merchants as setting such a price. A commentary on Aristotle by the twelfth century Byzantine scholar Michael of Ephesus suggested that *chreia* (Aristotle's term for use or need) should be recognized as relative and measurable by its monetary value—something that fluctuates and shows up as market price in normal situations.[8] This idea defined the just price in the context of an empirical world reflecting actual merchant transactions as constrained by history and current sociopolitical events. A just price for a given commodity could vary, over time and place, because arbitrary uniformity itself was perceived to be unjust.

The Byzantine state innovated finances in a number of ways to improve social welfare. In the sixth century, it ran various productive sectors (mines, quarries, textiles, and dying), distributed food (wheat /bread, oil, wine lard, pulses: *annona*) to the poor in Constantinople, and regulated credit and banking as well as its currency. Between the eighth and tenth centuries, the Byzantine state regulated profit margins, calculated as the difference between prices paid by merchants and prices charged to consumers. This margin was based on prevailing market prices for imports purchased by merchants for resale. Regulations in the *Book of the Prefect* spoke of "just profit" and established the rate for a number of commodities and transactions at less or equal to ten percent. This policy also incorporated corrective justice by insisting that the rates for the rich had to be lower than those for the poor. This unusual policy forced merchants to make their profits through turnover rather than profit margins. The regulation of profit margins was only done in Constantinople and disappeared during the tenth century.[9]

While the regulation of profit margins did not endure beyond the tenth century, the regulation of interest rates did. By the postclassical period, Roman law, based on a currency reform under Constantine, had set the highest legal rate (*centesimae usurae*—Byzantine *hekatostiaios tokos*) at a fraction of a gold *nomisma*, for example, 1/24 or 4.17 percent per month. This practice was adopted in the Justinian code and became the norm in the Byzantine Empire, though Basil I (885/6) explicitly banned the receipt of interest by anyone other than orphans and minors (the earnings on their assets managed by others). The ban was lifted and the rates restored by Basil's successor Leo VI the Wise.[10] These precise ratios may even early on have been regularly ignored and four percent or its multiple twelve percent used instead.

The standard in the Byzantine Empire came to be that sea loans were regulated at twelve percent and others between four and six percent from the sixth century until late in the eleventh century when the rates rose to 16 2/3 percent and 8 1/3 percent, respectively. It is worth noting that loans made by aristocrats in this century rose only to 5 11/20 percent from four percent.[11] The Rhodian Sea Law[12] provided that a creditor was not a partner and in consequence if goods were lost the creditor had no recourse to the partners' assets for compensation. The loan was not viewed as "safely on land" and so lenders could not make the same claims as on such loans. This regulation built directly on the Greek dichotomy between loans in the Agora and the Piraeus. It was the enhanced and well-understood risk, and non-liable status of the partners, that justified the higher rate for sea loans.[13]

The Byzantine version of the *commenda*, the *chreokoinonia* (corresponding to the classical *commenda* with distinct traveling and investing partners), continued to be used by merchants throughout the Byzantine period.[14] A Venetian version, the *collegantia* dating from 1073, stipulates that all accrued profits plus the initial capital must be reinvested by the partner for the duration of the contract. If that partner acted professionally and there were losses he had no liability, but if he were not professional he was liable to the other investors for double their losses (in profit and capital).[15] In the twelfth century, a new partnership began to be used in Byzantium in which some investors shared only in profits but not losses—investor returns were guaranteed or at least came first.[16]

Byzantine law for partnerships was flexible and at times it was unclear whether a more informal association (*koinonia*) or a more formal partnership (*hetaireia*) was involved.[17] Speaking inclusively, both types of partnerships could be formed even verbally and might involve all allowable arrangements for sharing profits and investments. Because these arrangements were understood to be for the purpose of making profits, all required each partner to share in profits. It was not necessary, in contrast, for all to share in losses—the personal risk one partner was subjected to by travel might allow that partner to avoid being liable for the losses of partnership capital. In this sense, a variety of partnerships might share in some of the advantages of a *commenda* including those sea loans financed by a non-partner creditor; for example, the traveling partner might not be indebted by losses even though all investors were at risk of losing their investments.[18]

From the eleventh century, the Byzantine Empire positively encouraged profit making and was more focused on eliminating distortions in the market prices that induced people to engage in obviously exploitative behavior. In emergencies or times of scarcity, the state imposed price controls on key staples or trade goods. Political fluctuations in prosperity and control of territory also led to policy changes impacting finances: in periods when the state controlled large amounts of grain producing territory there was state involvement in the shipping of grain but little else while when grain was more scarce due to either environmental issues or territorial diminution the state exercised more financial control of the grain trade.

Also in accordance with a greater move toward privatization from the eleventh century, taxation involved significantly more tax farming and less direct collection by the state.[19] Tax farming can itself be seen as a loan of usufruct made by the state in return for payment (quasi-interest) in advance. This advance payment and the surplus later kept by the tax farmer obscured the credit nature of the transaction and thus kept the transaction out of any charge of usury. The early Byzantine Empire viewed justice toward its residents as an important obligation of state and elaborated sophisticated ethical principles and laws to implement this obligation.

It should still be no surprise that in periods such as the eleventh century many tax farmers egregiously abused state regulations imposing additional taxes and fees for their own profit. The scale of tax farming ranged enormously from the award of most taxes linked to Thessalonike in 1081 to a contender for the throne (Nikephoros Melissenos) all the way to the lease of quite modest sources of taxes to private parties. A mirror practice was the granting of tax exemptions to individuals or monasteries who usually then collected local taxes for themselves and who in return owed political or military, rather than direct financial, support to the state.[20] During the Komnenian period, government relied heavily on this institution, the *pronoia* or tax exempt benefice.[21]

Recognizing the loan characteristics of tax farming makes it possible for us to ask a number of significant questions usually missed in discussions of this form of state financing. The Byzantine state defined and implemented justice, provided that it did not directly contravene scripture or its standard interpretation, and in so doing many issues of transparency were assured by the state. Liability was now a legal obligation solved on the one hand by state authority supporting the tax farmer's activity and the prepayment of the tax farmer's liability to the state. The recourse to the state of those paying the tax farmer, if abused, was also assured by law and remained as a potential liability for the tax farmer who did not follow state guidelines. Risk was also transparent and not legally shared by the state though famines or droughts regularly led tax farmers to seek relief and the state to provide it, as part of its obligation to provide justice (mercy) rather than as a legal obligation to the tax farmer himself.

In comparison, the annuities increasingly used for finance by cities and states in Western Europe from the twelfth century (in Italy) provided low risk for their wealthy purchasers and a fixed return, usually based on entailing specific revenue streams, plus the option of selling the annuity to someone else at going market rates. The explicit use of both tax farming and the imbrication of state and private finance represent a more general issue: credit involves both the construction of social or political capital as well as of monetary profit and the two as modern theory holds have long been somewhat interchangeable. At even higher levels, the enormous levels of inter-gifting by Byzantine and Muslim potentates represent a further level of sociopolitical capital construction.[22]

OTTOMAN FINANCES

The Ottoman Empire, like other Muslim states, enthusiastically encouraged private mercantile activities but the Ottomans nevertheless retained a major economic role for the state. Like the Byzantine state it practiced tax farming and many tax farmers were ethnic minorities such as Greeks or Jews. In a pattern not too dissimilar to that of the Byzantine Empire it displaced, the Ottomans defined any land that could be ploughed as "*miri*" or under eminent domain and therefore owned by the state. Such lands were typically leased to cultivators using a *tapu* contract which obligated the cultivator to pay taxes. While a *tapu* contract was heritable and could not be overridden by local authority it was still leasehold. Thus, technically, the state became a great lender of property and taxes served as de facto interest on the loan. While the Ottomans did this explicitly following a traditional Islamic effort at transparency, later Western states have tended to imagine a primordial contract citizens sign implicitly at birth that justifies the collection of taxes, including real estate taxes. The Ottoman state, like other Muslim states, divided the productive rural area into those parts that had been conquered from non-Muslims, defined as *kharaj* lands, which paid between 1/5 and 2/3 of yields and those assigned to Muslims which were taxed 1/10 of yields.[23]

The Ottomans took over from the Byzantines a practice of providing lands to support families of the military who instead of paying tax would render military service. In this variant of credit, there were two levels, the first (*timar*) a prebend involving authority and some tax revenues from a wider area, and second a right to cultivate a smaller area, viewed as (*hassa çiflik*), for the direct benefit of one's family. The right to the direct benefits of cultivated land was to be paid for in service and in the usual case the land would revert to the state at death unless a new family member provided military service. The Byzantine version of the *hassa çiflik*, a *pronoia*, required only irregular service and so worked even for lands that required significant male labor on a regular basis. Both were a loan of usufruct, but the Ottoman version, *hassa çiflik*, obligated the *sipahi* to campaign most of the year and so usually required vineyards, meadows, fruit trees, or flour mills: assets that readily yielded marketable products which would allow the military to support themselves while serving. Peasant households (*çift hane*) with tax obligations rather than military service were also viewed as obliged under the *hassa çiflik* system so there was a clear idea of substituting service for taxes as well as an explicit practice of granting lands to support military service.

The Ottoman system had a number of variants on the prebendal system in addition to the *timar*. Imperial demesnes were themselves referred to as *hass-i hümayun*, even as prebends for dignitaries such as viziers and begs were simply referred to as *hass*. Lesser commanders received *ziamets* just as the *sipahi* received *timar*.[24]

Religious institutions and elites also frequently received endowments, *vakf*, that similarly had associated, if different, obligations. Like the Byzantines, the Ottomans often felt that religious endowments served the state through their activities and therefore might not be obligated to pay taxes. Technically, such lands became private (*tamlik*) and exited from the *miri* system though often the poll tax, as opposed to the productive taxes, was still to be paid. Some elites received endowments for services rendered. More typically a request for such an endowment was made to a high official, usually to establish a religious institution but also for private benefits. Such *vakf* not only did not pay taxes, they also were off limits to local authorities with the consequences that they attracted population from the surrounding areas that were welcomed and used to help develop the lands. Grants of *tamlik* were given with conditions, for example, to keep the land in cultivation, and would be revoked if the conditions were not met for three consecutive years. Thus, even if they were nominally private land the state retained *rakaba* (*dominium eminens*).[25]

Some individuals, by contrast, were endowed with tax generating areas that were expected to produce state taxes even as the individual retained a part for their own benefit, though the award did not involve competitive bidding as in tax farming. Endowments were a decision of the Sultan and almost certainly reflected issues of social and religious capital being exercised to support state policies. Endowments made to religious institutions tended to be stable while those to elites were much more likely to be volatile and more difficult to renew.

Another category of state loan was the endowment of waste or empty, *mevat*, lands to elites. In this case, the return obligation was development; often irrigated works were required, but even livestock raising in some areas might suffice. While the benefits of the development accrued directly to the developer, the increase in productivity enriched the market, stabilized population in peripheral areas, increased demography, and generally was thought to benefit the state. Many border estates were created in this fashion to facilitate Ottoman control as it expanded. This, too, was essentially the same policy as that followed by the Byzantines on waste, *klasmatic*, lands. Once developed, future usufruct in the area, if no longer on the frontier, could be provided as *hassa çiflik* to new generations providing military service.

Generally, the Ottoman Empire, especially in the early centuries, followed Islamic practices in terms of private finance including the common use of the *commenda* partnership. The multi-ethnic character of the Ottoman Empire and its major role in the Mediterranean meant that Jews and Christians within the empire were quite free, among themselves, to follow other financial practices including new ideas from Italy. Ottoman international trade and customs rates were regulated both in Ottoman ports and in foreign ports giving rise to potential disputes: thus, when currency devalued and foreign ports wanted to change rates accordingly Ottoman authorities viewed this as *bida'at* (heretical innovations).[26] On the currency side, the Ottoman *akçe* went through a massive debasement, relative to other currencies in 1585–1586. Historical evidence also suggests that prices in Istanbul went up fourfold between 1450 and 1600 so rates over this period based on quantities of each good transiting customs could easily change from moderate to inconsequential from a merchants point of view and inadequate from the perspective of the state.[27] Thus, there is some reason to believe the traditional orthodox views about finance continued to have significance even in the face of radical financial changes.

The role of traditional Islamic financial tricks (*hiyal*) also remained important and we have to assume that, like state revenues from real estate there were ample opportunities for financial activities that were technically illegal or formally resembled lending at interest. Thus in 1485, a money changer sold rubies and pearls worth 64,500 *akçe* to a merchant in Tabriz on credit for six months with a second merchant pledged as surety. The arrangement included hidden interest in the repayment schedule as if the sale was a loan and a penalty clause for late payment that added interest on top of the accumulated amount due (interest on interest). Letters of credit, *havale*, were much in use and clearly provide an opportunity in the specified exchange involving currencies prevalent in different places for interest to be surreptitiously inserted. Yet, the concern over this possibility may explain why the Ottoman version of the earlier Persian letter of credit, the *suftaca,* was not approved by orthodox jurists.[28]

Around 1501, there is a record of bankers in Ottoman Pera taking out loans at 15 percent a year when short of cash.[29] This could not have been too unusual. In the sixteenth and seventeenth centuries, even pious foundations frequently lent money at interest. Such foundations were common in cities and especially in Istanbul. Similar changes were occurring in Europe. In the seventeenth century, a new variant of these pious lending foundations involved lending money to urban quarters to defray taxes and taking as collateral the housing of the borrowers, thereby gradually building up charitable endowments through defaults. Some religious scholars felt the direct charges of interest were illegal and it may be that this variant better addressed their religious concerns. Private lenders also were common in these centuries. By this time, in the loans both by religious institutions and private parties, no effort to conceal interest charges seems to have been necessary. Religious endowments typically charged 15 percent per annum while the loans in the private sector varied between ten and twenty percent.[30]

SCHOLASTIC VIEWS ON USURY AND FINANCE

The Byzantine, Ottoman, and West European states all viewed usury as something that prevented people from receiving appropriate value in transactions. Early positions derived much from Aristotle's outright denigration of interest on lending of currency as something intrinsically unnatural (*pecunia non parit pecuniam*) as well as from Plato's claim that lending at interest promotes social injustice. Usury prohibitions remained an important part of Islamic financial law as we have seen in chapter six of our first book. The Byzantines and Ottomans innovated significantly when they relied in large part on the state to implement justice in lending and the Byzantines went so far as to institute different interest rates for the rich and the poor—providing lower profits for the rich to increase the public utility of credit.

In Western Europe, a reliance on the Greek view began to change by the eleventh and twelfth centuries. Duns Scotus (1266–1308) suggested that the just price reflected the cost of production as well as the risk incurred in production and supply.[31] The theory of the just price, though contentious even as applied to normal commodities, was gradually extended in Western Europe to include money and credit. The Italian tradition transcended Platonic and Aristotelian attitudes toward interest in a gradual and cumulative way that almost reached modern perspectives in the scholastic work of Thomas Aquinas (1225–1274), Richard of Middleton (1249–1308), St. Antonine (1389–1459), Luis Molina (1535–1600), and the School of Salamanca in Spain.

Some scholars have argued that the scholastics introduced almost as much resistance to as progress toward modern views.[32] We provide some examples of such resistance in our discussion of the School of Salamanca (toward the end of this section). Unlike such scholars we find this modern conservative view anachronistic and believe that positions that have been viewed as resistance toward the modern view (e.g., that the market automatically sets the correct value on commodities as well as on money and interest rates) reflect instead a legitimate concern with important issues of justice and a more accurate understanding of reality. The medieval position attributed to Aquinas was that justice has two aspects; commutative justice involving relations between individuals and distributive justice involving the community's obligations to its members.[33] Typical issues involving distributive justice included the role of society and government in responding to the implications of the concept of a just price including the need to make a distinction between levels of interest acceptable in loans for production and those suitable for consumption loans. From our perspective, the scholastics proceeded with legitimate caution even as they introduced the key elements of the modern position; a position that has shown an unfortunate tendency to ignore far too many of the scholastic arguments for distributive justice.

We discussed the acceptance of many loans at interest in the Byzantine and Ottoman Empires, yet it is important to note that even as usury became a key focus for Western European scholars it underwent almost continuous transformations in definition. Even as in the East the Bosphorus area made the transition from a Christian Byzantine Empire to a Muslim Ottoman Empire, on the western end of the Mediterranean, Iberia made a converse transformation from Muslim Andalusia to Christian Iberia. The following chapter examines the reasons Iberian scholars largely, if not entirely, came to ignore the Islamic and Jewish traditions of Andalusia. Here we note that the Byzantine example may not have been held in high esteem in Western Europe in part because the schism in the Church militated against such a perspective and in part because the active role of the Byzantine government in assuring that just prices prevailed was far more difficult for western monarchs to accept from a church without comparable secular power. These two points by no means adequately explain this issue which involves many additional historical factors beyond the scope of this book.

Later chapters focus on the practical innovations in finance throughout Western Europe and North Africa so we devote the remainder of this section to the theoretical ideas which transformed Western European thinking on finance and credit. Table 1.1 summarizes the key issues and arguments leading to the gradual and partial rehabilitation of loans at interest in the Western European tradition. It provides most detail for the arguments that gradually carved away at the prohibitions on usury but begins with the classic views against usury and ends with a few informative exempted contracts.[34]

The classical arguments against usury that begin Table 1.1 are premised on the notion that there is potential harm to society from lending of money at interest though they do not agree on the nature of that harm. Plato felt that it was socially deplorable because it discouraged honorable generosity by rewarding those without such inclinations while Aristotle viewed it as logically repugnant and unnatural. As noted in Chapter 5 of *The Roots of Western Finance*, Christian and Jewish biblical texts were actually ambiguous but were interpreted in early medieval Europe as unambiguously opposed to lending at interest. The Christian focus was initially on the potential for exploitation in loans at interest while the Islamic focus had been on the unfairness of one party being legally assured a return while the other party's return remained legally at risk. It is worth noting that Aquinas and others accepted that the person borrowing at interest did not commit a sin, provided they had a good purpose in mind for the money.[35] None of the classic sources could be interpreted as suggesting that a pastoralist who loans a flock of sheep to a shepherd could not morally expect, given his investment, to get back both his sheep and some of the new lambs even if all the work were to be done by the shepherd.

One could of course argue that this bucolic practice might have been less than perfectly generous, but European scholars focused their attention on mercantile activities and may often have had an inclination to use lending at interest as a basis for spurning Jews. The concept of *turpe lucrum* (shameful monetary gain) captures the notion that usury was a particular excess profit that shared in the immoral character of any excessive or exploitative extraction of profit by nature of its intrinsic uncharitableness.[36] The early opinions about usury were soon premised on substantive distinctions between money and other goods and a traditional concern over inappropriate profit margins shared as we have seen with Byzantine scholars. Muslims went on to generalize the basic immorality indicated by Plato, it harms society and offends God, to all loans at interest regardless of the commodity being loaned. Yet, Western Europe took a different route mostly derived from Aristotle that strove to tackle the problem as they saw it—lending of money at interest.

Aquinas took the first (Aristotelian) step by defining usury as only relevant to lending of money.[37] It took a series of innovations before, between the sixteenth and eighteenth century, Christian consensus reached the point of viewing money as a commodity whose value varied locally with the quantity available across time and space (a quantity theory of value). This view implied that money might be seen as having a just price like any other

Table 1.1 Summary of Usury Motivated Arguments.

Usury arguments	Gloss	Source, greatest elaboration
Against usury		
Uncivil	Plato thought that loans should be based on trust and that monetary loans at interest, which were common, damaged the society	Plato (c.427–347)
pe*cunia non parit pecuniam*	Money does not beget money, so interest on money is unnatural	Aristotle (384–322 BC)
Theodosian Code	A major compilation of Roman law that put restrictions on allowable rates of interest	Emperor Theodosius (AD 438)
Corpus Juris Civilis	Four-volume code of Roman law; a key basis of canon law also defined moderate rates for allowable interest	Byzantine Christian Emperor Justinian (AD 430s)
Turpe lucrum	Shameful gain: usury as extreme case, selling at other than just price, usury on monetary loan is like any other unjust sale	Corpus Juris Civilis Council of Nicaea (AD 325)
Psalm 14	"Lord who shall dwell in thy tabernacle? He that hath not put out his money to usury"	Old Testament
Arguments for usury		
communis aestimatio vs *laesio enormis*	Just price set by *market*, unjust if 50% or more above or below, may include considerations of future uncertainty: more nuanced than the simple notion that *major harm* could occur if just prices were not available	Corpus Juris Civilis Petrus Placentinus (–1192), Thomas Aquinas (1225–74)
Monetary focus	Usury only involves interest on money	Thomas Aquinas (1225–74)
damnum emergens	*Unforseen losses* due to enacting loan; imagine lending to the loser in a political struggle	Roman tradition, many scholastics
propter periculum	Legitimate justification for profit in trade but loans that primarily put borrower at risk are usury, this issue of whose risk is later expanded	Huguccio (1188), Giles of Lessines (d.1304), Alexander Bonini (c.1307)
publicum utilitatem	Public utility: loans for charity, promotion of common good, may charge interest	Thomas Aquinas (1225–74) Jean Buridan (1300–58)
poena conventionalis	Penalty for late payment is okay, even a rebate from just price to hasten payment ok	Roman jurists, Thomas Aquinas (1225–74), other scholastics

(Continued)

Table 1.1 Summary of Usury Motivated Arguments (Continued)

Usury arguments	Gloss	Source, greatest elaboration
return gifts licit	Borrower could give lender free gifts, if not contractually obliged to do so, originally in money, later it was suggested that most returns might be envisaged as friendly obligations. This was an argument in limited form made to argue for the legitimacy of the *compagnia*	Hostiensis (–1271) Luis de Molina (1535–1601) Leonard Lessius (1554–1623)
loco pignoris	Deposition of a *pledge* or *guarantee*: when loan is made to facilitate these a premium is legal: benefit to borrower is disproportionately large and risk is minimal	Thomas Aquinas (1225–74)
raritas, virtuositas, complacibilitas	Sources of economic value: *scarcity, usefulness,* and *desirability* (basis of concept of subjective utility).	Thomas Aquinas (1225–74) St. Antonino (1389–1459) Pierre de Jean Olivi 1248-98) Jean Buridan (1300-58)
Time preference	Under valuation of future goods implies extra compensation due on a loan.	Thomas Aquinas (1225–74) San Bernadino (1380–1444)
industria, solicitudo, labores, pericula	*Diligence, responsibility,* and *labor, risk*: ethical justifications for merchant profit.	San Bernadino (1380–1444)
lucrum cessans	*Loss of income*: missing funds earn no profit, initially used to justify loans with returns for charity then for all business, then on all loans, develops into the full idea of opportunity cost.	Pierre de Jean Olivi (1248–98) Alexander Bonini (1270–1304) Conrad Summenhart (1465–1511) Cardinal Cajetan (1468–1534) Azpilcueta Navarrus (1483–1586),
intent	Not usury if perpetrator does not know it is or if loan is in the public interest.	Cardinal Cajetan (1468–1534, Bañez de Mondragon (1527–1604)
carentia pecuniae	Losses due *to absence of money* (*liquidity*).	Leonard Lessius (1554–1623)
Generally Exempted contracts		
societas	Partnership without general liability, investors risk their own property so returns not usurious.	Early Republic of Rome, Aquinas

mutuum	Pure loan, okay temporary transfer of ownership, usury if risk born by borrower.	Huguccio (1188)
commodatum	Lease, transfer of usufruct	Huguccio (1188)
census	annuity, guaranteed normal risk covered by recipient of funds.	Gabriel Biel (1430–95) Conrad Summenhart (1465–1511)
compagnia, soprocorpo	New form of partnership with non-partner investors guaranteed returns.	Florence, Italian city states

Table created by Thomas K. Park.

commodity—suggesting both a justification for exchange and for a rate of interest.[38]

A number of concepts elaborated by Aquinas were critical to this further intellectual process. Aquinas, like Michael of Ephesus, argued that ethics required the weighing of empirical contexts in the light of reason and revelation. In regard to the lending of funds, this meant that profit could be legitimized either by a) the necessity of making a living, b) a wish to acquire funds for charity, c) a wish to serve the public good (*publicum utiltatem*) considered as a reward for work (*stipendium laboris*), d) efforts to improve the object traded, e) inter temporal or interlocal differences in value, or f) the need to compensate for risk (*propter periculum*).[39] Other than the first justification, all provisions go beyond Aristotle's considerations and can be applied to lending of money just as easily as to loaning goats. Such provisions however opened the way for a re-evaluation of usury precisely because they clearly applied to the valuation of all commodities. In due course, Aristotle's notions about the singularity of money (unnaturalness of expecting it to generate profit) fell out of favor.

Lenders who incurred unforeseeable capital loss (*damnum emergens*) due to the loan might be considered within their rights to demand compensation but, initially, the majority of scholastics did not agree that the mere risk of losing capital justified a preemptive right to compensation. Nor did they feel the mere absence of the funds for a period of time (*lucrum cessans*) justified compensation. In twelfth-century Europe, the mercantile notion that profits were very much about timeliness and seizing opportunities had not yet displaced the social obligation to be charitable.

Aquinas, however, opened a small door in these objections by suggesting that a loan for the purpose of enabling a borrower to deposit a pledge or guarantee (*loco pignoris*) could justify a premium to encourage such socially constructive lending: since the risk was guaranteed to be minimal by the nature of a pledge this should not be seen as explicitly involving compensating the lender for risk.[40] The argument thus began by supporting socially positive activity such as pledges for such admirable expenditures as a dowry but this could be expanded to encouraging economically positive activity, for example, trade, and thus added to the arguments already adduced for the legitimate earning of profit on money.

An issue to which much more intellectual attention was paid in the Islamic world is that of risk: to lender and to borrower. By the time of Aquinas, the term *propter periculum* was used to gloss the potential risk to a lender and their consequent claim to some compensation beyond return of their principle.[41] At the same time, there was a consensus that putting borrowers at excessive risk through exorbitant rates of interest was immoral, yet there was no concern that the risks of the two parties should be explicitly balanced. The European discourse on risk in lending took much of the thirteenth century to evaluate what were seen as two distinct issues: it seemed sufficient to keep the borrower's risk moderate and to compensate the lender reasonably for their risk.[42] In the Islamic world, all risks were required to be made explicit and fairly divided between lender and borrower within the larger context of the activity financed; including the allocation of liability, labor, and profit. As we have seen, Byzantine contracts showed considerable similarity in approach to traditional Islamic perspectives, and this was even more so for Ottoman contracts.

Although the Byzantine Empire put serious thought into the notion of the just price, it was able to rely on government guidance even after the eleventh century when greater market flexibility was encouraged. In western Europe, scholars from the late eleventh century, and twelfth century on, relied on *communis aestimatio* (the estimates of the market community) as the basis for a just price. They argued that this never implied a single price for each commodity—given variance in quality this would never have worked. Instead, they imagined a deviation from the mean of no more than 50 percent as sufficient to guarantee a just price in normal circumstances. Prices outside this range could gouge consumers or bankrupt sellers and constituted *laesio enormis*.[43]

Aquinas, in the thirteenth century, and Buridan, in the fourteenth century, made more thorough arguments for the legitimacy of loans at interest that had charitable purposes or promoted the common good (*publicum utilitatem*). Scholastics suggested it was equally unproblematic to legitimize penalties for late payment (*poena conventionalis*) since the funds provided in a free loan might easily be needed later and some motivation for timely repayment seemed beneficial rather than immoral. The flexibility of this perspective was often illustrated with Aquinas' response to a question about a merchant who rushes to bring food to a famine area and charges high prices. The question posed included the stipulation that the merchant in question knew many other merchants would soon be on site and asked whether the merchant was morally obliged to let the buyers know that other merchants would soon be offering the same foodstuffs. Aquinas replied that the merchant had no such obligation for otherwise there would be diminished incentives for merchants to rush to alleviate a famine and the social consequences would be far worse if this were the case. In short, the famine struck community was free to buy or not and in so doing establish a just price and the greater social good helped justify that just price.[44]

The most admirable loan was free; a gift qualified as charity as long as the recipient had no contractual obligation to repay the gift. This issue raised many possibilities and was even the basis for a new partnership, the *compagnia*, developed in twelfth-century Italy and discussed in a later chapter, but the full potentials of the gift exemption were not fully elaborated until the fifteenth and sixteenth centuries. A key issue was what was meant by an obligation to repay. Initially, the focus was on individual contractual obligations but as the finances of cities and states were increasingly done through raising funds in the private sector rather than from taxes or customs duties the issue became more complicated.[45] A feudal style lord might be gifted with an estate but had obligations tied to this gift, such as military support. Similarly, a bank might lend funds to a sovereign king and expect something in return, for example, interest on the loan or, instead, a grant of monopoly in some segment of the market to serve as profits on the loan; producing both principle and a return because in the usual case, the loan itself would not be repaid. Each could be seen as a loan at interest. Eventually, reasonable returns on gifts were deemed not usurious when the gift could be seen as a civil obligation—regardless of how explicit this was in contract documents.

In the thirteenth and fourteenth centuries, Pierre de Jean Olivi introduced the very modern sounding triad of scarcity (*raritas*), usefulness / utility (*virtuositas*), and desirability (*complacibilitas*) as the basis of value. The Latin term *virtuositas* implies utility for good purposes and the term *complacibilitas* similarly meant desirability from the perspective of morally defensible purposes. Using these concepts, he argued for a supply and demand determination of value (and prices) and introduced the abstract concept of capital (*capitale*) as a fund for business investment.[46] In the fourteenth century, Jean Buridan (1300–1358) argued for a subjective theory of money and generalized the concept of *complacibilitas* to the principle of subjective utility suggesting that two parties to an exchange can each benefit even if it does not fit the traditional definition of a just exchange. Viewed in the larger perspective the notion of *complacibilitas* as subjective utility implied that most trades and allowable activities including most forms of *cambio* should be licit if it's good for society.[47] Olivi's trifold basis for value enlarged the debate on the valuation of services, such as money lending or credit, as well as the valuation of goods. If these three could be used to establish a just price for a good then why could they not be used to establish a just price for a service.

In the fifteenth century, San Bernadino added a further basis for valuation, time preference[48] viewed as a premium placed on the use of time for a particular purpose. He argued explicitly that undervaluation (discounting) of future goods by people explained why people would happily borrow to have a commodity now and agree to pay back more in the future. Put another way; empowering their current time is valued more than having funds to empower their future efforts. The implications of this for a just price on credit are enormous. Thus, rather than St. Antonino's vague claim that encouraging capital usage was in the public good, San Bernadino proposed a subjective justification for mercantile practice that did not involve injustice. In current economic terms, this is the primary reason adduced for people being willing to enter into a mortgage but it is little understood that the idea was around in the fifteenth century.

San Bernadino also argued that merchant diligence (*industria*), responsibility (*solicitudo*), labor (*labores*), and risk (*pericula*) represented the primary reasons merchants earned their mark up and that this premium had to be seen as part of the just price. The argument also was applied both to goods and to services.

Although discussed for centuries, no full consensus on some issues was reached until late medieval times. In the fifteenth century, a number of scholastics in Italy and Spain; for example, St. Antonino, Cardinal Cajetan, Conrad Summenhart, Azpilcueta Navarrus, and Luis Molina in the sixteenth century[49] had worked out a consensus on two other justifications for profit and interest on loans. They argued that both *damnum emergens* and *lucrum cessans* justified a premium on lending which could be seen as in the public interest since credit stimulated capital growth.

The more difficult question was how much premium could these concerns justify. San Bernardino's justifications for mercantile premiums lent themselves to reasonable estimates compatible with the returns to other activities but these last two issues were considerably more difficult to transform from theory into practice. Following Aquinas' teaching on the need for empirical contextual evaluation of ethics, the scholastics felt a need to evaluate carefully the context in a quantitative as well as qualitative sense. While in time this became the idea of opportunity cost, the statistical and quantitative apparatus for calculation of just premiums remained deficient until the modern era. In practice, in subsequent periods European states began to arbitrarily define legal (non-usurious) and illegal levels of interest.

As Christianity established itself more homogeneously across Iberia, the School of Salamanca began to contribute its own perspective to European financial thought. Early on with Cardinal Cajetan (1468–1534), it began to provide an interesting mixture of conservative views, reflecting Islamic traditions and progressive arguments that can be seen as in some measure responses to Italian and German opinions.

Cardinal Cajetan elaborated on the idea that intent was relevant to an assessment of what constituted usury.[50] He argued that certain forms of exchange (money paid in one currency and received elsewhere in another, e.g., by the same person) were also non-usurious. A later Salamancan, Domingo de Bañez de Mondragon (1527–1604) elaborated this idea more fully. In 1594, Bañez made the general case for the significance of intent and held that expectation of profit on a loan was legal as long as the expected profit was based on an expectation of gratitude not an obligation to pay in excess of the loan.[51] Cajetan also vindicated *lucrum cessans;* in the case of a loan by a businessman that entailed potential subsequent losses by that businessman due to unavailability of funds; the loan could legally charge interest.[52]

On the conservative side Cajetan opposed setting prices solely by the market; he endorsed as it were the possibility of unjust prices within a market and supported the notion of the just price. Though resident in Italy, Cajetan's views initiated many financial innovations in the School of Salamanca.

In his opus, *De justitia et jure* (1553), Domingo de Soto (1494–1560) argued that prices are determined by their utility but maintained nevertheless that the labor, trouble, and risk involved in their production should also be factored in and that, ideally, approximate prices should be set by "prudent and fair minded men" rather than simply by the market. Even as he introduced the idea that foreign exchange rates represented movements toward purchasing power parity, on the grounds of justice he argued for banning foreign exchange speculations (*cambio*) as usurious.

Martin de Azpilcueta Navarrus (1493–1586) wrote an appendix, *Comentario resolutoio de usuras*, to a manual on moral theology that introduced a quantity theory of money (rather than the Aristotelian theory that money was a measure of other things) and thereby suggested that money should be treated as a commodity. Following up on the notion of time preferences, this implied that lending at interest involved merely a just exchange for a good now versus a good of lower value in the future plus a compensation to make the exchange equivalent. His conservative side expressed itself in an absolute opposition to any annuity (*census*) as usurious in as much as it *obligated* a return greater than the investment.

Luis de Molina (1535–1601) a Jesuit who taught at the University of Coimbra in Portugal, argued that the just price is simply the common market price, endorsed the purchasing power parity determination of foreign exchange, and widened the scope of risk and *lucrum cessans* as justifications for charging interest. On the conservative side, Molina insisted that if the loan is not intended as an investment it is not permissible to charge interest.[53] The conservative positions expressed by scholastics in the Salamancan school find their direct correlate in traditional Islamic insistence on a fair and transparent division of profit and risk which precluded any contract with unforeseeable divisions of either between partners, any contract excluding one party from profit as in a loan for consumption, or any contract in which one party, regardless of events, had an obligatory return; that is, the risk was not shared.

A final scholastic refinement made in the late sixteenth and early seventeenth century had primary importance for the banking community. It would be hard to argue for concern related to *damnum emergens* or *lucrum cessans* in the case of a major bank but the reduction in liquidity due to lending out high proportions of deposits and assets could pose a problem that at the extreme might involve bankruptcy. Leonard Lessius (1554–1623), of Salamanca, introduced the more general term, *carentia pecuniae* (absence of money) as a justification for interest on credit that relied on the potential harm a shortfall of funds could impose on a lender both due to opportunities lost and due to continuing concern over the risk that the money would be lost. He further argued that the Bourse at Antwerp provided a reasonable valuation, of 6–12 percent, for this absence of money.[54]

Known historical exceptions to concerns about usury in finance also facilitated some of the above arguments. In the Roman *societas,* individual partners were solely liable for their own activities yet all partners risked the assets put into the *societas*. It was long the practice for partners to get an average return on *societas* investments based on the collective set of activities engaged in by the various partners. The consensus remained that this ancient and common arrangement did not constitute usurious lending because the profit of all partners was equally at risk even if the practice did regularly involve returns greater than that invested.

A related argument applied to the *mutuum* which Roman law saw as a temporary transfer of ownership that might provide benefits via the creation of *gratia*. This was not thought to constitute lending at interest *unless* the risk was entirely born by the borrower—in which case it was not a *mutuum*. Huguccio (1188) made a related argument about the *commodatum* which involved a lease or short term transfer of usufruct. In Roman law, the *commodatum* had been viewed as an *officium amicitiae*, or benefice between friends and so qualified as a gift even if some obligations were incurred (payment on the lease). Since the recipient of the usufruct paid for its lease it might be viewed as a usurious contract.[55] Huguccio argued on classical lines that it was not usurious. From an ethical point of view the operative issue was that the *commodatum* involves durable goods not easily lost or consumed so risk was radically reduced.

These particular examples helped to motivate the acceptance of the Thomistic argument that usury only involved lending of money and required some injustice as well. Another common medieval European practice, the annuity (*census*) in which a person might loan funds to a city council or to a state in return for a monthly stipend, it could be argued, though as noted above some disagreed, was non-usurious both because it served the public good and because risk did not play a significant role: the borrower was a city or a state and they were good for the loan. A medieval exception along similar lines, the *compagnia*, is discussed in more detail in a later chapter.

MEDITERRANEAN AND WEST EUROPEAN CONTRIBUTIONS TO FINANCE IN THE MIDDLE AGES

When finance is misconstrued as being merely or even primarily concerned with the accounting of monetary flows, issues of authority, legitimacy, value, ethics, and justice tend to be neglected. Financial planning may guide the flow of money but, to differentiate itself from mere robbery, making profits while benefitting from trust requires much else. Social capital and reputation which are cultural constructs are as important as money itself and much of financial planning in the past like the present was as concerned with social capital, reputation, and trust as with money or commodities. Both could grow or be put at risk as well as be used to enhance credit worthiness. In the intimate imbrication of state and private finance awareness of this usually proved critical.

Nevertheless, there are several core differences between modern finance and ancient finance that developed primarily in the Middle Ages. Ancient societies had state and temple based financing on a major scale, but private finance tended for ethical and practical reasons to be much more limited. Ethical issues had been more thoroughly explored in the Islamic world than in the Christian or Judaic traditions but by the medieval period they ended up in all three traditions having critical importance for the expansion of private finance. The state had been given great leeway in defining the ethical status of its own financial activities, but prior to this period the private sector had not been in the position to contravene or explicitly define financial proprieties. As private commerce often funded states (including the Papal state) scholars felt increasingly that it behoved them to evaluate the practices of commerce.

For Muslims around the Mediterranean there were constraints not faced by Jews, these were created by the dual concepts of *dar al-islam* (the realm of Islam) and *dar al-harb* (the realm of war) which divided the world into two areas: in one of which Islamic law prevailed and in the other of which it did not. Literalist jurists reached the conclusion that Islamic contracts could only hold within *dar al-islam* and thus that Muslims could not engage in trade with Europe since any contractual obligations entered into in *dar al-islam* would be invalid outside in *dar al-harb*.[56] While a minority legal opinion, this motivated some Muslims either to avoid trade with Christian realms or to use intermediaries, such as Jews, as partners to facilitate trade in areas where Islamic law might not be respected. Spain and Byzantium provide some obvious counter examples where interreligious commerce flourished.

The Byzantines and Ottomans contributed in important ways to state finance and managed to produce stable systems that included incentive structures for private production. Each state recognized that trade in the private sector was essential to social prosperity without imagining that it was wholly sufficient or naturally just. They both adapted financial rules readily to changing circumstances while maintaining a concern with justice. Both states were also multi-ethnic and receptive to merchants and merchant practice from a range of religious and ethical perspectives. In many ways, this openness and tolerance combined with an acute awareness of social justice were essential to their centuries of prosperity. We should not, however, imagine that intellectual progress in finance precluded either corruption or injustice in either society any more than it did in Western Europe.

Ethical considerations can potentially be seen to be relevant to the structure of rewards, liability, risk, and investment in any financial enterprise. Ethics may also be deemed to vary based on location and the identity of participants, for example, Muslims might travel on the Sabbath but not trade in alcoholic beverages while Jews might not travel on the Sabbath but could trade in alcoholic beverages. Such considerations have particular implications as well for financial activities involving a mix of religious identities. Similarly, trade in some commodities might be illegal or constrained in particular times and places, for example, the grain trade was frequently regulated by the state. Illegality, even where it might not otherwise be deemed unethical, changes the risks and those risks may differentially impact financial partners. The Islamic world was the first to carefully incorporate this broad range of issues into its financial guidelines, but this evolution of financial transparency directed the Islamic world down a different ethical path than that of Western Europe.

It is difficult to avoid being anachronistic in evaluating economic thinking. Economists are wont to evaluate scholastic intellectual accomplishments in the financial realm as somehow defective—as if their failure to seize on the idea of viewing the market as providing not only a just price but a just salary, a just rate of interest, perfect hedges for liability and risk, and tools for a perfect management of the economy was a failure of insight.[57]

We would do better to ask the basic question of why there was resistance in each of these areas and, as we have seen, the answer was usually not intellectual failure but rather attention to some ethical principle that has gone missing in much recent economic discourse. The introduction of a quantity theory of money, subjective utility, time preference, and recognition of the role of risk constitute major advances in economics that were applied by the scholastics to the financial sector as well. The introduction of intent as a critical piece of the definition of usury expanded the role of commutative justice while the concern with the potential for loans to be exploitative and the emphasis on a societal obligation to promote distributive justice hardly constituted simple obstructionism.

The scholastics followed, in their own way, one classic tradition developed more fully in the Islamic world; the illicitness of taking unjust advantage of others. A loan to facilitate a pledge was so helpful that a charge for that loan, if it did not disadvantage the recipient, was quickly deemed non-usurious. In contrast, a loan at interest for consumption had little chance of itself generating a profit for the recipient and so it was deemed usurious until the bitter end. The party potentially disadvantaged also mattered. An annuity which paid out interest was quickly deemed non-usurious both because the recipient of the interest (revenue stream) was at little risk and because the recipient of the loan, for example a city, had numerous ways to make the funds profitable. The key was that there were few reasons to worry about injustice despite the formal similarity of an annuity to a loan at interest. Similarly, a loan at moderate interest for business, which could indeed be expected to generate a profit, met with much less resistance and, as the initial extract summarizing St. Antonine's position indicates, was deemed non-usurious. This fifteenth-century insight, as the citation from Schumpeter early in this chapter notes, was critical in linking rates of interest to rates of profit themselves.

Despite the subtlety of thinking and the practical needs that drove European reworking of finance, not all issues broached in the Islamic world were seriously considered. There was no sustained ethical drive to balance risk and returns, little attempt by the scholastics to address equality of liability as an issue of justice, nor any attempt to ensure that the distribution of profits was transparent and proportional to the amount invested by each party (money, goods, or time). While gifts were considered praiseworthy, the scholastics failed to see them as a part of successful merchant activity that promoted trust and reputation. In this, they were far less sophisticated than their Muslims predecessors and displayed a naïveté about their own Roman heritage.

The Greek heritage, from the Agora and Piraeus, of a hidden and a public financial realm shows continuity in the European focus on the regulation of public activities by financial actors through attention to a just price in the market with less regard for balance and transparency between partners in an undertaking. The Islamic emphasis even when loans at interest were condoned, for example in the Ottoman Empire, remained focused on transparency and balance between partners and on orienting the law to ensure both: implicitly assuming this and market competition would suffice to promote the public good.

NOTES

1. Schumpeter, *History of Economic Analysis*, 105.
2. Abulafia, *The Great Sea. A Human History of the Mediterranean*, Chapters 3–5 of Part Three.
3. Reynolds, *Fiefs and Vassals. The Medieval Evidence Reinterpreted*, 64 ff.
4. Laiou and Morrison, *The Byzantine Economy*, 140.
5. Ibid., 158.
6. Ibid., 146, 157–59 suggest that the increase in tax farming and outright gifts of estates to elites from the late eleventh century on weakened the state but not the economy which merely became more privatized.
7. Ibid., 114.
8. Ibid., 162.
9. Ibid., 33, 38, 62.
10. Gofas, "The Byzantine Law of Interest," 1096–1100.
11. Laiou and Morrisson, *The Byzantine Economy*, 140.
12. Rhodian Sea law, *Lex Rhodia*, was a set of regulations governing navigation in the Byzantine Empire whose initial development was begun in the seventh century, further refined for several centuries and influential through the twelfth century after which it gradually became obsolete as Byzantine maritime trade declined.
13. Laiou and Morrisson, *The Byzantine Economy,* 73; Maridaki-Karatza "Legal Aspects of the Financing of Trade," 1112.
14. Already by the last quarter of the tenth century the *commenda* had become the standard European contract for long distance trade. Ballard, "A Christian Mediterranean: 1000–1500," 186.
15. Lopez and Raymond, Trans. *Medieval Trade in the Mediterranean World. Illustrative Documents*, 176ff.
16. Laiou and Morrisson, *The Byzantine Economy*, 140. See also discussion of the *compagnia* contracts in a later chapter which also first appears in Italy in the twelfth century; presumably the two are variations of the same contract.
17. Papagianni, "Byzantine Legislation on Economic Activity Relative to Social Class," 1089.
18. Maridaki-Karatza, "Legal Aspects of the Financing of Trade," 1112–20.
19. Laiou and Morrisson, *The Byzantine Economy*, 140–41, 161–62.
20. Oikonomidas, "The role of the Byzantine State in the Economy," 1022, 1040–41, 1048.
21. Laiou, "Political History: An Outline," 22–23.
22. Laiou, "Economic and Noneconomic Exchange," 681–96.

23. Inalcik, *An Economic and Social History of the Ottoman Empire, 1300–1914*, 110–13.

24. Ibid., 141.

25. Ibid., 122–30.

26. Veinstein, "Les marchands étrangers dans l'empire Ottoman (XVI–XVIIIe siècles) Questions de Prix." In eds. Faroqhi and Veinstein, *Merchants in the Ottoman Empire*, 57.

27. Pamuk, *A Monetary History of the Ottoman Empire*, 150, 121.

28. Inalcik, *An Economic and Social History of the Ottoman Empire, 1300–1914*, 206–08.

29. Ibid., 241.

30. Ibid., 490–92.

31. Rothbard, *Economic Thought Before Adam Smith*, 78.

32. Two conservative authors unhappy with scholastic reservations about their new ideas are: Chafuen. *Faith and Liberty. The Economic Thought of the Late Scholastics* and Rothbard. *Economic Thought Before Adam Smith*. We find both the new ideas and scholastic reservations equally important and like Schumpeter's (*History of Economic Analysis*, 73–142) do not find the latter detract from the value of the former.

33. An excellent discussion of these two aspects can be found in Chapter 8 of Chafuen's *Faith and Liberty. The Economic Thought of the Late Scholastics*.

34. This table and much of the related discussion is based on Chafuen. *Faith and Liberty: The Economic Thought of the Late Scholastics;* Rothbard. *Economic Thought Before Adam Smith*; Cajetan *On Exchange and Usury;* and Schumpeter. *History of Economic Analysis*, 73–142.

35. Aquinas, "Summa Theologica," 33.

36. Papal Decretals from Alexander III (1159–1181) through Gregory IX (1227–1241) and the works (1250–71) of Cardinal Henricus Hostiensis de Segusio make much of this problem first discussed, as noted in the table, in the fourth century.

37. This point is discussed in Rothbard. *Economic Thought Before Adam Smith*, 54–55.

38. Key figures in this development were Luis de Molina (1535–1601), Domingo De Soto (1494–1560) and Azpilcueta Navarrus. See Chafuen. *Faith and Liberty. The Economic Thought of the Late Scholastics*, 61–71.

39. Schumpeter, *History of Economic Analysis*, 91.

40. Ibid., 103–05.

41. Ibid., 91.

42. Aquinas seems to have had some such notion when he suggested that ownership of capital used jointly with a working partner was retained by the investor because of risk—in this case risk shared by the two partners. Rothbard (*Economic Thought Before Adam Smith*, 56) seems to have missed the significance to Aquinas of shared risk even though this retention was the norm in the *commenda* common long since in both the Islamic world and in medieval Europe.

43. Rothbard notes in *Economic Thought Before Adam Smith* that Petrus Placentinus (–1192) established the 50 percent acceptable range, 40.

44. Ibid., 55.

45. As both Hicks (*A Theory of Economic History*, 81–100) and Lopez (*The Commercial Revolution of the Middle Ages*) suggest the commercial revolution in Western Europe diffused wealth and limited state tariffs and taxes to a fraction of the potential revenue needed and this pushed governments to seek private finance—in return for finite term monopolies on state natural or political resources.

46. Rothbard, *Economic Thought Before Adam Smith*, 60–61.

47. Ibid., 72–73.

48. The key passages are: "*Tempus proprium venditoris ab eo licite potest vendi, quando temporalem utilitatem temporali pretio apretiabilem in se includit*" and "*Quaedam duration applicabilis alicui rei, quae duratio, atque usus est alicui concensus ad eius opera excercenda: et hoc modo tempus est proprium alicuius et huismodi tempus licite vendi potest*" Saint Bernardino of Sienna, Opera Omnia (Venice, 1591), Sermon 34, De *Temporis Venditione*, 322 cited Chafuen. *Faith and Liberty. The Economic Thought of the Late Scholastics,* 125 notes 4 and 6.

49. Both de la Cruz, (*Tratado Unico de Intereses, Sobre si se Puede Llevar Dinero por Prestallo),* and Leonard Lessio (*De Iustitia et Iure*, bk. 2 chap. 20, 3–19) sourced this idea to St. Antonino who taught that merchants were not, therefore, obliged to sell goods on credit at the same price as for cash.

50. Cajetan (*On Exchange and Usury,* 71) similarly argues that if the intent of the loan is merely a hope of amicable return greater than the amount lent this is not usury. Other examples of where intent can make the difference between usurious and non-usurious actions include some forms of *cambium* (money changing) (xxvff, 35–44, 53–52).

51. Domingo de Bañez, De Justiciaet Iure Decisiones. Salamanca 1594 is cited in Chafuen. *Faith and Liberty. The Economic Thought of the Late Scholastics,* 126, note 17.

52. Rothbard, *Economic Thought Before Adam Smith*, 101.

53. Ibid., 99–115.

54. Rothbard, *Economic Thought Before Adam Smith*, 99–125; Chafuen. *Faith and Liberty. The Economic Thought of the Late Scholastics*, 124.

55. Verboven, *The Economy of Friends*, 238.

56. Udovitch, *Partnership and Profit in Medieval Islam*, 229.

57. Rothbard, *Economic Thought Before Adam Smith,* despite its many virtues, provides a representative example of this anachronistic perspective.

Chapter 2

Credit and Faith in Medieval Iberia
The Road Not Taken

For over seven hundred years during the Middle Ages interactions and conflicts among Muslims, Jews, and Christians made and remade Iberia. In AD 711, Muslim armies invaded and quickly conquered Iberia. Under Islamic rule, Muslims, Christians, and Jews developed a thriving international trade with the Middle East, and beyond, that by the tenth century had made Córdoba, the capital of al-Andalus, the most populous and prosperous city in western Europe. One of the major puzzles of the middle ages is how the interactions between Muslims, Christians, and Jews contributed to the commercial revolution in Western Europe that allowed Christians ultimately to reconquer Iberia and to wrest control of the Mediterranean trade away from Islamic dominance. In seeking answers to these questions, this chapter specifically focuses on the influence that Jewish and Islamic trading practices had on Christian trade, but also examines how differences in their legal traditions may have shaped the very distinctive path that Christian commerce ultimately took.

In examining these issues, although our discussion necessarily focuses on the technologies of trade and the role that Islamic practices played in the so-called "commercial revolution," we are not attempting in this chapter to explain the transformation of feudalism into capitalism, nor are we making a Henri Pirenne[1]–style commercialization argument[2] which holds that feudalism represents a historical rupture with the intrinsic logic of the market, or its more refined forms as put forth by Max Weber and Fernand Braudel[3] that focus on the factors that impeded the development of capitalism. These bigger arguments are beyond the scope of this chapter, and would entail a much broader examination of factors of production, and not just technologies of trade. Instead, we limit our concerns to the political and urban dimensions of credit, and the role finance played in politics. We begin this chapter with a description of the Caliphate of Córdoba in the tenth century; since we provide a description of Western European feudalism in another chapter, we then launch into a discussion of how the Reconquest, Crusades, and commercial revolution remade feudal Iberia.

THE CALIPHATE OF CÓRDOBA

In the tenth century, Islamic Iberia and Western Europe were worlds apart. The feudal economies of Western Europe were rooted in the land, in the extractions of rents and tribute. Although trade existed, its scale was nothing like that in the Islamic world. The cities of al-Andalus were centers of commerce and industry and linked through trade to the Mediterranean world. Its

Figure 2.1 Folio from a Qur'an Manuscript, Spain, late thirteenth to early fourteenth century. Ink, opaque watercolor, and gold on parchment. *Source*: Sold by Mrs. Kamer Aga-Oglu, 1942 to the Museum of Modern Art, accession number 42.63. http://www.metmuseum.org/art/collection/search/450486.

merchants carried on an extensive trade with North Africa, Cairo, Alexandria, Baghdad, the Near East, Byzantium, and beyond.[4] When most villages or towns in Western Europe had populations of 500–2,000 inhabitants, and even Rome, the largest city in Catholic Europe had perhaps 25,000 people,[5] Córdoba toward the end of the tenth century was more comparable to a Baghdad or a Constantinople, with a population of perhaps 250,000.[6] Córdoba, of course, was the capital of the Caliphate that had some twenty-one provinces, and many great cities: Sevilla, Toledo, Malaga, Lisbon, Zaragoza, Tortosa, Almeria, and Valencia.

Córdoba was a jewel of Islamic civilization.[7] It was the largest, wealthiest, and most civilized city in Western Europe. It was a walled city adorned by magnificent palaces and mansions, hundreds of mosques and baths, aqueducts, gardens, fountains, as well as lighted and paved main streets.[8] Tens of thousands of shops lined its narrow streets that ran through its many neighborhoods. Its central market was filled with both local commodities and imported goods: Persian carpets, Damascus metalware, Chinese silks, fine leather, jewelry, and slaves.[9] Córdoba was also a great center of learning, having established the first university in Western Europe. As one contemporary (al-Masudi, AD 893–956) observed, "During the times of the ancient Greeks and for a little while during the Byzantine [i.e. Roman] empire, the philosophical sciences kept on growing. ... They developed their theories of natural science ... until the religion of Christianity appeared ... they then effaced the signs of philosophy, eliminated its traces ... changed and corrupted what the ancient Greeks had set forth in clear expositions.[10]" At a time when the largest library in Christian Europe held at most 600 manuscripts, Córdoba's caliphal library, one of the seventy libraries in the city, had some 400,000 volumes.[11] As a cosmopolitan city, its society was highly stratified, and was religiously and ethnically diverse. The social gamut ran from the aristocracy to professional classes, to humbler classes. There were religious scholars (ulemas, priests, and rabbis) lawyers, architects, astronomers, physicians, bureaucrats, merchants, and craftsmen; and its commoners included among others, petty shopkeepers, street vendors, day laborers, and slaves.[12]

During the Caliphate, Jews and Christians were allowed a degree of self-governance and tended to live in their own neighborhoods.[13] They had their own governing bodies, own courts, and magistrates. As *dhimmi,* that is, as monotheists to whom God had also given scriptures, they were not compelled to convert to Islam, and were allowed to practice their own faith provided they paid a special tax not required of Muslims and observed certain restrictions. They were not to proselytize Muslims, build new places of worship, practice their rituals publicly, ring their bells, or display their symbols. Apart from these restrictions, Jews and Christians were allowed to engage in all aspects of social and economic life, a fact that opened vast opportunities to them.[14] Both Jews and Mozarabs (assimilated Christians) learned Arabic and shared in Islamic life and culture. Many highly educated Jews came to hold exalted posts in government as viziers, ministers of finance, tax farmers, and ambassadors.[15]

In AD 929, the Umayyads declared the Caliphate of Córdoba, and severed their allegiance to the Abbasid caliphate of Baghdad. To rule over its twenty-one provinces, the Caliphate set up an administrative structure modeled on Byzantine forms and practices, thought to be the most evolved and sophisticated system of the time.[16] The system was headed by the Caliph, beneath him was a *hajib,* a kind of prime minister or chamberlain who supervised a corps of royal *viziers*, specialized in various fields that carried out the day-to-day administrative business of the chancellery dealing with matters of public finance, providing administrative services, and handling the political and military matters of the provinces and frontiers. Four principal *viziers* worked with the *hajib:* one, to handle correspondence from provincial officials; a second, to handle matters of defense of the frontier and coasts; a third, to execute decrees approved by the caliph; and a fourth, to receive and forward petitions to the proper officials for their consideration.[17]

As civil and financial matters had moral and ethical dimensions, religious courts had jurisdiction over them. The Islamic jurists, or *qadi,* were religious scholars who held their courts daily in a corner of the mosque, and gave their opinions on civil matters to those who came to them for advice. Their powers, however, were quite limited. They had no authority to compel anyone to appear in their court, nor did they have any power to enforce their rulings. Rather, their task was to determine with regard to any given matter what was obligatory, recommended, permissible, disliked, or forbidden based on the Quran, *sunna*, and *ijma*.[18] If the case raised complex issues, the *qadi* might consult with other legal scholars who, relying on precedents, issued their written opinions. Jewish and Christian communities in al-Andalus similarly had their own jurists and courts that interpreted their respective canons. Nevertheless, Muslim courts had, as across the Islamic world, jurisdiction in cases between Muslims and non-Muslims.[19]

Financial administration under the Caliphate of Córdoba was based on the logic of a tributary state.[20] The monies that flowed into the public treasury came from a variety of sources: tributes, tolls, tariffs, taxes, and levies. A portion came from taxes on trade; however, the bulk came from taxes on land and from the special levies on Christians and Jews. While provincial governors were officially responsible for such collections, much of the actual work was done by tax farmers—most of whom were Jews—who advanced revenues (as a form of credit) to the state in return for this privilege.[21] After the governors deducted their own expenses, they remitted the remainder to the public treasury in the alcazar of Córdoba. The public treasury also received revenues from minting fees, earnings from special monopolies, such as the production of *tiraz* (a fabric that functioned as an emblem of state power), and from trading in special commodities, such as grains.[22]

The Caliph's private funds came largely from his own landholdings, and were administered separately from the public treasury. A secretary (the *khazin al-mal*) administered the public treasury and it was his duty to make required disbursements when needed to the court, to the civil administration, to the army and navy, or for public works and building projects.[23] The funds of the mosque were also administered separately from the public treasury, and were under the control of its director who used the revenues from alms giving (*zakat*) for charity to the poor and to support the foundations established for the upkeep of the mosque and other public buildings.[24]

During the Caliphate, although as in Western Europe agriculture was the backbone of the economy, its technologies were far more advanced. Following the Muslim conquest, from those areas that had put up resistance, the state took a fifth of the lands. These lands were then cultivated by tenants under sharecropping arrangements. The remaining lands were distributed among Muslim troops. In some regions, particularly in the Levant, around Toledo, and in the Ebro valley, large latifundia were common. In the northern and central parts of the peninsula smallholdings predominated.[25]

Muslims continued to grow the crops that had long been part of Iberian agriculture—wheat, olives, and wine grapes (which they continued to appreciate despite religious prohibitions). They also planted many new crops including citrus fruits, figs, sugar cane, rice, flax, cotton, asparagus, artichokes, coffee, and saffron; and, used advanced agricultural techniques such as crop rotation, terracing, pruning, and splicing to create special fruits and to increase yields.[26] Moreover, they repaired and extended Roman aqueducts and systems of irrigation (that the Visigoths had preserved), and improved them by adding new technologies such as waterwheels and windmills. They introduced new insects for sericulture (silk production) and apiculture, and imported the ass from Egypt. Expert herders and breeders, they also improved breeds and significantly increased the production of wool, meat, cheese, leather, etc. In addition to its agricultural products, Al-Andalus was also renowned for its leather, swords, armor, carpets, glassware, silk, and paper as well as its mines that produced gold, silver, lead, copper, iron, and mercury.[27]

Because Al-Andalus was integrated into an Islamic trading sphere, it functioned as the Western trade entrepôt between Muslims and Christians, making it the conduit for Eastern spices, textiles, paper, and other assorted goods from across the Mediterranean and beyond. Both Muslim and non-Muslim merchants from all around the Mediterranean came to markets in al-Andalus, and likewise its traders ventured far and wide.[28] Although its economy was primarily oriented toward the Muslim world, its merchants also traveled to markets in Castile, Galicia, León, Navarre, and Portugal. Both Christian and Muslim rulers protected commerce along these roads. Besides a wide assortment of itinerant peddlers, traders, and shopkeepers that traded in Andalusian markets, there were a variety of merchants engaged in international trade.

International merchants fell into two broad categories, those involved in overseas commerce, and those trading using overland routes. Whereas overseas merchants specialized in certain high-value commodities, the itinerant traders who carried goods across borders between Christian and Muslim regions seem to have chiefly handled inexpensive household goods.[29] There is good evidence that Andalusian merchants exported textiles, spices, ceramics, paper, and gold to Christian Europe, and imported slaves, furs, and other raw materials from Christian kingdoms.[30] Commerce between Muslim and Christian kingdoms was scant during the tenth century, and was limited to a few Jewish merchants and even fewer Muslim merchants who rarely ventured beyond the Pyrenees.

Though the Mediterranean has been described as a "zone of free trade" in that Muslim and non-Muslim merchants were free to travel with their goods, this was not a "free market." Merchant activities were always circumscribed by government regulations. Government officials administered port facilities, performed cargo inspections, and collected taxes, duties, tolls, and fees. Foreign merchants were subject to particular restrictions governing their movement, conduct, and even accommodations.[31] This was an administered trade with price controls on particular commodities, and trade in others limited to particular persons. Overseeing these activities was the *sahib al-mazalim* or lord of injustices. He headed a hierarchy of officials including market inspectors who oversaw market transactions,[32] and whose duties were to ensure fair prices, to prevent swindles and deceptions, to see to it that weights and measures were honest, and that disputes were settled peaceably.[33]

Trade was organized by networks (typically comprised by co-religionists) who specialized in particular commodities. International trade was commonly carried out through *commenda* partnerships in which an established merchant worked with a traveling partner[34] who acted as his agent and supplied the services required for a commercial venture.[35] Even though Muslim, Christian, and Jewish merchants competed with one another, they also would cooperate with each other; for example, in shipping goods; and, even occasionally would enter into partnerships with one another. Because these networks were built upon kinship and friendship ties, they were somewhat clannish and so formed fairly closed-trading systems in which members were generally known to one another.[36]

Of necessity such trade involved a great deal of trust, and commerce depended heavily on social capital expressed as reputation. Merchants freely exchanged information and provided one another trade-related services as these both built their social capital and lowered their risks and transaction costs.[37] Even though Jewish, Muslims, and Christians had access to their own courts, their jurisdictions were limited to their own cities and communities, often making enforcement difficult, costly, or next to impossible. Even if they could take their case to court, few merchants did so. They much preferred to rely on informal mechanisms of enforcement: gossip and complaints to their peers.[38] Reputation, in fact, was so important that to protect it, Jewish merchants would pay compensation, if the performance of one of their family members or agents was unsatisfactory.[39]

Preserving one's reputation required scrupulously adhering to "merchants' law," which consisted of informal rules and practices that prescribed how to behave in an honest and trustworthy fashion in business dealings. These practices and customs if followed ensured that transactions were clear and transparent to all parties involved. Such practices included conducting important transactions in front of witnesses, and keeping separate books for each venture. To document and carry out transactions a wide variety of written documents were used such as bills of lading, receipts, letters of instruction, contracts, releases, and account books. This kind of commerce required high levels of literacy and mathematical skills, as well as great familiarity with the foreign markets, and laws governing trade for each commodity in each place. Not surprisingly, many merchants also had other careers that they practiced alongside their commercial activities—many were also scholars, government officials, physicians, ship owners, or soldiers.[40]

CREDIT UNDER ISLAMIC RULE

Despite Islamic proscriptions on usury, credit played an essential role in trade. Broadly defined, credit is simply an advance of goods, services, or money against a promise to repay these at some future time, with or without interest. The terms of credit, however, may entail a host of other requirements: collateral, penalties if payments are not made as specified, and forms of payment, among many others. Many of these—such as the price put on the goods advanced—may conceal interest or other equivalent benefits. During this period, as Goitein notes, business in the Mediterranean was routinely conducted on the basis of credit; and, in wholesale trade, deferred payment was absolutely necessary. When Maimonides was asked if deferred payment was religiously permissible since it often concealed hidden interest, he replied that "without it most livelihoods would come to a standstill."[41]

The problem presented by interest payments was complicated for Muslim, Jewish, and Christians jurists alike as scriptural proscriptions against usury are found in all three traditions. Part of the problem, however, was to whom did such strictures apply. While all three traditions agreed that they applied to members of their own faith, for whom a brotherhood standard clearly applied, they differed regarding others. For example, Muslims were clearly forbidden from engaging in usury; and, were even discouraged from doing business with non-Muslims, unless transactions were done according to Islamic conventions, effectively extending this ban to their participation in commercial projects with non-Muslims if they transgressed Islamic norms.[42] By contrast, Jewish jurists permitted usury in relations with non-Jews while Christian sensibilities did not need to surface in Islamic Iberia since Christians agreed with Muslims on the illegality of lending at interest though like Muslims they could receive a loan at interest from a Jew because it did not bring them profit from the interest paid.

Because interest payments could be veiled in financial transactions in many ways, Islamic jurists were particularly concerned with broadening both the equity and the fairness that a brotherhood standard implied, and were particularly insistent upon transparency as a means to ensure this. Given this, Islamic financial instruments tended to require very detailed specifications. As usury was forbidden, any transaction where shares were unequally distributed was suspect. Related to their concerns with equity, jurists had an aversion to speculation and gambling, and any kind of transaction where risks could not be foreseen (making them non-transparent) was also not permitted.[43] As the following cases from al-Andalus illustrate these concerns are clearly evident in the *responsa* by the Islamic jurists to questions posed to them:[44]

> 208. A person brings to the market and offers printed cloth to a merchant for 50 dinars, provided he splits the earnings from the sale with him. Response: *His participation in the earnings is illegal ... it can only be legal if in the case of loss he will bear the consequences in the same proportion as in the planned share of the profit.*[45]

What is proposed in this case is a kind of partnership, which under Islamic principles of law requires both equal participation and equal shares in both risks and benefits. This case clearly violates these dictums so it was not permitted.

> 300. Selling of goods that the buyer wants to pay little by little in exchange for dying other clothes that the seller gives him to be dyed. Response: *Such an operation is not allowed.*[46]

The issue in this transaction is that it is not transparent. One cannot determine the quality of the work that the buyer may present in exchange as the purchase is in advance of the payment which is not in coin, so fairness cannot be determined.

259. Purchase on credit of loads of onions ready to pick, payable once they have been resold. Response: *This transaction is legal if it is done by a merchant, if not then the date of payment must be specified.*[47]

The issue is that merchants have on going and predictable payment arrangements and often sell on credit—others introduce unpredictability without specification of the date of payment as well as specification that the onions are ready to pick: lack of either would be like gambling, which like interest is not allowed.

299. A storm forces passengers to throw part of their cargo overboard. Do those passengers who were carrying gold or silver coin have any liability. Response: *The assessment of what to jettison should only take the weight of the goods into account, and not a person's coin, as it was the weight of the goods that put the ship in peril.*[48]

Here again it is fairness and transparency that are at issue. Thus, the jurist holds that as weight of goods causes risk not the value of what is transported, the coins passengers carried should also be excluded in calculations of liability.

THE RECONQUEST

Between the eleventh and thirteenth centuries the interplay among three major processes the Reconquest, the Crusades, and the commercial revolution reshaped Iberia and Western Europe. By the thirteenth century, Western Europe had followed the Iberian example and become significantly urbanized. Some Spanish historians date the beginning of the reconquest to the kingdom of Asturias's defeat of Muslim forces at Covadonga in AD 722, others somewhat more objectively note that for the next 300 years the Christian kingdoms of the North were in no position to offer effective opposition to Muslims in Iberia, and only began to have military success once the Caliphate of Córdoba fell apart in 1031, politically shattering into twenty-one to twenty-three *ta'ifas* that fought amongst themselves. In 1085, Castile and León captured Toledo, and controlled over a long stretch of the Tagus River. Facing advancing Christian armies, Muslims sought military assistance from the Almoravids, a Berber dynasty based in Marrakesh. Almoravid armies soon arrived, and while they halted Christian advances,

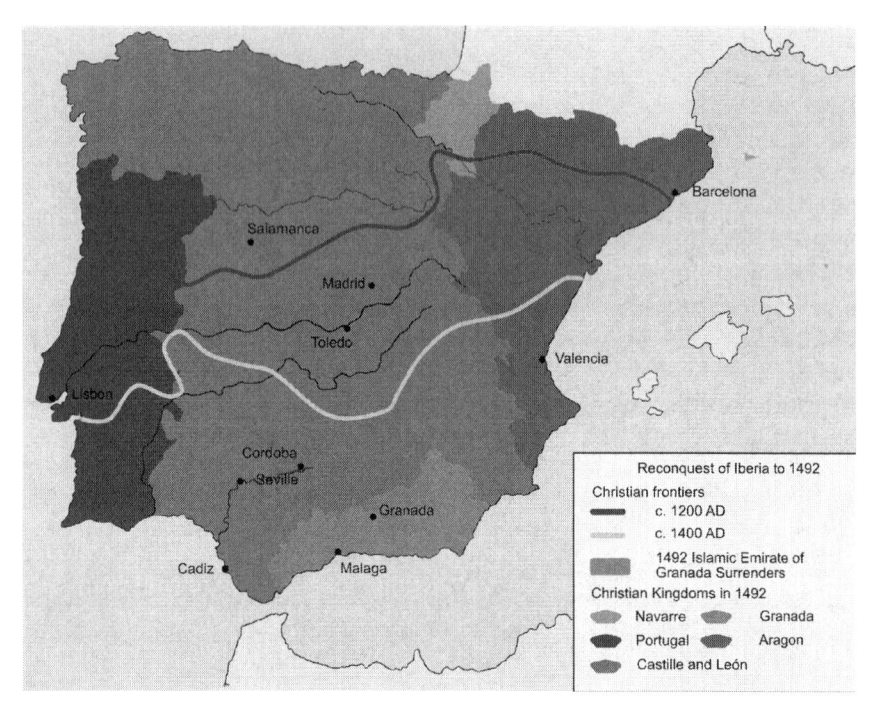

Figure 2.2 The Reconquest of Iberia, AD 1200–1492. *Source*: Map drawn by Thomas K. Park.

they did not retake Toledo. What they did do was to absorb the petty *ta'ifa* kingdoms, and reunify what remained of al-Andalus under their rule.[49]

In the meantime, and especially after 1150, a more peaceful "co-penetration and synthesis" was going on which produced a new proliferation of Christian, Jewish, and Muslim quarters especially in Muslim ruled cities across the northern half of Iberia. This process was driven by population increase in Christian Europe accompanied by large levels of mobility as the underdeveloped parts of Europe attracted cultivators whose life chances were poor where they had been born.[50] It is a reasonable conjecture that the advanced urban development of Iberia had its own influence on the development of cities throughout Western Europe via the gradually increasing acquaintance of Christians with Iberian cities.

While the Almoravids were consolidating their rule over al-Andalus, the Crusades got underway. The first was launched in 1095, followed by four other major crusades in 1144, 1190, 1204, and 1213. The crusades opened up a new theatre of warfare and cultural exchange with the Islamic world. The finances required also stimulated the development of international banking and trade, services which made the Templars both wealthy, and the target of jealous kings.[51] While the first crusade took Jerusalem and succeeded in setting up the Latin Kingdom of Jerusalem, the city was retaken by Saladin in 1187. In 1291, after another century of war the Latin Kingdom's last outpost in Acre fell. In the twelfth century, Almoravid power also began to wane. Christian kingdoms again renewed their attacks on Islamic Iberia. In 1118, Aragon conquered Zaragoza. In 1147, Portugal's king with the aid of crusaders on their way to the Holy Land took Lisbon.

After this, numerous Papal bulls were issued equating the Reconquest with the Crusades. Again, there was an appeal to Muslims in Morocco for help—and in this same year, Almohads came from Morocco, and soon began to take over. By 1163, they had established themselves and moved their capital to Sevilla. Though the Almohads achieved a great victory in 1212 over the Christians at the battle of Alarcos, their victory merely set back Christian ambitions; and, in 1236 Castile and León captured Córdoba, then Jaén in 1246, followed by Sevilla in 1248. Meanwhile, Aragon had seized the Balearic Islands and subjugated Valencia in 1238. Thus, by the middle of the thirteenth century, with the exception of the Kingdom of Granada in southern al-Andalus—which would ultimately fall in 1492—Christian kingdoms ruled Iberia.[52]

This series of dates and places, kingdoms and battles, while telling us about the when, where, and who the players were, provides little insight into more fundamental questions: How did these Christian kingdoms muster the resources required to overcome their seemingly more sophisticated and powerful Muslim opponents? What role did the commercial revolution play in the Reconquest and Crusades? To begin to answer these questions we need to examine the Reconquest more closely, and consider questions such as what role did finance and trade play? This requires giving some consideration to what Christians may have learned from the Islamic world about statecraft, trade, and finance. It also requires giving some thought to why Christian methods of commerce, laws, and forms of organization ultimately took a different path.

The stereotypic portrayal of western Catholic Europe in the tenth century is one where rural manors and villages had become the principal units of production and consumption, as an era in which towns and cities had virtually disappeared due to centuries of political turmoil. In this picture, although periodic markets existed, they were few and far between, and though a cadre of itinerant merchants attended them, trade was anemic for several reasons: (1) traveling with goods was dangerous; (2) there was a lack of coinage in circulation; and (3) few Christians were literate,[53] and so lacked skills required to conduct international trade, and as a result the trade that did occur was largely conducted by literate Jews.[54]

As tempting as it is to contrast the economic development in the Islamic world with the backwardness of Western Europe in the tenth century, underlining such differences ignores the forces that were shaping the rise of commerce in Europe. Western Christian economies were far more dynamic than has been imagined. Trade might have been scant, but populations were growing rapidly partly due to a period of milder climate,[55] because of advances in agricultural production such as the heavy plow that allowed the tilling clay soils which opened new areas to cultivation, and also because of changes in diet; eating a greater variety of grains, beans, and greens provided people with greater food security. As population increased more intensive forms of production were required—clearing of forests and draining of swamps involved new land that had to be taken from others through warfare.[56]

The Reconquest set in motion a long familiar logic of accumulation by dispossession where, as conquered peoples flee, the victors appropriated their houses, lands, and property.[57] The subjugated population that remained paid tribute and taxes, increasing the victor's wealth and capacity to wage war. The obverse held for the losers. Even so, the Reconquest and Crusades were more than a series of wars and battles, as Muslims and Christians engaged one another, there was also an ongoing, profound, and centuries long cultural encounter between their worlds.

To understand this long cultural encounter; however, the dynamics of the relations between Muslim and Christian kingdoms need to be appreciated. The Reconquest was a punctuated conflict in which there were periodic wars, truces, and times of peace. Its politics was messy, and did not always pit Muslims against Christians. Christian Iberia was divided into rival kingdoms which at times fought each other. In such wars, rulers would seek to form alliances with other rulers and power brokers; Christian or Muslim if expedient. Within these kingdoms as well, wars over succession were common—and could be particularly nasty as alliances between kingdoms regularly took the form of marriages between royal houses. Rivals for thrones looked for backing wherever it could be found, and Muslim rulers—reading the political winds—often found good reasons to support one pretender over another. The opposite was also true. Once the Caliphate splintered into *ta'ifas*, Muslim polities were rife with political rivalries and would-be power holders also looking for political support wherever it could be found.[58]

One of the profound results of Christian military victories was their impact on society itself. As Muslim cities fell, many residents fled, but others stayed. Those who stayed included Mozarab Christians, Jews, and Muslims (called Mudejars or Moors). Each conquest brought these groups into Christian kingdoms in greater numbers. How they were treated varied from kingdom to kingdom, from city to city, and changed over time as their integration engendered social conflicts and tensions within these societies.[59] The negative aspects of this are well known: the rules imposed on Mudejars and Jews on the practice of their religion, bans on inter-marriage, restrictions on their economic activities; attempts to segregate them and force them to live into special quarters; and to wear distinctive dress.

This is documented in their experience of pogroms, in records of forced conversions, in Jewish and Muslim persecution by the Inquisition, and ultimately in expulsion.[60] Less known are its positive dimensions. Many Jews, Mudejars, and Mozarabs were literate. Toledo, for example, at the time of its conquest in 1085 was the most important crossroads for Jewish, Muslim, and Christian scholars in Europe. Almost immediately, its new archbishop undertook a vast project that sought to translate philosophical, scientific, and literary works from Arabic into Latin and Romance languages.[61] As important as this project was, its impact pales in comparison to that which the incorporation of vast numbers of Jews, Muslims, and Mozarabs had on these societies. As al-Andalusi merchants, scholars, physicians, and assorted craftsmen came under Christian domination, their previously rare skills and talents reinvigorated the economies of these kingdoms.

In this long encounter Christians, Jews, and Muslims came to use much the same technologies of trade—*commenda* partnerships, letters of credit, bills of lading, banks, monies of account, etc. Nevertheless, there were substantial and profound differences in their political and legal systems that raise fundamental questions about how these divergent traditions shaped trade.

THE COMMERCIAL REVOLUTION

Among the grand processes reshaping the medieval world between the eleventh and thirteenth centuries was the so-called "commercial revolution"[62] that ultimately helped provide the economic resources that the Reconquest required, and fueled by mass transfers of wealth from the reconquest, this revolution also made it possible for Christian kingdoms to dominate the Mediterranean trade. These grand processes also entailed population growth, advances in agricultural production, the spread of minting and coinage (absent since the fall of the Roman Empire in many areas), increasing literacy,[63] the founding of Christian universities,[64] infusions of knowledge from classical and Islamic sources, the rediscovery of Roman law, the establishment of fairs,[65] the diffusion of the techniques and practices of long-distance trade, and the evolution of new ways of organizing business ventures. As a result, by the second half of the thirteenth century, Christian Spain was well positioned to take advantage of the growing international commerce that was developing from Western Europe to China.[66]

Roman law contained principles and rules that were better suited to regulate the complex commercial transactions, commercial litigation, partnerships, and the problems of credit and debt that developing trade required[67] than those codes that had governed commerce in Christian kingdoms during earlier centuries, and this helped put Catholic Europe on a different trajectory from the Islamic world.[68] Roman law decontextualized from Roman concerns about honor and reputation[69] proved to have few restrictions and pushed traditional issues of justice and fairness to the periphery. It could, thus, be tailored to fit the needs of new kinds of associations.[70]

This was a time of competition not just between states and religions, but also between moral, political, and economic discourses. Christian kings found in Roman law the means to carve out a distinctly secular space, a domain separate from the religious and moral authority of the Church, over which they could legitimately claim power to rule the increasingly diverse population of Christians, Muslims, and Jews living in their kingdoms. Moreover, Roman law entailed the principles of governance that also helped bolster their claims to absolute power and authority.[71]

In Spain, the *Siete Partidas* of Alfonso X, King of Castile and León (1252–1284), was the most famous result of this Roman influence. Even though the *Siete Partidas,* addressed many of the same concerns found in Islamic law governing commercial transactions such as fair treatment, just price, and the issue of usury, its approach to such questions is based upon a profoundly different approach. Instead of viewing these issues as moral questions, the *Siete Partidas* places them into the decidedly political arena of secular law. In contrast to Jewish law where a brother standard applies to transactions between co-religionists, the Roman approach is to see the other party as an enemy or stranger. In both Roman and Visigothic law parties to transactions are seen as opponents. Thus, in the *Siete Partida*s we find:

> Selling is a form of conflict that men frequently use with each other, and is done with consent of the parties, for a price that the buyer and the seller agree upon. ... Unless this agreement is voluntary it is void.[72]

Likewise the seventh century, Visigothic *Liber Iudiciorum* states:

> No one shall attack the validity of the transaction by declaring that he sold the property for less than it was worth.[73]

The implication is that because commercial transactions are a form of conflict, if buyers and sellers agree, it is by definition fair to both sides. The role of law, given this stance, is to guarantee fair treatment—but here this merely means seeing to it that the form of sale is proper, that the terms of the agreement are met, and that the goods are delivered at the agreed upon time and place in the condition specified. If buyers and sellers are engaged in a form of conflict, then it is logical for competitors to keep secrets, and transparency is foolish, so *caveat emptor*—let the buyer beware! While Islamic jurists worried about speculation and risk, from this position risk and speculation are inherent parts of doing business. Similarly, if all parties freely entered into an agreement, however it may be structured, it is by definition fair. If this is the case, then any Islamic legal requirements of equity in inputs, profit, liability, or risk simply cannot apply.

Medieval banking[74] developed in the Italy in the twelfth century, and offered a variety of simple services—money changing, deposits, loans, processing bills of exchange, and transferring payments from one merchant to another.[75] As these services were vital both for trade and for warfare, banking quickly spread. By the thirteenth century, banks were to be found in Catalonia, and its maritime commerce developed in competition with Genoa. Catalonia's commercial empire soon extended across the Mediterranean. However, following the failure of its principal private banks in 1381, Catalonia went into decline.[76] While a number of other factors were involved in the contraction of Catalonia's economy, for example, the plague, the pogroms of 1391, and rivalry from Genoa, the failure of these banks and the subsequent decrease in the availability of credit certainly contributed.[77]

In the shadow of *caveat emptor*, Bankers sought to protect themselves from risk by creating a variety of new forms of lending better suited to commerce such as "sales with the power of redemption or with guarantees, advances on life annuities or redeemable securities, loans on mortgages, and, above all, loans on a limited partnership basis, of security of specie or against a bank deposit, and loans on bottomry, the last being used in the great enterprises of sea commerce."[78] Merchants for their part sought both to lessen their risks and maximize their profits by pooling their resources in various new ways within commercial societies with limited liability that brought together investors, merchants, and their agents. They formed guilds or societies for mutual defense and protection and, later, merchant trading companies and federations to monopolize trade; most famously the German Hanseatic League.[79]

Nonetheless, there were certain types of risks that bankers and merchants could not easily resolve. They faced the uncertain demands of kings, lords, prelates, and other power holders. Forced loans were common, and too often went unpaid. Such defaults ruined many banks and wealthy merchants. Against these risks were the rewards—the protection and patronage of popes and kings. In return for loans, bankers and wealthy merchants were in a position to receive special privileges and exemptions. As the Jewish experience attests, all such advantages could vanish in the ever changing political winds. By the thirteenth century, Jewish merchants were compelled to conduct business according to Christian laws.[80] Compared to the Italians, even as moneylenders, they played a minor role. In fact, during the Middle Ages "the more economically advanced a country was, the fewer Jewish moneylenders were to be found there."[81]

The changes to the financial landscape that were at play during the Reconquest set in motion fundamental changes to trade routes across the Mediterranean. Prior to the thirteenth century, the east-west maritime trade routes that linked al-Andalus to Egypt ran along the Maghribi coast and passed through the crucial hubs of Tunisia and Sicily. In the eleventh and twelfth centuries, Christian conquests of the eastern coast of Iberia, of Sicily, Majorca, Ibiza, and Minorca opened an alternative northern route across the Mediterranean to Muslim ports that Christian merchants favored.[82] Christian domination of the Mediterranean trade was further helped along as the Reconquest deprived Muslim ship builders of access to Iberian timber.

Although some suitable forests still existed in Morocco, northern Syria, Lebanon, and Crete, and Muslims continued to build some ships in Kingdom of Granada, Papal bans on selling to Muslims commodities that had military applications (wood, arms, and ships) prevented Muslim ship builders from procuring timber from Christians through trade,[83] and probably also helped to tip the naval balance of power in the Mediterranean in the Christian favor.[84] As well, simulated by the expansion of trade, a Christian shipbuilding industry developed in Barcelona, Sevilla, Dinis, and Lisbon that by the late thirteenth century had improved the design of Christian-built ships in the Mediterranean, which took on characteristics of those in northern Europe, being studier and more seaworthy than their Muslim counterparts.[85]

By the late twelfth century, Jewish and Muslim merchants were increasingly compelled to use Christian vessels to ship their cargos. As a result, by the later part of thirteenth century, the role al-Andalus played as an entrepôt for eastern commodities to Christian Europe had been eclipsed by Christian Mediterranean ports. More and more goods were shipped on Christian ships to such ports as Genoa, Marseilles, and Barcelona, and from there to secondary markets, including Muslim ports in Granada.[86] In the face of growing Christian competition, and the decline of the trade route between Egypt and al-Andalus that the Almohad hegemony had maintained, Maghribi Jews began to turn away from the less profitable trade with Iberia, and to concentrate their efforts on the Indian Ocean.[87] Following the Christian victories of the thirteenth century, which opened the strait of Gibraltar to Christian shipping, a Christian north-south axis developed between Mediterranean markets and Europe, the importance of which soon overshadowed the shrinking east-west trade.[88]

The rise of western European kingdoms to dominate Mediterranean trade, however, was not simply due to better ships or other physical factors, but also had to do with both financing and forms of commercial organization. In contrast to Jewish and Muslim merchants whose trade was structured into fairly closed networks in which social capital in the form of knowledge of members and their reputations formed the basis of trust and exchange, as the channels of trade in Christian world rapidly grew, they soon outstripped the capacities of trade built on relationships among "friends." As buyers and sellers were often strangers, Christian merchants in Iberia turned to Roman commercial law[89] and its derivative contracts to build an institutional framework for commerce including corporations, merchant guilds, and courts that could enforce and mediate relationships among often distrusting parties.[90]

THE SPECIAL PROBLEM OF USURY

The negative valuation of usury constrained the development of commercial trade.[91] It was the subject of Church canon law, and so a matter of moral concern. However, because it was an integral part of commerce, the state also sought to regulate it—an issue that often put church and state at loggerheads. Church bans on usury had existed since the Ecumenical Council of Nicaea in AD 325, and were reaffirmed at the Second, Third, and Fourth Lateran Councils in 1139, 1179, and 1215. The Church looked at usury from the point of view of an agrarian society, where borrowing for consumption was something the poor did out of desperation. Basically, Catholic Church objections were manifold and have been examined in the previous chapter Although canon law banned Catholics from engaging in usury, the changing definitions of usurious commerce applied only to the faithful, and so excluded Jews. The regulation of Jewish usury fell to kings, placing it squarely into a political sphere.[92]

During the thirteenth century, Spanish (Christian) kingdoms took a variety of positions on usury from banning it to regulating it, which because they were driven by various political interests differed from nation to nation and often changed from one reign to the next, or even from one day to the next. As commerce increased, and it became increasingly apparent that lending could have productive benefits, a number of Spanish kingdoms rather than ban usury, followed the example of the Codex Justinian, which accepts the payment of interest on a debt as a useful practice, and attempted to merely regulate it, either through legal definitions of what constituted usury, or by setting a cap or range for the legal interest rates that could be charged.[93]

Alfonso X, for instance, in his *Fuero Real,* while forbidding Christians to make interest-bearing loans, permitted Jews and Muslims to charge up to 33.33 percent per annum on loans. This provision, however, did not make it into his *Siete Partidas*.[94] From the twelfth century, the Church extended the ban on usury to include lending against collateral, specifically targeting consumption lending by pawnbrokers. This prohibition, however, did not apply to merchant bankers to the degree that the financial instruments they dealt in were not without risk and did not guarantee interest.

One core concern about consumption lending by pawn brokers was the interest gained without risk by the broker—from a contractual perspective it was noted that risk of capital loss was impossible in the pawn brokerage. This focus on risk opened the door to risky lending for commerce, and to contracts that had implicit interest bearing features within Iberia and elsewhere. Since Christian commercial law refused to demand the transparency that Islamic law emphasized, a cottage industry flourished in Iberia, as elsewhere in the Islamic world,[95] to hide interest payments in a variety of ways.

The triple contract was the most famous of these simulations. It entailed three different transactions: a partnership (*societas*) contract for an investment, an insurance policy on the amount of the investment, and a contract to sell an uncertain future gain for a lesser certain sum. Each individual contract was valid, but when combined, simulated a risk-free loan. We find interest hidden in mortgages and fictitious sales, in structured purchases, and refinancing over time, disguised as rent, as prepayments, and veiled as mixed payments of cash or kind, as transaction costs (damages and expenses), and in usufruct rights to property held as collateral.[96]

JEWS AND CREDIT

The Jews were often the scapegoat used to divert attention from the larger set of political and economic processes transforming societies in the Middle Ages. Small Jewish communities existed among the feudal kingdoms of Catholic Europe long before the Reconquest. However, this was only possible where they had kings and lords as patrons—as without their protections they were exposed to attacks from all quarters.[97] As Christian kings reconquered Iberia, and because literacy was rare among Christians, they looked to the Jewish communities in their new lands where they found a highly literate population with great administrative skills and financial expertise, and soon employed them "as physicians, counselors, envoys, tax collectors, and entrusted them with a major responsibility for organizing supplies for the armies sent against Muslim Spain."[98]

In Castile, for example, Jews from about 1075 to 1375 were regularly appointed to high offices.[99] They were often chosen to head the Royal treasury.[100] Likewise, they filled the ranks of the king's accountants (*contadores*). Often a Jew would serve as the *almojarife mayor* who oversaw tax collection. As well, taxes were collected by tax farmers who guaranteed the Crown a specified sum for the privilege and most of these were Jews.[101] Jewish courtiers were in a position to compete for royal favors with Christian knights, and were even rewarded for their services with houses and estates in reconquered lands.[102]

Jewish communities understood that whether they prospered or not turned on patronage. In this game, patronage was key both to protection and to power and money. It demanded loyalty, expressed by services rendered.[103] Spanish kings regularly exacted forced loans from Jews to finance military campaigns, diplomatic missions, royal marriages, and the like.[104] Arguably, whether forced or not, because such loans were part of the currency of patronage, having a king or an important lord in one's debt, reinforced an ongoing relationship that was very useful whether the loans were repaid or not.

Royal patronage, however, came at a price. As under Muslim rule, Jewish communities paid additional levies, not required of Christians; besides annual head taxes that Jewish communities paid as a lump sum (and apportioned among its households according to their ability to pay), communities also had to pay thirty silver coins a month "in memory of the thirty pieces of silver paid to Judas for the betrayal of Christ."[105] Moreover, Kings considered Jews to be their personal property, so these taxes and levies were paid directly to the Crown. A clear formulation of principal is found in Teruel's *fuero* (municipal charter) from 1176: "The Jews are the slaves of the Crown and belong exclusively to the royal treasury."[106] Although they were under the king's protection, he was free to give other secular and ecclesiastical authorities permission to settle Jews on their lands, to collect taxes from them, or to utilize their services.

During the Reconquest, the political structure of Spain underwent a profound transformation that ultimately had deep repercussions for its Jewish communities. At the beginning of the eleventh century, Christian kingdoms had a predominately feudal character; by the end of the thirteenth century, several large Christian states with a decidedly more modern legal and bureaucratic structure dominated most of the Iberian Peninsula.

Up to the thirteenth century, Spanish sovereigns had ignored the Church's council that Jews should not be named to offices that gave them authority over Christians, that usury should be forbidden, that Jews should not be allowed to eat, live, or marry with Christians, and certainly not be allow to build synagogues.[107] However, anti-semitism had deep roots in Christian Spain, and with the commercial revolution, as Christians and Jews came increasingly into direct competition, anti-Jewish sentiments rose. Ultimately, Jews were victims of their own success—despite enjoying Royal protection, they were hated by their Christian rivals at court, by other merchants, and especially detested as tax farmers by the commoners,[108] who blamed Jews for all the ills that had befallen them. This hatred and bigotry soon gave rise to blood libel—and stories of Jews killing children.[109] In 1230, following the death of Alfonso XI all the Jewish communities in the kingdom of León were destroyed. León, wasn't the first, but it presaged the great pogroms in 1354 and 1391.[110] Throughout this period, usury remained a point of contention.

Kings were under constant pressure from Christians to do something about usury. Even Jaime I of Aragon (1213–1276) who had actively recruited Jewish settlement in his realm with promises of new charters, tax breaks, and various privileges bowing to such pressures in 1228 issued a series of anti-Jewish decrees.[111] He set the rate of interest Jews were allowed to charge at 20 percent, which was at the time the rate Florentine merchants charged. He prohibited Jews from collecting debts on their oath alone, and required them to present written evidence or witnesses. As well, he forbad Jews from holding public offices or from employing Christian women as servants.[112]

In 1254, Jaime I, following the lead of Louis IX of France, who had just expelled all Jews from his kingdom and cancelled all debts owed them, confiscated all debts owed to Jews, supposedly as a punishment for violating royal edicts, the sums they owed instead were to be paid to the Crown.[113] Driven by competing political and economic considerations, the stance of Jaime I on usury vacillated during the years that followed: the concession granted to moneylenders one year, would be succeeded by strict enforcement of the bans in another.[114] However, rather than seeing the behavior of Jaime I as idiosyncratic—it should be viewed as being symptomatic of the changing forces Spanish monarchs faced.

As increasing trade and integration into larger markets transformed feudal societies, kings had to wrestle with very different logics: one, the *status quo* based on a tributary mode of production rooted in extraction of agricultural surplus and limited by its constraints;[115] the other based on commercial relations and the logic of trade with a wider world that offered far greater potential rewards if its transactions could be taxed and regulated.

Sandwiched between these logics stood the issue of usury—and therefore the treatment of Jews. Under the tributary logic, usury posed threats to the mode of production: peasants borrowed for consumption when their production failed to stretch to the next harvest—so interest would not only make their recovery harder, but it would compete directly with the extraction of tribute. Under the logic of trade, credit was put to productive use: it allowed merchants to buy and sell in greater quantities, augmenting their profits, and speeding up the cycle of accumulation as well. For monarchs, at the time these logics were embodied by different kinds of people: on one side, the church, noblemen, peasants, and commoners; on the other merchants, bankers, and moneylenders. During the Reconquest the politics of usury, thus, was the arena of competition between Christians and Jews as the interests groups tied, respectively, to feudalism and mercantilism.

By the middle of the fourteenth century, the tide of anti-Jewish sentiments pushed Alfonso XI, King of Castile and León to enact a new law prohibiting Jews and Muslims from charging interest on loans. This 1348 law also forbade government officials from collecting on debts owed to Jews, and called upon the Church to use its powers of excommunication to assist in its enforcement.[116] It didn't take long, however, for the consequences to be felt throughout the economy, and within three years the king was petitioned by cities to nullify these measures and to return to the *status quo antes*.[117] None of this altered the growing anti-semitism that was spreading through Christian kingdoms.

In 1354, the Jews of Sevilla were attacked by a mob who accused them of having desecrated the host.[118] The virulence of the rhetoric only increased: It was said that when the taxes are allocated at the royal court, Jews come "who are ready to drink the blood of the poor Christians, flaunting the contracts made with them and promising gifts and jewels to the king's favorites." The bishops needed money and themselves urged the king to farm the taxes out to the Jews as those most capable of increasing the royal revenues. The Jews promised to augment the income of the royal treasury by three millions more than were collected in the previous year, and the king approved, for "the poor man does not realize that all this blood comes out of his own side."[119]

In 1377, under continuing pressures to prevent circumvention of laws against usury, the Cortes of Castile prohibited Jews and Muslims from accepting notes of obligation of any sort from Christians. None of these measures lessened the hatred of Jews. Enflamed by the plague and wars of the late fourteenth century, the poor laid the blame for all their troubles on the Jews, and in 1391, a pogrom that started in Sevilla soon spread leaving thousands of Jews dead in its wake in Carmona, Écija, Córdoba, Jaén, Úbeda, Cuenca, Burgos, Madrid, and Logroño among other cities.[120]

Following these pogroms, fearing for their lives many Jews became Christians. However this result seems to have encouraged, over the next decades, ever harsher anti-Jewish measures to be passed—forbidding Christians to act on behalf of Jews, and forbidding Jews to act as tax farmers or from receiving any documents from Christians that mentioned debts owed them.[121] In 1412, supposedly to protect these new converts from the corruptive influences of their Jewish brethren, the Laws of Catalina were issued which required Jews to wear distinctive garments, to live in enclosed ghettos, and which forbade Jews from tax-collecting, practicing medicine, working for Christians, attending their weddings or funerals, or even talking idly with them. The intent of this ordinance seems to have been to both encourage conversion—"No Jew shall prevent another from being baptized"—but also discourage flight, so Royal law also specifies that any "Jew ... departing from my kingdom and dominions, and taking in the road or any other place, shall lose whatever they have with them, and be my slaves forever."[122]

Yet, even the forced conversion of Jews did not resolve the underlying class jealousies. New Christians (*conversos* formerly Jewish or Muslim) now were free to participate in Christian societies—and quickly rose to positions of power and influence in both Church and state, and continued to excel in the commercial world. New charges were invented—of backsliding, and that *conversos* were secretly continuing Jewish or Islamic practices. In time this developed into the Inquisition, which continued long after the expulsion of Jews from Spain in 1492.[123] Politically what these repressive measures did was to drive financially savvy Jews or Muslims out of the most lucrative sectors of the economy, and open up those areas to Christian domination.

IBERIA'S COMPLEX FINANCIAL IMPACT ON WESTERN EUROPE

At the outset of this chapter, we raised two basic questions. How did interactions among Christians, Muslims, and Jews in Medieval Iberia contribute to the commercial revolution in western Europe? Why did Christians and Muslims ultimately follow different paths? Although Muslim and Jews played a broad role in transmitting best business practices, borrowing from Islamic law was probably a non-starter in Catholic Europe—and this may have been an issue in taking from the Jewish cannon as well, given that Christian doctrine held that Christ's teaching and the Church's cannon law supersede Jewish law. The Islamic concerns with fairness, transparency, and the sharing of risks also seem to have been problematic under a legal regime that emphasized *caveat emptor*. One might speculate that a brotherhood standard also problematized Jews and non-Jews or, alternately, Muslims and non-Muslims sharing the same ethical and legal principles—the partiality in treatment was not seen as well suited to regulate inter-ethnic competitors in an emerging transnational commercial world. The complexity of the Muslim-Jewish-Christian accommodation in Islamic Andalusia proved impossible to translate. The rediscovery of Roman law gave the development of commercial law an independent secular realm beyond Church doctrine, and its standard of fairness, favoring more palatable versions of partiality, emphasizing that simple agreement among parties resolved issues of fairness in deals between competitors.

Jews had long played a central role in the diffusion of the technologies of trade. In the Islamic world their status as *dhimmi* allowed them to participate fully in both its economic and political spheres. The Catholic church as well had offered some begrudging recognition to Jews—as Christ and his apostles had been Jews—but policies toward Jews were always in political flux. Jews were initially welcomed, and indeed recruited by Christian monarchs, during the initial phase of the Reconquest because they possessed both financial and administrative expertise that were scarce commodities in Western Christian Europe prior to the eleventh century. They played an important role in putting Royal finances on a firm footing, and so made a substantial administrative contribution to the Reconquest, but they also contributed economically as skilled merchants whose interactions with Christians helped to transmit the fundamentals of merchant practices.

As Christians and Jews came increasingly into direct competition, anti-Jewish sentiments rose, against which even the patronage of kings offered little protection. In this struggle, Jewish lending became the point of contention between two very different logics—one based in a feudal view in which people borrowed due to misfortune, and moneylenders compounded their misery with usury; the other, based on the logic of trade, saw credit as a means of making productive investments and generating greater rewards. Unfortunately, as these new technologies of trade transformed feudalism, Jews and Muslims became the convenient political scapegoats. This blanket scapegoating contributed to Iberia's failure to bring Islamic commercial ideas about full transparency into the European mainstream.

As discussed in the previous chapter, the scholars of Salamanca, who produced Iberia's greatest medieval commercial thought, came late to the table after most of the commercial brilliance of Andalusia had been replaced by distrust between religious communities. Their contributions to rehabilitating lending at interest were considerable and reflected an interesting mix of progressive ideas and conservative ones. Their positions were also more in line with the Islamic prohibition on usury based on differentials in risk, profit, liability, or inputs that arguably facilitated injustice in finance. The scholars of Salamanca, contributed to the gradual loosening of rules against lending at interest but may have also provided a significant brake on too rapid progress. Andalusia's financial scholars were not entirely ignored in Europe's march toward a liberal market, even if some modern conservatives view them in part as reactionary opponents of progress.[124] Nevertheless, it was the adoption and dissemination of classical Roman adversarial positions toward financial contracts that most clearly inserted an intellectual obstacle to any appreciation of the economic, cultural and moral benefits of the Islamic focus on financial transparency.

NOTES

1. See Pirenne, *Medieval Cities*.
2. Wood, *The Origins of Capitalism*, 11–21.
3. See Weber, *Economy and Society;* Braudel, *Civilisations matérielle, économie et capitalisme, XVe–XVIII, Les Jeux de l'Echange*.

4. See Curtin, *Cross-Cultural Trade in World History.*

5. Cantor, (ed). *The Enclyopedia of the Middle Ages,* 411.

6. Córdoba's population in the tenth century is a matter of guesswork. The lowest estimate pegs its population at a 90,000 inhabitants, but an estimate of a million is not unreasonable if the Census ordered by Almanzor is to be believed. It records 213,067 houses occupied by poor and middle class families, and 73,070 palaces and mansions belonging to aristocrats, high officeholders, and rich merchants. See: Gonzalez-Zymla, *Año 929 El Califato de Córdoba,* 137–8; Crow, *Spain: The Root and the Flower,* 55–56; Erdoes, *AD 1000: Living on the Brink of Apocalypse,* 46–47; O'Callaghan, *A History of Medieval Spain,* loc. 1797.

7. In 756 the Umayyads acknowledged the Abbasid caliphate of Baghdad, and al-Andalus became one of its provinces, and though ruled by Umayyad emirs or governors they were technically subservient to the caliph in Baghdad. See: Menocal, *The Ornament of the World,* 81.

8. Menocal, *The Ornament of the World,* 32.

9. Lewis, *God's Crucible: Islam in the Making of Europe,* 304–05.

10. Cited in Gutas, *Greek Thought, Arabic culture,* 89.

11. O'Callaghan, *A History of Medieval Spain,* loc. 2622–32. See also Menocal, *The Ornament of the World,* 33.

12. Lewis, *God's Crucible: Islam in the Making of Europe,* 306.

13. Visigothic persecution of Jews, led many Jews to welcome Muslim rule. Although during the Caliphate of Córdoba Jewish communities were protected as *dhimmi,* after 1146 under the more fundamentalist Almohades faced persecution, and fled to Christian kingdoms of the north by the thousands. See, Pérez. *Los Judíos España,* 52–53.

14. Menocal, *The Ornament of the World,* 72–73 and 85; O'Callaghan, *A History of Medieval Spain,* Loc.1444.

15. Crow, *The Root and the Flower,* 62.

16. These provinces were basically the same ones established by the Romans, and also adopted by the Visgoths as administrative units.

17. Gonzalez-Zymla, *Año 929 El Califato de Córdoba,* 73–74; O'Callaghan, *A History of Medieval Spain,* loc. 2286.

18. . There were three major sources of Islamic canon law. The Koran—seen as the will of God; the *Sunna* (the tradition of the Prophet's conduct, habits, and behavior as handed down by his companions); and the *ijma* (the consensus of the community). Beyond the Islamic canon, however, there also existed a body of customary law, that covered commercial practices. Islamic jurists, however, were generally suspicious of customary law, and in their responsa and rulings they usually looked to the canon rather than customary law for justification of the proper procedures and correct forms of commercial relationships and transactions. See also Park and Greenberg, *Roots of Western Finance,* Chapter 6.

19. O'Callaghan, *A History of Medieval Spain,* loc. 2334–84.

20. Wolf, *Europe and The Peoples Without History,* 79–88.

21. Goitein, *A Mediterranean Society,* 73; O'Callaghan, *A History of Medieval Spain,* loc. 2384–96. See also Chapter 2 of this book for a more detailed discussion of tax-farming.

22. Constable, *Trade and Traders in Muslim Spain*, 147–48.
23. Ibid., 127.
24. O'Callaghan, *A History of Medieval Spain*, Loc. 2384.
25. Ibid., loc. 2540–51.
26. Phillips and Phillips, *A Concise History of Spain*, Loc.1117–23.
27. Erdos, *AD 1000: Living on the Brink of Apocalypse*, 42–43.
28. Most of what we know about merchant behavior during this period comes from the Geniza papers, documents left by Jewish merchants in Cairo who carried on an extensive trade with Jewish, Muslim, and Christian traders in al-Andalus. The geniza ("depository" in Hebrew) contains about a thousand contracts, price lists, traders' letters, accounts, and other documents that reflect trade in the Muslim Mediterranean. Greif, *Institutions and the Path to the Modern Economy*, 60.
29. Constable, *Trade and Traders in Muslim Spain*, 54.
30. Ibid., 138–9; 159; 199; 204–06.
31. Ibid., 112.
32. Ibid., 116–17.
33. O'Callaghan, *A History of Medieval Spain*, loc. 2358–84.
34. Constable notes under Islamic law formal partnership took a variety of forms. In one type, two or more people invest both capital and labor, and split all profits according to relative investment of each partner. In a more elaborate arrangement one party provided the capital, and the other party did the work, however, the profits were divided unevenly, with most of profits (2/3) going to the partner providing the capital for his greater risks. Constable, *Trade and Traders in Muslim Spain*, 71.
35. Goitein, *A Mediterranean Society*, 166.
36. Constable, *Trade and Traders in Muslim Spain*, 64.
37. Greif, *Institutions and the Path to the Modern Economy*, 59.
38. Ibid., 62–71.
39. Ibid., 356.
40. Constable, *Trade and Traders in Muslim Spain*, 55.
41. Goitein, *A Mediterranean Society*, 197.
42. Udovitch, *Partnership and Profit in Medieval Islam*, loc. 4641–52.
43. Ibid., loc. 642–61.
44. The following *responsa* (*fatwa*) or legal opinions from al-Andalus were compiled by Ahmad al-Wanšarīsī a Maliki jurist and scholar born in Tlemcen (present-day Algeria) who died in 1506.
45. Lagardère, Lagardère, *Histoire et société en occident musulman au moyen âge*, 342, #208.
46. Ibid., 178, #300.
47. Ibid., 170, #259.
48. Ibid., 359, #299.
49. Constable, *Trade and Traders in Muslim Spain*, 9.
50. Robert Fossier, *The Cambridge Illustrated History of the Middle Ages 950–1250*. Chapter 6 and pp. 258ff.
51. See Chapter 3 of this book for more detailed discussion of the Templars and Italian banking.

52. See further details on the Reconquest. see Collins, *Early Medieval Spain*; Lomax, *The Reconquest of Spain;* MacKay, *Spain in the Middle Ages;* O'Callagham, *A History of Medieval Spain.*

53. See Cantor, *The Encyclopedia of the Middle Ages,* 129; Davies, *A History of Money: From Ancient Times to the Present Day,* 116–17.

54. Pirenne, *Medieval Cities,* 11.

55. Mann et al. "Global Signatures and Dynamical Origins of the Little Ice Age and Medieval Climate Anomaly," 1256–60.

56. See: Lopez, *The Commercial Revolution of the Middle Ages,* 36–48; Hodgett, *A Social and Economic History of Medieval Europe,* 12–23.

57. Harvey, *The New Imperialism,* 139; Graeber, *Debt: The First 5000 Years,* 226–32.

58. Numerous examples of such alliances between Christians and Muslims are documented by O'Callaghan, *A History of Medieval Spain,* loc. 2017; 2122–32; 4126; 5963; 6466; 6486; 6525; 6961; 7310; 9189.

59. Constable, (ed). *Medieval Iberia,* 134–15; 279–83; 298–302; 393–98 present a variety of surrender treaties, *repartimento* documents, and *fueros* (rules of governance) that set out how these groups are to be treated, what they will be permitted or not permitted to do, and what rights they have.

60. See O'Callegan, *A History of Medieval Spain,* loc. 4841; Netanyahu, *The Origins of the Inquisition in Fifteenth Century Spain,* 296–97.

61. See Márquez Villanueva "La escuela de traductores de Toledo," 23–34.

62. See Lopez, *The Commercial Revolution of the Middle Ages*, 56–84.

63. Following the collapse of the Roman Empire in the West, coinage ceased to be minted in much of Europe for several hundred years. Although some Islamic and Byzantine coinage circulated during the early Medieval period, minting was reintroduced under Charlemagne around 800. Christian rulers in Spain, with the exception of Catalonia that began minting coins under Charlemagne around 800, only started minting their own coinage as the reconquest got underway: Aragon under Sancho el Mayor (1000–1035); León y Castile under Alfonso (1065–1109); Navarre under Sancho el Mayor (1000–1035), Valencia under Jaime I (1246). See Gerli, *Medieval Iberia: An Encyclopedia*, 240–46; Davies, *A History of Money: From Ancient Times to the Present Day.*

64. Following the fall of Toledo in 1085, universities seem to have sprung of rapidly across Europe. A rash of colleges and universities began to pop up at the end of the eleventh century including Bologna (1088), Oxford (1096), Salamanca (1134), Paris (1170), Montpelier (1150), Vinceza (1204), Cambridge (1209), Palencia (1209), Padua (1222), Naples (1224), Toulouse (1229), Siena (1240), Valladolid (1241), Northampton (1261), Murcia (1289), Macerata (1290), Cambria (1290), Alcala (1293), Lleida (1300). Dates of founding are the subject of some debate, in part because definitions vary, and also because there may be different phases in a universities history. The University of Salamanca, for instance, could thus be dated either to its earliest mention in 1134 or to the date of its royal charter in 1218. In the foregoing I have used the earliest documented date of its activities (See de Ridder-Symoens, "A History of the University in Europe").

65. See the discussion of trade fairs in Chapter 3.
66. Abu-Lughod, *Before European Hegemony,* 3–4; 33–34.
67. Burns and Robert, *Las Siete Partidas,* vol. 4, xxxiv–xxxv.
68. Following the collapse of the Roman empires, initially under the Visigoths Hispano-Romans continued to be subject to Roman law, and Visigoths to their own Germanic laws. In the seventh century, the Visigoths influenced by Germanic ideals rewrote Roman law, producing The *Liber Iudiciorum* that introduced German court procedures and treated civil suits as private matters. With the fall of the Visigoths, the *Liber ludiciorum* fell out favor. Partly because few Christians were literate, and there was a resurgence of customary law. Customary law, though much of it was never written down, prevailed until about the eleventh century when with the spread of literacy there was a rival of Roman law. See O'Callaghan, *A History of Medieval Spain,* loc. 877–911; 6446–51; 7849–53.
69. See Park and Greenberg, *Roots of Western Finance,* Chapter 4.
70. Islamic *commenda* partnership (which typically were imagined as being between two partners that are in different places and prescribed that they share profits and losses in appropriate proportions) allowed some flexibility. See Constable, *Trade and Traders in Muslim Spain,* 70–72, Park and Greenberg, *Roots of Western Finance,* 214–17.
71. Although canon law might guide Christian conduct, imposing it on Jews and Muslims was fraught with difficulties; and as the Reconquest progressed and increasing numbers of Jews and Muslims became part of the kingdom their status as self-governing communities became ever more problematic for Christian rulers.
72. Burns and Robert *Las Siete Partidas,* vol. 4, Fifth Partida Title V, Law I, II.
73. Khindaswinth, King of the Visigoths, *Liber Judiciorum,* Book V Title IV Law VII, 86.
74. We take up the subject of medieval banking in chapters 1 and 3 so only offer a brief discussion of this topic here.
75. Pounds, *An Economic History of Medieval Europe,* 409–15.
76. O'Callegahan, *A History of Medieval Spain,* Loc. 10988–994
77. Ibid., loc. 10820–828.
78. Boissonnade. *Life and Work in Medieval Europe,*166.
79. Ibid., 162–63.
80. Ibid., 252–55
81. Pirenne, *Medieval Cities,* 131.
82. We offer a more detailed discussion of this shift in trade routes in chapter 1.
83. Constable, *Trade and Traders in Muslim Spain,* 133.
84. Ibid., 196–97.
85. Ibid., 29.
86. Constable, *Trade and Traders in Muslim Spain,* 34–35; 241–42; O'Callaghan 2013: Locations 8397–8400.
87. Constable, *Trade and Traders in Muslim Spain,* 10.
88. Ibid., 241.
89. See chapter 1 for a more detailed discussion of Roman law and partnerships.
90. Grief, *Institutions and the Path to the Modern Economy,* 388–89.

91. Park and Greenberg, *Roots of Western Finance*, provides great detail on how the opprobrium on usury developed despite its long history of approved practice.

92. Even so, economic justifications needed to be found. St. Thomas Aquinas provided one such rational in his *Summa Theologica* in examining the problem why a lender should be paid for the length of time it took for a loan to be repaid, Aquinas recognized that if loan was to be repaid at a set date, then late payment entailed a loss for the lender of money he could have made had he not lent it, which he termed the *damnum emergens* which in modern economic parlance would be called opportunity costs. Although Aquinas rejected this solution because it entailed a hypothetical gain on money the lender did not have, ultimately others found it useful. See Hodgett, *A Social and Economic History of Medieval Europe*, 65.

93. See Chapter 1 and also Pounds, *An Economic History of Medieval Europe*, 405; Hodgett, *A Social and Economic History of Medieval Europe*, 65.

94. Garcia Diaz, "El Fenomeno del mercado en la obra legislativa de Alfonso X, El Sabio," 117.

95. Park and Greenberg, *Roots of Western Finance*, Chapter 6.

96. Rubin. "Institutions, The Rise of Commerce and the persistence of Laws: Interest Restrictions in Islam and Christianity," 1314–315.

97. Yitzhak, *A History of the Jews in Christian Spain*, 45.

98. O'Callaghan, *A History of Medieval Spain*, Loc. 4841.

99. Netanyahu, *The Origins of the Inquisition in Fifteenth Century Spain*, 65.

100. Example: Samuel ha-Levi during the reign of Pedro I, of León-Castile 1350–1369. See: Netanyahu, *The Origins of the Inquisition in Fifteenth Century Spain*, 94.

101. O'Callaghan, *A History of Medieval Spain*, loc. 7948–971.

102. Baer, *A History of the Jews in Christian Spain*, 140.

103. Ibid., 123; 307–08.

104. Rubin. "Institutions, The Rise of Commerce and the persistence of Laws: Interest Restrictions in Islam and Christianity,"1314; Baer, *A History of the Jews in Christian Spain*, 179.

105. O'Callaghan, *A History of Medieval Spain*, loc. 8112–125.

106. Baer, *A History of the Jews in Christian Spain*, 85.

107. The Council of Coyanza as early as 1055 forbade Christians to live with or eat with Jews; 1081 Pope Gregory VII warned King Alfonso VI not to allow Jews to exercise public authority over Christians; the Third and Fourth Lateran Councils of 1179 and 1215 forbade intermarriage between Christians and Jews and recommended that Jews should be required to wear a distinctive dress. See O'Callaghan, *A History of Medieval Spain*, Loc. 4841.

108. Netanyahu, *The Origins of the Inquisition in Fifteenth Century Spain*, 61–65.

109. The first documented incidence of blood libel stories of this type that originated in Northern Europe circulating in Spain was in 1250. See: Baer, *A History of the Jews in Christian Spain*, 149.

110. See Netanyahu, *The Origins of the Inquisition in Fifteenth Century Spain*, 66–79.

111. Baer, *A History of the Jews in Christian Spain*, 138–144.

112. Ibid., 147.

113. In the years which followed, Jaime I policies on usury continued to vacillate. At times, he would make concessions to Jewish moneylenders, in total disregard the debtor's interests or his own previous decrees, and at times he would insist on strict execution of the law at the Jewish creditors expense. Ibid., 149.

114. Ibid., 149.

115. Wolf, *Europe and The Peoples Without History,* 79–88.

116. Baer, *A History of the Jews in Christian Spain,* 360.

117. Netanyahu, *The Origins of the Inquisition in Fifteenth Century Spain,* 95.

118. Baer, *A History of the Jews in Christian Spain,* 362.

119. Ibid., 368.

120. O'Callaghan, *A History of Medieval Spain,* loc. 9405–415.

121. Netanyahu, *The Origins of the Inquisition in Fifteenth Century Spain,* 177–79.

122. This applied to Muslims as well. See Netanyahu, *The Origins of the Inquisition in Fifteenth Century Spain,* 191–95; O'Callaghan, *A History of Medieval Spain,* Loc. 10674–689.

123. See Netanyahu, *The Origins of the Inquisition in Fifteenth Century Spain* for full treatment of the inquisition.

124. Rothbard. *Economic Thought Before Adam Smith,* 99–115.

Chapter 3

Early European Finance 1050–1650

The period between 1050 and 1650 saw innovations in banking and finance on a scale without historical precedent as Europe urbanized and its population grew. The innovations we examine in this chapter facilitated a scaling up of finance that became critical in the age of exploration and the subsequent Industrial Revolution. Italian bankers helped finance the development of north western Europe and the age of exploration but new forms of finance including the *compagnia*, royal monopolies including the Staple of London[1] (founded 1248), new forms of maritime finance, insurance, annuities, and other loans secured by shares in civic or state revenues, and eventually joint stock companies facilitated the expansion of investors in trade and industry.

The great Italian banks (*monti*) began as trading companies with a minor part of their capital in finance and evolved to combine both trade and finance while adding industrial production within Italy, for example, of finished textiles of increasing sophistication. In this chapter, we focus on the role of newly innovative private firms in the development of new forms of finance, their imbrication with medieval states, and their influence in Western European development.

HISTORICAL CONTEXT

Few scholars suggest that capitalism existed in Europe at the beginning of our period, even if there was accumulation of capital involving new financial techniques and new ethical justifications. We will define capitalism as a socioeconomic system, as usual facilitating particular forms of inequality, in which the price structure of core factors of production (e.g. land, labor, and capital) is efficient enough that commodities can be purchased on the market

58   *Chapter 3*

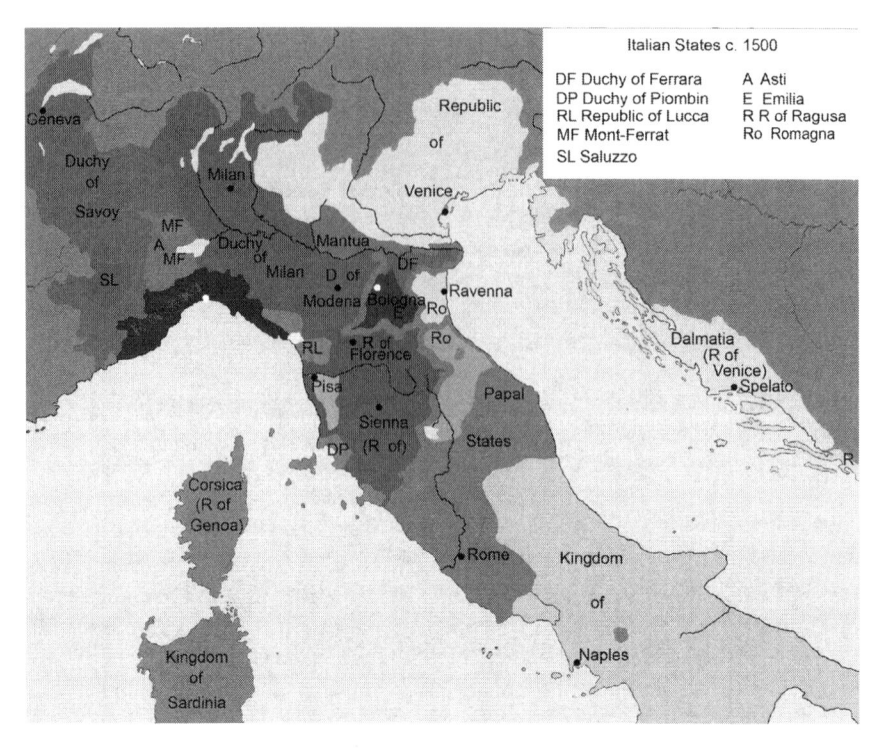

Figure 3.1   Italian States c. 1500 AD. *Source*: Map drawn by Thomas K. Park.

at prices that allow their profitable productive use—without reliance on influence, monopoly, or, more generally, state or private power.

The latter, even today, provide ample sources of additional profit, but, prior to the capitalist period prices were so far from efficient that state granted monopolies or corporate influence kept the possibilities for significant capital accumulation without influence quite minimal. More particularly, while profits in trade were only moderately dependent on influence, the possibilities for profitable industrial investment were seriously hampered by the inefficient price structure of the factors of production as a result of monopolies of one form or the other. Agricultural land was so tied to elite status that its productive capacity was secondary and did not determine its price, natural resources such as mines were tightly controlled, and the supply of labor was constrained in countless ways that radically affected its price in the market. Land and labor were largely locked up in feudal obligations and arrangements. Radical change in many forms was to come but in this chapter we will focus only on the transformations of the financial sector and their important contributions to the formation of a capitalist economy in Italy and Western Europe.

A key to financial change was that the budgetary resources available to governments were inadequate to their growing needs.[2] Technological and economic change was reflected in the cost of government and motivated long-term growth in the state. As wealth accumulated in the hands of merchants, the old taxes oriented to feudal obligations were increasingly inadequate to the needs of an expanding state. Revenue in kind was inadequate and inappropriate for this era where money and credit could provide everything in sufficient quantities and in a more timely manner. As trade over land and sea proliferated, easily assessed goods were increasingly unrepresentative of overall trade. States, if they wished to be considered legitimate, were constrained in what revenue innovations they could impose. Many had to resort to the "forced loan" imposing specific payments on wealthy people, cities, or regions as "interest free loans" given the emergency needs of the state—though all knew this was an implicit tax.

Holding absolutist ideologies, most sovereigns, from a modern perspective, abused power, denied justice regularly, and were notoriously slack about repayment of their debts. Typically, they exchanged monopoly trade positions for loans they had no intention of repaying and at the death of a sovereign or prince the heirs frequently abrogated all extant debt contracts. Typically, funds were raised by leasing tax farming positions to elites or entailing specific revenue streams to a creditor; who might hope to earn thereby both interest and principle given the small chance the principle would be repaid.

While the financial benefits to the state of such financing varied in the short term, tax farming and entailed revenue streams did empower the financial elite and tie them to the state. Nevertheless, once the major capital exchanges of Antwerp and Lyon had developed to the point of providing a market assessment of credit worthiness, with few exceptions (e.g. the British monarch) the princes and sovereigns of Europe were assessed as unworthy of credit—imposing higher interest / rates of return from entailed revenue streams than the rates available to those with good credit.[3]

Efficiencies in the credit market seem to have long preceded those in the labor market which were tied to the slowly increasing efficiencies in the price of machinery which imposed, in slow sequence, low wages and then the option of better wages, more regular pay, and finally a rising standard of living, toward the end of the nineteenth century. Such options came to exist only after major societal sacrifices, the growth of wider bases for societal power and significant social transformations outside the focus of this chapter.

The multiplicity of currencies in Europe meant that the alternative of financing the state through monetary debasement worked best for local jurisdictions and even so this led precious metals to abandon any debased mint for mints where the *seigneuriage* fees were less in real terms. The existence of strong international currencies like the florin (b.1252) or the Venetian gold ducat (b.1285) may also have strengthened the position of Italian merchant bankers relative to that of Western European monarchs attempting to raise funds through debasement.

To put this in historical context, it was not until the eighteenth century that the state began to have the taxing power to raise adequate revenues for its expanding needs. By the twentieth century, state expenditures had reached such a size relative to their economies that taxation was needed to prevent inflation and, as paper currency and credit predominated, the mint and the taxing authority became parts of a greater financial policy that responded quickly to international financial and economic events in ways that would have been quite impossible in earlier centuries.

KNIGHTS TEMPLARS AND HOSPITALLERS: A GEOPOLITICS OF CORPORATE BANKING

Among the motors of change propelling the rebirth of trade in Europe, were the crusades and long-distance pilgrimages. Between 1095 and 1272, there were eight crusades to defend Christendom or liberate the Holy Land from the Infidels. Supplying these great movements of men and arms required the opening of trade routes across Europe from West to East. At the same time, great pilgrimages to shrines in France, Spain, Italy, and the Holy Land also opened more local circuits of trade. The fourth crusade (1202–1204), which never reached the Holy Land, but instead sacked the Christian city of Constantinople, poured the wealth of the Byzantine Empire into many hands including those of the Doges of Venice, and substantially increased the supply of gold in Western Europe.

The banking needs were met by two religious corporations: the Knights Hospitallers, formed in 1094 to care for the wounded of the Crusades, and the Knights of the Temple of Solomon, commonly known as the Templars. The Templars was formed by Crusaders in Jerusalem in 1118 to maintain the safety of trade routes and shipping lanes used by pilgrims to reach Palestine, and to defend the Holy Land from the Infidels. Both orders started life as Benedictines, gained fearsome reputations on the battlefield, and quickly evolved into independent orders that answered only to the Pope.

The avowed mission of these orders, viewed as among the most sacred causes in the medieval world, rapidly drew financial support. Papal bulls, for example, allowed the Templars to keep any spoils they captured from the Infidels. Rich and poor alike, to assure their place in heaven, gave gifts, bequests, and estates to the Templars and Hospitallers. Among the properties of these two orders were the vast estates bequeathed them by King Alfonso I of Aragon (1104–1134), and by King Stephen of England (1135–1154).

By the time of the Second Crusade (1147–1149) the Templars were acting as bankers not only to Christians but also, because they were generally regarded as being exceptionally honest by many Arab merchants as well. Often, knights going off to the Holy Land would leave their last will and testament on file with the Templars, and should they not return; the order would act as their executor. Both orders often acted as agents for their depositors, managing their financial affairs during their absence.[4]

Perhaps the most infamous gift bestowed was to atone for the murder in 1170 of Thomas à Becket, the archbishop of Canterbury. Henry II granted the Templars enough money to support two hundred knights a year, and left an additional 15,000 marks (or approximately 10,000 pounds of silver) to the Templars and Hospitallers in his will. To support their work in the Holy Land, both orders not only maintained their own military forces, but had their own ships, depots, storehouses, as well as strategically located castles. By the thirteenth century, the Templars alone owned 870 castles and manors scattered throughout Europe and the Mediterranean. Because the same ships that carried armies and provisions to the Eastern Mediterranean could also be used to carry cargo back to Europe, their infrastructure enormously increased the volume of trade across the Mediterranean. Both orders, naturally, charged fees for their services and soon were functioning essentially as banking institutions.[5]

The Templars ran afoul of King Philip IV (the Fair) of France in the 1290s. Philip (1285–1314) had chronic financial problems linked in part to his bellicosity. One untapped source of revenue was church lands and, even as the Papacy was beginning to insist that everyone, noble or base pay tithes, Philip decided he could tax all property including that of the church. He had numerous confrontations over this with Pope Boniface VIII (1294–1303).[6] Though the principle in dispute remained unresolved, ever since this period the state's right to tax the general population, if not charitable institutions, has been accepted in Europe. Philip debased the French currency in part to help raise money for his war with Sicily (1282–1302), his conquest of the lands of the Count of Flanders to the north (of Paris) and his conquest of the region of Guyenne in the south.

To restore the currency he needed gold and silver, so he turned to the Templars, who managed his finances, for a permanent loan. When they refused in 1295, he withdrew his money and established a royal treasury in the Louvre. Because the Templars enjoyed the backing of Pope Boniface VIII, any confiscation put him at loggerheads with the church. In 1302, a papal bull, *Unam sanctam*, ruled that the pope had jurisdiction over all secular sovereigns.[7] In 1303 Philip, after being excommunicated, turned on the Lombard merchants (moneylenders of north Italian origin) seizing their goods; and then took aim at the Jews; first seizing their property and then expelling them from France in July of 1306. When Pope Boniface VIII died in 1303, Philip had his successor Benedict IX poisoned and then engineered the election of Pope Clement V, the Archbishop of Bordeaux, whom he felt would do his bidding.[8]

With the backing of the new pope, Philip moved against the Templars, and in 1307 arrested them throughout France in a mass raid. He then seized all Templar lands, property, and wealth in France. In the Inquisition style trials that followed, the Templars were accused and tortured into confessing to every perversity and moral offense imaginable to the medieval Christian mind: including heresy, trampling and spitting on the cross, sodomy, and devil worship. In 1312, Pope Clement V issued a bull *Ad providam* that dissolved the order, and transferred their properties to the Hospitallers.[9] At the end of the trials in 1314, the year of Philip IV's death, the captured Templars were burnt at the stake (where they all recanted their confessions). At the end of the trials there was little left in France to turn over to the Hospitallers.

Philip was less than cutting edge when he expelled the Jews from France in 1306; Edward I had already expelled the Jews from England in 1290, after first having forbidden them to engage in usurious financial practices.[10] Unlike Lombards and Jews who were convenient scapegoats and easy targets for rapacious kings, the Templars constituted a genuine threat to the feudal establishment. Many knights and nobles who joined the Templars left their lands and estates to the order, thus depriving the Crown of its feudal base of power. Through this process not only did the Knights Templar come to possess castles, houses, churches, chapels, oratories, lands, and granges, they also held dominion over cities and towns, and so truly constituted a competing political force.

ITALIAN MERCHANT BANKS AND THE DEVELOPMENT OF NEW FINANCIAL INSTRUMENTS

As coins could be debased, and in any case varied greatly in weight, purity, and condition—some being new; others being old, worn, or clipped—foreign exchange required the expertise of money changers. Foreign trade, however, required more than the accurate assessment of money, it required secure and trustworthy methods for transferring funds, so merchants turned to the bankers, who could transfer money between their accounts, settling their transactions on the spot without the use of cash. The banker's bookkeeping (*scritta*) not only facilitated transfers of money, but permitted overdrafts for established clients.

Banking, of course, was hardly a new invention. The earliest well-known deposit bank, that of House Egibi, dates to 635 BC in Babylon. As we noted in our first book, Jewish moneylenders were major operators in the Islamic world well before their reappearance in the West. Although Jews met with opprobrium and even expulsion especially in the thirteenth and fourteenth century, the church understood that Catholic religious prohibitions on usury applied only to Christians. As Jewish merchants in particular had networks of trading partners all across the Mediterranean, and expertise in handling complex economic transactions, private and government clients frequently asked them to make financial arrangements. As the demand for these services grew, they too began offering banking services as part of their other activities.

In the thirteenth century, all deposit banking services were private arrangements, extended to trusted clients, and were based largely on bills of exchange and money changing. Private bankers were also speculating with (investing) money entrusted to them. Such operations were usually profitable. Once Europe began to grow its way out of the dark ages, cities and states frequently saw advantages to raising money to improve infrastructure and promote economic prosperity.

When he ascended the throne in 1272, Edward I of England was already in debt from expenses incurred during the eighth crusade. To finance wars in Wales and France, Edward turned to the Riccardi of Lucca, his royal bankers, but soon drove them into bankruptcy. Edward then turned to the Frescobaldi family of Florence, who had opened a branch in London in the 1270s, and made them his royal bankers. Between 1302 and 1310, the Frescobaldi bank lent Edward I and II £150,000. In return, however, they demanded as security the revenues from customs worth about the same as *seigneuriage* on the royal mint. When they were also granted lands, honors, and privileges, the House of Lords passed an act that prohibited the assignment of customs revenues to foreigners, and authorized the arrest of foreign merchants and confiscation of their goods. The Frescobaldi fled to France.

By the 1330s, England was again offering concessions to foreigners for financial aid. Edward III desperate for money to finance the Hundred Years' War, turned to English, Flemish, and Italian bankers for hefty loans. In particular, in return for the assignment of customs and tax revenues, the Peruzzi and Bardi houses of Florence made Edward III large loans. They continued to lend Edward III money even as the cost of the Hundred Years' War multiplied. By 1340, Edward III owed Peruzzi and Bardi "the value of a kingdom," over £1,400,000.[11] Although Parliament granted him new taxes, when these failed to yield the expected financial returns, the king defaulted on his loans. To make matters worse, the king of Naples defaulted on his loans to the Peruzzi and Bardi houses as well. Without both revenues, the Peruzzi and Bardi houses were unable to meet other obligations. The king of France helped his royal kin and confiscated the goods of the Peruzzi and Bardi houses and exiled them. In England, agents of both banks were arrested for bankruptcy, and were only released when the Peruzzi and Bardi houses relinquished all claims upon the English crown for debts and interest payments. Royal collusion could do what individual kings could not.

One of the earliest new ways to finance states was through the sale of annuities. These involved a creditor providing capital in return for a part of a revenue stream. On the creditor side, when sold by a creditworthy entity the annuity provided a secure return to capital. Although the creditor alienated capital if necessary (it was often written off as a sale), the annuity could be sold to someone else at a profit or discount as the market conditions determined. This twelfth-century innovation in Italy spread throughout most of Western Europe (in sixteenth-century France they were extremely widespread and termed *rentes*).

The other early innovation first appearing in Italian city states was the *monte*: an organization of merchants willing to raise funds for investments made in the form of loans. In the twelfth and thirteenth centuries large and small firms began to focus a large part of their funds on financing states.[12] An early *monte* making a loan to the Venetian Republic in 1164 involved seven people with the following shares: 2, 2, 1, 1, 1/2, 1/4, and 1/4. As *monte* became institutionalized they were regularly approached whenever civic financing was needed. The Monte del Paschi di Siena was set up in 1472 and as of this writing is still functioning as a bank. Yet, as civic institutions *monti* in time became involved in lending in less exalted circles and even to the poor. The establishment of the Bank of England in 1694, which involved the incorporation of all of the crown's creditors as the Governor and Company of the Bank of England, might be said to have established the ultimate traditional *monte*.[13]

The annuity met with little religious opposition for reasons discussed in our first chapter while the *monti* also benefited from their origin in lending for the public good and to public institutions as well as from the participation of elites as the source of funds and recipients of returns. The work of the scholastics was clearly critical in the acceptance of such financing to the point that even the Papal state ended up having its own *monte*. Yet, neither of these innovations was incompatible with the feudal order. Other innovations which flourished best in more unconstrained economic circumstances provided the seeds that pushed Europe toward a capitalist economy.

In the medieval and Renaissance period, clients could deposit money with private bankers, for safekeeping, with instruction to pay other merchants, as an investment or as part of more complex financial arrangements. During the thirteenth century, the growing demand for banking services led to the creation of new banking houses in Florence, Venice, Genoa, Siena, Lombardy, and Lucca. In Florence alone, there were some eighty great banking firms including the Peruzzi, Bardi, Frescobaldi, and the Medici. Italian bankers soon covered Europe with a network of counting houses which not only handled bills of exchange, but also gave loans both to individuals and corporate entities, received deposits, kept current accounts, and even assisted states in recovery of taxes.[14] Public banks soon followed—in 1401 the Bank of Barcelona was established; followed by the Bank of St. George in Genoa in 1407. Keeping good accounts was critical. Bookkeeping was not just a tool of bankers, it became an essential technology of commerce.

Merchant capitalists did not yet inhabit a world where it was normal for private citizens to hire productive labor at a reasonable price on the open market. Nor was it, even in the late fifteenth century, a world in which it was normal for capitalists to command labor in the way that kings or nobles of the period might. The existence of such a society, which developed in England out of an amalgam of private plantation production based on slave labor in the Caribbean and early industrial production in England,[15] was however not so far off.

The most important involvement in a state-owned productive process by the Medici family came when a godson of the Pope, named Giovanni da Castro, discovered mountains in Tolfa, within Italy itself, that were loaded with alum, used as a mordant in setting dyes. Since the early fifteenth century, the Genoese had virtually monopolized the supply of alum through their ties with the Ottomans who controlled the major alum mines of Phocaea in Anatolia. In 1465, the Medici family was asked to manage the new Italian mines and their profits from the mines were a key source of income through the end of the fifteenth century even though the ownership of the mines remained in the hands of the pope. Similarly, Jacob Fugger of Augsburg became the preeminent banker in Germany in large part by managing the silver mines in the Tyrol (from 1487) though the mines remained legally in the hands of the Archduke Sigismund.[16]

Beginning in the twelfth century, but expanding dramatically in the thirteenth century Italian merchants began not only to trade in Western Europe and the Eastern Mediterranean but developed accounting techniques that facilitated international transactions and provision of credit. In the late thirteenth and early fourteenth century, Italian merchants began to keep individual accounts in bilateral form: one column for debits and one for credits.

One of the key innovations of the fourteenth century was the development of double-entry bookkeeping. Double-entry bookkeeping was based on a simple procedure of recording every transaction twice. Records of equity in individual accounts were complemented by general profit-loss or income-expenditure records for defined units of time, such as a month, thus providing a picture of how the equity was performing. When goods were bought, they were added to the ledger as an asset, and at the same time, their cost was entered in the profit-loss ledger as a deduction. In theory, profits should regularly exceed losses but when they did not the cause was more easily pinpointed if the extra records were maintained. While the origins of double-entry bookkeeping are obscure, in essence it involved multiple ways of representing the same numbers and it probably derived from insights implied by Islamic works on algebra translated at the end of the twelfth century.[17]

F.B. Pegolotti published a guide to commercial practice, *La Pratica della mercatura*, around 1315 and others soon followed making new techniques and suggestions for profitable avenues of investment widely available.[18] By the end of the fourteenth century, many Italian accountants were already using double-entry bookkeeping but by the nature of the accounting which initially involved multiple account books, the incomplete historical record often makes it difficult to be sure that double-entry bookkeeping is being employed.[19] By the time of the Medici bank (1397–1494), most Italian merchants were also using double-entry bookkeeping which added summary accounts for tangible assets and credit operations to the array of bilateral personal accounts.[20] Keeping these more sophisticated accounts made it far easier to know not only if things added up but also which investment or exchange transactions were most advantageous.

In 1494, Friar Luca Pacioli published his *Summa de arithmetica, geometrica, proportioni e proportionalità* which included explanations of bills of exchange as well as an exposition of double-entry bookkeeping that became so popular it was later published separately in 1504 and then in English in 1543 and 1553.[21] W. Schweicker published a German discussion of double-entry bookkeeping, *Zwifach Buchhalten*, in 1549.[22] This spread of this new financial tool allowed merchants, for the first time, to keep accurate accounts of multiple aspects of their economic lives. One had only to look at one's books to know instantly where one stood in terms of assets and liabilities or return on investments. Such knowledge allowed merchants to take control of their business in ways that were not hitherto possible.[23]

Accurate bookkeeping facilitated another key innovation—money of account. Money not only served as a medium of exchange and store of value but now also served as a unit of account. Coins, of course, embody all three of these aspects of money. When commodities are expressed (priced) in terms of units of account, like money they function as mediums of exchange and stores of value. Money of account, however, allowed trade partners to buy and sell goods by simply recording the transaction in terms of money of account as a debit or credit. Such monies of account were expressed sometimes in particular currencies such as ducats or florins, but they were often not based on actual real money, but on so-called ghosts—commonly ancient currencies no longer in use such as the Roman solidus.

Such ghost currencies might be defined against bullion standards, such that twenty solidus were equivalent to a pound of silver,[24] usually they were defined indirectly (e.g. a number of ancient ducats of a specific gold content) in terms of a convenient specific weight of precious metal.[25] Ghost currencies did two things. First, because the value of real coins fluctuated with exchange rates and precious metal content, expressing deposits and debits in ghost money created a more stable standard for payments and one that was removed from the politics of debasement. By way of brief illustration, say a merchant in Florence had contracted to buy a vat of wine from a French merchant at the next harvest for 100 solidus; if in the meantime the value of the florin fell, the French merchant would be still guaranteed his 100 solidus worth of florins as payment for the wine. Second, as merchants valued their inventories and goods in money of account or ghost currencies they in effect added stability to the financial situation. Depreciation or appreciation of modern currencies disturbed merchants less to the degree that they had their resources farmed out as credit (i.e., invested in commodities or in direct loans) repayable at rates that by definition had to be adjusted for depreciation of currency. Money of account could of course be cancelled out through bookkeeping transactions but if it had to be it could also be paid in either currency or commodities, at market adjusted values. Since financial paper took up no precious metal the system both stabilized and enormously expanded the effective money supply.

A bookkeeping device or paper asset such as a credit contract stimulated the economy as it would if it were official paper money pegged to the most stable currency available. Such book money also undermined royal control over money. Although kings may have controlled the mints, all their gold and silver coin represented but a fraction of the value of commodities tracked by merchant monies of account. Moreover, although the state could easily seize tangible properties, credit wealth was nearly invisible, existing in books and slips of paper representing credit dispersed among a network of traders large and small as well as far and near, so it was much more difficult for the state to seize or control. Philip the IV was one of the few kings willing to take on a large credit network and as we have seen he gained only marginally by the attempt, and then only in the extreme short term.

The new accounting techniques provided better tracking of funds but also increasingly substituted for currency at the local level. Even within a town, merchants would frequently pay each other off by transfers of credit. In Florence, even artisans kept meticulous accounts and payments could be made by offsetting on private accounts.[26] The existence of accounts enabled transfers of funds and credit—a merchant who had confidence in the flows of funds into an account could provide credit to a client in excess of the current account balance (by recording a debit) and the credit provided could be used to pay bills or make profits elsewhere.

Initially this worked only for two merchants having accounts in the same bank but soon transitive arrangements were made available via intermediary accounts that linked the two principles' accounts. Thus if "C" had an account with the same bank as "A" and another account in the same bank as "B" the two bankers could arrange transfers from "A" to "B" via "C"'s account. One record of such a scheme in 1466 involves a chain of four intermediary parties to effectuate a payment between the first and the last members of the six person chain without any cash involved.[27] Credit transfers required the existence of credit accounts and a network of bankers willing to trust each other.

Surviving instructions of Bartolomeo de' Bardi (mid-fifteenth-century Florence) advise caution in deciding who is lent money suggesting that merchants are more creditworthy than the Curia and Romans, in particular, are to be distrusted.[28] This advice, like early Medici policy to avoid loans to princes, references the chance of being repaid, many loans to princes and to the Curia were nevertheless made because social networking had its own returns. Where overlapping accounts were not available, a merchant's best alternative was a bill of exchange.

BILLS OF EXCHANGE AND TRADE FAIRS

Merchants in fairs began to issue their own credit notes though the full chronology of this practice is unclear. They were known in France, where they apparently were first seen in the sixteenth-century Brabant fairs, as *cédules obligatoires*. The notes obliged the merchant to pay a given amount within a specified time period.[29] As these notes could themselves be traded they came in time to be called simply *assignations*.

The proper bill of exchange was an early instrument[30] that developed from a preexisting contract referred to as a *cambium*, which was a notarized contract, rather than a simple letter, and, unlike the bill of exchange, referenced no third party[31]—only the drawer and drawee are mentioned and they were members of the same firm.

In its basic form, the bill of exchange was a fairly informal and flexible agreement between the buyer and the seller of the bill in which each agreed that the buyer's funds to purchase goods in another place would be obtained by redeeming the bill at a later date, at the offices of the seller's firm in that other place, and in local currency. In its initial form, bills of exchange were justified because they clearly saved on the risky transport of funds from place to place. Goods were harder to steal and more difficult to convert than coins so using a bill of exchange redeemable where one wished to purchase goods minimized risk.

From the thirteenth century, Italians began to standardize the bill of exchange to fit their international trade networks. They refined it into a multipurpose credit tool that escaped strictures against usury. By the fourteenth century, the bill of exchange was a transaction among four designated parties:[32] A) deliverer, B) taker, C) payer, and D) payee. Typically B and C might run branches of the same merchant bank in different locations. In a standard exchange A provides B some florins in return for a bill of exchange which A sends to D who turns it over to C in return for payment of a comparable amount in local currency, say pounds sterling. The bill of exchange only works because B has credit with C and each adjusts their books accordingly. The original account credit might derive from trade profits deposited in each account or from profits on exchange and could be used to transfer funds within the firm from one partner's account to the other.

Originally, bills of exchange were drawn up as notarized contracts for use in cities and fairs, and required the merchant or his agent to come to the fair in person. The earliest versions of the bill of exchange date to the thirteenth-century practices of Italian merchants in the Champagne fairs.[33] Braudel has documented the origin of real markets for financial paper, a bourse, to the fourteenth century in cities such as Pisa, Venice, Florence, Genoa, Valencia, and Barcelona.[34] It should be noted that medieval bills of exchange were not initially negotiable instruments, and so could not simply be signed over to a third party. Early on, they could be discharged only by the original lender or an agent acting for him.[35]

Since most transactions were based on verbal face to face discussion many merchants knew well who might serve as the agent of another and were in a position to finalize transactions with an agent as readily as with the principle. Bills of exchange initially were non-negotiable: that is, not sold and resold at discounts to serve in effect as currency in the sense of a storehouse of value. Eventually, merchants began to send these contracts to one another for collection. For example, a merchant in Venice wanting to buy goods in Bordeaux, could if he had obtained a bill of exchange from another merchant there, use this bill to have a seller in Bordeaux provide his agent with the desired goods either by using the bill to obtain the local currency or by paying with the bill of exchange which the seller of the desired commodities could themselves redeem for cash or credit.

A version of a bill of exchange, and one more likely to be suspected of being usurious, that was common by the fifteenth century[36] was referred to as dry exchange (no commodities involved nor travel required) or *cambium et recambium*.[37] This might involve a loan of ducats in return for a promise of Flemish groats at a specified time—the exchange between groats and ducats might fluctuate and provide a profit on the loan. Unlike the bill of exchange, it did not rely on movement of credit through accounts. The key was simply a loan for a few months in return for a repayment involving a premium nominally tied to exchange rates so it could involve no travel at all by either party as it only required public information related to the exchange rate in question. This transaction roused suspicions of disguised interest even though it deliberately did not specify a rate of return. Although the Medici professed to deal only in lawful exchange, several clear cases of dry exchange are found in the ledger of the Bruges branch.[38]

Studies of the accounts of the Medici Bank (1397–1494) however show no instances of a negotiable bill of exchange.[39] In early years most exchanges were done at the major fairs but gradually financial activity moved West and south to the European cities as new developments in trade empowered the port cities of Western Europe. In the thirteenth century actual discounting of bills of exchange was impossible because it would elicit a charge of usury.[40] As Italian commerce grew in Western Europe, first in the internal fairs and then in the port cities trade in commodities such as finished textiles, in part gave way to importation of raw wool from England and then Spain to be finished in Italy. In 1321, the wool guild ranked first, and far above the other guilds, in terms of tax contributions.[41] A number of merchant banks in this period established industrial production facilities within Italian urban areas using imported raw goods.

By the end of the sixteenth century, after a long series of increasingly sophisticated usages of bills of exchange, new procedures were standardized. A producer of goods (say Spanish wool dispatched to sell in Italy) might get paid first in Spain with a bill of exchange dated three months after it was drawn up by the firm of the actual purchaser of the wool in Italy. The receiver of the wool needing three months to realize its value (through resale) would date the bill of exchange, given on receipt of the expedited wool, three months hence.

This meant that the provider of the wool, if short of cash, might be willing to sell this bill of exchange redeemable three months hence at a discount—opening a space for a profit margin for any intermediaries. The intermediary might send the bill of exchange to an associate in the Italian city where it could be redeemed. The associate would, after redeeming the bill, use the cash to buy a new bill of exchange also at a discount but working the trade circuit in reverse (perhaps advancing cash to a merchant trading Italian cloth to Spain and unwilling to wait three months for his Spanish bill of exchange to be redeemable at face value).

Those selling discounted bills of exchange in their home area benefitted by not having to transport cash and the pair of intermediaries benefitted because of their financial savvy and their dual location which could make them a little over 5 percent on their cash each six months or 10.38 percent a year without themselves risking the transport of cash.[42] By the seventeenth century, bills of exchange issued by reputable firms had become so negotiable that they were used to a significant degree much like commodities and were bought and resold multiple times at discount.[43]

The initial advantages of a bill of exchange went beyond facilitating trade: one such advantage was that the exchange rates on bills to non-partners both provided a measure of profit to the company and escaped the onus of usury. Since information travelled slowly and the relative values of the currency at the moment of deposit and payout would be less than certain, a margin could always be estimated. That the exchange might end up in a loss made the transaction more legitimate because it did not involve profit without risk for one party, such profit was thought to be a key characteristic of usury by Christians as well as Muslims. The theoretical possibility of loss (i.e., risk) was often sufficient to disarm the charge of usury even if on average the exchanges were quite profitable. Exchange profits accrued to the writer of the bill since his international account, kept in debasement proof money of account, would only be debited at the prevailing exchange rate while his local account would receive greater value if the hedging on the expected future rate of exchange provided a profit.

Bills of exchange were regularly used for this purpose in late medieval trade fairs. Such trade fairs grew to prominence in the twelfth century, and reached their highest numbers in thirteenth century before gradually being displaced by urban bourses. In effect, bills of exchange not only reduced the need to carry large sums of money from place to place, they helped existing supplies of hard currency to work harder, effectively increasing the velocity of circulation. Business worth millions could be settled with a hundred thousand gold écus (the principle gold coin of France from 1385 until the early modern period: it displayed a crowned shield or écu on one side). Any remaining debts would be settled by either a new bill of exchange or a promise of future payment.

Because trade brought revenues to the lords under whose auspices they were held, many lords were only too glad to guarantee the peace of the fair, and to negotiate with their neighbors the safe conduct through their territories of all those who wished to attend the fair.[44] The rebirth of trade "was a momentous period for medieval civilizations when furs of Smolensk and the dried whale of Greenland reached Bruges in Hanseatic ships, while the cloths of Flanders were exchanged in Africa for Guinean gold and the linens of Rheims were exchanged for the silks of China in the heart of Asia."[45] Because merchants traveled from fair to fair, in a circuit of fairs, they developed their own financial institutions for the arbitration of disputes, so that eventually bills of exchange drawn up at one fair could be used anywhere in the system of fairs across Europe. By 1400 the practice of clearing debts through correspondence had become standard practice, and large trade fairs had declined.[46]

In 1460 the center of the exchange market, under pressure from the French king Louis XI moved from the Geneva fair to the fair in Lyon.[47] One of the greatest of fairs, the Besançon fair, which originated perhaps as early as 1534 at a town that was a stepping stone between Lyon and Genoa, soon became the most important for financial transactions. The sixteenth-century fairs of Besançon under Genoese control became purely places for financial paper and served to settle accounts and contracts of all sorts.[48] Braudel describes these fairs as a confrontation of several hundred thousand gold écus of debt where each debt annihilated the other as they evaporated like snow in the sun.[49] The Besançon fair was moved south by the Genoese to Piacenza, on the territory of the Duke of Parma near Genoa, in 1579. There the fair remained under the control of the Genoese until 1621, though it continued to be referred to as the Besançon fair. The critical role of the Genoese reflected their enormous financial power as well as their widespread presence in Iberian cities which gave them the inside track on financing the Spanish Hapsburg monarchy which itself controlled Flanders (after 1556).

These fairs became the place where, among other debts, the debts of major sovereigns, such as Philip II of Spain were settled (negotiated). Philip II had urgent and continuing needs for funds in Flanders from 1566 and the Genoese had installed their banking facilities in Madrid and quickly became Philip's primary and indispensable bankers. Their indispensability showed up when in 1575 Philip tried to abrogate (annul) his agreements with his Genoese bankers and switch to financing by Fugger. The Genoese successfully blocked needed transfers of gold to Flanders and, in December 1577, the king agreed to a compromise (such frequent negotiations were seen to constitute a *medio general* in which debts were paid at some negotiated discount). From the Genoese perspective, their victory negotiated at the Piacenza/Besançon fair was seen as demonstrating the incompetence of the Castillian bankers and their Fugger allies who had failed to come up with an adequate solution to Philip's financial troubles.[50] Other Italian firms from Venice, Genoa, and Florence, as well as other cities, also played critical roles in the internationalization of finance and the development of new technologies of credit.

To round out the discussion of the bill of exchange we need to mention that by the eighteenth-century bills of exchange not only enabled trade between Britain and India they also had become fully discountable (as we will see in the next chapter London had fully discountable credit through the tally system from the twelfth century). An Indian merchant could send the funds through an Indian bank to a merchant bank in London, who would pay the British merchant. The ability of the Bombay importer to pay the London exporter with a bill of exchange depended typically upon the willingness of the London merchant banker to accept the bill and extend credit to the Bombay merchant banker. Often, however, rather than wait months for funds to arrive, the merchant might prefer either to borrow against the bill or sell it to the London merchant bank at a discount. If the bank accepted the bill as collateral for the loan, typically they would limit the loan to no more than two-thirds of the bill's face value.

By this time, when a merchant bank would buy a bill, they would often sell it in turn to a discount house. The merchant bank's acceptance of the bill became a crucial endorsement of its value. When a banker accepted a bill, he assumed responsibility for its eventual payment to the holder of the bill. In fact, each endorsement and assignment further guaranteed its payment, increasing its security and liquidity as a negotiable instrument. Such transactions promoted close ties between merchant-bankers and other banks, in addition to empowering the expertise about the commodities being sold and accurate knowledge of prices for them in particular markets.[51]

THE COMPAGNIA

Bills of exchange, however flexible, were insufficient for financing the bulk of commerce. The centuries old yet conceptually simpler Rhodian Sea Law, long forming the basis of Byzantine and Venetian credit arrangements for maritime shipping, specified allowable and relatively high rates of interest to cover general risk. It also provided flexible financing from non-partner creditors who could estimate the rough likelihood of losses to weather and piracy and hope to come out ahead due to the high rates allowed. It may be that this seemed ethically defensible primarily because the risk in question was in part due to storms and in part due to piracy all of which might be thought true risks predictable only by God, so risk remained for all parties.

In 1274, a less-flexible sea loan responding to cultural and religious pressures in Venice specified that the Constantinople-based partner was to send goods purchased with the capital advanced plus a fixed 25 percent profit in money to Venice or owe double the sum advanced; at 25 percent interest each year until paid. This loan put the recipient of the loan at greatest risk by insisting on a payment of a 25 percent additional profit—over and above the benefits of buying cheaply in Constantinople and selling at a profit in Venice. The only concession by the lender was that the shipper was not liable for losses at sea of goods shipped.[52] That the provider of the initial funds was not at risk for his interest but only for his principle must have taken some argumentation.

Quite early, Italian merchants tried to address the least appealing features of sea loans in more practical terms via the development of a more flexible form of partnership useful for long-distant trade. This new partnership, using a preexisting term, the *compagnia* came to replace both the *societas,* a partnership with limited liability, and the Venetian sea loan. It seems to have been initially developed in twelfth-century Italy and had a number of features designed to encourage investments by assuring returns to non-partner investors. In some ways, it may have borrowed from the more flexible Byzantine sea loan. A major obstacle to investment had been knowledge and liability: only those with adequate knowledge of the products and markets involved, as well as their associated risks, could be tempted to invest as partners or assume liability for partnership activities. These were key limiting factors addressed by the new instrument. In Florence, merchants elaborated additional ways to finance the *compagnia* which could pass muster as non-usurious and attract a broader range of investors:[53]

The details of each partner's contribution and expectation, including the calendar of activities, were precisely stated to allow potential investors to decide in which enterprises / voyages they wished to invest.

In addition to the equity of the partners, the *compagnia* was financed by earnings reinvested in the business, additional funds invested by the partners (*fuori del corpo della compagnia*), and most innovatively by time deposits accepted from outside investors (*depositi a discrezione*) who, not being partners, had no liability.

Each of these three additional types of investment were paid different rates that varied between 5 percent and 10 percent but they were all paid out as gifts given to the investors as inducements rather than as interest on a loan or as part of a contractual agreement yet the payments to outside depositors always took precedence over disbursements to partners. The *compagnia* allowed a number of Florentine merchant banks to earn between 14 and 20 percent per annum even as it allowed them to leverage their deposits. Obviously, a lot of social capital and discourse went into getting the *compagnia* deemed a non-usurious enterprise and its advantages soon spread to other Italian city states.

This practical innovation amounted, despite the subterfuge, to the payment of an assured (if unspecified) return (interest) to attract the capital investment of those who had neither time nor expertise nor inclination to become partners.[54] This contract in some forms appeared as early as 1109 in Venice and 1143 in Genoa.[55]

Analysis of the sources of capital in the various branches of the Medici bank suggests that there were three basic revenue streams available beyond the initial partnership investments: reinvested profits held over and not paid out to the partners, additional funds provided by the partners, and funds provided by outsiders whose accounts on the Medici bank books would be invested and paid out first as *discrezione*. These additional funds more than doubled the initial partnership capital.[56]

Perhaps, the most important point revealed by a scrutiny of a Medici account in Lyon of the early 1490s, for Ymbert de Batarnay, Seigneur du Bouchage, is that money deposited by non-partners earned income for them but that the percentage earned (the *discrezione*) varied based on how well investments did each year. In this case, his deposit of 10,000 écus au soleil does not promise a specific rate of return and in actuality earned him 1,640 écus au soleil for a two-year period (about eight percent non compounded) and apparently about 7.5 percent for a less well defined preceding period. In other words the deposits earned variable rates as the market determined—but presumably earned enough to be attractive and were paid out with priority— hence payment was assured to the degree possible even if a precise payment was not.[57] This absence of a fixed rate on the books would have provided, as with dry exchange, an escape clause from usury since the investment clearly remains at risk—at least as far as particular levels of profit are concerned.

The clever construction of the *compagnia* with its external investors adding to the initial *corpo* established by the partners also provided only modest alarm as to its potential for moral harm since the investors were wealthy and their prioritized returns were initially disguised as regular gifts. The socioeconomic advantages of this institution also counted heavily in deliberations and, like international exchange contracts, the public good provided by expansion of trade was difficult to oppose when no one was seriously disadvantaged.

Sometime before 1250, maritime insurance was also available in Genoa with premiums at 10 percent of the local value of the insured cargo and we know thirteenth-century insurance premiums as high as 100–200,000 florins were paid.[58] In the Islamic world, leveraging like that provided by the *compagnia* was not to appear in any significant form until the twentieth century.[59] Commercial expansion in the Islamic world was constrained by laws which insisted on proportional sharing of risk and profit—something that typically demanded either close and informed participation by the investor or a near foolhardy disregard for risk.

PAPAL FINANCES AND THE NORMALIZATION OF INTEREST

The dominance of the Catholic Church in the medieval period and the tithes it collected across Europe provided a critical entrée for Italian merchant banks. The Papacy's finances were enormous and its international reach second to none. Tithes needed to flow to Rome, other than during the papacy of Clement VI in Avignon (1309–1377), and always were handled by the Italian banking establishment. Indeed during the exile in Avignon there were estimated to be 250 Florentines present of which fifty were independent bankers linked to the Curia's finances (*mercatores romanum curiam sequentes*).

In the fifteenth century, the post of depositary general or "first Papal banker" was almost always filled by a Florentine.[60] Expenses for the Catholic Church in its entirety entailed counter flows and these two flows were ideally suited to establishment of reciprocal credit arrangements across Europe. Merchant bankers would receive funds in Italy and dispense them from appropriate international accounts to minimize physical transfer of gold or silver. Details of this financing are available only for some periods but the best known periods are likely to be reasonably representative. An extensive study of Papal finances during the papacies of two Florentine (Medici) popes, Leo X (1513–1521 and Clement VII (1523–1534), and the Papacy of Paul III (1534–1549) may be taken as moderately representative.

Official doctrine on usury followed scholastic thinking slowly. On May 4, 1515, at the tenth Session of the 5th Lateran Council led by Pope Leo X, the church approved the non-usurious character of *Montes pietatis* or lending institutions that made loans both to the poor and to the church—on the grounds that their practices did not qualify as usury, redefined as when: "a thing which produces nothing is applied to the acquiring of gain and profit without any work, any expense or any risk."[61] This allowance specifically applied to organizations providing public benefits and charging moderately for doing so.

A more general solution was provided in the *Vix pervenit* encyclical of Pope Benedict XIV (November 1, 1745) by recourse to the concept of extrinsic interest which could be allowed as involving costs external to lending (not intrinsic to the loan) defined as required additions to the return of the principle which made the benefits to the recipient of the loan equal to those received by the lender. These, in time, were seen (posited) to include most of the issues addressed by the scholastics.[62] Equality of benefits in lending was defined as justice, inequality as injustice.

By the beginning of the sixteenth century salaried functionaries no longer collected Papal taxes and instead private individuals and groups collected the funds; in effect the funds were collected by tax farmers. The Papal financial structure received funds from Apostolic collectors; tax farmers for indirect taxes (*gabelles*, from Arabic *qabala* or liability/responsibility) were divided into Roman (e.g. in Rome), provincial, and salt as well as indirect taxes from Papal state monopolies such as alum. The depositary general of the Apostolic chamber was both the top Papal banker advising the pope and the Apostolic chamber but also the top comptroller of the depositaries of the city of Rome, the *monti*, Papal colleges, for example, the College of Cardinals and Papal provincial treasuries.[63] From Clement VII the Papal state expanded its system of taxation so that Papal territories were directly taxed, culminating in the Triennal Subsidy of 1543 (under Paul III).

The Papacy, as well as many Italian city states, established a number of *monti* to facilitate financing. These institutions controlled specific revenue streams and were invested in by the wealthy who then received monthly dividends while their investments provided loans to the city or state.

The Monte della Fede managed the Papacy's public debt.[64] The Papal State had significant resources and revenues but it also had major expenses; not least, the unavoidable basic costs for the importation of grain and other foodstuffs.

Secular and Papal states relied on a network of interconnected creditors who received direct and indirect benefits ranging from influence or patronage and international trust to direct interest returns and benefits on loans. We know the *mercatores* in the sixteenth century provided huge loans in return for 12 percent interest per annum, a *donativo* or premium of 3–4 percent and a commission of 2–3 percent but the surviving records do really tell us if the signatories to the loan documents represented a large group tied in through separate arrangements or if the signatories gathered the funds for the loan out of their own resources and social capital.[65]

Through the first half of the sixteenth century, the Olivieri family figures prominently in the position of Depositary of the Apostolic chamber. The accounts of the Olivieri family company include sections for transactions as Depositary of the Apostolic chamber as well as accounts for other company business within the same account book—suggesting that the Olivieri had the Papacy as a client rather than being a salaried functionary of the Papal state.

We should view such early merchant banks as aspects of enterprises in which the construction and exploitation of social and political influence could also be tightly tied to financial success. This was as true of the greatest as well as of the smallest. Even at the height of his influence, Cosimo De' Medici still felt a need to improve his position:[66]

> Whatever his supplicants chose to believe, Cosimo could not simply appoint people to office, requisition money for projects he favored, or have his wishes enacted into legislation. Both public and private records show that he was obliged to pursue these ends with the aid of his partisans in a roundabout way, respecting the constitution and the opinions of the *principes civitatis*.

The distribution of wealth shown in the 1427 *catasto* of Florence is remarkably similar to that of the United States in 1995; the top 20 percent had 84.2 percent and 83.9 percent, respectively, of the total wealth and wealth in the other quintiles was similarly distributed. A recurrent theme in Florentine governance was the appearance of "new men" (*gente nuova*) and 5000–8000 names (in a population of about 50,000) went into the electoral bags from which those to fill official posts were selected. While Florence was no democracy it was clearly not a tight oligarchy either—even if a small set of families, with both rural and urban roots, were clearly most prominent in financial and political affairs.[67] It is probable that in medieval and Renaissance Italy, as in the Republic of Rome, the construction of social capital was as important as that of financial capital.

While many states touched by the reformation began to deem moderate interest rates non-usurious, no sixteenth- to eighteenth-century European state, to our knowledge, openly viewed a net benefice on a loan reaching an explicit range of 17–19 percent as non-usurious—though it should be recognized that the *donativo* and commission were one time fees not annualized interest. Needless to say, it probably took little "guided introspection" by a state to see that financing the state, Papal or secular, could be justified as in the public good.

IN BRIEF

From the eleventh to the eighteenth century, an elaborate series of improvements in the instruments of credit expanded the scale of finance in Western Europe to take advantage of the intellectual developments discussed in our first chapter. These core technologies were basic to more audacious ideas developed later but shared the recognition that scale was tied to trust and that the state could not only itself benefit from credit but could benefit the financial community and the public by allowing protections for those who otherwise might not dare invest in unfamiliar ventures.

The Roman concept of respect among *amicitia* evolved into official recognition in Western Europe for networks of social capital that enhanced the scale of finance but this, subsequently, paved the way for the outrageous speculative bubbles examined in the next chapter. In many ways, England arrived at solutions similar to those in continental Europe but it greatly elaborated other ideas, such as discountable tallies, and eventually established London as a preeminent banking center. In the following chapter, through a focus on England, we examine the financial trajectory of the western Industrial Revolution and the early era of globalization that produced the international trade framework on which modern finance has subsequently relied.

NOTES

1. Power, *The Wool Trade in English Medieval History,* 96–103.
2. Hicks, *A Theory of Economic History*, Chapter VI. Land and labor were largely locked up in feudal obligations and arrangements. The Finances of the Sovereign deals at length with medieval state financial shortfalls and the reason state after state resorted to borrowing rather than relying on taxation for its finances.
3. Ehrenberg, *Capital and Finance in the Age of the Renaissance,* his chapters on Antwerp and Lyons provide copious documentation of this point.
4. Weatherford, *The History of Money: From Sandstone to Cyberspace,* 67.

Early European Finance 1050–1650   79

5. Ibid., 67–68; Davis, *A History of Money: From Ancient Times to the Present Day*, 52–54.
6. Wood, *Philip the Fair and Boniface VIII*.
7. Papal bull *Unam sanctam*, 1302.
8. Philip IV seems to have liked to torture people. Of the many possible illustrations available, the two knights accused of adulterous relations with his daughters-in-law who were castrated, flayed, and quartered are apparently not untypical (See de Bertier de Sauvigny, *History of France*, 55).
9. Papal bull, *Ad providam*, 1312.
10. It is only subsequently that, Jews were expelled from Spain and Portugal: in 1492 and 1496 respectively.
11. Boissonnade, *Life and Work in Medieval Europe*, 169.
12. Goldthwaite, *The Economy of Renaissance Florence*, 232–33.
13. Ehrenberg, *Capital and Finance in the Age of the Renaissance*, 47, 355.
14. Boissonnade, *Life and Work in Medieval Europe*, 288.
15. Mintz, *Sweetness and Power*.
16. Jardine, *Worldly Goods*, 115–16, 284.
17. In Spain, Gerard of Cremona (ca. 1150–1190) translated into Latin the work of the Islamic mathematician Muhammad ibn-Musa al-Khwarizmi from whose book *Hisāb al-jabr w-al muqābalah* (the mathematics of the unknown and exchange) we derive the term algebra. By the beginning of the thirteenth century this work was circulating throughout Europe.
18. Schumpeter, *History of Economic Analysis*, 156.
19. Crosby, *The Measure of Reality*, 206. De Roover, *The Rise and Decline of the Medici Bank*, 97.
20. De Roover, *The Rise and Decline of the Medici Bank*, 1397–1494, and De Roover *Money, Banking and Credit in Mediaeval Bruges*, 13 provide the earliest detailed records for Italian merchant bank accounting practices are those studied by De Roover for fourteenth century Bruges. Jacks and Caferro, *The Spinelli of Florence*, using archival materials dating from 1430–1535 and Kent's *Cosimo De' Medici and the Florentine Renaissance* provide detailed analyses of archival material illuminating the cultural and political accomplishments of two of the most important Florentine banking families (Spinelli and Medici).
21. Davies, *A History of Money*, 234. A friend of Leonardo Da Vinci's, Pacioli also discusses such topics as the golden mean, defined as a division into two parts such that the ratio of the smaller to the larger is comparable to that of the larger to the whole (e.g. 8:13). Pacioli's next work, *Divina proportione*, included illustrations by Da Vinci.
22. Schumpeter, *History of Economic Analysis*,156.
23. Crosby, *The Measure of Reality*. 208.
24. Chown, *History of Money from 800 A.D.*, 18–19.
25. Braudel, *Civilisations matérielle, économie et capitalisme*, Tome 1, 409, notes that ghost moneys (monnaies imaginaires) were always defined in terms of a long absent currency of known metallic content.
26. Goldthwaite, *The economy of Renaissance Florence*, 458.

27. Ibid., 459.
28. De Roover, *Money, Banking and Credit in Mediaeval Bruges*, 90.
29. Braudel, *Civilisations matérielle, économie et capitalisme, Tome III*, 128–29.
30. De Roover, *Money, Banking and Credit in Mediaeval Bruges*, 48–52.
31. Ibid., 49.
32. Goldthwaite, *The Economy of Renaissance Florence*, 211.
33. Ibid., 213.
34. Braudel, *Civilisations matérielle, économie et capitalisme, Tome 2*, 79.
35. Neale, *The economy of Renaissance Florence*, 51–52.
36. Goldthwaite, *The Economy of Renaissance Florence*, 220.
37. De Roover, *The Rise and Decline of the Medici Bank*, 1334–1335. See also Goldthwaite's discussion in *The Economy of Renaissance Florence*, 219 who notes that this was also referred to as fictitious exchange.
38. de Roover. *The Medici Bank*, 38.
39. Ibid., 31.
40. Barron Baskin and Miranti, *A History of Corporate Finance*, 41.
41. Goldthwaite, *The Economy of Renaissance Florence*, 265.
42. Braudel, *Civilisations matérielle, économie et capitalisme, Tome 2*, 119.
43. Kindleberger. *A Financial History of Western Europe*, 41. For an example see, Braudel. *Civilisations matérielle, économie et capitalisme, Tome 2*: 119.
44. Chown, *History of Money from 800 A.D.*, 116.
45. Bautier, *The Economic Development of medieval Europe*, 146.
46. Chown, *History of Money from 800 A.D.*, 123–25.
47. Jacks and Caferro, *The Spinelli of Florence*, 89.
48. Goldthwaite, *The Economy of Renaissance Florence*, 225–7.
49. Braudel, *Civilisations matérielle, économie et capitalisme, Tome 2*, 72.
50. Braudel, *La Méditerranée et le monde méditerranéen, Tome II*, 183–89.
51. See Chapman, "Financial Restraints on the Growth of Firms in the Cotton Industry, 1790–1850," 50–69; Jones, *British Multinational Banking*, 33–34; Neal, *The Rise of Financial Capitalism*, 5–7.
52. Lopez and Raymond, *Medieval Trade in the Mediterranean World. Illustrative Documents*. 171ff.
53. Discussed inter alia in Baskin and Miranti, *A History of Corporate Finance*, 38.
54. In conjunction with the arguments from Aquinas and others, the Catholic Church began relaxing its prohibition on usury in the thirteenth century, redefining it as exorbitant amounts of interest but it was clearly pushed in this direction by the financing needs of Italian states. As early as 1403, a renowned lawyer and theologian, Lorenzo di Antonio Ridolfi won a case on behalf of the Republic of Florence and many rich creditors the gist of which was that periodic payments in the course of a long loan were legal interest and not usury. Clearly arguments for public utility and civil obligations are relevant in such a case. This method of raising money in a lump sum and paying it back, with something added, in many periodic payments was later adopted in France as the system of "rente." Davies, *A History of Money* 219–20.
55. Fossier, "The Leap Forward," 313.
56. De Roover, *The Medici Bank*, 52.

57. Ibid., 55–56.
58. Fossier, "Clouds Gather in the West," 27.
59. Modern Islamic banking provides such an instrument though it is structured in a more biased way toward benefiting the banker, who gets to spread his risks while the smaller depositors do not, whereas in western banks all risks and profits are averaged for all depositors.
60. Bruscoli, *Papal Banking in Renaissance Rome,* 3, 7.
61. The text is available on line at papalencyclicals.net: Search 5th Lateran Council (1512–1517 A.D.) Session 10.
62. The text is available on line at papalencyclicals.net: Search Pope Benedict XIV, encyclical *Vix pervenit*, points III, IV and V especially.
63. Bruscoli, (*Papal Banking in Renaissance Rome,* 129–44) provides an analysis of the records of the treasuries of Perugia, Umbria, Romagna, Parma and Piacenza as well as a brief discussion of others.
64. Ibid., xviii, 145–66.
65. Ibid., xxii.
66. Kent. *Cosimo De' Medici and the Florentine Renaissance*, 350.
67. Goldthwaite, *The Economy of Renaissance Florence,* 546ff, 562.

Chapter 4

Transcending Feudal Finance in Western Europe

There is little consensus either about when the feudal period began or about how far it extended in Europe for any given period between the eighth and the sixteenth century. An eminent scholar has suggested that, "Starting our investigation of phenomena by focusing on particular words is a sixteenth-century habit that needs to be dropped."[1] Certainly, England after the Norman invasion cannot be said to be typical of any other time or place. In fact, most experts agree that in the eleventh-century England was decidedly atypical for Europe—as, they also suggest, was every place else.[2] It is also likely that the academic construct "the feudal period" is something that well describes only a small subset of medieval Europe—small in timespan and in area. England under the early Normans was quite different than England even a century later. Likewise, fifteenth-century Italy had major differences from fourteenth-century Italy.

We should note that for our purposes the particular social relations of production and rights in property turn out to be a bit less important, and more local, than the developing instruments of commerce and credit. The kingdoms, duchies, and empires of medieval Western Europe were interconnected commercially, culturally, and politically even when their tenure infrastructures differed or changed in different ways and at different rates. We will use the term feudal in this chapter in a decidedly lax fashion while we focus on finance. Space does not allow an adequate coverage of Western Europe so our intent is to use a few illustrative examples: including some key continental fairs and financial technologies in the private sector while we focus on the development of British government finance. London became one of the key financial centers in Europe in part through its own financial innovations and in part due to its response and adaptations of financial developments originating elsewhere such as in Italy.

By grants of privilege, feudal rulers actively encouraged the formation of merchant guilds and associations "such as the wholesale mercers and the merchants who frequented the River Loire in France, the Staplers and Merchant Adventures in England, and the Hansards in Germany."[3] German merchants, for instance, formed *hanses* (associations) in a hundred or so towns, the foundation of the Hanseatic League. Originally, the Hansards simply sought to protect their goods from robbers and pirates during transit. To secure protection for their commercial activities, they made loans and gifts to foreign rulers. In return, they were granted certain privileges and trade monopolies. Soon, they controlled the trade across northern Europe in grain, timber, furs, tar, honey, cod, flax, copper and iron, and sundry manufactured goods such as cloth. As this trade expanded, the balance of power shifted. By the fourteenth century, the League's control over trade in Northern Europe was such that they were able to use threats of withdrawal of trade, embargoes, and even blockages to protect their commercial interests.

By the fourteenth century, the face of Europe had changed beyond all recognition. Commercial networks linked merchants in cities throughout Europe, and extended into the Levant and Asia, and increasingly across northern Africa and down its western coast. Merchants in Hanseatic cities of northern Germany and on the North Sea traded for furs, for grain, and for iron around the Baltic Sea, and with England for its wool. Cities in northern Italy traded with the Levant for species, semitropical foods, cotton, and goods such as silk from Asia. As trade flowed over the Alps and up and down the Rhine and Rhone rivers, commercial networks tied the cities of the Mediterranean to those of the north.[4] Not only were such commercial networks important for international trade, within feudal states, but the social ties that promoted credit and credit based trade also helped to reshape the constellation of feudal society.

Large-scale trade transformed feudal societies along several dimensions. Such trade requires an infrastructure not just to handle money, credit, bookkeeping, shipping, and information, but also to enforce contracts, collect debts, and settle disputes. As trade expanded so too did the medieval cities that provided these services. The history of world capital, as Braudel notes, can be written by following the rise and decline of its urban centers.[5] Trade also seems to have been a factor in population growth. The medieval social and political world consequently changed dramatically over the centuries.

When late medieval kings "reached into the countryside for taxes and soldiers, [they] found well-established commercial connections [they] had little part in creating, and could not completely control."[6] In this new social world, commerce provided both new avenues to wealth and status and new ties of patronage to protect it. Social status was no longer dependent solely on conquest or political patronage. By 1540, a change had begun to occur in

England such that many professions whose occupants had acquired significant wealth were assimilated to the ranks of the gentry. The newcomers to high status were resented by the landed gentry who created the new category of squires to keep themselves superior to the newcomers.[7]

Where feudal technologies of power used threats and force to exact rent and tributes, commercial hierarchies were constructed organically from the bottom up, and were tied both to supra-local systems of credit and local relations of production. This is not to say mercantile technologies of power were any less abusive, or did not use threats and force. However, usually, they depended on the state and its courts for these sanctions. This is also not to say that relationships were any less exploitative, but simply that exploitation was more subtle, and more apt to be hidden in the details of a transaction. Though tied to international or regional trade these commercial networks reached into the countryside, into villages and towns, more directly, and more extensively, than did earlier feudal structures.

As rulers and merchants at times competed, but sometimes joined together in this complex mode of wealth generation, their technologies of power became increasingly wedded to one another. Merchant classes provided the financial assistance and services needed by medieval princes and kings and, in return, received increasing backing from the state. Wealthy merchants and bankers moved in the circles of power, not simply because they had money to lend to feudal lords and kings, but more importantly because they had the financial expertise in organizing and managing fiscal systems that rulers needed for administrators and financial agents. These services elevated them to positions of prominence in social life, earliest, as we saw in the last chapter, in the Italian city-states, because of the complex financial needs of the Papacy.[8]

STATE FINANCE IN GREAT BRITAIN

Almost every English school child knows that in 1066, the Normans defeated the Anglo-Saxons at the battle of Hastings. Many know as well that the Anglo-Saxons arrived in England in the mid-fifth century largely from Denmark and Germany and that the Normans, though French, had come to France from Scandinavia and had only established their domination of Normandy itself in 911.[9] What is less well known are the financial consequences of these invasions. Among his first acts, William the Conqueror (1066–1087) seized the lands held by Anglo-Saxon nobles who had supported King Harold II[10] and distributed them among his Norman followers.[11] This effectively destroyed the Anglo-Saxon nobility. It also massively concentrated land ownership. More than 4,000 Anglo-Saxon lords and knights lost their lands and were replaced by around 180 Norman barons.[12] This massive transfer of land created a new hierarchy of Norman nobles who owed their allegiance to the king, greatly enhancing the monarchy's power, and ultimately transforming the English state.

The king as paramount lord granted his barons, tenants-in-chief,[13] overlordship of vast lands. For these grants or loans, they were duty bound to pay the king homage and support him militarily by providing him with knights and soldiers when needed. Their obligations also included annual payment of such taxes, aids, or reliefs[14] as might be required, and the provision of other personal services when called upon to do so. The kings' tenants-in-chief, in turn, had tenants of their own with whom they had similar relationships. Among these subtenants, vassals of their lord, were thanes or knights, and in exchange for their services they normally received rights to a fief consisting of a manor and attached serfs. At the bottom of this social hierarchy were villains, cottagers, and serfs; who, in return for working the manor's fields received land under various forms of free or unfree tenure arrangements.[15]

In 1085, to more effectively administer (tax) his kingdom, William I ordered a detailed assessment to be done of England. The intent of the survey was to provide the king with full knowledge of the rights he possessed as King Edward's heir; to facilitate the levying of taxes. William set his commissioners the enormous task of assessing the taxable capacity of all lands in Norman England. Because, like the last judgment, this survey for most nobles seemed to entail a final reckoning, the record that was compiled soon became known by the millenarian title of *The Domesday Book*.

Under Anglo-Saxon rule England had already been divided into shires or counties, and these were further subdivided into *wapentakes*[16] or hundreds. Hundreds were often formed around districts comprising large blocks of land fifty to 100 square miles which seem to have already existed by the seventh century.[17] Though each hundred itself contained numerous villages and manors, the land was divided into hides, a land unit of about 120 acres, which typically consisted of a farm supporting a free peasant (*ceorl*/churl) and his family. It was the hide, or groupings of twenty or more hides with special obligations that traditionally served as the basis of tax assessments. The huge payments made to the Danes in the 990s, called Danegeld, were raised on a fixed rate per hide and this levy was later used to support standing armies. Before *The Domesday Book* there had been careful records of tenure kept in many kingdoms perhaps as early as the seventh century, though one of the few to survive (from the eighth century), *Tribal Hidage*, dealt only with a single kingdom—in this case that of Mercia.[18]

William the Conqueror built on this tradition. In each shire the commissioners were assisted by a reeve (an agent of the king charged with enforcement of specific regulations either appointed by the king or elected by the peasants), the sheriff,[19] and a local jury. As they visited each hundred, six villains[20] from each manor were called in and questioned. They were asked the name of their manor, who it was held by during the reign of King Edward, and who held it currently. They were questioned about how many hides of plowed lands, meadow, pastures, and woods, as well as fish ponds and mills were on the manor; how many hides were held by the lord of the manor in the demesne,[21] and how many hides were worked by its residents. They were interrogated about how many villains, cottars, freeman, and serfs lived there; how many oxen, cows, pigs, goats, sheep, and so on there were; and, how much they paid in rents. And, for each question about land, people, animals, and rents, inquiries were made, about how these had changed from the time of King Edward to the present (roughly the last forty years).

The Domesday Book as a geld (payment) book or crown tax roll was a remarkable instrument for the exercise of power. It not only provided the king information about the taxable capacity of every scrap of land in England, it told him who could be held to account; and allowed him as well to judge whether the value of these lands had risen or fallen over the previous decades. Because the king's revenues were collected from his tenants-in-chief, lands in *The Domesday Book* are recorded under their names. Thus, if the king wanted to know what lands Robert Malet held, although his lands were scattered in sundry hundreds in the shire of Norfolk, all were listed under his name with a detailed description for each of his manors. This listing made it easy for the king to consult the record, and enabled him to drive a hard bargain with his tenants-in-chief over how much rent, taxes, and tribute he could expect from them.

What *The Domesday Book* did, in effect, was to institute for the first time in Western Europe since the fall of the Roman Empire a transparent, nationwide, system of taxation, or civil debt to the government. Under King William, manors were assessed a levy of six shillings per hide. Since the lord had to pay the land tax, he had incentives to collect this debt from those who worked the land. It is clear from *The Domesday Book* that although money circulated, England was far from having a fully monetized economy. Manors were organized to be largely self-sufficient. Most exchanges were based on obligations or bartered transactions. Peasants, serfs, smallholders had to support their lords, the church, and their own poor kin by providing goods and labor. While coins might have been rare, money's presence is seen in *The Domesday Book* as several tributes are recorded or valued in money. Most manorial products cannot unambiguously be valued in money because most products did not transit through a competitive market and so what monetary prices existed reflected arbitrary local factors not abstract value in any sense.[22]

Chapter 4

MONEY, MINTS, AND ROYAL PREROGATIVES

Coin gave rulers the necessary liquidity to meet the exigencies of warfare. When Athelstan (925–940) through a combination of alliances and conquests became the effective ruler of England and most of Scotland; he expanded the number of mints in large measure to buy off the Danes.[23] Because many of these mints were located in previously independent feudal domains, Athelstan established a single national currency to make his control over them explicitly plain. With this act, England became the first major country in Western Europe to establish a national currency in post Roman times.[24] The minting of money became, henceforth, a royal prerogative. Just as taxes later allowed William to tap the wealth of the kingdom, the minting of money was another technology of power that benefited the king.

William I operated fifty-seven mints. These mints, however, operated very differently from those of modern states. If an individual had bullion and needed coin, he would take it to the mint, where the royal moneyers, after assaying and refining it, would convert it to coins, keeping a fee for minting known as seigniorage.[25] Moneyers paid the Crown for the privilege of minting, and the king bore none of the costs directly; and, mints made it possible for the ruler to require his tenants-in-chief to pay their levies in cash.

Both taxing and minting are related parts of government finance, and so were highly contested. When Henry I died in 1135, a civil war (1138–1158) ensued between the supporters of his nephew, King Steven (1135–1154), and his daughter, Matilda. To finance their military campaigns, powerful barons on both sides issued their own coins. One of his successor's (Henry II) first tasks following the civil war was to close the provincial mints operated by barons. To reassert royal control, Henry began to concentrate minting in London.[26] Constraints ultimately limited how much tax could be extracted from subjects. The demands on the king's purse were almost limitless yet kings were expected to be fair, even generous. Their largesse was an indispensable method of securing the continued loyalty of their vassals. The conspicuous consumption of the king and his court was an essential display of power and a warning to those who might challenge him. Given these extensive needs, a great temptation, when kings could not raise the funds they required through other means, was to use their royal control over mints to debase coinage.

The principle advantage and often the primary reason for debasement was to devalue existing debts. Unfortunately, all too often, given these apparent short-term advantages, to stay ahead of creditors, one round of debasement followed another. This was especially true on the Continent where, between 1100 and 1300, feudal coinages swiftly degenerated.[27] Although William the Conqueror (1066–87) and his son William II (1087–1100) resisted the temptation to debase the currency, opting instead to impose new land taxes, the quality of English coinage declined during the reign of Henry I (1100–1135). Coins were so wretched and their silver content so untrustworthy that people were forced to cut into them to see whether they were genuine, or merely silver plated. By 1124 public confidence in the king's money was so low that scapegoats had to be found. On Christmas day, Henry summoned all 180–200 mint masters in the kingdom to Winchester, and according to accounts, punished about half of them by chopping their right hand off. As barons operated their own mints, during the civil war following his reign, the quality of coinage declined even further.[28]

Bureaucratic records, tax rolls, accounting systems, and usurious forms of money, Biddick (1990) argues, were the "new" technologies of power during the twelfth century.[29] They allowed the state not only to occupy strategic nodes in the shifting intersections between local and central forms of power, but ultimately redefined time, and space in the medieval world, and lay the foundations for the revival of trade in Europe in the following century. In the thirteenth century new forms of taxation, based on revenue, and movable property, were developed in England (first assessed in 1166) and under Edward I (1272–1307) customs duties that had been instituted as temporary war measures under Richard the Lionheart (1189–1199) and John (1199–1216) for the first time produced a normal peacetime revenue for the crown.[30] Yet, this tax base soon enough proved inadequate for government needs.

The reformation initiated at Wittenberg, beginning with Luther's protestations (1517) against Papal schemes to raise money by selling indulgences, opened a new argument for separating commercial profit making from religion. Although Luther felt that the selling of indulgences took advantage of credulous folk's faith in the church and was itself exploitative (e.g., both usurious and unchristian), at some level he was inadvertently making a case for other authorities than the Pope to make judgments about what constituted usury. On October 31, 1517 Luther even appealed to Archbishop Albrecht of Mainz to have the practice stopped; apparently unaware that the profits on the sale of indulgences was being used to pay off the Archbishop's debt of 26,000 ducats incurred to Fugger (of Augsburg) for a loan used to purchase the position.[31] This was irrevocably an age when the elite increasingly saw commerce as the creator of prosperity.

In many places, it soon became generally acceptable to charge interest up to a specified rate and only charging more than that rate was regarded as usury. Initially, the rates fluctuated but within a few centuries moderate levels of interest on loans became acceptable in much of Europe. England was fairly representative. When Henry VIII broke away from Catholicism in 1534 lending at any interest rate became potentially legal, but it was only with an Act of 1545 that this became official, and the state set the upper limit at ten percent, while still vigorously forbidding "usury" itself (higher rates of interest). Later Edward VI restored the prohibition on any lending at interest in 1552 (in effect making charging interest and usury synonymous). Elizabeth I made lending at interest legal again in 1571. Charles the II reduced the legal limit to 6 percent in 1660.[32]

What was most distinctive about English policies is that they were breaking with tradition, and expanding on a Reformation critique, by declaring this a secular and national matter not a religious one. The controversial nature of such a claim is clear from debates in Parliament which led to the repeal in 1552 of the 1545 law. In 1549, for example, Robert Crowly argued the case explicitly in Parliament:[33]

> Alas, that ever any Christian assemblie should bee so voyde of Gods Holy Spirit that thei shoulde alowe for lawfull any thyng that Gods Worde forbideth. Be not abashed (most worthy counsellors) to call this act against usury into question agayne. Scan the wordes of the Psalmist. 'He that hath not given his money unto usury, and hath not taken giftes and rewardes against the innocent'.

The Renaissance period saw a huge growth in commerce and acquisitiveness among the elite. Europe for elites became a consumer society, and merchants for the first time acquired the prestige they had long enjoyed in the Islamic world.[34] As commerce grew in scale, it stood to benefit from broader participation even by those who were not the specialists in a particular trade and so could not properly estimate its risks. As we have seen in discussion of the *compagnia*, Italian firms apparently were the first to recognize this as a serious obstacle to commercial growth. In their search for a way of attracting greater and broader bases for investment by insuring investors against risk, merchants across Europe ran up against the strictures on usury and added pressure to modernize commercial law and church doctrine. Viewing usury as financial exploitation, instead of as interest on a socially beneficial loan is basic to understanding the European angst about usury though it is also important to separate church doctrine and scholastic thinking from local secular and church practice both of which varied greatly both over time and in space.

HENRY II AND THE EXCHEQUER

When Henry II ascended the throne in 1154 (he reigned until 1189), the finances of the kingdom were in need of reform. Shutting down provincial mints, Henry undertook a general reform of the coinage, replacing all the coins in circulation. To further consolidate his political and economic control, Henry reorganized his sheriffs, and he strengthened their powers to collect taxes. In a move to reduce his reliance on barons for military support, he pressured them to provide cash payments called *scutage* in lieu of the forty days of military service owed him by tenants-in-chief and their retainers. These reforms resulted in a steady flow of funds into the Royal Treasury, and its operations came to provide the Crown with ready credit, and generated a discount market for its receipts.

Although prior to 1300 the Royal Treasury and the Royal Mint were a part of the king's household, the treasury was the first part of the royal household to become a clearly separable, though closely related, Department of State.[35] During the reigns of Henry I and Henry II, bureaucrats in the royal household instituted new forms of accounting that further extended state control over the economy. As we are told in the *Dialogue of the Exchequer* (written in the 1170s) the Treasury was organized into two sections: the Exchequer of Receipt, also called the Lower Exchequer, and the Exchequer of Account or Upper Exchequer.[36] The Lower Exchequer was responsible for the receipt and payment of money, assaying coin received, and the safekeeping of the coin. The Upper Exchequer authorized the money to be spent, kept records, and audited accounts.

The Exchequer's basic procedure was to issue a summons for a sheriff to collect monies. He would execute the summons, and attempt to collect the amounts specified. Some debts could take years to collect. Debtors were permitted to make installment payments, or defer payment for some years if there were a good excuse, but eventually the day of reckoning would arrive, and the debtor would be either forced to pay, or the sheriff would seize sufficient possessions or property to satisfy the debt.

As we learn from the *Dialogue*, sheriffs were directed to satisfy debts by first expropriating surplus crops or luxury goods; only if these were not available, would they seize tools, equipment, and beasts of burden. The sheriff was instructed to leave the debtor with the necessities of life for himself and his family. Analogously, a knight would be left his horse to preserve his dignity; and, if he personally performed military service, his armor was exempt from seizure. Husbands were not only responsible for their wives' debts contracted during their marriage, but unless the wife had died, and an heir had inherited her property; the husband was also responsible for debts she incurred during previous marriages. Only, if the debtor had nothing to expropriate, could the sheriff swear an affidavit that the debtor was insolvent, and only then would the exchequer release the sheriff from responsibility for its collection. This was not done while there was even the faintest hope of collection.[37]

The collections sheriffs and other officials made were delivered to the Exchequer of Receipt. There the money was counted, compared with the writs, summons, and tallies presented, and an accounting made. The exchequer, in fact, takes its name from the counting table. It was a five-by-ten-foot-long table covered with a checkered cloth that was used like a primitive abacus. Squares on this table represented different sums: pence, shillings, pounds, twenty pounds, hundred pounds, thousand pounds, and ten thousand pounds. By moving coins, or silver and gold tokens for larger amounts, from square to square, like a croupier, computations of revenues and expenditures could be easily made by the king's calculator, as the official who did the counting was called when counting the money, the amount received was recorded in writing, and a tally made.

The tally (French *taille*) as used by the Exchequer was initially a government receipt usually made from a stick of hazel wood, about eight or nine inches long at one end of which notches of varying sizes were cut to represent different sums. To represent £1000 a notch the width of a man's palm was cut (i.e., four inches); for £100 the notch narrowed to the width of a thumb; for £20 it was the thickness of an ear; for £1 it was the size of a swelling of a grain of barley; for a shilling even less; a penny was marked by an incision. By varying the angle at which notches were cut tallies also recorded whether payment was received in gold or silver. However, the crucial feature of a tally was that it consisted of two parts. When the cuts were completed, the resulting tally was carefully split lengthwise into two parts, so that the notches on the two halves would line up. While the notches on the two halves tallied, the sticks themselves were of different lengths. The longer one, with its uncut handle, or stock, was retained by the creditor, the shorter one, called the "memoranda tally" was given to the debtor (e.g., the state).[38] If wood seems archaic for the time it was not, the key to the tally was that it provided, through nature's complexity and the uniqueness of any piece of raw cut wood, a readily understood security against counterfeit unavailable at the time in manufactured instruments of credit.

The real story, however, of the tally system concerns how such government receipts came to be used as full-fledged instruments of credit. By the reign of Henry II (1154–1189), the Exchequer of Receipt was becoming less a counting house than a clearing house for writs and tallies of assignment. The initial step was to assign a tally stock (reflecting a debt of the king) to others as a way of payment for debts owed by the king. As yearly taxes became increasingly institutionalized; the Crown began to routinely issue tally, stocks in payment of debts, while keeping the shorter tally that then could be referenced by recipients of the tally stock in payment of future taxes. Initially, it would seem that tally stocks were given to tradesmen who furnished goods to the court as a way to conserve cash and postpone or even obviate cash payment for products received. The recipient could redeem such tally stocks for cash by going to a king's debtor at a later date or could return it to the Exchequer by using it to pay taxes.

Generally, since tallies initially involved a royal debt the holder of tally stocks could use them to pay taxes or government rents when these fell due. In this usage, tallies stretched the quantity of currency available to the economy and established a government credit system. Sheriffs used exchequer tallies not only to aggregate shire payments into larger sums, but also to limit the risks of being robbed on the way to the Exchequer with large amounts of coin. Thus, when sheriffs went to the Exchequer to account for their receipts, they would deliver a mix of coin and tallies. If the sheriff's tally stock matched the half held by the exchequer, he would be given credit for the payment—and obligations would be cleared from the books.

As tallies were used to represent debts owed by the king, and were physically created in the Exchequer, people could also increasingly use tally stocks to pay many creditors or even to get credit from the king, that is, later repay a debt incurred to the king. In effect, by transferring tally stocks, tallies of assignment evolved into negotiable instruments. The recipient of the creditor's half of the tally could collect the money owed, could use the tally stock to pay someone else, or could hold on to it and apply it toward paying next year's taxes. The tally system had the advantage of discouraging theft since a thief could only use the tally in an elite circle of people, it had to correspond to written records, and the tally had much less convertibility and more accountability than cash.

One problem was that holders of Exchequer tallies in a remote place might have to travel to London to collect on them—unless they could find someone else that would accept them as payment. This inconvenience gave rise to an elaborate system of discounting tallies, centered in London, which undoubtedly contributed to London's later specialization in banking discount houses. In this system, people unable to travel to some distant town to cash in their tally stock or unwilling to wait to be paid until the exchequer asked for its anticipated taxes, could sell their tally at a discount. Because technically the seller of the tally stock was the original lender (and not in debt to the buyer of the tally—the Exchequer still owed the amount), the buyer was simply someone willing to take over the debt if paid for the inconvenience of collecting on it. Although the transaction might appear to involve "hidden interest," it was not considered usury because it had transformed the loan into a transaction having the form of expected profit on a sale.

The tally offered an even more direct way of skirting prohibitions against usury at a time when charging usurious interest rates was not only forbidden, but subject to serious punishments. The method used by officials working in the Exchequer to disguise interest bearing loans to the Crown, involved exchanging, for cash, tallies that were redeemable at a later date for 125 percent of the cash paid into the Exchequer. In this case, because there was no third party assuming the loan, the Exchequer officials were clearly engaging in hiding interest payments owed by the state. The advantage offered by the tally was that it was more circumspect than a written contract and provided no incriminating evidence—it established only a debt at a particular level. Historians have, however, found enough evidence to be confident that this was a common official use of the tally.[39]

When added to the Crown's control over taxing and minting, what the Exchequer tally did was to create a state system of credit that effectively increased the money supply without debasement (though the tally was not immune to inflation). In perfecting bureaucratic techniques of accounting the English state took control not only of its revenues and debts, but of time itself. Not only did this allow the state to spend against future revenues, but as an incipient discount market developed in London for such tallies, these rigid wooden but financially flexible instruments multiplied the efficient use of the coin in circulation, and freed the creation of wealth from limits imposed by minting. As Biddick notes, interest projects the value of money into the future, accounting conserves such projections for future scrutiny.

These simple but powerful techniques constituted a revolution that not only reorganized social life, but changed perceptions of both money and time itself. As money was made to reproduce itself, goods were no longer valued simply on their current value, but also their future worth.[40] The British tally system was the earliest system of fully discountable credit instruments. As pointed out in the last chapter a system of discountable bills of exchange began in the sixteenth century and was only widespread in Europe in the seventeenth century while a fully functioning tally system was in use in London by the end of the twelfth century.

CREDIT AS A QUASI-COMMODITY

The hallmark of modern credit is that it is treated as a commodity. It is bought and sold and circulates independently from the personal relationships and goods from which it is abstracted. Yet, unlike real commodities it is not in any full sense alienated from its producer (the lender) as Marx suggested was the case for traditional commodities. Relationships of continuing power are fundamental to credit. In traditional credit systems, debts between specific people, are not necessarily transferable, and vary in degrees of informality and trust. By contrast, negotiable debts may be bought, sold, and assigned, so the debtor may have no relationship to the holder of his debt other than obligations to pay him. Banking and negotiable forms of credit have a long history, as we have documented in preceding chapters—but what turned credit into a quasi-commodity was its institutionalization as a central technology in national economies.

This appears to have become significant by the fifteenth century with the establishment of public banks in Italy, and then spread across Europe by the seventeenth century. It took on ever greater importance in England following the Glorious Revolution of 1688, the aftermath of which saw the formation of the Bank of England and the transformation of the sovereign's personal debt into public debt. It also led to a reworking of legal systems that allowed a matrix of credit institutions and forms of credit to develop and come into use on an unprecedented scale interconnecting merchant banks, acceptance houses, stock markets, mortgages, letters of credit, shares, bonds, annuities, insurance, and so on.

Modern credit has particularly developed along two dimensions: negotiability and abstraction.[41] Negotiability refers to the wide gulf between credit based on personal relations between lender and borrower, and contractual forms of debts, which may be assigned for collection to others, and even bought and sold. The ability to sell debts to third parties turns debt into a quasi-commodity. This trick also turns debt into a new type of asset, a form of money. However, such negotiable forms of credit-money are necessarily based on formal, contractual obligations, and so depend upon institutional matrices, such as financial markets for stocks, and courts for enforcement.[42]

Abstraction refers to the increasingly symbolic forms that capital investment and credit may take. As houses are to mortgages, such forms come into being when financial instruments come to represent physical assets and become negotiable themselves. Because these forms are conceptual, they are dimensionless, perfectly mobile, and may be combined and divided in ways that physical things like land or houses are not.[43] These negotiable and abstract forms of credit have become dominant forms under modern capitalism and given their institutional character are imbued with strong class dimensions of power.

In arguing that these two dimensions are characteristic of modern forms of credit, we are not arguing that these had no predecessors, or that personal credit is not a part of modern economies. We recognize that even as new forms of credit have emerged and older forms, rather than being replaced by newer ones, coexist. New relations overlay old, and may even combine to produce new hybrids. We also recognize the world is more complex than such simple divisions, and that personal relations are part of even the most modern forms of credit, and play across and through modern institutions, especially in areas of access, terms, and payments.[44]

In rest of this chapter, we explore how modern credit has changed capitalist logics of production, transformed social relations, and affected law, government, and politics. We begin this journey into these particular roots of modern credit by focusing on the development of banking and commercial credit in Western Europe. In a following chapter we look at the development of consumer credit.

RETHINKING THE ECONOMY

Despite an arsenal of financial tools, up to the end of the seventeenth century, the continued existence of the feudal order and its logic remained the chief obstacle to the development of both capitalism and modern credit. Land and labor and state revenues were largely locked up in feudal obligations and arrangements. The Crown granted monopolies and administered trade. Constant warfare in Europe meant that monarchs always in need of money, borrowed heavily, and often resorted to forced loans. As God's ordained representatives, monarchs abused their power, identified justice and self-interest, and felt no obligation to repay debts. So before modern forms of credit could really flourish, there had to be a profound transformation of the social order. There had to be a rule of law, more flexible state finance and confidence that credit transactions would be profitable in one way or another.

If the philosophers of the enlightenment may be seen to have had a unifying project it was to imagine alternatives to feudal society and its ideas of divine order? Rejecting old arguments for morality based on religion; these thinkers sought to establish the foundations for morality based on reason or nature. Thomas Hobbes[45] and John Locke[46], for example, sought to locate the basis for government and society in self-preservation and the social contract. Philosophers raised questions about the use of power, the basis of society, the rule of law, natural rights, and the relation between the state and its subjects.

Standing in opposition to those who advocated a continuance of feudal obligations thinkers like John Locke, David Hume,[47] Charles-Louis Montesquieu,[48] Benjamin Constant[49], and Jean-Jacques Rousseau[50] argued for natural rights, personal freedom, and liberty. Because feudal ruling classes would often seize property, grant monopolies, demand tribute, impose taxes, abuse power, and deny justice many philosophers argued for justice and "rule of law." Locke argued that the social contract between the state and the individual entailed the rule of law, and so required respect for personal liberty. Locke, went as far as to argue that property rights are created through labor, and because such natural rights to property precede those of governments, states cannot justify taking property arbitrarily.

Much of economic history can be read as a debate over what powers are appropriate to the state, and the role it should play in the market. Just as the enlightenment sought to free labor from feudal obligations, to define new relations to property, and to ground law, and morality in secular social relations, thinkers such as David Hume, Adam Smith, and later David Ricardo sought to free the market from state control and its practices of administered trade. To reduce state control over the economy, they argued that the invisible hand of the market obeyed natural law and that unfettered trade would spontaneously create broad benefits—the "wealth of nations" as Smith put it.

THE GLORIOUS REVOLUTION AND THE INSTITUTIONAL MATRIX OF MODERN CREDIT

The Glorious Revolution of 1688 laid the foundations for the rule of law, and established the financial institutions needed for modern credit. With the overthrow of James II, ideas about the divine of rights of kings went into exile with him. When William of Orange took the throne as William III, the deal he struck with Parliament was that he would accept constraints on his authority and respect Parliament's laws. This shifted fiscal power decidedly toward Parliament.[51] Under William III, who brought Dutch advisors with him, Dutch techniques of finance such as foreign and inland bills of exchange, transferable stocks in corporations, government borrowing through annuities, lotteries, and tontines were adopted wholesale, creating a financial revolution in England.[52] Before 1688 "the king's debt was a hodgepodge of different arrangements, often negotiated separately with individual lenders."[53] Following the Glorious Revolution, Parliament took responsibility for government debt, and it ceased being the king's personal obligation. A Promissory Notes Act was passed that both provided parliamentary guarantees to all government debt, and made all debts negotiable and transferable.[54]

In 1694, the Bank of England was established as a private joint stock company by Royal charter. It was the offspring of a marriage of convenience between London's merchant community and the government, which urgently needed money for its war against Louis XIV. The Royal Charter was given in exchange for a loan of £1.2 million at eight percent interest, which would be repaid by taxes raised by the Tonnage Act on wine and ships, tonnage and large casks or "tuns." The money was raised from subscribers who bought the bank's stock. Effectively, this loan turned royal debt into a national debt, backed by Parliament's promises to pay. The enabling legislation, which made the Bank the instrument for handling government loans, and for assuring promised payments, also imposed restrictions: the Bank could not lend the Crown money or purchase Crown lands without the consent of Parliament.[55]

The long-term loans, it should be noted, also constrained what a later parliament might do, effectively tying their hands. Not only was "the sovereign's personal debt transformed into a public debt, but through its incorporation into the Bank of England, this debt was ultimately transmogrified into public money."[56] This neat trick both assured government funding, it turned the bank's debts, its promissory notes, and stocks into negotiable credit-money fueling the economy, and increasing the effectiveness of circulating hard currency.[57] This trick put government finances on a firm footing, and gave it unprecedented access to funds. Between 1688 and 1697 government, borrowing increased more than tenfold.[58]

The success of the financial revolution that followed the Glorious Revolution created the institutional and legal frameworks needed to support modern credit. The Bank of England both provided "a stable mechanism for creating and allocating credit,"[59] and served as a model for establishing joint-stock companies, notably the New East India Company in 1698 and the South Sea Company in 1711. In return for permanent loans, the government granted these companies economic privileges.[60] As stocks in these companies were fully negotiable financial instruments, a thriving stock market came into being. The trade in stocks and annuities, and the need to mediate sundry financial risks, also led to the formation of insurance companies, such as Lloyd's of London established in 1688. The growth of this financial market was remarkable. Where securities trade averaged £300,000 per year in the early 1690s within a decade, the volume averaged £3,400,000 per year; by the early 1710 the volume reached £11,000,000 per year.

Even after the South Sea Bubble collapse, market volumes from 1715 to 1750 remained higher than before 1688. Banking likewise grew quickly following the establishment of the Bank of England. By the 1720, there were twenty banks in London, thirty by 1750. After 1750, banks began to be founded outside London as well.[61] This financial revolution put government financing on solid ground, and the explosion of credit-money that followed not only fueled the Industrial Revolution, but caused a shift in power from the monarchy toward the merchant classes that saw money lending and profits as being virtues and not vices.[62]

The South Sea Bubble: Credit and Speculation

The Glorious Revolution unleashed capital, putting government financing on firm footing, and creating the capital funds and institutions needed for large-scale financial enterprises. The Revolution's principal weakness was that it also encouraged huge financial experiments, wild speculation, and innumerable fraudulent scams. The South Sea Bubble of 1720 in which an orgy of speculation led to the worst stock market crash in English history is the classic case of this.[63] In outline, in 1711 the South Sea Company received a royal charter that granted it a monopoly over trade with Spanish colonies in South America. At the end of the Wars of Spanish succession, as part of the settlement under the Treaty of Utrecht (1713), the South Seas Company was granted an *asiento* to sell duty free 4,800 slaves and as much merchandise as could fit into a 500 ton ship per year for thirty years.

When England and Spain again went to war in 1718, and the Company's prospects dimmed, its directors began to eye the possibilities that financial markets held. Debts the government had incurred because of these wars presented an opportunity. Although the Bank of England and the East India Company held around 13 percent of the government's debt; the rest was held in private hands as either redeemable government bonds or irredeemable long-term annuities that paid high interest. To lighten the burden of these debts on the Treasury, the government was naturally interested in ways of renegotiating them.[64] In 1719, the South Sea Company proposed to assume the government's entire public debt.

After a bidding war with the Bank of England, and a good deal of bribery of peers of the realm and members of Parliament, in March of 1720 the South Sea Company was empowered to purchase £31 million of privately held bonds and annuities. As part of this deal, the Company agreed to charge lower interest than the Treasury paid to holders of these annuities, and as a sweetener pay to the government some £7 million. The trick was to persuade the holders of these bonds and annuities to surrender their assured interest rates in exchange for South Sea stock. To lure these holders into this exchange the Company began to drive the price of their stock up through artificial means—through new subscriptions, offering stock on margin and extended terms, by spreading stories of trade with Spain designed to give the impression that the stock soon would go much higher. And as Dutch investors also clamored for South Sea stock, the price of stock rose.[65] As the South Sea Company had some £40 million in working capital, the largest amount ever amassed in England, investor confidence that this was a financially sound exchange was high. Between February and August, the price of South Sea stock rose tenfold. Everything, however, depended upon the value of South Sea stock continuing to rise.

Unfortunately, the rise of South Sea Company stock inspired imitators hoping to cash in on the speculation mania. Overnight, many new joint-stock companies were founded, some for real enterprises, others for bogus schemes. As scams were bad for the speculation business, on June 11, 1720, under pressure from the South Sea Company parliament passed the so-called "Bubble Act" on June 11, requiring a royal charter of all joint-stock companies.[66] When the act was enforced on August 18, 1720, there was immediate downward pressure on the price of shares of the affected companies. "Since the shares were mostly held on margin, sales hit the share of all companies, including the South Seas, in a scramble for liquidity."[67] A meltdown of the market began. Between September and mid-October, the price of South Sea Company shares fell from £775 to £170. While commonly, the South

Sea Bubble is cast as a story of greed, the underlying speculation is a direct product of the abstractions which create modern credit. When a deed is used symbolically to represent a piece of property, this entails some loss of information about its particular character. Similarly, when debts as promises to pay are rolled into stocks as securities, the true value of the assets may be less than transparent. The meltdown of the stocks of banks and mortgage companies built on subprime loans is a contemporary example of the potential consequences of the same type of opaqueness.

MODERNITY AND THE ARMATURE OF CREDIT

If we take one approach to the definition of capitalism, following Eric Wolf,[68] and say that it comes into being when capitalists are able to exert sufficient control over the means of production to force workers to sell their labor at efficient prices (low enough to enable capitalist profit), then certainly capitalism had come to dominate the English economy by the second half of the eighteenth century. Yet, it is also clear that the changes that led up to this did not happen overnight. For a capitalist to lay hold of the means of production at reasonable cost, required historical transformations in which land, labor, and capital came to be perceived as commodities, processes that in Britain took centuries.[69] Changes to land tenure and feudal obligations required not merely the fundamental reworking of legal systems and institutions, but for the capitalist to lay claim to the mode of production, it arguably also required the development of an arsenal of credit arrangements and institutions: merchant banks, acceptance houses, stock markets, mortgages, letters of credit, shares, bonds, annuities, insurance, and so on; all which were partially developed by the beginning of the eighteenth century.[70]

The creation of banks, joint-stock companies, stock exchanges, commercial law, and court enforcement of contracts provided the armature to separate credit from personal ties and networks. As negotiable financial paper came to symbolically represent goods and debts a basic transformation of feudal order was set in motion that would replace rulers living off of feudal obligations with bureaucratic nation-states, living from a monetized economy, redefine subjects as citizens with national obligations; and thus create the institutional matrix required for capitalism to flourish.

SPREAD OF BANKING AND THE INDUSTRIAL REVOLUTION

As population growth began to create burgeoning towns, and with them flourishing markets for agricultural products, prices rose steeply. Lords living on fixed rents soon felt the pinch from taxes and the cost of living. They dealt with this problem in two ways. They raised rents, and saddled their tenants with new labor services or reimposed old ones from which they had been able to buy exemptions.[71] This often involved remeasuring lands and arguing that peasants had illegally expanded their holdings while no one was looking (clearing forest or encroaching on the demesne). Alternatively, lords moved to take over the direct management of their estates—though they often found that lands were buried under leases and money rents, and that peasants had settled on or collectively held substantial portions of the demesne.

Not surprisingly, when lords attempted to recover demesne lands, they encountered fierce resistance from their tenants.[72] The legal courts of Henry II grappled with the questions of how land tenure was connected to personal relations. Ultimately, they rendered decisions that uncoupled them. In so doing, they severed "the link between land and personal service, the touchstone of early medieval social relations," and "land left the sphere of personal relations and became property."[73] In time, the separation of tenure from personal status, allowed lords with the backing of the state, to enclose their lands. Because of traditional practices of partible inheritance peasant holdings looked like a crazy-quilt of scattered small fields. These were consolidated, and in some cases further rationalized by imposing impartible inheritance. The "liberation" of the rural workforce through dispossession provided the labor force for the Industrial Revolution. The Poor Laws (1598–1601) kept the unemployed alive and available for industrial labor.

The spread of banking in Britain was closely associated with the rise of industrial capital. In 1750, outside London, barely a dozen banking houses existed in England and Wales. As the Industrial Revolution gained steam, private banking houses quickly proliferated across Britain. By 1784, there were 119 private banks, 280 by 1793, and 783 by 1810. Most of these were setup by provincial merchants and small manufactures, usually in partnership with a lawyer because like the London scriveners they were used to handling such transactions.[74] They founded banks partly because they allowed them greater access to capital and credit, but also because they desperately needed banking services to deal with the many forms of currency in use. As Davis reminds us at the end of the eighteenth century, the state of currency was deplorable. There was a widespread shortage of hard currency, particularly of silver, and copper coin. Market transactions often involved the use of promissory notes, shop tokens, company notes, notes issued by banks, and quasi-banks, foreign coins, and bills of exchange.[75]

The credit these banks offered usually was for the short-term rather than for long-term investments.[76] At the time, most of the long-term investment capital for manufacturing and other business enterprises came from profits plowed back into business, from family, and friends, or sometimes from selling of stocks. What the spread of banking did do was to create channels that permitted an increasing trade in promissory notes, and inland bills (which were bills of exchange drawn and payable within the country) to flourish, and facilitated the concentration and movement of savings from one part of the country to another to meet the needs for short-term capital.[77]

BANKING, CAPITALISM, AND NINETEENTH CENTURY GLOBALIZATION

If the variety of currencies, notes, and inland bills in circulation domestically in Britain required private bankers, International trade required the even great expertise of merchant bankers.[78] The latter part of the eighteenth century saw a rapid rise in merchant banking houses in London specializing in international trade. As London began to flourish as a financial center, merchant bankers—particularly from Germany and Holland but from other countries as well—such as the Barings, Rothschilds, Schroders, Warburgs, Hopes, Raphaels, Brown Shipley, Seligmans, and the Morgans to name but a few began to concentrate in London.

What these merchant bankers provided was real expertise in the ins and outs of buying and selling abroad. Merchant banks (also known as acceptance houses because of their dealings in bills of exchange) financed foreign trade and specialized in the issue of foreign loans. Through their own business dealings, merchant bankers had built extensive networks abroad with correspondent banks, and in turn for equivalent services, acted as their London bankers for trade finance and payments.[79] Because of their long, personal, and family involvement in trade, these merchant bankers had intimate knowledge of the credit worthiness of foreign bankers.[80] This knowledge and capacity were further enhanced because they maintained commission agents overseas who were in day-to-day contact with the local market. By the mid-nineteenth century these, London merchant bankers were associated with 1,500 firms of British commission agents around the world. They dealt in everything from bullion trading to underwriting, to bonds, and to arranging foreign loans.

Prior to the 1820s the impact of the Industrial Revolution was fairly circumscribed.[81] Manufacturing was largely provincial; and the Napoleonic Wars had retarded international trade.[82] Even so, new opportunities were opening. The colonial revolutions that shattered Britain's and Spain's monopoly of trade with their former colonies also opened the doors for British trade in Mexico, the Spanish West Indies, Central America, and Latin America.[83] In 1825, the Bubble Act of 1720, which had forbidden the formation of joint-stock companies without a Royal Charter and had essentially confined commercial undertakings to individuals and partnerships, was repealed. Within a year of its repeal 624 new joint-stock companies had been formed, and Parliament, following the prevailing laissez-faire ideology stepped away from its attempts to regulate the market. New investments were not only being made within Britain, but British capital was investing abroad. Capital was flowing into Europe to rebuild businesses and governments, but also being invested in risky ventures in Mexico[84] and Latin America.[85]

As Britain turned it attentions to empire building following the Napoleonic Wars, British banking helped finance foreign trade. Up to the 1830s, merchant-banking houses in London handled British overseas transactions through their networks of commission agents and correspondent banks abroad were usually family businesses. Beginning in the 1830s a new type of multinational bank, organized as joint-stock companies, began to compete with merchant banks. Unlike merchant banks, multinational banks established branch offices overseas that were directly controlled from their corporate headquarters in London.

In the wave of globalization that ensued with the Industrial Revolution, multinational banks followed the British Empire into its colonies. Initially, multinational banks established branches in Australia, Canada, and the West Indies. Between 1841 and 1871 as Great Britain embarked on a vast program of accumulation by dispossession, occupying or asserting control over New Zealand, the Gold Coast, Labuan, Natal, the Punjab, Sind, Hong Kong, Berar, Qudh, Lower Burma, Kowloon, Lagos, Sierra Leone, Basutoland, Grigualand, Transvaal, and established new colonies in Queensland and British Columbia multinational banks followed and spread quickly across much of the world into Latin America, China, and the Balkans.[86]

This expansion, not only opened new markets for British goods, but also new sources of cheap raw materials and food to fuel British capital.[87] This trade was greatly encouraged by multinational banking and the development by the British treasury of uniform rules for banking across the empire, so by 1914 some thirty British banks owned more than 1,000 branch banks spread across the globe.[88] The advent of multinational banking took a good chunk of the business from merchant banks. While merchant bankers in London continued to finance much of the trade between Europe and the United States, they also began to specialize in the issuance of foreign loans.[89] But contrast, British multinational banks rarely participated in issuing loans to foreign governments, issuing only four loans to Latin American governments between 1880 and 1914.[90]

No merchant banking house better illustrates the scope of foreign operations than Barings. The Duc de Richeleau, acknowledging the role the Barings played in sponsoring a loan of 315 million francs to the French government in 1815 after Napoleon's defeat, is reputed to have said: "There are six great powers in Europe, England, France, Prussia, Austria, Russia, and the Baring Brothers."[91] The Barings, like many merchant bankers, were German Jews who had come to England in the eighteenth century. In 1762, they established a merchant banking house; and, by the beginning of the Napoleonic Wars, they had become one of the strongest merchant banks in London. When Napoleon, hard pressed for cash, proposed to sell Louisiana in 1803 to the United States for $15 million, it was to the Barings, and to Hope & Company[92] in London that the American government turned to for financing.[93] Technically, the $15 million purchase was made with US Bonds, which Napoleon to get cash then sold to the Barings at a 13.50 percent discount.

While merchant banks such as those of Rothschild and Barings dominated the issuance of foreign government and railway loans during the first half of the nineteenth century, in the second half, the Hambros and the Anglo-American house of Morgan became serious competitors, particularly in Latin America. Initially, these houses preferred to issue loans by themselves if possible; however, as the size and complexity of these loans increased, these banks formed syndicates to handle them.[94] International lending, however, was not without significant risk. During the nineteenth century, the British economy was racked by financial crises in 1810, 1825–1826, 1839, 1865, and 1873 which threatened banks and caused some to fail.[95] In the 1890s, "There were major financial crises in almost every region of the world where British multinational banks operated."[96]

In 1890, Barings got into serious trouble because of its overexposure to debt in Latin America. During the 1880s, British investment in Argentina rose from £25 million to £150 million, constituting nearly half of Britain investments abroad, a great proportion of which was financed by Barings. In August of 1890, when The Buenos Aires Water Supply and Drainage Company Limited in which Barings had invested heavily failed to complete its contract a financial crisis ensued. Although the Argentine government proposed to buy the company, inflation, and the costs of servicing its foreign debts meant that it only could do so with a hefty foreign loan. Barings could not make this loan unless it unloaded its debentures, but the crisis meant there was no market for them. As word spread of Barings' problems, large depositors such as Russia who had £3 million on deposit began to withdraw their funds. By November 24, 1890, Barings was within twenty-four hours of bankruptcy. The Bank of England raised a guarantee fund of £17 million from the Britain financial community to provide short-term loans. Barings liquidated their assets, averting a major crisis in London. To save itself from complete ruin, the company was split in two: Baring Brothers & Company was liquidated, and a new limited liability Barings company was created.[97]

ABSTRACTION OF CAPITAL, SOCIAL CAPITAL, AND ETHICS

It is sometimes forgotten that in Adam Smith's (1776)[98] and David Ricardo's (1817)[99] original liberal visions of free trade, land, labor, and capital were assumed to be national, and it was mere commodities that moved and were traded. Reacting to mercantile policies advocating tariffs, Adam Smith argued for the advantages of free trade in most commodities but accepted the need for tariffs to protect infant industries producing goods important to national defense. His 1776 ideas prevailed in England only by mid-nineteenth century. Ricardo introduced a new idea, comparative advantage (c. 1820s), that has had enormous influence up to the present. He imagined a situation in which both England and Portugal could produce wine and wool and Portugal could produce wine much cheaper than England and wool marginally cheaper. In this situation he thought the old idea of absolute advantage (for both commodities this would be Portugal's advantage) should be replaced by a policy of investing capital in the areas of greatest comparative within-country advantage.

In other words, Portugal should invest its national capital in wine production and buy its wool from England. The assumption of mobility of capital and labor within countries but not between them was fundamental to the argument. The puzzle that needs addressing is why in more recent eras, despite the failure of these fundamental assumptions of the international immobility of labor and capital, the theory of comparative advantage is still so popular among economists.

The neoliberal perspective is represented by Hernando de Soto, who noted that capital is more than the physical wealth embodied in buildings, property, inventories, which following Marx he calls "dead capital."[100] de Soto imagines that dead capital becomes optimally useful only when it can be rendered abstract and turned into a commodity. This requires a neoliberal legal regime and in his view a lack of such a regime is the key problem for economic development in most poor countries. de Soto, argues that "why capital succeeds in the West and fails everywhere else," is that while less developed nations may have wealth, they lack the legal frameworks needed to turn physical assets into abstract, financial capital. By representing physical assets as abstractions such as mortgages, stocks, and other instruments that could be easily subdivided (discretized), these abstractions were turned into flexible commodities that could become security for loans and could be mobilized and deployed in ways in which physical assets could not.[101] These processes of abstraction, in his view, create genuinely new commodities, that are optimized for investment and for collateral for loans; however, they also require special institutions to process them. In our view, such abstractions open up new opportunities for inequalities in exchange that can motivate or discourage and seem to have empowered the latter most frequently: for example, contributing to the enrichment of slum landlords and the inexorable peripheralization of slum dwellers themselves.[102]

The chronology of these new financial ideas (of abstraction and discretization) may be best understood by looking at analogous developments from the seventeenth to eighteenth century in mathematics. Calculus as developed in England and the continent showed that complex abstract problems, such as the area under a curve, could be better understood by dividing that area into smaller and smaller vertical strips and introducing the notion of limits. This discretization program, freed mathematics from the constraints of traditional geometry, and made many new sorts of calculations and more rigorous proofs possible.[103] Capitalism underwent an analogous process of discretization as these new ways of abstraction led in the nineteenth century to marginal analysis as a way to understand prices and value. Economists began to look at enterprises as being comprised of discrete and separately calculable and manipulable elements, and began also to create ever more abstract representations of assets.

What Smith and Ricardo did not foresee was that capital's own program of discretization would substantially free it from geography and dependence on place by creating two kinds of new mobilities. The first involved seeing productive processes as composed of separable components (labor, materials, business specializations, etc.) that could be moved to the advantage of any capitalist anywhere.[104] The second involved, substituting profound abstractions of physical capital for already mobile symbolic assets. These two ideas elaborated earliest in Great Britain increasingly permitted capitalists to evaluate their investments against ever wider geographic and industry comparisons not just in terms of rates of return, but also in terms of security and the costs of their component elements. With the evolution of ever more powerful technologies of information transfer, comparisons of investment alternatives across time and space have become ever easier.

Although comparative advantage makes no sense in a world of labor and capital mobility, it still serves as a banner idea for rationalizing investments and enhancing capital utility within country, and, conveniently, also between countries. Opening markets has continued to be pushed using the increasingly inadequate idea of comparative advantage because opening markets is not obviously beneficial. Although a global market without barriers will provide increasing advantages to scale, that is, to alliances of big capital, it will not provide any automatic national advantage. When Adam Smith advocated free trade for Britain he never claimed that the same policy would be beneficial to all countries whatever their stage of development, it was the genius of Ricardo to introduce an idea that later scholars could pretend suggested just this.

Unlike the social and biophysical wealth located in specific sites and spaces, discretized, forms of capital, because they are based upon symbolic representations of assets are essentially unidimensional.[105] Although such forms of money and credit are symbolic and numerical abstractions, they are imbued with the power to summon together labor and materials. Lacking physicality, they can be easily transported to another spatial location to initiate another and different production process. With the evolution of more powerful technologies of information transfer, the numerical representations of capital (such as rate of return on investment, cash flow, contracted interest, etc.) make it relatively easy to compare the returns on invested capital in light manufacturing in London, Mexico China, or Brazil, comparisons that drive "globalization." As corporate planners, retirement managers, and investors crunch the costs of labor, land, supplies, transportation, inventories, interest rates, and the business skills of local partners, these initially local and contextual elements[106] are turned into one dimensional numbers that may be easily compared.

The discretization and abstraction of capital is no longer about the advantage of place, but about empowering larger scale group relationships, and institutions. It is through these, that financial capital is created and information about risks and opportunities flow.[107] Unlike physical commodities, symbolic representations such as stocks are eminently divisible. Moreover, since there is nothing to haul to market, billions of dollars in shares, securities, and futures can be moved electronically across the globe. Such financial markets provide the information on risks and opportunities that empower big capital to shift quickly between investments.

In recent times land, labor and capital have become increasingly mobile as well as increasingly abstract. Even land has its version of mobility in the form of export processing zones (EPZs) which can exist in country A but have the quasi-legal status of land in country B: so that labor and environmental laws of country B can be instantiated while the EPZ is located in country A to facilitate logistics and eliminate entry tariffs to country A's market. Modern labor mobility is itself imbricated in systems of control and constraints on human rights. The new forms of abstraction have been explicitly designed to facilitate the exercise of self-serving influence by national and global elites.

The key flaw in the neoliberal ideology has been the almost certifiable refusal to examine issues of power and ethics and this has led, not surprisingly, to the rapid post–World War II growth in inequality within the United States where the neoliberal legal apparatus is most developed. The upside of these new abstractions for the rich, as well as the downside for the poor, has always been contingent upon legal, political, social, and financial arrangements and the explicit or implicit goals on which they are based. The suggestion that facilitating access to, and control of, the factors of production will increase global wealth represents a popular faith in top down transparency, associated in academia with extensions to Bentham's Panopticon, an institution optimized for surveillance of prisoners. Exclusive focus on the governance advantages of top down surveillance obscures the issues of distribution and justice that are not improved by technologies providing short-term advantage to global elites and managers of large-scale capital.

NOTES

1. Reynolds, *Fiefs and Vassals,* makes a strong case for legal heterogeneity in medieval Europe in terms of geographic differences, differences in rates of change over time, and differences between secular estates and clerical estates (from which most records of the feudal period come). She also traces the new perspectives on property to their origin in practices on clerical estates.
2. Reynolds, *Fiefs and Vassals*, Chapter 8.
3. Boissonnade, *Life and Work in Medieval Europe*, 283.
4. Neale, *Monies in Societies*, 49.
5. Braudel, Civilisations matérielle, économie et capitalisme, Tome 3, 24.
6. Tilly, *Coercion, Capital, and European States,* 128–29.
7. Morrill, "The Stuarts," 327–98.
8. Boissonnade, *Life and Work in Medieval Europe*, 169.
9. After years of Norman invasions of what were the remnants of the Carolingian Empire, the Treaty of St. Clair sur Epte in 911 ceded that part of Modern France thenceforth called Normandy to the Normans as the Duchy of Normandy implying only some vague theoretical acknowledgement of the Carolingian king's suzerainty. The Capetians soon took over the Carolingian kingdom and it was under Philip I (1060–1108) that the Norman conquest of Britain occurred (de Bertier de Sauvigny, *History of France*, 36, 43).
10. Harold II reigned for only a few months in 1066 after the death of Edward the Confessor (1042–1066).
11. William I retained about 20 percent of the land in England under his personal control.
12. Gillingham, "The Early Middle Ages," 120–91; Peters, "Henry II of Cyprus, Rex inutilis."
13. In addition to the barons, roughly 100 major churches were tenents-in-chief (Ibid., 158).
14. Under Henry I (1100–35) in 1129–1130 about 50 percent of royal income came from land rents (in the broad sense) while only 13 percent came from taxation in its various forms. By Edward I's reign (1272–1307) the proportions had significantly changed with land rents amounting to 33 percent and taxation, including the new revenues from customs, bringing in over 50 percent. Reliefs were payments to the King for approving an inheritance. The amount of any patronage based appointments were initially negotiable and often a large part of the sum was never collected—allowing

the King, as debt holder, to move to collect the debt immediately should the noble take the wrong side in a dispute. In 1215 baronial reliefs were fixed at £100. (Ibid., 143–45).

15. Tenure relations were more complex than this brief description suggests. Although free tenants held lands at the will of their lord and could in principle be dismissed if they failed in their duties just as the lord could, their "rent" or "services" were fixed, typically at so many days' agricultural labor in the lord's fields each year. By contrast, unfree tenants were bound to their lord and could not leave his service without his approval, and never knew what they might be called upon to do.

16. A hundred generally did not have one hundred "hides"—those where reality conformed to theory were the exception not the rule. Wapentake is derived from Old Norse "*vapnatak*" referring to the ceremonial brandishing of weapons when a chief assumes office. It was used in place of "hundred" primarily in the areas long held by the Danes: the Northern Danelaw—centered around the area of York and established between 865 and 878. The southern part of the Danelaw was retaken by Edward the Elder in 918 but it was not until 954 that Eodred drove out the last Scandinavian kings from York. King Cnut (1016–1035) who gained control of all of England was the last Danish king in England—though the Normans were themselves originally Danish.

17. Blair, "The Anglo-Saxon Period," 65.

18. Mercia was at its height under King Offa (757–96). (Ibid., 96).

19. Sheriff is an abbreviation of shire-reeve a position, roughly the King's head bailiff for each shire, created in the reign of King Aethelred (979–1016) "the Unready." (Ibid., 94).

20. Villains / villeins /villani were free peasants lower in rank than a thane (a free retainer owing military service) but typically holding twenty to forty acres and higher than a sokeman (typical free villager) or cotter (a peasant who has a cottage and small landholding in return for services). In the late eleventh century, villains comprised 41 percent of the recorded population and held 45 percent of the land. Cottars comprised 32 percent of the population and held 5 percent of the land. Sokemen comprised 14 percent of the population and held 20 percent of the land. Slaves holding no land comprised 9 percent of the population. The elite, two hundred laymen and one hundred bishoprics, abbeys and priories, held rentier rights to about 75 percent of the assessed value of the entire country (Gillingham, "The Early Middle Ages," 157–58.)

21. The demesne was that part of the lord's manorial lands not allocated to his serfs or freeholder tenants. It could be scattered among the serfs' land or could be a separate area, the latter being more common for pastures and orchards.

22. The best study of this is Kula, *An Economic Theory of the Feudal System.*

23. Davies, *A History of Money*, 127–33. Athelstan operated thirty mints. By the reign of Edgar (959–975) the number increased to forty. Aethelred II (978–1016) faced with Danish invasion needed to operate seventy-five mints just to produce the 40 million silver pennies need to pay the Danegeld or tribute to the Danes.

24. Ibid., 129.

25. Chown, *History of Money from* 800 *A.D.*, 10.

26. Davies, *A History of Money*, 141.

27. Chown, *History of Money from* 800 *A.D.*, 28.

28. Davies, *A History of Money*, 138–39.
29. Although Biddick, "People and Things: Power in Early English Development," 7, calls such technologies new; many of these existed in antiquity and were still used in other places such as Byzantium; and so were not so much new as rediscovered in feudal Western Europe.
30. Gillingham, "The Early Middle Ages," 147.
31. Jardine *Worldly Goods,* 337.
32. Kindleberger, *A Financial History of Western Europe,* 43–44, Davies 1995:221.
33. Cited in Jardine, *Worldly Goods,* 373.
34. Ibid.
35. Davies, *A History of Money*, 146–47.
36. Much of our knowledge of the Exchequer is based upon *The Dialogue of the Exchequer*, a detailed description written in the 1170s by Richard FitzNeal, Bishop of London, Treasurer of England.
37. Hollister, *Anglo-Norman Political Culture and the Twelfth-Century Renaissance,* 250–72.
38. The earliest mention of the Exchequer dates from 1110 (Gillingham, "The Early Middle Ages," 145).
39. Davies, *A History of Money*, 148–51.
40. Biddick, "People and Things: Power in Early English Development," 7–8.
41. Because there are innumerable dimensions along which modern and pre-modern economies might be distinguished, it is probably a mistake to imagine that there this a clear divide, especially in terms of instruments of capital. Contractual and abstract form of credit predates capitalism, but it is their prevalence in modern economies which is distinguishing.
42. The negotiability of debt came about slowly. It involved incremental changes that spread from the Islamic world into Italy in the fourteenth century and through Holland to England. While bills of exchange were used widely in trading networks in the middle ages, they depended on personal endorsements on the bill. Nonetheless, such bills detached payment from particular goods. When these bills became payable to the "bearer," debt detached from person-to-person relationships, and became negotiable, turning debt essentially into money (see Ingham. "Capitalism, Money, and Banking," 76–96; Carruthers, *City of Capital,* 127–31).
43. Gold and silver, Marx argues, when considered in terms of the labor-power and the social means required to produce them constitute an expense for capital and to the degree that the costs of monetary production are decreased this will benefit the social product. See Marx *Capital,* Volume 2., Part Two, Chapter 17, 420.
44. Finn. *The Character of Credit.*
45. See Hobbs, *Leviathan.*
46. Locke, *Two Treatises of Government.*
47. Hume. *Hume's Political Discourses.*
48. Montesquieu, *The Spirit of the Laws.*
49. See Constant, *Constant Political Writings.*
50. Rousseau, *The Social Contract.*

51. Dickson, *The Financial Revolution in England,* 48–73.

52. Gelderblom Jonker. "Completing a Financial Revolution: The Finance of the Dutch East India Trade and the Rise of the Amsterdam Capital Market, 1595–1612," 642.

53. Smith, *A History of the Global Stock Market from Ancient Rome to Silicon Valley,* 18–19.

54. Ibid., 19–20.

55. North and Weingast, 820–821, "Constitutions and Commitment: The Evolution of Institutional Governing Public Choice in Seventeenth-Century England;" Davies, 261, *A History of Money*; Carruthers, 45, "Rules, institutions, and North's institutionalism: state and market in early modern England."

56. Davies, *A History of Money*, 149; Ingham, "Capitalism, Money, and Banking: A Critique of Recent Historical Sociology," 89–90.

57. Ingham, "Capitalism, Money, and Banking: A Critique of Recent Historical Sociology," 84.

58. North and Weingast, "Constitutions and Commitment: The Evolution of Institutional Governing Public Choice in Seventeenth-Century England," 805.

59. Smith, *A History of the Global Stock Market from Ancient Rome to Silicon Valley,* 19.

60. Broz and Grossman, "Paying for Privilege: The Political Economy of Bank of England Charters, 1694–1844," 48–72.

61. North and Weingast, "Constitutions and Commitment: The Evolution of Institutional Governing Public Choice in Seventeenth-Century England," 826–27.

62. Smith, *A History of the Global Stock Market from Ancient Rome to Silicon Valley,* 18.

63. See Neal, *The Rise of Financial Capitalism*; Flood and Garber, *Speculative Bubbles*; Willcox and Arnstein, *The Age of Aristocracy 1688–1830*; Sornette, *Why Stock Markets Crash.*

64. Hoppit, "The Myths of the South Sea Bubble," 143.

65. Hoppit, "The Myths of the South Sea Bubble", 143; Sornette, *Why Stock Markets Crash*, 10–13.

66. Sornette, *Why Stock Markets Crash,* 10–13.

67. Flood and Garber, *Speculative Bubbles,* 48–49.

68. Wolf, *Europe and the People Without History.*

69. Marx *Capital,* Vol I, Part Eight, Chapter 29; Wordie, "The Chronology of English Enclosure, 1500–1914"; Martin, *Feudalism to Capitalism*; Hilton, *Bond Men Made Free*; Brenner, "The Origins of Capitalist Development," 30–75; Brenner, "Agrarian Class Structure and Economic Development in Pre-Industrial Europe," 10–63; Blaut, "Colonialism and the rise of capitalism," 260–96; Duchesne, "Remarx on the Origins of Capital," 129–37.

70. Roseberry, "Political Economy," 163–69.

71. Boissonnaide, *Life and Work in Medieval Europe*, 239.

72. Gies and Gies, *Life in a Medieval Village*, 45–47; Gillingham, "The Early Middle Ages," 158.

73. Biddick, "People and Things: Power in Early English Development," 9.

74. Davies, *A History of Money*, 285–87 argues this rapid rate of bank formation lends support to Rostow's view that British capitalism experienced the world's first take-off in to self-sustaining grown. Rostow, in *The Stages of Economic Growth*, however, posits that this take off was based on a rise in the rate of domestic savings. This overlooks the strong role that foreign investment, particularly from Holland played in Britain's industrialization (Brezis, "Foreign capital flows in the century of Britain's industrial revolution: new estimates, controlled conjectures," 53–55.

75. Davies, *A History of Money*, 292.

76. Pollard, "Fixed Capital in the Industrial Revolution in Britain," 307–08.

77. Shafaeddin, "How did Developed Countries Industrialize?" 7.

78. In Europe, merchant banking before it became prominent in London had existed for hundreds of years. International banking practices were developed in the late middle ages in Italy by Italian grain merchants and Italian banking houses such as Bardi, Peruzzi, and Medici. In the sixteenth century these moved into southern Germany and then the Netherlands.

79. Jones, *British Multinational Banking, 1830–1990*, 5.

80. Davies, *A History of Money*, 344–45.

81. As Reddy argues, "The structure of a cultural crisis: thinking about cloth in France before and after the Revolution," in France despite rapid commercial expansion during the eighteenth century, there was little or no change in the predominant modes of production either before, during, or after the French Revolution. Industrial capitalism was almost nonexistent in France in 1789 and was still quite rare in 1815.

82. Cannadine, "The Empire Strikes Back," 185–86.

83. Gallagher and Robinson, "The Imperialism of Trade," 7–9.

84. Greenberg, "Medio Mileno de Credito entre los Mixes de Oaxaca," traces the role credit played among the Mixes in shaping their trade interactions with the wider world over 500 years.

85. Davies, *A History of Money*, 306; Smith, *A History of the Global Stock Market from Ancient Rome to Silicon Valley*, 92.

86. Gallagher and Robinson, "The Imperialism of Trade," 2–3.

87. Ibid., 7–9.

88. Jones, *British Multinational Banking, 1830–1990*, 1–19.

89. Ibid., 5.

90. Ibid., 120–21.

91. Davies, *A History of Money*, 346.

92. Hope & Company was one of the strongest merchant houses in Europe, and fled to London in 1795 when the French invaded the Netherlands, and subsequently formed close ties with the Barings.

93. Davies, *A History of Money*, 346.

94. Jones, *British Multinational Banking, 1830–1990*, 119.

95. Laider, "Rules, Discretion, and Financial Crisis in Classical and Neoclassical Monetary Economics," 17–19; Neal, *The Rise of Financial Capitalism*, 169–181.198–206.

96. Jones, *British Multinational Banking, 1830–1990*, 63.

97. Davies, *A History of Money*, 348–49; Ferns, "The Baring Crisis Revisited," 24(2): 241–273; 260–262; Jones, *British Multinational Banking, 1830–1990*, 63.

98. Smith, *The Wealth of Nations*.

99. Ricardo, *Principles of Political Economy and Taxation*.

100. de Soto, *The Mystery of Capital*.

101. Ibid., 46–52.

102. Davis, *Planet of Slums*, Chapter 4. Illusions of Self Help and Chapter 6. Slum Ecology.

103. Lakoff and Nuñez. *Where Mathematics Comes From*.

104. Carrier and Millers, *Virtualism*.

105. Hornborg. *The Power of the Machine*.

106. Smart, "Local Capitalisms: Situated Social Support for Capitalist Production in China."

107. Karen, *Situating Global Capitalism*, 68–96.

Chapter 5

Mercantile Credit and the Atlantic Slave Trade

In this chapter we first review the big picture, establishing the economic and social significance of the slave trade to states in Africa, Europe, and the Americas, when black slaves "were the strength and sinews of this western world,"[1] and then focus on the role of credit in the early financing of the Atlantic slave trade. We hope to show that this economically important, and ethically deplorable, activity that contributed so much impetus to the Industrial Revolution would never have succeeded without major financing and that this financing required an unprecedented ethical blindness. An early trope in discussions of the Atlantic slave trade was to argue that African leaders were prone to pillage and enslave their own people and so slaves bought for the Americas were escaping a worse fate. Thus following a purchase of 300 slaves in the late nineteenth century, the French agent in the Senegambia, André Brüe, noted.[2]

Negro princes always have a ready resource which allows them to procure more slaves; they sell their own subjects. They never lack pretexts to justify their violence and rapine. The Damel used this method because he was already deeply in debt to the Company, and he knew his credit would not be extended.

Already in the seventeenth century the Italian Gio Antonio Cavazzi who was on the coast of the Congo from 1654 to 1667 reported that for a coral necklace or a bit of wine the Congolese would sell into slavery their parents, their children, their sisters, or brothers.[3] In the early eighteenth century, it was standard for European Companies to advance goods on credit: guns and horses being then the most desirable imports into the Senegambia just as slaves were the most valuable exports. These debts rarely exceeded the price of one hundred slaves and when they did in 1720 this provided a justification for cutting back on the extension of credit.[4] The notion of debts explaining the sale of slaves may have seemed a little more understandable to Europeans than the practice reported by Cavazzi. Current Wolof proverbs such as that "the king is not a kinsman" or "the king is not dangerous his vassals are" give some indication of the historical situation but we should not forget that some West African societies, for example, the Sereer in Senegambia, adamantly refused to participate in the slave trade.[5]

This trope of the unjust Africans as a justification for New World slavery faded in popularity with time as moral arguments against slavery eventually led the British to outlaw the slave trade in Parliament (1810), to propose its abolition in the Congress of Vienna (1815) and to try actively to abolish it on the high seas after 1830. In reality, African leaders much preferred slaves from far away as enslaving their own greatly increased both the chances of escape and of social disruption. This partly also explains the preference within Africa for female slaves who were valued for their agricultural and domestic labor; their reproductive capacities and their greater docility compared to male slaves.[6] The latter two virtues enhanced their social assimilation.

Within Africa, there were slaving societies more and less affected by the Atlantic slave trade. Between 1667 and 1710, the Kingdom of Kongo transmuted into a new sociopolitical structure with a huge domestic slave population[7]. Yet, a contemporary society far from the Atlantic, the Sultanate of Dar Fur (at its peak in what became the western Sudan between 1700 and 1850 during which time it enslaved approximately 750,000 people) and a supplier of slaves north to Egypt, gives the lie to claims that all slavery in Africa was benign or caused by the Atlantic slave trade. A song sung in the Sultanate that came down to us in an Arabic manuscript titled "The Slave's Lot" has been translated and goes in part as follows:[8]

> The slaves must do the work in the house; if they are unwilling to work, they must be beaten with the whip or must be beaten with the stick. Then they begin to cry (they) are willing to work. Their language is difficult; people don't understand them. If we find a girl among them, who pleases us, then she doesn't need to do any housework. I make her my wife, so that we can sleep together and "eat the skin" (have intercourse) so that we will have children. Then she becomes pregnant and has a child. If it is a boy, then everything is fine.

When in 1865, Amadou, son of Umar Tal the Muslim general who spread Islam across the Sahel, in extending Islamic territory captured Toghou in Mali, his slaughter of at least 2,500 Bambara men and enslavement of 3,500 women and children were easily as violent and merciless as anything in the Americas.[9] It is important to remember that Africa was exposed to several millennia of trans-Saharan slave trading and to at least a millennium and a half of slave trading up the east coast of Africa or across the Red Sea as well as to almost four centuries of the Atlantic slave trade. While slavery within Africa was undoubtedly influenced by these flows, it had ample time as well to develop its own internal social dynamics. It is quite possible that many societies practicing slavery within Western Africa, and elsewhere in Africa, left slaves with more considerable reason to hope for a near-term future amelioration in their life than was the norm in plantation agriculture or in mines in the Americas.

ECONOMIC CONSIDERATIONS IMPACTING THE ATLANTIC SLAVE TRADE

The benefits to European development of the Atlantic slave trade were much praised in the eighteenth century, and the substantial profits at every step of the "commodity" chain were often substantial and far above the norm in most other trades. While profit margins could be as high as 100 percent and may have averaged close to 40 percent the slave trade was still risky and provided much smaller profit margins than the East Indies trade conducted by the Dutch East Indies Company which occasionally reported profits of 5000

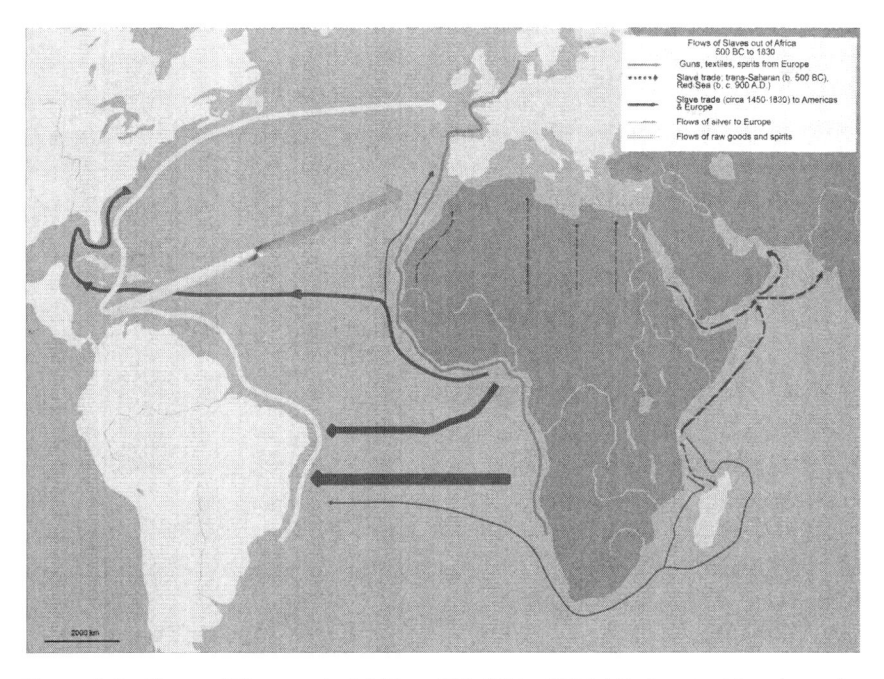

Figure 5.1 Flows of Slaves out of Africa, 500 BC to 1830 AD. *Source*: Map drawn by Thomas K. Park.

percent. Bankruptcies were frequent and credit essential, a report in 1795 assessed the trade as follows:[10]

> The African Commerce . . . holds forward one constant train of uncertainty, the time of slaving is precarious, the length of the middle passage uncertain, a vessel may be in part or wholly cut off, mortalities may be great, and various other incidents may arise impossible to be foreseen.

When scholars[11] who define capitalism as being primarily about high rates of return on investments (accumulation of wealth) look at the mercantile age, they note great continuities with earlier periods. They view commerce and see European merchants among others using banks, letters of credit, forming companies, issuing stocks, and conclude that capitalism organized the world even in this period. This however, focuses on realms of circulation and exchange but ignores some of the structural incentives behind why goods were produced.

By contrast, scholars[12] who focus on modes of production, argue that we cannot talk about capitalism until capitalists come to dominate the means of production, and can force people both to work for them and buy from them. In short, they follow Karl Marx's view that when labor-power (not labor) becomes a commodity sold like any other commodity then we have capitalism. Thus, they argue that the system of capitalism grew up in Europe after 1500, as capitalists seized control of production, and only became dominant after 1750.

Neither perspective relies upon the not so subtle notion that prices in a capitalist economy should be efficient in the sense that they reflect their productive value such that marginal returns to investment equal marginal productivity from investment. In a capitalist economy, neoclassical economists think this efficiency shapes and guides all decision making. The notion that slaves in particular were priced globally at a price point where their marginal productivity equaled their owner's marginal returns does not withstand a moment's scrutiny as the often exorbitant profit margins attest. Obviously, slaves did not voluntarily offer or sell their labor-power or their labor. Although we can agree that the seeds of capitalism could be found in the fifteenth to nineteenth centuries, we would argue there are truly significant differences between the mercantilistic and capitalist worlds.

This earlier era was decidedly not one of free markets or free trade. Though the replacement of the British Royal Africa Company by the Company of Merchants was a nominally free trade success in Britain[13] it actually represented a success of the private sector vis-à-vis a royal monopoly and did little to establish a price point in the slave trade resembling the efficient pricing Adam Smith and his economic heirs advocated. This was still a world of administered trade with protective tariffs and royal prerogatives. European and African rulers regulated trade for their own benefit. They controlled access to markets by issuing licenses and contracts, and by granting monopolies. A boat could not even set sail except by their leave. Although a merchant might, for example, be granted a right from the king of Portugal to buy slaves in Africa or an *asiento* from the king of Spain to sell slaves in the Spanish colonies, he would still have to negotiate permission to trade with African rulers who were just as interested as European royals in what would be in it for them. While Adam Smith made an argument for more general free trade in many commodities in 1776, it was not until the 1850s that the British government repealed mercantilistic policies. It is worth noting that there seems to be good evidence that African states on the coast experienced increasingly good terms of trade between the eighteenth and nineteenth centuries as they over time procured slaves more cheaply from the interior and sold them for a better price to Europeans.[14]

It is worth noting that the advent of a general free trade policy, appearing earliest in Britain, postdated all except the tail end of the Atlantic slave trade. The general quantitative chronology of the Atlantic slave trade has been worked out by Curtin and refined subsequently by others.[15] Curtin's analysis based on known shipping records suggests that it began with annual low numbers on the order of 1000 in the fifteenth century rose gradually over subsequent centuries to reach an annual peak over 60,000 around 1780 and then declined gradually to 20,000 by 1840 before being eliminated by British patrols and disappearing around 1870.[16] Subsequent work estimating deaths in the middle passage and unrecorded trans-shipments has shown Curtin's calculations to underestimate the probable numbers by at least 20 percent and maybe as much as 50 percent.[17] These analyses raise the total trans-shipped slaves over all centuries to perhaps 15 million instead of 10 million.[18] Nevertheless, Curtin's quantitative chronology for the Atlantic slave trade, viewed as a histogram, has been little challenged other than to point out the obvious chronological variability in annual numbers across the sending regions.

This chapter's focus on the Atlantic and the role of credit in the slave trade cannot do justice to key factors tied to local economics and politics within Africa. While the diversity of local conditions near the west coast of Africa and during the sixteenth to nineteenth centuries was enormous, two of the most important uses of slaves within Africa were for military purposes and for productive (agricultural or domestic) labor. Each African state had its own goals and internal politics that to a significant degree determined its participation in the slave trade. The great productive contributions of slaves in the Americas and to the European economies don't correlate (positively or negatively) well with the economic trajectories in Africa. Still, there is little doubt that the Atlantic slave trade empowered states with access to the coast at the expense of those further inland nor that it had reverberations across much of Africa for we should remember that slaves destined across the Atlantic were also sought along the East coast of Africa.

Still, slavery within the African continent has been shown to have had a different chronology not just in that it long predated the Atlantic slave trade but also in that the quantitative peak of slavery came late in the nineteenth century instead of late in the eighteenth century. The disappearance of the trans-Atlantic slave trade as well as the trans-Saharan slave trade, or that up the east coast to Somalia and the Arabian Peninsula, might have provided an impetus to greater use of slave labor within Africa but historians have amply documented the indigenous trajectories of economic growth, as well as state, religious and lineage dynamics. As Braudel has suggested the apparatus of domination is much more than the state and is a sum of hierarchies, politics, as well economic and sociocultural structures.[19] There can be little reason to imagine that these cessations in slave trade across the Sahara or the Atlantic determined the overall pattern of nineteenth century increases in slave-based production within Africa.[20]

THE ROOTS OF THE ATLANTIC SLAVE TRADE

The African slave trade had been a going concern even in Europe, long before it crossed the Atlantic. Slavery was a component of medieval society as well as an element of the social structure in the ancient world. In the ninth to eleventh centuries, a Jewish group the Radhaniya traded white slaves from Europe (slavs called *saqaliba* in Iberia) and black slaves from Africa destined almost entirely for the Islamic world (known as *'abi*d) across the Mediterranean world.[21] The same group went on to buy slaves from as far away as India for the Mediterranean market. Both the Byzantine and Islamic worlds provided a sufficiently diverse society that the obligations, rights, and opportunities available to slaves ranged from miserable all the way up to positions of high responsibility. The Islamic world, like the West African world during the era of the Atlantic slave trade, preferred female slaves and a consequent reverse sex ratio prevailed in the trans-Saharan slave trade (roughly 2:1 female) between AD 650 and 1900 than that which later prevailed in the trans-Atlantic slave trade (roughly 2:1 male).[22] The total numbers of slaves involved in each trade were also comparable even if annual numbers were much higher for the few centuries of the trans-Atlantic slave trade. West African societies in the era of the Atlantic slave trade provided ranges of opportunities for slaves analogous to those they had encountered in the Islamic world: from high positions in the military or the government down to arduous agricultural labor performed naked and on minimal food—as well as sex servitude for girls and women.[23]

Despite the much discussed Biblical passage, "There is neither Jew nor Greek, there is neither bond nor free, there is neither male nor female: for ye are all one in Christ" (Gal. 3:28), the Byzantine Empire allowed slavery[24] and Western Christianity took until early in the nineteenth century, when the economic advantages of slavery were on the decline, to abandon it. The Byzantine Empire despite its emphasis on state obligations to promote a just society did not view Christianity as incompatible with slavery. Yet, it was in the same ninth- to eleventh-century period that, along with its turn towards a more individualistic economy, the notion that freedom (to follow Christ) might preclude slavery began to spread in the Byzantine world.[25] Muslims in West Africa, despite more than a millennium of condoning slavery in Islamic societies were among those who most adamantly initially opposed its increase in the era of the slave trade. Early in this period the minority Muslim community in Senegambia was the most vocal about the practice of enslaving members of civil society, or worse enslaving Muslims,[26] but less concerned about the importation of slaves from elsewhere. Notions of religious schismatic differences were regularly used to justify conquest and the taking of slaves in areas already Islamized.[27]

As a continent, despite giving birth to humanity, or maybe because of the diseases that long accompanied this development, Africa has in most areas been labor short and land abundant. This need for labor could have facilitated the lengthy internal recourse to slavery, but if so it is hard to attribute this internal trade to outside influence. A considerable agency must be attributed to Africans.

In the remainder of this chapter, we will focus on the financial structure of the early Atlantic slave trade. We will examine the role of finance in the development of what came to be a major industry providing enormous benefits to Europe and the Americas at significant cost to Africa. We will also note how, despite the long close ties between finance and ethics, it exemplified an important example of the limited application of ethical considerations in financial thinking.

THE EARLY ATLANTIC SLAVE TRADE UNDER EUROPEAN DOMINION

In the fifteenth century, the geo-political configuration of the Iberian Peninsula was one in which Muslim Moors confronted Christian rulers, who since the twelfth century had been engaged in a campaign to reconquer the peninsula. Still, Europeans had been buying slaves as well as gold, spices, and ivory from Barbary Coast merchants for centuries. In fact, during the reconquest, as Moors fled from reconquered territories, the demand for African slaves rose. Thus, only eight years after the Moors were driven out of Portugal in 1250, Moorish traders were selling African slaves at fairs in northern Portugal.[28]

The usual portrayal of the "Age of Discovery" focuses on the Portuguese exploration and mapping of the African coast, but tells us very little about the motivations, and even less about financing and administration. In 1415, Henry, "the Navigator" seized Ceuta, a major terminus for the trans-Saharan trade, and then began sponsoring exploratory voyages down Africa's west coast, hoping to discover a way to flank the hated Muslims and unite with Prester John, the purported Emperor of Ethiopia, whose kingdom Henry mistakenly thought lay in West Africa, Henry began financing voyages down the West African coast but this was not an easy matter even for a prince. In part, the required monies came from Henry's monopolies on tuna fishing along the Algarve coast, and from his monopoly on a fishery on the Tagus. However, it was the Order of Christ—a knightly order founded to carry on the war against Islam—of which Henry had been named Grand Master in 1420 that provided the bulk of the finances required.[29] Between 1419 and 1441, Henry continued to finance exploratory voyages though they yielded little profit.

In 1441, Prince Henry's fortunes took a turn for the better, and Africa's for the worse. Along the northern coast of Mauritania, one of his captains captured a group of twelve black Moors, and ransomed three of them back for ten black slaves, some ostrich eggs, and the first gold dust procured by any of the voyages.[30] The financial success of this voyage persuaded Lisbon merchants that the African trade could be profitable. That same year, Lançarote de Freitas, a customs officer backed by group of Lisbon merchants, formed the Lagos Company and applied for a royal license to trade along the West African coast. Obtaining this license in exchange for twenty percent of the profits, Freitas then set sail in command of a flotilla of six ships. Although Freitas found no gold or ivory in Senegal, he did abduct 235 black moors from islands off the coast. Prince Henry received forty-six slaves as part of his share of the loot.[31] The success of this expedition, spurred expansion of the slave trade; and, by 1450, the Portuguese were shipping between 1,000 and 2,000 African slaves to Portugal.[32]

As the African trade grew in importance, the Portuguese crown both sought to consolidate its control over this trade, and to protect its interests from rival European powers. To do this, the Portuguese began seizing islands off the African coast—first, in 1445 the island of Arguin, off the Mauritanian coast; there, in 1461, they built the first fort and trading post on the African coast. They then seized of the islands of São Tomé and Príncipe in 1470 in the Gulf of Guinea; and, in 1471, took the island of Fernando Po at the mouth of the Niger River. Major trading posts then followed at Elmina in the Bight of Benin in 1482, and at Axim in 1503.[33]

Simultaneously, as it established control over the African coast, the Portuguese Crown also sought diplomatic recognition of its claims to Africa. In 1452, the Portuguese enlisted the support of the church. Pope Nicolas V issued a Papal Bull blessing the king of Portugal's efforts to subdue pagans and other non-believers. In 1454, a second Papal Bull was issued, which gave Portugal a monopoly over Africa, with the expectation that its populations would be converted to Christianity. In 1462, Pope Pius II stipulated that Christian converts in Africa must not be enslaved. In 1479, Portugal gained uncontested control over the African trade under the Treaty of Alcaçovas, which limited Spain's penetration of Africa to the Canary Islands.[34]

Thus, Europeans were already engaged in a thriving African slave trade when Columbus landed on Hispanola in 1492. Initially, the conquistadors in their search for gold pressed Indians into forced labor or enslaved them to work on the plantations they established. However, the native population of the Americas was soon decimated by European diseases. So by 1517 when Fray Bartolomé de las Casas, who had been named "Protector of the Indians," pleaded to Spanish authorities to provide some relief to the Indians of Hispanola, he argued that they would soon disappear from the island if their enslavement and forced labor continued. The remedy Las Casas proposed was that African slaves be used in their stead.[35] Albeit eventually, his arguments to protect Indians would find expression in the New Laws of the Indies, which in 1542 prohibited the enslavement of Indians, sadly his proposed solution also became a reality.

Even with these laws the Aboriginal population of the Americas continued to decline, so by the end of the sixteenth century native populations, it is estimated, were only ten percent of pre-conquest levels.[36] As populations fell, the demand for African slaves for Spanish mines and plantations grew. The demand for African slave labor also soared in Portugal's colonies. By 1520, the sugar plantations and sugar mills that the Portuguese established along the Northwestern coast of Brazil had become the largest consumer of slaves in the Americas, not only because of the labor these enterprises required, but also because slave mortality was so high in them that their population had to be replaced every twenty years.[37] What at the beginning of the sixteenth century had been a demand for a few hundred African slaves a year by century's end had become an annual demand for thousands.[38]

Even when African rulers granted permission to trade, price negotiations were peculiar. No exchange houses or banks existed to convert cowrie shells to pieces of eight. No international price for slaves had any reason to correlate with the local value of slaves. There was also no basis for direct equivalence or price ratios between the other trade goods. Barter was usually for an assortment of items as a lot, and negotiations were over the size of the lot, roughly how many of which items went into the pile. This depended very much on local political and economic needs that changed continuously. So, it was difficult if not impossible for Europeans to estimate profits until the goods they procured were finally sold. The risks for both deaths of slaves in transit and losses of sailors either to disease or absconding at the most convenient port in the New World were so high that early attempts at accurate estimates of profit were well known to be futile.

If a particular voyage turned a profit, other costs and risks were related to maintenance of long term trade. Protecting investments required fortifications and armed forces. By the time trading companies arose in the late sixteenth century, corporate battles often involved armed conflicts in which cutthroat competition had a literal meaning. Getting slaves to market was not easy. They had to be fed and guarded from the time they were captured until they were sold, and many sickened and died, or committed suicide. This made time of the essence and within Africa motivated the production of grain and foodstuffs. The longer it took for a slave to pass along the commodity chain, the greater the costs of maintenance and the greater the risk of loss. Cutting one's losses, when applied to this commerce led to a deplorable logic in which sick slaves might be thrown overboard in the hope of preventing a contagion from spreading; and, slaves who could not be sold might be left to starve to death.

To understand the crucial role of credit in the Atlantic slave trade we will explore the slave trade of the sixteenth to early nineteenth centuries—a time when Portugal still dominated the acquisition of slaves in Africa, and when Spain was their major client state. What we discover is that before ships could ever sail to Africa or trade in the Americas, several elements had to come together. The proper Royal licenses and permits had to be obtained. Financing had to be found. Ship owners had to be persuaded to provide ships. Crews had to be recruited. Trade goods had to be procured. Credit and social capital were key to all this.

Obtaining Permits

Business, then as now, required permits and licenses. As Portugal claimed a monopoly on the African trade—which Spain at least recognized—a royal license to buy slaves had to be acquired first. If one wished to sell them in the Spanish colonies in the New World, one had to solicit the permits to import slaves from the king of Spain; for example, Charles I, as well. At first glance, all this might seem to involve familiar requirements; a part of the apparatus states have always used to regulate trade and derive revenues. However, licenses were not intended to regulate free markets, but quite the opposite, to grant the holder a monopoly over a certain area for a specific period of time. Acquiring permits was not merely a matter of walking in, making an application, and paying the required fees; the monopoly they conferred made them valuable, and hard to obtain unless one had the right connections, patronage, and capital, specifically social capital. These licenses also provided the Crown a way to build its own social capital: to play favorites, to reward loyal followers; and, punish enemies.

Examining the first license issued to import slaves directly to the Indies from Africa may provide some indication of how this system worked. In 1518, Charles I granted licenses to transport 4,000 African slaves to the new world, to his friend, Lorenzo de Gorrevod. Gorrevod who was a Flemish courtier, and the majordomo of the royal household, was as well the governor of Bresse in Burgundy. Gorrevod, however, was not a merchant, and had neither ships nor slaves. So, he sold his permits to Juan López de Recalde, the treasurer of the Casa de Contratación. Using the Treasurer of Madrid as an intermediary, Juan López de Recalde resold these licenses to a group of Genovese merchants living in Sevilla for 25,000 ducats. Since under terms of the Treaty of Alcaçovas between Spain and Portugal, Spanish ships could not legally go to Africa to buy slaves, the Genovese merchants resold these licenses to Portuguese slave dealers and sea captains who had the necessary licenses from Portugal to purchase slaves in Guinea—the price, 300,000 ducats.[39]

Eventually realizing the value of these licenses, in 1528, Charles I sold another monopoly license for 4,000 African slaves to representatives of a German Banking house for 20,000 ducats.[40] As did the Genovese merchants, the Germans turned around and sold them to the highest bidders. By 1537, Charles seems have concluded that selling these exclusive licenses to merchants who simply resold them—if the price they paid was any indication—gave the Portuguese merchants exorbitant profits, and allowed them greater access to the markets of the Indies than was desirable, so he switched to a policy of awarding permits to import a limited number of slaves to an assortment of individuals and groups—with the proviso that such licenses could not be resold. This policy lasted until 1578, when Charles I's son Philip II who had financial problems, resurrected monopoly licenses. In 1595, he sold a license to deliver 4,250 African slaves a year for nine years to Pedro Gomez Reynal for 100,000 ducats.[41]

Almost from the beginning, because of the substantial capital that such trade required, Italian bankers and merchants were heavily involved with the financing of the slave trade. And, no matter whose name was on the license, it was a small circle of Portuguese slave dealers and Italian bankers who were initially behind these enterprises.[42] Since the thirteenth century, Italian merchants and bankers had perfected the technique of using credit to capture regional economies by advancing money to sovereigns.[43] By the fifteenth century, Italian trade diasporas were well established in Europe, and were strongly represented in Spain and Portugal. Since trade and especially credit requires strong bonds of mutual trust, we find that much of international commerce was carried on between diaspora members. Diaspora members shared a common culture, ties to their home cities, frequently intermarried, and formed enduring personal relations. Long years of residence abroad allowed them to acquire the local knowledge as well as the political and financial ties needed to conduct their businesses.[44]

SHIPPING AND FINANCING TRADE

At the highest levels of finance a small circle of Italian bankers and merchants were heavily involved in financing the slave trade; however, it would be a mistake to think that they provided all the capital involved. At lower levels of finance many others were involved. Because the slave trade was a risky business, to spread their risk other merchants and ship owners were brought into trading expeditions—and each vessel formed a ship's company for the duration of the expedition. These ship's companies typically were based on shares of cargo space, and the eventual profits calculated upon a ship's return. Ship owners received two-thirds the cargo space, the remaining third was divided amongst the captain, officers, and crew—though not evenly. If the ship owner were a merchant, he could fill his cargo space with his trade goods. More often, he would lease some his space to other merchants, reducing his risks should the ship or cargo be lost.

Sailors were commonly offered a mixture of incentives to sign on including some cash in advance, cargo space, rations, and a share of the profits at the end. Like ship owners, they if they could afford to buy trade goods could fill their allotted space with them or they could rent their space to a merchant for cash. This was often preferred because it provided cash up-front without risks. Moreover, any cash they received might be the only money their families would see for many months. Cash was needed to pay off debts, which allowed their families to obtain new credit while awaiting their return. They payment of the crew, thus involved substantial use of credit. While they received ten to twenty percent of their expected earnings in advance, the remainder was paid upon return, they thus advanced eighty to ninety percent of their labor to the enterprise.[45] As they sailed "with the luck of the ship," their earnings were far from certain.

Upon the ship's return, to calculate the profits all monies earned from the freight charges were first summed; and, then the expenses incurred for the benefit of the enterprise as a whole were deducted. Deductions included such expenses as ship repairs, bureaucratic fees and taxes, stevedores, alms for patron saints, and the services of pilots, scriveners, and gunners. Once deductions for common expenses were made, another ten percent was taken out for "stockings." Three-fourths of the "stockings" went to the master or captain of the vessel; the remaining fourth was divided among the crew. After all of these deductions had been made the remaining profits were split three ways—two-thirds for the ship owner, one third for the crew.[46]

While this system may look like a partnership, it entails a simple credit transaction in which the crew advanced their labor against future payment. This reduced the ship owner's capital outlays before the voyage, and forced the crew to share the venture's risks. When the voyage went well, sailor collected their shares; however, if it went badly, they suffered. For example, if a ship sank, even if a sailor were lucky and escaped with his life, he had no right to compensation. However, if part of the cargo were saved, his claims to a share of freight charges had a higher priority than those of merchants or even ship owners. Interestingly, towards the end of the sixteenth century a new system of compensation came into use, which, in effect, separated labor from capital. Under this new system, the crew ceased to be co-participants in the venture—and sailors were recruited for fixed pay. As in the old system, they advanced their labor, and were paid at the end of the voyage. And, while ordinary sailors still received rations as part of their pay, they no longer enjoyed rights to cargo space or shares of their ship's profits.[47] As the benefits owed sailors deteriorated, it became harder and harder for ships to recruit men, particularly on slave ships which were foul smelling, disease ridden boats, and on which rarely less than a fifth of the crew died during the voyage. Increasingly to man these ships, sailors were either shanghaied or recruited by getting them into debt, and threatened with imprisonment if they didn't choose to sign on.[48]

TRADE GOODS AND CREDIT

The merchandize required to trade for slaves was drawn from throughout Europe. Portuguese ships bound for Africa carried textiles from England, Ireland, Flanders, and France but they also carried Indian, Chinese, and Japanese silks, satins, and taffetas. Cargos often included brass utensils, brass anklets called *manillas*, and nine-inch iron bars from Sweden. Flemish and Italian glass beads were another favorite trade item. In the nineteenth century, guns, tobacco, and alcohol would come prominent parts of such trade merchandise.[49]

Assembling this merchandise—not only meant moving goods through commercial networks all across Europe and beyond, but depended heavily on the use of credit. Thus, letters of credit issued by Portuguese merchants to their Genoese representatives in Antwerp allowed merchants to buy Manillas made in Germany for the trade.[50]

THE AFRICAN SIDE OF THE SLAVE TRADE

Permissions

Even if a merchant had been able to procure the required licenses for his ships to sail to Africa from the Portuguese Crown, before his representatives could do any trading, they still had to negotiate for "permission" with African heads of state, and these were no less complex and demanding than European royals. African rulers were playing a gate-keeping game. While the power of African rulers varied, like their European counterparts they sought to control trade within their realms, and to extract what benefits they could from it.[51]

Although the details varied from place to place, African authorities meeting Portuguese ships attempted to isolate Europeans from direct dealings with slave traders. For example, in Dahomey, arriving European traders would be met by the king's representatives, and porters would carry their goods to a depot in town. During their stay, although they were given servants and attendants to pander to their needs, they were not allowed to leave town except with the king's permission.

At the same time, slave traders from the interior were not allowed to enter the town, nor were they allowed to independently trade in slaves. Trade, rather, was conducted under the supervision of royal officials, with the king setting prices for goods and slaves.[52] When African rulers allowed trade, they decided when and where trade could take place. In Benin, for instance, where there were separate markets for a variety of commodities including male and female slaves, the ruler could open and close these markets at will. The negotiations for the king's permission to trade usually required a series of well-placed gifts to the ruler and his officials. Although, as an act of friendship and a demonstration of their power, rulers often bestowed valuable gifts in return, this was also a way of ensuring that they would have first choice of European trade goods, and would receive a special deal, both for their own goods and any they might purchase. Thus, for example, if commoners were offered eight-inch iron bars, the king would be offered twelve-inch ones at the same price.[53]

Middlemen

African heads of state were able to insert themselves in a position of profit and control by separating buyers from sellers, and preventing direct dealing between them without royal permission. This opened a number of opportunities for middlemen and brokers of one sort or another, both private and official. Although this separation put officials in a position to exact "gifts" for their services, a number of other elements, both cultural and economic in character, required the expertise of middlemen and brokers. Initially, many of these brokers were Portuguese *lançados*, merchant's agents and sailors who had jumped ship when they discovered that African rulers were quite willing to give them private concessions and let them to trade on their own.[54] The complex nature of trade negotiations and transactions required real expertise, making the services of these intermediaries all the more essential.

Assortment Trading and Credit

These complexities commenced with the lack of coinage. While Islamic states in northern Africa had had coinage for ten centuries, coins were seldom if ever used for trade along the African coast, and the few European coins that did find their way into trading depots were usually made into bracelets or necklaces.[55] Although cowries, brass bracelets, and iron bars were used as "standards of value" against which to gauge the value of other commodities, their values changed constantly. While Europeans brought them to Africa to use as a local means of payment, they were not about to take them back to Europe—so as these accumulated in Africa—their value declined.[56] European commerce had its own complexities—goods were purchased in a variety of coinages, but valued in their books in terms of theoretical accounting currencies whose exchange value in terms of real coins could be adjusted to the inflation of the latter. The complexities of placing values on slaves—young, old, men, women, strong, weak, healthy, or sickly required its own fictitious accounting standard of one good slave.

Negotiations involved first establishing value equivalents. Generally, this was expressed as slaves per yards of cloth, per number of iron bars, brass bracelets, etc. Once these equivalences had been established, bargaining turned to deciding the composition of goods (how many of each sort) each side would accept in trade. For example, even if Europeans might want to buy slaves, if African traders could not supply the numbers desired, negotiations would turn to what other merchandise—such as ivory, gold, or spices—would be offered as part of the mix. In this pattern of assortment trading, just as European merchants attempted to maximize their profits by trading for goods with the highest demands and best prices in their home markets, African traders likewise understood market conditions in their world and sought to maximize the assortment of European goods that they thought would sell best.[57]

Even with assortment trading, because traders often wanted more of one item or another than was available, or had more merchandise to sell than buyers wanted, credit became an important tool of trade. European merchants, for example, advanced goods to their African trading partners against future delivery of slaves. The goods advanced on credit, then, would be used to trade for slaves. Typically, the assortment of goods advanced for "one good slave" would be less than would be paid in a simple batter transaction—in effect, hiding interest paid on these loans in the price of goods. Credit, however, also followed in the opposite direction. When African slave traders advanced slaves against future payment, they received more for their slaves than they would have otherwise.[58] While in Islamic areas, there were prohibitions on usury; there were many ways around these injunctions. Partners in trade, for example, could exchange gifts; and, as long as these "gifts" were not a formal part of their agreement, the extra payment they might represent not only was not considered usury, but would be seen as demonstrating Muslim virtues of generosity.

Advancing goods on credit to Afro-Lozano brokers and African middlemen on the coast also made sense in terms ensuring future supplies of slaves. Trading with trusted middlemen on the Coast had other advantages. As foreigners, there were few sanctions Europeans could apply to force Africans to repay loans other than withhold further credit. If collecting from coastal traders with whom one was familiar was difficult, sometimes, extending credit to slave traders from the interior was an even riskier proposition; the costs of trying to collect from distant traders made such loans impractical. It was much better to have middlemen who were part of such trade networks undertake these risks.[59]

Aside from risks that goods advanced would not be repaid, the slave trade was inherently risky. Goods advanced might be stolen, destroyed, or lost before they could be traded for slaves. Even if slaves could be procured, delivering them alive, much less in good health was problematic. To bring them to the coast, not only did slaves often have to be marched hundreds of miles, but also they had to be guarded and fed. And, if buyers were not available to receive them, they had to be maintained until they came. Because of such risks, the purchase of slaves also included negotiations over how such risks would be shared. One way this was commonly done was for the trader who advanced the goods to assume all risks until the merchandize advanced was traded for slaves; thereafter, the borrowing trader merely became an agent for the lender, and the lender assumed the risks of any losses that might occur bringing slaves to market. In essence, because buyers who advanced goods to traders were buying slave futures, if they shared such risks, they could negotiate a better price for them.[60]

Credit, Caravans, and the Slave Trade

Traders within Africa faced not just a whole gamut of chicanery, but brigandage, and warfare as well. These threats made security a prime concern, and trading with trusted partners essential. The solution to both concerns lay in forming trade networks that provided both trading partners and places of security and tying this together with credit—the promise of future returns lessened the advantages of outright chicanery.

The trade networks that moved slaves from the African interior to the coast were typically based on trade diasporas in which particular ethnic groups would send colonies of traders to live among other peoples, usually along particular trade routes. Several such ethnic trade networks have left abundant traces in the historical record: the Aro of the Niger Delta, the Julaa of the Asante hinterland and the Jahaanke of Senegambia. Typically, the members of these trade networks either congregated in a section of major settlements, or they formed a separate settlement adjacent to a host community, so-called double towns. These diaspora settlements not only provided resting places and security for caravans in the lands they passed though, but provided trusted trading partners along their route. If we were to travel with a diaspora trade caravan to the coast, we might find as many as 600 to 800 slaves, broken into units of thirty to forty slaves tethered together by the neck, guards, porters, donkey drivers, their animals. In large caravans, for example from the Sahel west to the coast, there might be many as 2000 people. Sometimes, a prominent merchant would organize and led a caravan, inviting others from neighboring villages to join him. More often, the initiator had no intention of going himself, and much like his European counterparts would conduct trade using the Islamic *commenda* model in which stationary partners provide the bulk of the goods and capital on credit to their traveling partners who accompanied the goods.[61]

We would find that two figures were key—the diaspora landlord-brokers who lived in settlements along their route; and, the caravan leader who was usually picked by the traveling merchants. The local landlord-broker was the chief of the local merchants in a settlement. He provided the facilities for the physical security of goods and slaves in transit at each stop, provided access to food supplies, protection from interference by local authorities, and possibly commercial credit or loans from moneylenders. Once chosen, the caravan leader's responsibilities included providing provisions, recruiting a military force to protect the caravan, bargaining with local authorities along the road for permission to pass unmolested through their territories, and even though each merchant had his own goods, he negotiated any sales for them with land-landlord brokers, African middlemen, and Europeans. For his services, the caravan leader received 20 to 30 percent of the final sales price received for goods sold.[62] While we might wonder for a moment about the logic of having the caravan leader bargain for them (and perhaps ponder why European merchants also had the ship's captain negotiate for them), we would quickly realize that this was a price fixing tactic used to prevent competition among the individual merchants, who otherwise might undercut each other. There was another reason as well, which we might not appreciate as readily. Merchants traveling with a caravan may or may not pass that way again. By contrast, the caravan leader, who because he did business with local landlord brokers, African middlemen, and Europeans year after year, had established the relationships of trust that were needed for trade goods to be advanced against slaves.

Slaves were obtained in three ways. First, captives taken in warfare between groups could be enslaved and sold, with one exception. In Muslim areas, only infidels could be sold though sectarian differences enabled conquerors to define the conquered as infidels. Second, those convicted of crimes could be enslaved. Among the Aro, for example, disputes over land, inheritance, blood feuds, accusations of witchcraft, sorcery, and murder, were judged by a local oracle, and those who the oracle found guilty—could be killed, fined slaves, or themselves sold into slavery. Finally, people could be enslaved for debts. The Aro, for instance, advanced credit to non-Aro. Should they be unable to repay the loan, they could be forced into slavery or be forced to sell a member of their family into slavery to pay off their debts.[63] Although we might wonder why a person would take such risks, the answer is that there were few other acceptable forms of collateral—most land was communal and in abundant supply relative to labor. Instead, wealth lay in claims to people and their labor. Although livestock could be used as collateral—the poor often had only themselves to pawn.

When the Aro caravan reached the coast, we would find that most of the slave trade with the Europeans was handled by Ibibio-speaking, Efik brokers. In Old Calabar, these were organized into a Leopard society which was a secret society not unlike a businessmen's club such as the Kawanis, Elks, Rotarians, or Masons—complete with wizards, that also wielded powerful religious and legal sanctions. In Old Calabar, which had neither king nor sacred oracle, the Leopard Society enacted laws, adjudicated important cases, punished crimes, protected the property of its members, and even enforced trade boycotts against Europeans when necessary. In fact, their power was such that some European traders found it advantageous to buy memberships. Society membership not only helped European traders avoid being sanctioned, but because the society also used its power to enforce the repayment of debts, such membership helped to ensure that any goods advanced on credit to Efik brokers would be repaid.[64] Old Calabar was only one of many African states with far reaching ties and long experience in trade. Like mercantile nations in Europe, these states were sophisticated about trade and competed ruthlessly with one another not just for trade and profit, but also for territory.[65]

THE EUROPEAN ROLE IN THE ATLANTIC SLAVE TRADE

The Middle Passage and Credit

In the modern era time is money, for European slavers on the African coast speed was also of the essence but the reasons were different. The longer Europeans stayed on the coast, the more likely they were to catch one of the many endemic and deadly fevers like malaria or yellow fever to which they had little resistance. Ideally, they wanted to quickly exchange their trade goods for slaves—and as we have seen the only way to do this was to advance them on credit. Timing was also important for the delivery of slaves. If slaves were delivered long before the next boat was due, then someone not only incurred the expenses of feeding, guarding, and housing them, but also many were likely to die before the ship arrived. In the terrible spreadsheet logic of transporting slaves to the New World, slavers tried to balance the costs of transportation (the per capita costs of which fell as the number of slaves that could be crammed aboard rose) against the losses from disease, which rose the longer the passage took. Slaves were packed and chained into coffin like spaces, and made to lie in their own excrement for anywhere from twelve to twenty weeks. Under these conditions, death tolls of 30 to 40 percent were not uncommon. High mortality rates were so much a part of this trade that *asiento* contracts awarded by the Spanish Crown usually made allowances for a death rate of 10 to 40 percent.[66]

While death was a partner in this trade, credit was used to incentivize productivity and increase reliability. To encourage captains to take good care of their cargo, their pay as well as that of some officers was typically a portion of the slaves delivered. Although the more slaves delivered alive the greater would be the captain's and officers' profits, this arrangement also meant they shared the risks of the venture. If losses were high, despite all the labor they had advanced, they would see little profit.[67]

Selling Slaves and Credit in the New World

Landing and selling slaves in Spanish or Portuguese colonies, was a familiar bureaucratic nightmare. In this highly administered trade, Spanish and Portuguese policies required the delivery of slaves at designated ports. Arriving vessels were subject to several inspections. First, royal health inspectors inspected the slaves imprisoned below decks to determine if they were infected with yellow fever, smallpox, elephantiasis, or other contagious disease, and only those considered "safe" could be landed in the customs area. Customs officials then checked the ships inventory, logs, permits, and questioned the captain about passengers, crew, and itinerary. The ship would then be searched for contraband. Those slaves judged to be salable would be thoroughly examined, and grouped according to age, sex, size, and physical condition, and classified for tax purposes as "one good slave" or some fraction thereof.[68]

The strategies merchants in the Americas used to capture product, mirrored those of African merchants and brokers. In the port cities were the great mercantile houses, middlemen, and brokers who were the terminus of commercial chains that stretch into the hinterlands. They handled the auctions and sales of slaves to colonial buyers, and as in Africa extended credit to a host of small merchants who came from the interior to sell sugar, indigo, cotton, ginger, coffee, and other commodities in demand in Europe. Timing was particularly critical for captains—constrained by winds, tides, and weather—they could afford to linger in port only for so long. While it was in the interests of European merchants to have their Captains remain in port as long as possible looking for the best prices both for the slaves they sold and for the cargo they bought, yet if they tarried too long, they might be forced to sell cheap before a ship sailed. If they were unable to sell their slaves fast enough or procure a return cargo of sugar, they were forced to accept credit as payment for their slaves and sail home with little or no cargo. In such circumstances, they preferred to have bills of exchange payable in twelve to eighteen months by a merchant or his agent in Europe.[69]

In the colonies, this commerce had other peculiarities. Because of the unbalanced trade relations with the mother land, although prices were calculated in familiar currencies such as Spanish reales and Portuguese escudos, little money was actually in circulation, and the few silver and gold coins that were tended quickly to flow abroad. Cash sales were rare, and most business was conducted using credit. Even for slaves sold at auctions, payment might be made with mixture of cash or credit (with property as collateral). Hundreds of small merchants from the colonial hinterlands would come to these ports to sell to commodities, attend auctions, and buy slaves. When these merchants arrived home because planters had little cash, they usually had to sell on credit, and advanced slaves against the plantation's future harvests. Although buyers often took a couple of years to pay; and then, usually offered a mixture of cash and commodities, while rarely settling their entire debt. This system allowed merchants to set the future price for such commodities well below the expected market price, essentially charging interest on the loan.[70]

Growing Competition among Europeans

To about 1600, Portugal and Spain dominated the slave trade and overseas activities generally. After 1600, there was a mad rush among northern European nations to establish their own colonies in the New World, by force if necessary. By 1650, England, France, and the Netherlands had established colonies in the Americas. Each colony was supposed to trade exclusively with its mother country, and in this administered trade not to compete in production with the European homelands. To supply their colonies with the slaves the colonists wanted, rival European states began to challenge the Portuguese monopoly. While France, England, Holland, Sweden, and Denmark all entered the slave trade, it was the Dutch; that were to dominate the slave trade in the seventeenth century. Dutch hegemony, however, was short-lived, and by the beginnings of the eighteenth century, Britain ruled this trade.

Competition among European powers for colonies and trade significantly increased both the cost of trade and the demand for capital. As colonies became going concerns, the growing scale and volume of transactions required ever-greater sums to sustain. Although private banks had existed for centuries, the growing volume of transactions was more than these institutions could handle. To meet this growing demand, public banks first appeared in Italy (1585), in the Netherlands and Spain (1609), in Germany (1616), in Sweden (1656), in England (1694), in Scotland (1695), and finally in France (1716).[71]

These banks handled currency exchange, processed foreign bills of exchange, and made loans. At this time, we also find a stock exchange (1592) and a Chamber of Insurance (1598) being organized in Amsterdam.[72] As these financial institutions were coming into being, the parastatal charter companies were also being formed: England (1553), Netherlands (1600), Denmark and Sweden (1625), and France (1626).[73] These joint-stock companies provided a double benefit to states: they not only produced a flow of revenues into the royal treasury, but since they had monopolies over trade and made their own arrangements with private traders, they simplified the state's regulation of trade—in effect, further maximizing the state's revenues and minimizing its administrative costs.[74] Because the slave trade continued to depend heavily on credit, the evolution of these institutions changed both the way capital was mobilized and transactions handled. By the 1630s, for example, there were Dutch banks in Brazil that could extend credit to planters, and process bills of exchange issued in payment for slaves or sugar.[75]

The Dutch West India Company

In the seventeenth century, Dutch companies achieved hegemony over the slave trade. Although in 1600, it was the Dutch East India Company that was organized first, primarily to meet the growing challenge from British privateers to the Dutch spice trade in Indonesia, it provided the blueprint for the Dutch West India Company organized in 1607 to compete with the Portuguese. While initially it failed after a few years, in 1621 the Dutch again went to war with Spain and Portugal, and Dutch West India Company was reorganized and given a twenty-four year monopoly over Dutch trade to Africa and the West Indies.[76]

As a parastatal company, the States General appointed the chairman of its nineteen-man governing council. The company, however, was not what we might expect. Instead of being a single firm, it was a collection of merchants that operated under a charter. The company was divided into five chambers, each from a different area of the Netherlands, each provided capital, but each was constituted of independent traders. Their say in control of company affairs was proportional to how much capital each chamber contributed to particular enterprises. Because the Amsterdam chamber contributed the most capital, its chamber dominated the company.

Not all its moneys, however, came from its chambers. The Dutch state also invested public funds in the company. The Dutch state also provided the company with war materials and soldiers, though the company paid their salaries. The Dutch and the Portuguese were almost constantly at war during these years and as rival powers competed over the African trade, warfare, and trade became nearly indistinguishable.

At the beginning of the seventeenth century, Holland was at war with Portugal and Spain. When Philip II prohibited Dutch vessels from entering Spanish and Portuguese ports, the Dutch forcibly acted to open trade.[77] The West India Company began by procuring most of their slaves by capturing Portuguese ships, which they sold in the New World.[78] Moving into Africa the Dutch attacked the Portuguese in Mozambique in 1607 and 1608; they seized Elmina, Axim, and Shama on the Gold Coast in 1637, and between 1641, and 1648 took control of the Angolan coast. As they tried to consolidate their hold on the African trade, the Dutch West India Company also attempted to establish their own colonies in the New World, not just in New York (1624–1664), but also in the Caribbean and South America. The Dutch also attempted to take control of the sugar trade. Although production in Brazil was in Portuguese hands at the beginning of the seventeenth century, the finances needed came from Flemish and Dutch sources. In 1624–1625, the Dutch attempted to seize Bahia outright, and in 1629 they seized the sugar districts of Pernambaco, occupying them until a revolt in 1654 of local Portuguese caused them to abandon their claims.[79]

While these incursions certainly weakened the Portuguese, it was Portugal's revolt in 1640 against Spanish Hapsburg rule that spelt the end of Portuguese domination of the slave trade. An irate Philip IV in revenge prohibited Spanish colonies from buying slaves from the Portuguese. Rather than attempt to set up his own African trade, and unwilling to do direct business with the Protestant Dutch or English, and at war with Catholic France, Philip IV moved to a *licencia* program which during the next twenty-two years issued over 100,000 permits. Soon Spanish vessels were sailing to Dutch, French, and English ports in the Caribbean and returning with more slaves than granted by their permits.[80]

Great Powers Competition for the African Trade

While deploying armed forces to seize control of trade and markets could be profitable, as we would discover it also was a very expensive enterprise. Following the debacle in Brazil, the Dutch faced its first 'real competition from Britain. In 1660, the Royal Adventurers into Africa were given a thousand year monopoly over English trade to Africa. In 1664, the French also entered the fray, chartering a number of companies to trade to engage in the African slave trade.[81] In this militarized climate to protect their trade from rival states, companies, or privateers, European powers not only had to fortify their trading outposts, but provide merchant ships with armed escorts. The costs of protection and the risks of trade/warfare were so great that only the best-financed companies could survive.

During the Second Dutch War, around 1666, the Royal Adventurers set about recapturing forts along the West African coast that had previously taken from them by Dutch and Swedish companies. The financial costs of these efforts, however, put the Royal Adventurers so deep in debt that by 1668 they owed over £100,000 pounds. And, in 1672, the bankrupt company was taken over by the Royal African Company (RAC).[82] Like its predecessor, the RAC raised capital by subscriptions—and there was a new floatation which raised over £111,600 pounds from 200 people—and it too was given a thousand year monopoly of English trade to Africa.[83] Although the RAC was one of the largest joint-stock companies formed at the time, even with capital raised through subscriptions, the costs of building and maintaining fortifications along the West African coast were larger than envisioned, and the company had to borrow to meet these costs.

From the beginning, interest payments on these loans amounted to a large portion of the company. Even with a monopoly, the capital needed to buy slaves on the scale required to make a profit was enormous. Dutch bankers provided much of this capital. To trade, captains required at least £100,000 pounds worth of goods per voyage. And as slaves were advanced on credit in the West Indies, turnover of capital was slow. Even so, the 1680s were good years for the RAC. Yet, every year, there were more interlopers both from foreign competitors and from private traders. By the end of the century, the RAC monopoly that was to last a thousand years, had been lost to independent English traders, who in theory were to pay a ten percent tax to the RAC on all exports to Africa, and in return were to have rights to use the companies forts. Soon, however, these "ten percenters" as these independents were know, were doing nearly four times the slave trade than was being done by the RAC.[84]

Asientos and Dutch Banking

Yet, the end of Dutch hegemony over the slave trade was not simply due to increased competition from the British or French, changes in Spanish policy also played role. Spain, which never found it worth its while to enter the slave trade itself, depended on other countries to supply its demands, making its *asientos* the grand prize of the slave trade. Under Philip IV, from 1662 to 1685, Spanish *asentistas* not only depended on the Dutch West India Company to deliver the slaves they had contracted for, but also on Dutch Banks for financing.[85] When the Spanish *asentista* died in 1685, the Dutch of Coymans was given the *asiento* for a large cash payment, and the promise to build ships for the Spanish navy. Doing business, however, with the heretic Dutch did not sit well with Charles II. And, by 1696, Spain's Charles II would tolerate the Dutch no longer. Yet, he was also frightened by the English, and at war with the French, and so he decided to return to the Portuguese as suppliers of slaves, and issued a new *asiento* to a Portuguese company in exchange for a much-needed loan for 200,000 pesos. However, before his death in 1700, Charles II, named Philip of Anjou, grandson of Louis XIV, to be his successor, opening the way for the French to become *asentistas*.[86] After a disastrous experience with the French, in 1712 the Spanish *asiento* was bestowed upon Great Britain as part of the peace accord, which we shall see was the prelude to an equally disastrous affair.

South Sea Company and the Bubble

At the end of the War of Spanish Succession in 1712, Britain was the most powerful member of the coalition facing Spain, and demanded the Spanish *asiento* as part of the peace treaty. The Crown turned around and sold the *asiento* contract to the South Sea Company for the princely sum of £7.5 million. The primary purpose of the South Sea Company, which had been formed in 1711, was to break the Spanish monopoly on trade to its American colonies. Because Britain also hoped the Spanish trade would wipe out its national debt, to help fund the company, £9 million in unfunded government securities were exchanged for shares in the South Sea Company.[87]

As part of the deal struck, the South Sea Company was to advance King Philip a payment of 200,000 pesos, and pay him 33.50 pesos in silver for each of the 4,800 slaves to be delivered annually to the Indies for the term of thirty years. Additional payments were made to the president of the Council of the Indies, and to the five members of the Junta de Negros. In this sweet deal,

King Philip V was allocated twenty-eight percent of the company's stock, England's Queen Anne received 22.5 percent, and the company also agreed to lend the Spanish king a million pesos to purchase his shares. The hoped for profits from this deal were so high that when Queen Anne died in 1714, her successor, King George I, not only inherited her shares, but also purchased more, as did the Prince of Wales. However, despite their large stock holdings neither monarch controlled the company.[88]

Sour notes soon sounded. The South Sea Company was not the great success hoped for. Permitted ships encountered bureaucratic obstacles, and were allowed only to enter Spanish ports during the infrequent trade fairs that took place less than yearly. Like the earlier Royal Africa Company, the South Sea Company not only had to compete with independent private traders and pirates, but also Dutch, Portuguese, and French companies.[89] To make matters worse, when war between Great Britain and Spain broke out in 1718, the Spanish Crown ordered the confiscation of all South Sea Company properties in its colonies. By 1719, the South Sea Company needed an infusion of new capital. Recognizing that debts (which are promises to pay) are themselves an asset, the South Sea Company offered to buy the government's outstanding debts at five percent until 1727, and four percent thereafter.[90]

Recognizing the value of this asset the Bank of England offered the government £5.5 million, but the South Sea Company countered with a bid £7.5 million.[91] With so much money owned to the company not only was abundant credit suddenly available, but the price of its shares rose. Holders of government securities rushed to exchange them for shares in South Sea Company. The whole stock market was in a boom. Between mid-1719 and mid-1720, some 200 new companies were formed. Speculative mania was such that South Sea Company stock rose from £128 to £1050 between January and August of 1720.[92] Its list of stockholders soon read like a *"Who is Who"* of Great Britain. Ironically, what caused the South Sea bubble to burst was the Company's own questioning of the legality of eighty-six new companies that focused attention on the weakness and credit-inflated value of those companies, more scrupulous attention to these issues revealed that the South Sea Company itself was the worst example. In the crash that followed, company stock had plummeted to £180, and as it fell—lords, noblemen, members of Parliament, statesmen, banks, directors, and insurance companies saw their fortunes evaporate.[93]

Although the South Sea Company limped along after the crash until 1752, during the nineteenth century nearly all the chartered companies set up by European states to engage in the slave trade proved to be financial failures. Despite the monopolies granted them, they failed to attract sufficient private capital, and had to be continually subsidized by states. The high costs of maintaining forts, defenses, and bloated bureaucracies made them unprofitable. Employees who put their own financial gains ahead of company interests undermined them. They were outmaneuvered on every side and unable to protect their monopolies not only from foreign competitors, but also from homegrown independent traders.[94]

CONCLUSIONS: ENOUGH BLAME TO SHARE

We began this chapter by asking whether mercantilism was distinctly different from capitalism, and by implication when did the economy transit out of mercantilism. It is clear from the way in which the Atlantic slave trade operated that despite the importance of credit and the growing prevalence of what came to be modern financial instruments, banks, companies, bills of exchange, bills of acceptance, insurance, checks, stock exchanges, etc., the game being played during this period was not a capitalist game. It certainly was not an efficient market for labor-power, nor a free market untrammeled by government policies or investments, nor even an exchange of most commodities at their global standard prices.

Rather, the mercantile game was rooted in royal privileges and rights in which states in Europe, the Americas and Africa attempted not merely to exact benefits but also to control and use commerce to their own political, social, and economic ends. What is also very evident is that by the nineteenth century, the scale of trade and the tactics of competitors had reached a point where neither states nor companies could maintain monopolies or protect their trade either through force or through administrative or financial means. It is also apparent as protected trade gave way in the nineteenth century to a "free market" in the sole sense of one in which private enterprise was king, capitalists realizing that they could not monopolize trade turned to monopolizing the means of production instead.

As we have seen, credit played a key role in almost every aspect of the slave trade. Credit was used not only to mobilized resources and launch enterprises even when coin was in short supply, but it helped to articulate modes of production, facilitating trade between economies without useful currency exchange rates. Credit not only helped to mobilize wealth, spread and shift risks, but in the emerging global system, credit was used as a political and economic weapon in the competition between companies and states to capture whole economies. The triangle trade would seem to offer a perfect example of such use of credit. The profits from the triangle trade rested on two basic uses of credit, credit for productive enterprises and credit for consumption. In the triangle trade, first we see consumer credit used to underwrite African consumption of European goods. Secondly, we see production credit—as African slave labor—invested in the Americas. Finally, we again see consumer credit used to enable both European consumption of sugar, rum, tobacco, etc., and African consumption of European manufactures through which profits were ultimately repatriated and returned to European coffers. This pattern in the use of credit played an integral role in the past but also established patterns of unbalanced trade and uneven development that still persist between these three continents.

NOTES

1. Calendar of State Papers, Colonial Series, V, 167. Renatus Enys to Secretary Bennet, November 1, 1663. Cited in Williams, *Capitalism and Slavery*, 30.
2. Cited in Searing, *West African Slavery and Atlantic Commerce*, 28.
3. Braudel, *Le Temps du Monde*. Tome 3, 374.
4. Searing, *West African Slavery and Atlantic Commerce*, 31.
5. Ibid., 17, 42, 37ff.
6. Within Africa, the violence linked to capturing slaves was high and retaliatory conflict often led to as many executions as enslavements. A plethora of firsthand accounts are cited or summarized in classic works on African slavery some of which are referenced in our text. An example from the early twentieth century is Dow, *Slave Ships & Slaving*.
7. Vansina, *Kingdoms of the Savanna*, 194.
8. O'Fahey, "Slavery and Society in Dar Fur," 83.
9. Meillassoux, *The Anthropology of Slavery*, 265 ff. The horrendous account comes to us from a French military officer also held as captive by Amadou.
10. Williams, *Capitalism and Slavery*, 37–38.
11. e.g., Braudel. *Economie et Capitalism XVe–XVIIIe Siècle. Tome 1–3*; Guyer. "Currency Interface and Its Dynamics," 1–34, Frank, *Dependent Accumulation and Underdevelopment;* and Wallerstein, *The Modern World System I*.
12. e.g., Wolf, *Europe and the People without History*; Tilly, *Coercion, Capital, and European States AD 990–1992*.
13. Williams provides a discussion of the politics involved in *Capitalism and Slavery*, 32ff.
14. Curtin, *Economic Change in Precolonial Africa*, 327, 336.
15. Curtin, *The Atlantic Slave Trade, A Census*. Many refinements of these numbers have been offered, a number of which have been collected in Inikori and Engerman *The Atlantic Slave Trade*. Many other overviews of the subject can be found including Searing, *West African Slavery and Atlantic Commerce,* and Klein, *Slavery and Colonial Rule in French West Africa*.
16. Curtin, *Economic Change in Precolonial Africa*, 155, 167–68.
17. Rout, *The African Experience in Spanish America*, 64–65.
18. Davidson, *The African Slave Trade*, 95–101.
19. Braudel, *Civilisations matérielle, économie et capitalisme, XVe–XVIII*: Tome 2, 494; *Tome* 3, 375ff.

20. The many contributions to Miers and Kopytoff. *Slavery in Africa* document the distinct dynamic of slavery within Africa and provide perspective on the range of influence the Atlantic slave trade or the trans-Saharan slave trade had on these internal systems of slavery.

21. Constable, *Trade and Traders in Muslim Spain,* 8, 86, 206.

22. Manning, "The Slave Trade: The formal Demography of a Global System," 255–79.

23. Searing, *West African Slavery and Atlantic Commerce,* 52–56; Ruf, *Ending Slavery. Hierarchy, Dependency and Gender in Central Mauritania,* 102 has even suggested that the practice among Mauritanian Bidan of manifold serial monogamy developed as a way to legitimize as "free" female slaves and their offspring. The increase in status at divorce has been maintained for all women giving rise to the oddity, shared with the Polisario but not with Morocco or Algeria, that a woman divorced multiple times has a particularly high social status.

24. Rotman, *Byzantine Slavery and the Mediterranean World,* 131 ff.

25. Ibid.

26. Searing, *West African Slavery and Atlantic Commerce,* 25.

27. Meillassoux, *The Anthropology of Slavery,* 244.

28. Rout, *The African Experience in Spanish America,* 4–6.

29. Ibid., 5; Thomas, *The Slave Trade,* 53.

30. Rout, *The African Experience in Spanish America,* 7.

31. Ibid., 8; Thomas, *The Slave Trade,* 22.

32. Palmer, *The First Passage,* 27.

33. Wolf, *Europe and the People without History,* 196.

34. Rout, *The African Experience in Spanish America,* 15; Palmer, *The First Passage,* 27; Curtin, *Economic Change in Precolonial Africa,* 61.

35. Baptiste, "Bartolomé de las Casas and Thomas More's Utopia: Connections and Similarities," 7–10.

36. Borah and Cook, *The Indian Population of Central Mexico, 1531–1610.*

37. Davidson, *The African Slave Trade,* 75; Wolf, *Europe and the People without History,* 197.

38. Davidson, *The African Slave Trade,* 65–66.

39. Rout, *The African Experience in Spanish America,* 37; Thomas *The Slave Trade,* 99.

40. Rout, *The African Experience in Spanish America,* 37.

41. Ibid., 39–42.

42. Ibid., 41–42.

43. Biddick, "People and Things: Power in Early English Development," 8.

44. Thomas, *The Slave Trade,* 119.

45. Pérez-Mallaina, *Spain's Men of the Sea,* 98–103.

46. Ibid., 8–101.

47. Ibid., 100–05.

48. Thomas, *The Slave Trade,* 310–11.

49. Ibid., 323–32.

50. Ibid., 320–23.

51. Thornton, *Africa and Africans in the Making of the Atlantic World,* 55–56.

52. Wolf, *Europe and the People without History*, 214–15; Davidson, *The African Slave Trade*, 164.
53. Thorton, *Africa and Africans in the Making of the Atlantic World*, 67–69.
54. Curtin, *Economic Change in Precolonial Africa*, 173.
55. Thomas, *The Slave Trade*, 323–24; Williams, 1997:211–12.
56. Law, "Cowries, Gold and Dollars: Exchange Rate Instablity and Domestic Price Inflation in Dahomeny in the Eighteenth and Nineteeth Centuries," 54.
57. Curtin, *Economic Change in Precolonial Africa*, 248–49.
58. Ibid., 303.
59. Ibid., 305–06.
60. Ibid., 75–91, 307.
61. Ibid., 272.
62. Curtin, *Economic Change in Precolonial Africa*, 273, 298; Curtin, *Cross-Cultural Trade in World History*, 55.
63. Wolf, *Europe and the People without History*, 219–20.
64. Latham 1973:39; Davidson, *The African Slave Trade*, 221–22; Wolf, *Europe and the People without History*, 219.
65. Davidson, *The African Slave Trade*, 213–14.
66. Palmer, *The First Passage: Blacks in the Americas*, 37; Davidson, *The African Slave Trade*, 112. Some sources (e.g., Dow, *Slave Ships & Slaving*) suggest that conditions for slaves in the middle passage were distinctly better than for indentured Europeans who had paid passage in advance and whose death therefor benefitted the captain but there can be little likelihood that conditions for either were anything but abysmal.
67. Pérez-Mallaina, S*pain's Men of the Sea*, 98–99.
68. Rout, *The African Experience in Spanish America*, 69–70.
69. Thomas, *The Slave Trade*, 440.
70. Ibid., 440–41.
71. Braudel, *Civilisations matérielle, économie et capitalisme*: *Tome* III, 295; Davis, *A History of Money*, 233, 271, 552–54.
72. Braudel, *Civilisations matérielle, économie et capitalisme: Tome* III, 208.
73. Braudel, *Civilisations matérielle, économie et capitalisme: Tome* II, 443–55; Curtin, *Economic Change in Precolonial Africa*, 100–05.
74. Thorton, *Africa and Africans in the Making of the Atlantic World*, 55.
75. Thomas, *The Slave Trade*, 165, 440–41.
76. Thorton, *Africa and Africans in the Making of the Atlantic World*, 57–66.
77. Isreal, *Dutch Primacy in World Trade*, 38–42.
78. Wolf, *Europe and the People without History*, 197.
79. Ibid.
80. Rout, *The African Experience in Spanish America*, 42–54.
81. Wolf, *Europe and the People without History*, 197.
82. Davies, *The Royal African Company*, 42–47.
83. Thomas, *The Slave Trade*, 200–01
84. Ibid., 202–06.
85. Rout, *The African Experience in Spanish America*, 45.
86. Ibid., 43–46.

87. Thomas, *The Slave Trade,* 236–38.
88. Thomas, *The Slave Trade*, 235–38; Rout, *The African Experience in Spanish America,* 54–55; Davies, *A History of Money,* 264.
89. Thomas, *The Slave Trade*, 239–40.
90. Davies, *A History of Money,* 265.
91. Ibid., 265.
92. Ibid., 265
93. Davies, *A History of Money,* 265–66; Thomas, *The Slave Trade*, 240–42.
94. Thomas, *The Slave Trade*, 225.

Chapter 6

Chayanov, Marx, and Hidden Interests in Rural Morocco

Social capital can be institutionalized in cultural and legal ways. What social scientists have come to realize is that some of this institutionalization can have long enduring impacts. As Acemoglu, Johnson, and Robinson have written:

> Many economists and social scientists believe that differences in institutions and state policies are at the root of large differences in income per capita ... A more detailed analysis of the effect of more fundamental institutions on property rights and expropriation risk is an important area for future study.[1]

In this chapter we do just this and examine the imbrication of economic stratification, whose roots stretch back in time, and the modern implementation of credit embodied in agricultural development strategy in a province of Morocco during the 1970s. Our approach is a little indirect due to the nature of data available for rural areas in Morocco. Our primary data are demographic from the census or economic from the rural tax office. Thus our approach will be first to assess the agricultural strategies pursued by rural households in terms of a simple notion proposed by Chayanov that household size influences the area under cultivation. Then we add in a number of other variables including the alternative of intensification via irrigation, class analysis to see if large landholders behave in significantly different ways than smaller landholders, recourse to credit and finally the historical patterns of market participation institutionalized in the run-up to independence. The latter variable, which also proves to be significant, suggests that long established patterns of social capital still are relevant explanators of rural strategies.

The data examined provide a rural comparison to the urban data examined in the next chapter for a similar time frame. The chapter provides a critique of the too simple idea that credit has a uniform impact across social class and its minor corollary that, at least above a certain economic level, access to credit enables households to improve economic strategy. The chapter compares indicators of economic class and the use of credit among 62,000 households in 624 villages for the Province of Essaouira, Morocco, to make the case that structural analysis is required if we wish to delineate the real patterns of hidden interest, the who benefits of any murder mystery. The chapter relies in part on data from credit agencies operating in the province during the 1970s and in part on government records of economic assets and strategies for the region during this period. It also incorporates archival material from the nineteenth century which illustrates class structure throughout the province and seems to help explain (from a statistical perspective) the distribution of agricultural responses to credit in the province. Overall, the chapter compares a Marxist or class-based explanation of the use of credit (those with money have access to credit) with a Chayanovian (household size and structure) explanation (those in need seek to expand production even if it means accepting a lower net return to their labor).

Chayanov's work in the Soviet Union in the 1920s brought him exile in Siberia, where he died in 1939, primarily because his model of peasant agricultural strategies seemed to exclude any role for class.[2] While Chayanov's ideas have had considerable influence in anthropology[3], Chayanov's model is still usually applied as if differential control over the productive process should not make any qualitative difference to the applicability of the model. A direct confrontation between a Marxist and Chayanovian[4] model ought, minimally, to compare the impact of class differentiation on the degree to which peasants[5] seem to conform to theoretical expectations derived from Chayanov's model. The key elements of that model are Chayanov's suggestion that there is an on-farm equilibrium point (a balance between marginal drudgery and marginal utility at the household level) which responds to numerous factors and determines agricultural strategy.[6] If a neglect of class is justified, economic stratification should not itself be a significant factor in determining the agricultural strategy employed.

There have been numerous attempts over the years to apply or test Chayanov's model,[7] but the norm has been to criticize the model when it proves insufficient to explain the "data" rather than to ask if lack of sufficiency is not really the point and that perhaps its value, like that of other models, lies more in the area of providing a partial explanation of behavior. This article combines critique with application through a rather narrow focus on the potential complementarity between class analysis and Chayanovian analysis in determining access to credit, with the implication that Chayanov may have been wrong to neglect class processes even if his model was brilliant in other respects. We argue, following Crummett,[8] that attention to class improves one's understanding of the role of household composition, Chayanov's on-farm equilibrium in agricultural decision making and thereby household recourse to credit.

The initial analysis that follows is based on demographic and production data for some 62,094 households in 624 villages of the Province of Essaouira, Morocco (located on the coast due west of Marrakesh). The data used is from the census, the agricultural credit offices, and the rural tax offices[9] which provide data on agricultural lands in production per household. While levels of production or numbers of livestock, on which taxes are based, are not reliably reported to the tax services, the areas owned and under production are the basis for qualifying for state subsidized and run agricultural credit so they are distinctly more reliable. This analysis measures the degree to which area under production fits household size. In a large census of households (in this case roughly 62,000), Chayanov's model would, barring some potentially mitigating factors,[10] predict that larger households should have more land under production than smaller households.[11]

This result follows from Chayanov's suggestion that more household labor and more mouths to feed both lead to higher levels of production. Since the vast majority of the land in the Province is semi-arid rainfed land growing barley, where extensification of surface areas is the primary way of increasing production, it would, following Chayanov, be reasonable to expect on average a direct relationship between area under production and household size—even if this by no means synthesizes Chayanov's model.

The final stage of the analysis takes the results of the first analysis and then calculates to what extent class and market factors explain the large differences between the way different *communes rurales* (counties) of the Province seem to bear out the initially hypothesized fit between household size and area under cultivation. The data used here are archival material or data from the rural credit and tax offices of the province. The latter sources give several ways of assessing economic stratification; a census of large landholders, comparative aggregate data on land per household, and the credit office's assessment of the number of households that qualify for intermediate levels of credit. Archives provide a 1918 census of German investments in the Province that prove to be highly significant statistically, reflecting an enduring relationship to the market for specific areas of the Province. This twofold analysis is not intended as a test of Chayanov's ideas, for which all of the numerous factors that he hypothesizes would impact the on-farm equilibrium point would need to be addressed.[12] Rather, it relies on the demonstration that some relationships predicted by Chayanov's model, even at its simplest, do seem to hold to varying degrees in Morocco but, the degree to which they hold seems to be clearly linked to economic stratification and structural differences of considerable historical depth.

AGRICULTURAL STRATEGIES IN THE PROVINCE OF ESSAOUIRA, MOROCCO

In the period studied, the Province of Essaouira comprized sixteen counties, *communes rurales*, plus two urban "*centre autonome*" (Essaouira and Tamanar). This study deals with fifteen of the sixteen *communes rurales*, one of the sixteen (Ait Daoud) was left out of the extended analysis because there were major discrepancies between the sources (census and tax office) in terms of how the data was aggregated. While this might not affect an overall average, it would affect any more detailed calculations. The Province includes great ecological variety, going from irrigated valleys to dry highlands, and this ecology is faithfully reflected in the different emphases put on agriculture, animal husbandry, and arboriculture in the different *communes*. The largest difference is one of scale between Shiadma (the Arabic-speaking eight northern *communes*) and Haha (the Berber-speaking southern eight *communes*). Average land holdings per family in Shiadma (with the exception of the *commune* of Korimat) are two to nine times as high as those in Haha. Further, all of the Shiadma *communes* include large landholders (those with more than fifty hectares) while in Haha only the *communes* of Neknafa, Ida ou Gourd, and Smimou have any large landholders.

Haha and Shiadma are fairly similar with respect to the numbers of domestic animals kept per household with one exception. Goats are about five times as abundant in Haha as in Shiadma. Less obvious, but well worth noting, is the scarcity of camels and cattle in Sebt Ait Daoud which has between a tenth and a twentieth as many camels as the other communes and by far the fewest cattle per household. If the two categories of land shown in Table 1 are added together one finds that the average land per household in Ait Daoud is only 3.99 hectares which is also far and away the smallest *commune* average for the Province. This may reflect primarily the major discrepancies between the census and tax office data for this county.

HOUSEHOLD SIZE AND AREA IN PRODUCTION

The differences illustrated by Tables 6.1 and 6.2 clearly affect the economic behavior of households in the Province. In this section I will focus on the four categories of land, into which land tenure data is categorized by the tax service. Two aspects of Chayanov's work on Russian peasants concern us here. The first was his general idea that rational optimizing behavior of peasant farmers is based on different criteria than that of farmers who are thoroughly involved in a capitalist market economy. Instead of producing for

Table 6.1 Household size and area under cultivation, Taftecht, Morocco.

	Relation between household size and hectare exploited for Taftecht		
	Test	Significance	Partial R
IRRIG	1.789	0.05	0.106
NIRR	3.128	0.005	0.266
DIRR	3.016	0.005	0.2519
DNIRR	1.689	0.1	0.0956

Statistical significance: R-squared = .391 F-ratio = 4.328 (0.05 significance). Table created by Thomas K. Park.

the market in the way described by classical cost benefit analysis increasing production when prices rise, decreasing it when prices drop and weighing costs versus potential profits peasant farms tended to weigh benefits against costs in a different way. This involves viewing benefits as rapidly decreasing once the basic needs of the household are met while simultaneously viewing costs (mainly the onerousness of labor) as rapidly rising once a significant degree of labor has already been performed. In Chayanov's analysis these two curves were empirically found to meet at a point corresponding to a relatively low production level beyond the critical needs of the household because less critical needs were balanced by high drudgery.

The second aspect of Chayanov's work of concern to us was his extension from the above observation to a hypothesis that individual households tended to expand production wherever possible when their life cycle provided the household with larger amounts of human labor (as children reached working age) or larger levels of basic requirements and to decrease production otherwise (when children were unborn or when some members became unfit for work or died). On average, larger households would have both greater needs and a larger work force. This would imply that Moroccan households in the Province of Essaouira, insofar as they behave economically like Chayanov's peasant households, should on average expand production when they have many members and decrease it when they have few.

The statistical evidence needed to test this hypothesis is available at the *douar* (village) level for the entire Province but it is not available at the household level. In fact, what must be done is to estimate the average household size in each village (from statistics on how many households there are in each village and the population of each village) and use this as a proxy for individual households. Aggregating population and the number of households at the village level means that only cumulative differences in the number of people in households will show up. Since there are many village in the Province the sample is large enough that a correlation, if it exists, should be apparent. Complementary data on land in use, aggregated by village, are available for the entire province from the Impôt Agricole.

Table 6.2 Credit and economic stratification by rural commune, Province of Essaouira.

Commune Rurale	C.R.C.A. Potential Receivers	Percent of Households	Large Landowners Number	Irrigated ha	Non-irrigated ha	German Rural Investments, historical	
SHIADMA							
Akermoud	141	2.32	2	0	690.9	4	2.49
Talmest	259	4.33	2	0.6	342	12	27.59
Had Draa	208	4.97	4	3.6	396	44	197.58
Mramer	255	8.22	6	7.1	1247.7	71	631.728
Takat	176	3.61	1	0	106.25	1	8.9
Korimat	288	6.88	18	56.9	3966.15	2	10.39
Taftecht	318	0.96	11	2.9	1784.9	7	92.45
Hanchene	228	4.05	7	3.8	979	3	157.63
HAHA							
Ait Zelten	136	4.5	0	0	0	0	0
ou Gourd	193	6.33	0	0	466.6	0	0
ou Tghouma	103	2.07	0	0	0	0	0
Sebt Imghad	92	3.05	0	0	0	0	0
Sebt Neknafa	157	3.76	3	2	1134.69	0	0
Smimou	122	3.36	0	0	7.985	0	0
Zemzem	123	5.32	0	0	0	3	96.7

Table created by Thomas K. Park.

The most direct test calls for a regression of household land holdings against household size for each village of the province. We would expect that if households in the Province behave in the way Russian peasants studied by Chayanov behaved, there would be evidence of significant correlations between household size and land holding.

The total land included in the four categories is only a fraction of the surface of the Province. For Shiadma this fraction amounts to forty-one hectares per square kilometer (41 percent) while for Haha it is about eleven hectares per square kilometer (11 percent). The rest fits into a number of categories: collective land used for grazing, land of no agricultural or grazing value, or National forest. In most cases, therefore, some expansion of agriculture into marginal areas is possible. Only a fraction of the surface area of the Province is registered in the Government's records as officially private land (the Immatriculation Foncière) though far more undoubtedly has been registered as such by notaries.

The analysis was done with data at the village level using population divided by the number of households as the dependent variable and the four types of land holdings per household (irrigated, non-irrigated for main crops, and diverse irrigated and non-irrigated used for miscellaneous minor crops) tabulated by the rural tax office as the independent variables. The analysis used 321 village from Shiadma and 303 village from Haha. This includes about 93 percent of the villages in the Province. A few villages had to be left out when the Census data and the Impot Agricole data did not correspond. The results for the commune of Taftecht, which turns out to have a high level of households pursuing a Chayanovian strategy, are shown in Table 6.1:

The t-statistics indicate that all four independent variables were significant. Although regressions are usually used to discover causal determinants of the dependent variable, they actually define degrees of relationship and the probability of a (possible) causal link between independent variables and the dependent variable.

In this case the model is not intended to explain the cause of variation in household size. Instead it highlights evidence that there may be a link between the amount of all types of land exploited by a household and the number of people in that household. The main proximate causes of household size are undoubtedly demographic: birth rate, infant mortality, and outmigration. Links between amounts of land exploited and household size may be interpreted as rational expansion of production in keeping with Chayanov's suggestions. Because the time series household level data are not available for the province at the household level we cannot simply follow individual households and see if they expand production when more labor power is available as children reach working age. Nevertheless, if such a pattern of expansion were frequent it would show up even when annual data are aggregated at the village level. This is the more so because the villages are not static and new villages are regularly formed by lower branches of extended families who are at different stages of the household cycle than the higher branches.

The R-squared statistic and the partial R-squared statistics are of little significance here because the model deliberately does not include the main demographic determinants of household size. In addition, we know that intensification of land use is an alternative to extension of land under production. It would, therefore, be surprising if the variables included explained a large proportion of the variation in household size.

The intent at this stage is to see if there is a significant link between the independent variables and the dependent variable. When we find such a link as in the case for Taftecht we can infer that it is possible Chayanov's suggestions are accurate estimates of household decision making in that particular *commune*. There is one alternative explanation, that in households with little land some members choose to migrate to the city to alleviate the pressure on the household land, which we will examine further in the following section. Without full information on levels of outmigration per commune it is impossible to accurately assess this possibility, but the evidence available does not indicate that levels of outmigration explain more than a fraction of the degree of confirmation received by the regression equation in the different communes of the Province.

The most important statistic for our purposes is the F-statistic which summarizes the degree of significance of the relation between all independent variables and the dependent variable. To determine the level of significance, the calculated F-statistic must take into consideration the different values for given degrees of freedom in the regression equation. The latter depend on how many cases and variables were included in the calculation. This means that a given level of significance (say 0.05) will correspond to different actual F-statistics for each county because there are different numbers of villages in each county.

The easiest way to compare the significance of the F-statistics for each *commune rurale* (District) is to take the ratio of the calculated F-statistic over the value it would need to reach to be significant at a given level I have used the "0.05" level. This ratio makes it possible to rank the counties according to the degree to which variations in household size seem to correlate with variations in the amount of land under use. These correlations will, for convenience, be referred to as the Chayanov correlations, though they are by no means an adequate measure of Chayanov's model.[13] Map 6.1 gives the normalized results (these ratios) for all the districts as well as the rank of each from highest ratio to lowest.

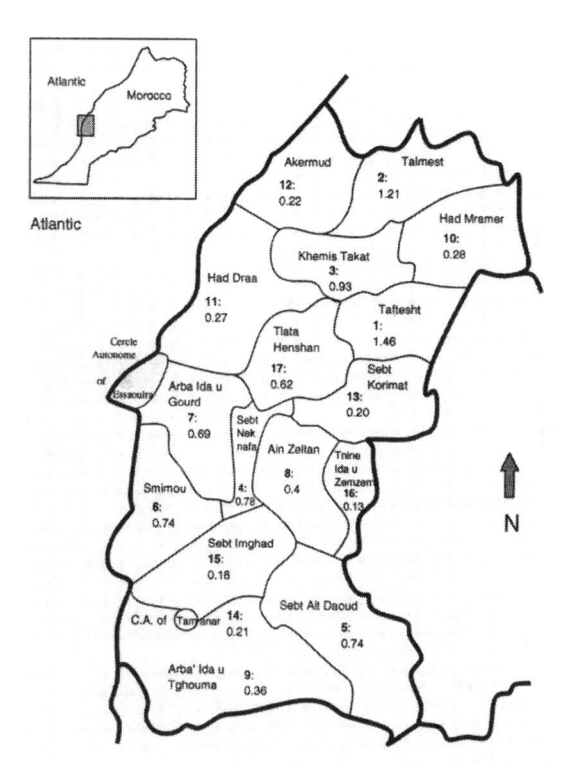

Figure 6.1 Degree of confirmation for model by commune and centre urbain in the Province of Essaouira, c 1980. *Source*: Map drawn by Thomas K. Park.

A cursory examination of map 6.1 indicates that the hypothesized correlation was confirmed at the 0.05 level in only two cases (Taftecht and Talmest: which have ratios greater than 1). In a number of other cases the hypothesis would be confirmed at only slightly lesser levels of significance (up to rank five) and in most of the additional cases it would be confirmed at moderate levels of significance (those with at least one t-statistic of 0.10 significance or more, including all districts up to rank 11). Only four cases showed none of the variables to be significant (based on t-statistics) to the 0.10 level or better. If we allow for the basic problem that we had to deal with data at the village level (averages for a village) rather than the household level, the level of confirmation the hypothesis received is impressive.

An obstacle to the analysis is the near certainty that the majority of the basic data is only roughly accurate. Every attempt to check officially collected data on rural income in Morocco has shown the official version to embody a consistent underestimation of reality.[14] It is quite possible, therefore, that had accurate household level data been available the hypothesis might have been confirmed even more strongly. Even so, it seems highly probable that the relative strengths of that confirmation would remain roughly the same. It is unlikely that unreliable data is a significant reason Henchane is ranked fifteenth and Taftecht (its neighbor) is ranked first. The weaker our model, in the sense of not including factors we would like to include, but cannot, or in having less than perfect data, the more persuasive any support for the model appears.

The rankings depict the degree to which expansion of surface area under use per household correlates with increase in size of the household. Clearly another way to increase production would be to intensify use of land already in production. Intensification of use can therefore be seen as another direct alternative to extension of the area being used. Only the extension of cultivation would necessarily show up in the official production statistics. Although irrigated land is distinguished from non-irrigated land, both types could be exploited more or less intensely. Thus, more hours weeding, irrigating and fertilizing irrigated land could increase yields. Several alternatives are usually available for using the non-irrigated land from cultivation, arboriculture, or planting of vines to grazing of various animals. One might expect, therefore, that the choice of extending surface area would be more necessary where the alternative of intensifying production was most difficult. The alternative of intensifying production on irrigated land is taken into consideration in the following section.

DETERMINANTS OF FIT BETWEEN HOUSEHOLD SIZE AND AREA IN PRODUCTION

Other determinants of the degree of fit that must be considered may be divided into two types. Determinants of the first type measure economic stratification (through measures of large and intermediate landowners and the amount of non-irrigated land available—aggregated at the county level). Such measures directly address the defensibility of neglecting class in Chayanovian analysis. Another possible group of determinants can be examined by measuring the most significant alternatives; market orientation or the significance of irrigation as an intensive alternative to expanding area under cultivation. One variable we will use measures market participation using archival material. We can also tease out the obvious alternative agricultural strategy; a small number of *commune rurales* (four) have both large amounts of irrigated land (greater than 11 percent of their land) and adequate amounts of non-irrigated lands (approximately one hectare per member of the household or greater).

In these cases, the amount of non-irrigated land would suggest there might be more of a link between household size and area under production than there is—if it were not for the presence of relatively large amounts of irrigated land. A binary variable can be included to allow a regression model to take this alternative, irrigation oriented strategy, into account.

The most obvious measure available for economic stratification is the number of large landowners and the hectarage they own. The data for this are carefully recorded in the books of the rural tax office (the basic definition is holdings superior to 50 hectares). All of Shiadma has large landowners, but only Sebt Neknafa, Arba' Ida ou Gourd, and Smimou among the Haha communes, have large landowners. The three land owners based in Neknafa are related. In fact, the vast majority of land in this county was acquired by Caid Mbarek b. Neknafi on the eve of the Protectorate and has since been declared the joint property of the state and the heirs. All the land listed for Arba' Ida u Gourd and Smimou belongs to this group of lands as well, so the number of large land holders listed for those counties is zero.

An understanding of the role of credit in the rural area we have only 1970s government data though the historical investment data by Germans represent credit as well though it is private credit not government credit. Our contention is that both factors, as well as the obvious economic data, delineate a financial structure that differentially benefits some households more than others. There are three main sources of credit available to the rural area in the 1970s. For major enterprises there was the Caisse Nationale which provides credit to important clients: cooperative associations, industrialists, etc.

More relevant to the Province of Essaouira are the Caisse Régionale (C.R.C.A.) and the Caisse Locale (C.L.C.A.). The former lent to all farmers who had a yearly taxable income superior to 2000 dirham (in other Provinces the bottom is usually 3000 dirham). The official limit for credit in this category is 180,000 dirham. The C.L.C.A. lent to farmers with a taxable income between fifty dirham and 2000 dirham. The great majority of farmers qualified for this latter level of credit so the figures do not reflect differences in wealth that are of use to this analysis. The administration of the CRCA., whose qualifiers are distinctly wealthier than the norm for the whole Province, was run from the Essaouira office of the Credit Agricole.

The number of farmers in a particular area who actually apply for and receive loans is in part a function of the area's outreach programs. Thus, one can only derive very tentative estimates of the relative well-being of farmers in various areas of the Province from such figures. More revealing is the number of farmers in each area who are deemed creditworthy in the two systems. Table 6.2, thus, provides the number of farmers deemed potential receivers of credit under the CRCA scheme as well as to what percent of the known households in that Commune these figures correspond.

The extension of credit was seen by Chayanov as indicative of the degree of penetration of the capitalist market system into the peasant economy.

Yet for this to be reflected as a simple relationship between credit and the postulated Chayanov correlation one would need a radically simple (perhaps an egalitarian) land tenure situation. That we do not have such a situation in the Province has meant that, in the regression context, the amount of credit given per household shows a complete lack of significance in explaining the linkage between household size and area under production. As we will see, the data on potential qualifiers for credit in Table 6.4 reflecting the relative distribution of wealth in the different Communes, do prove to be significant.

While it would be quite possible to estimate local market involvement by doing a current survey, it is probably more instructive to substitute historical levels of market participation documented in the archives. This has the advantage, it turns out, of demonstrating that structural differences between parts of the Province are of considerable antiquity. German commercial penetration of Morocco began in earnest in 1890. The next year German vessels tripled their visits to Moroccan ports. In 1889 only three German boats visited Essaouira while in 1890 there were twenty-eight. For Morocco as a whole the numbers went from fifty-two in 1889 to 163 in 1890. These numbers increased steadily until 1897, when the total for Morocco was 327 and that for Essaouira was fifty-two, and then leveled off.

The main difference between the activities of German firms or nationals and those of other countries were twofold: (a) they were more willing to extend credit and (b) they entered into contractual arrangements with locals in the rural areas on an entirely different scale than their rivals from other European countries.

The difference in scale had little to do with the total size of German commerce. Both British and French trade was greater and remained so. Yet the difference can most easily be seen in the attitude which developed toward German trade among Moroccan notables in the South. Germany was clearly perceived as the only alternative to a French takeover even though the German government gave no more signs of being interested in acquiring a piece of Morocco than did Great Britain. The reason Britain and Germany were so differently perceived in southern Morocco was entirely due to the vigorousness with which Germany's merchants pursued the business of making contractual commercial/political alliances.

The French decided to nationalize all Austro-German holdings in French Morocco shortly after the start of World War I and pursued this goal in the post war years in pursuance of their interpretation of the Treaty of Versailles provisions. As a result, French administrators in Morocco (a Protectorate lasted from 1912 to 1956) succeeded in obtaining from post war Germany all the papers and account books of German firms that had been operating in Morocco. The nationalization effort succeeded in obtaining repayment of most outstanding debts and it leased out those of the Austro-German rural land holdings which could be located until the invested principal was repaid.

The simplest way for German firms to operate in Pre-protectorate Morocco was to loan money to local merchants and rely on them to collect the raw produce and sell the imported materials. This mode of operation was used throughout the period and was the classic method used by foreigners to operate in Morocco. The drawback to the simplest form of this system was that if the local had Moroccan nationality and was not granted foreign protection (in this case German) as either a *semsar* or a *mukhalat* (two categories of officially recognized agent for foreign powers) the lending firm ran the risk of losing the money extended and was without any effective recourse whenever local caids decided to exact particularly large road taxes, brigands decided to simply steal the commodities or when the local himself decided not to repay the loan.

As a result, the simple system was usually "improved" by arranging to have the local given foreign protected status. This meant that any legal matters could be settled in Consular courts and that any robbery or undue extortion would directly involve foreign nationals. Such direct involvement put the matter on an international level and usually resulted in a ruling by the sultan in favor of the foreign nationals and compensation of the loss either by the parties at fault or by the sultan himself.

Direct loans for commercial purposes were only a part of the effort by Austro-German merchants at penetrating the Moroccan economy. In addition, they contracted various types of profit sharing arrangements with people in the rural areas. These ran the gamut from buying half shares in some sheep and sharing the profits from the offspring to buying part or whole shares in prime pieces of land and then either sharing in the produce of that land or hiring someone to make it produce for them. These arrangements ran the same risks as direct loans as well as the risk that the purchases in whole or in part of real estate would be declared illegal because in principle such purchases were forbidden or because the presumed seller would turn out not to be the legal owner. A further serious risk was that once the purchase was made, a local zealous or greedy caid would decide to confiscate the land in question. Such actions seem to have been generally well received by the populace and so may have provided a simple means for caids to increase their wealth without incurring as much popular disapproval as the more traditional methods of over taxation and corvee labor.

The only perceived solution to these problems was to arrange protected status for the part owner of the property and to vigorously pursue confiscations of property fully or partly owned by foreign nationals at the international level. Just as important was the continued extension of credit. Generally, this meant that loans and commercial operations in a particular area were most likely to remain undisturbed if the local authorities (caids and sheikhs) were themselves party to the activities and if credit arrangements erred on the liberal rather than on the conservative side. As a result many of the documents testify to the involvement of Moroccan officials, at all local levels, in German commercial activities. In principle this was forbidden. A letter of Ramadan 1, 1312 (February 26, 1895) from the *na'ib* (assistant) of the qadi of Essaouira to the sultan's wazir Sidi Musa explicitly acknowledges the rule that no official was to enter into any commercial relationships with foreign nationals or have protégé status. In practice, all the grand caids and most of the minor ones in southern Morocco acquired protégé status, and security of land tenure, from one or another country well before 1912.

Caid Guellouli, centered in Talmest had German protégé status. In addition Caid Anflus (centered in Neknafa) asked for and received both French protégé status and German protégé status. This plus his activity against the French led to him being branded as a great traitor and hastened his demise as the French prepared to take over Morocco. The other more minor caids of the province also vacillated but generally sided with Mtougi (the Grand Caid whose region of influence began on the eastern borders of the Province) and so ended up in the French camp on the eve of the Protectorate.

The total number of Austro-German firms operating in Essaouira may be put at 23 plus two banks: The Deutsche Bank and the German Postal Service which dealt in funds and credit as well as providing postal services. Of these firms, the figures make it clear that two, Mannesmann and Marx, had far and away the greatest amount of activity. Their share of the extended credit amounted to 7.4 percent and 86.3 percent respectively. The Grand total of £22,254 is a respectable sum for the period. It corresponds to about 8 percent of the value of total exports from Essaouira for the year 1912. If we consider that Germany's share of trade from Essaouira in 1912 was only 18 percent this means that at a given point in time almost 40 percent of the value of exports was out on credit from German firms. Since most loans were for specific trade in a particular season, it is likely that the great majority of German trade was done on credit.

When it came to rural investments the number of firms involved was quite different. Only three firms engaged in purchases of rural real estate. These were Mannesmann, Marx, and Von Maur. Although all three invested in land throughout much of southern Morocco from Essaouira to Marrakech and in the Sous (the area due south of the Anti-Atlas mountains) we will be concerned only with their activities in the Province of Essaouira. There the French took pains, from 1914 to 1925, to locate the actual property mentioned in each of the Arabic titles held by these three firms. Although they were not always successful, in many cases the clarifications they made can be directly applied to the modern map of the Province. In other cases the location mentioned in the deed has to be tracked down by using a list of all the villages in the Province and reference to any other topographical material that is included in the Arabic deed. For the great majority of the cases we have been able to estimate hectarage for each of the sites and decide which properties were in each of the Communes of the Province with a high degree of confidence. The rural investments in the Province were largely confined to Shiadma and except for significant investments in Ida ou Zemzem did not occur in Haha. The main explanation for this is likely to be the rather radical differences between the quality of land in Shiadma and Haha; Zemzem is a highly irrigated clear exception.

Table 6.2, thus, also includes the total amount of rural investment by the three firms per *commune rurale* in the Province (between 1890 and 1914). The figures are really no more than fairly accurate estimates because a small number of properties simply cannot be reliably located. The figures given are hectares and number of properties because the prices paid were often not directly reflective of the value of the property or were difficult to assess usually protégé status would have been included as part of the transaction in cases of part ownership and the market value of protection was entirely relative. The French tried to assess the values of the properties they located, but their assessments of hectarage are more likely to be accurate.

The figures in table 6.2 and the figures for dryland per household from table 6.1 plus the binary variable mentioned at the beginning of the section provide a basis for a persuasive explanation for the degree of fit between household size and area under production. The working hypothesis, that there is a relationship between economic stratification and the degree of fit can be refined given the data available.

The proportion of potential receivers of C.R.C.A. levels of credit and the proportion of large proprietors in the population will be unlikely to have the same impact. Large landholders in this part of Morocco are generally absentee landlords who employ people to work their land on a sharecropping basis. Since most of the land is semi-arid, there are normally diminishing returns to intensification that are aggravated by sharing returns with the landlord. This tends to make the alternative of outmigration more promising than it would be were the landowner operated. An additional reason may be that landlords save on labor-monitoring costs by optimizing the amounts of land allocated to sharecropping families such that they are forced to devote maximal labor to survive; hence optimizing the landlord's returns on the total land. This practice would restrain the opportunities to expand the area under production, for the landlord would prefer to force intensification on all his land. Thus, a reasonable hypothesis would be that high levels of land owned by large landlords would decrease the degree to which households tended to expand agricultural production in line with growth in household size. Rather than relying on expanded agricultural production to feed more mouths they might be constrained to rely increasingly on revenues from remittances. By contrast, owner operated lands that have access to a relative abundance of land and resources would more closely resemble the Russian peasant farms, which had a relative abundance of land, and so might be expected to behave as Chayanov predicted. Accordingly, a reasonable hypothesis would be that high levels of potential receivers of C.R.C.A. credit should correspond to high levels of fit.

The final indicator of economic stratification to be used is the amount of Dryland available per household. At the level of a province, there is the consideration that there are important differences in land tenure but fairly equal access to migration. This should, were a Chayanovian dynamic general, result in the migration alternative looking relatively more promising in areas with the least promising agricultural options. Clearly, given the logic of Chayanov's model, it would be reasonable to hypothesize that counties with higher levels of Dryland in production per household would be most likely to be able to pursue Chayanovian strategies. Thus, the hypothesis would be that high levels of Dryland correspond to high degrees of fit.

In order to account for the degree of fit, it helps to take into account alternative strategies. These include a reliance on the market and significant available alternatives in irrigation intensification that will thus not show up in figures for area in production. The first alternative may be measured with a variable for hectares of German investment calculated as a proportion of the land in the county. The expectation would be that high reliance on market participation would correlate negatively with the degree of fit. The second alternative is dealt with by the binary variable mentioned above. The model thus formulated gives the following results (Table 6.3):

As can be seen (from the t-statistics) the variables are all highly significant, all the hypotheses are confirmed, and the F-statistic (16.8 with a probability of .00034) is well beyond the point generally accepted as persuasive (.01). There is, therefore, little chance that the variables considered are neither significant determinants of the degree to which farmers in different parts of the Province expand or contract their hectarage as their households grow and contract in size nor proxies for such determinants. In the current model, the variable for German investment is explicitly intended as a proxy for market participation while the other variables are assumed to measure the role of economic stratification and irrigation intensification. It is worth noting that it is to be expected that the "Dryland" variable would be a significant explanator since it was one of the four variables included in the model generating the dependent variable (Chayanovfit). Yet, a stepwise regression indicated that the "Dryland" variable brought the R^2 to only 34 percent while the additional variables brought the model up to an R^2 of 90 percent. Further, it is to be remembered that "Dryland" was significantly related to household size in only a subset of the *communes rurales*.

Discussion

The model tested provides persuasive evidence that in the Moroccan case examined there is indeed a direct link between economic stratification and the degree to which households expand or contract production in line with household size. The high degree of confirmation for the binary variable confirms the hypothesis that in some cases irrigated land provides a significant alternative to expanding "Dryland" production. In the more typical case, where this is not an option, the signs of the coefficients suggest that the large proprietors (negative coefficient) do not follow a Chayanovian production strategy while the middle class (positive sign for CRCA) do and that the more "Dryland" available the more likely the household will be to pursue a Chayanovian production strategy.

The most likely interpretation of these results is that they imply that the middle class are more likely to follow Chayanovian production strategies than either the poor or the wealthy. Across the province there is a better fit the greater the proportion of people who qualify for the CRCA level of credit. Similarly, the higher the average holdings of "Dryland" the greater the correspondence between household size and area under production.

The negative coefficient for German investment confirms Chayanov's and neoclassical economists' expectations that those producing primarily for the market will not be basing production strategies on Chayanov's on-farm equilibrium. What is most striking about this result is that the data document German investments in the Province of Essaouira between 1890 and 1914 yet prove to be significant explanators of the degree of fit in the 1970s. The explanation for this apparent oddity is simply that these areas of the province have been oriented toward the market ever since. The Germans sought out export oriented sectors for investment and these, not surprisingly, turned out to be areas that had comparative advantages in producing export or market oriented crops relative to other areas of the province. The primary reasons were ecological, abundance of fertile or even irrigated soil. These factor endowments have not changed significantly since.

The Moroccan case has some implications as well for the more general question of the defensibility of ignoring class, or economic stratification based on control of production, in Chayanovian analysis. It appears that Morocco, with its long tradition of rural exploitation, has an abundance of impoverished peasants, who have few if any opportunities to expand production, and significant numbers of wealthy rural elites whose strategies preclude a significant role for the on-farm equilibrium model. It is unlikely that very

Table 6.3 Explanators of Peasant Economic Strategies.

| Dependent variable: Chayanovfit, independent variables in order of significance ||||||
Ind. Var.	Coefficient	Std. Error	Beta Coeff.	t-Statistic	Probability
Binary	0.64280559	0.12885	0.698038657	4.98887	0.000750286
LrgPropr	11.25006458	2.47102	0.685417642	4.55281	0.001380384
Dryland	0.025167433	0.00491	0.571214218	5.13093	0.000618803
CRCA	11.88163607	3.74093	0.537629402	3.17612	0.011254775
GInvest	80.30758964	26.57926	0.461675903	3.02144	0.014445629

Notes:
Chayanovfit = the overall degree to which households size per *commune* explains level of production as exemplified by the normalized F-statistics ratios shown on map 6.1.
Binary = a binary variable where 1 signifies the presence of appreciable amounts of irrigated land in this case 11 percent or more of land is irrigated- combined with adequate non-irrigated land, roughly one hectare per household member.
LrgPropr = the hectarage owned by absentee landlords and very large land owners expressed as a fraction of total arable land in each *commune*.
Dryland: non-irrigated area hence not usually subject to intensification.
CRCA = the fraction of farmers qualifying for credit under the Caisse Régionale criteria
GInvest = the hectarage purchased by German firms from 1880 to 1914 as a percentage of total arable land in the *commune rurale*.
Significance. R^2: .903412538, R^2 (d.f.): .849752838, F-Ratio: 16.83595928
Probability: 0.000340846.
Table created by Thomas K. Park.

many countries differ significantly from Morocco in this respect. Harrison[15] suggests that the data on which Chayanov's analysis was originally based suggest that both significant economic inequality and large variations in the role of outmigration by region play significant economic roles ignored by Chayanov's model. Harrison[16] also provides support for the suggestion that even in the Soviet Union, Chayanovian analysis may well have been improved through a focus that was less exclusively oriented toward the household.

Despite these obvious limitations, the initial analysis based on roughly 62,000 households in 624 villages received impressive support for a basic implication of Chayanov's model. Given that the analyses at the county level were based on village averages the high level of confirmation of a link between household size and area in production for several counties, along with significant confirmation for most counties, must be seen as a strong indicator that Chayanovian strategies may play a very significant role.

The use of government credit by those deemed worthy and poor enough to need it, the middle class, clearly allowed households to expand production and follow a Chayanovian production strategy involving fitting area under production or intensification of production to household size. At the same time, the economic structure revealed by our analysis suggested that those too poor to qualify for credit could not expand area under production, or were constrained not to do so by long established hidden interests, and that there was also a complementary class so rich that it had no need to make use of government credit schemes—its sources of benefit already gave a greater return than was available via government credit. It is this general structural analysis which delineates the sources of hidden interest within which credit provides one component whose rate of interest must, even as in the Roman case, be contextualized within the greater set of interests available to economic actors.

The advantage of a Province-wide analysis of the sort presented is that it highlights the extreme heterogeneity between different counties and provides the means for explaining this heterogeneity in structural terms. There is something of the nine blind men and the elephant in this; had Taftecht alone been studied we might have concluded that all Moroccan peasants follow Chayanovian strategies while fieldwork in other counties might have led to similar, somewhat different, or even radically opposite conclusions. We would argue that such narrowness of scope is a regular failing of anthropological research that all too often results in a retreat from generalization. The model presented suggests that despite enormous heterogeneity there are regularities worth discerning because they reveal the deep structure of hidden interests. It also allows us to understand the degree to which access to credit depends on power and even on power structures established in earlier circumstances and by earlier governments. The analysis suggests most generally that social capital shapes both income and credit usage, and in this it emphasizes one of our main points about the likelihood, despite the historical paucity of appropriate data, that many financial and economic patterns have deep roots.

NOTES

1. Acemoglu, Johnson, and Robinson "The Colonial Origins of Comparative Development: An Empirical Investigation, 1369–1401" provides a now classic study of the legacy of institutional power and its impacts in the present using comparative data from the colonial period and recent development data for 75 countries. The German colonial effort in southern Morocco is well discussed in Guillen, *L'Allemagne et le Maroc*.

2. Thorner, Kerblay, and Smith, *Chayanov on The Theory of Peasant Economy*.

3. Donham, *History, Power, Ideology*, provides one of the more persuasive examples of the value of comparing a Chayanovian analysis with a Marxian one and has provided some incentive for this chapter.

4. See Patnaik, "Neo-Populism and Marxism: The Chayanovian View of the Agrarian Question and its Fundamental Fallacy," 375–420.

5. The questions of peasantry as a category has been critiqued by Ennew, Hirst, and Tribe, "'Peasantry' as an Economic Category," 295–322.

6. Durrenberger, "Chayanov and Marx," 119–29; Harrison, "Chayanov and the Economics of the Russian Peasantry," 389–417; Harrison, "The Peasant Mode of Production in the Work of A.V.Chayanov," 323–36; Harrison, "Chayanov and the Marxists," 6–100; Pertev, "A New Model for Sharecropping and Peasant Holdings," 27–49.

7. Durrenberger, "An Analysis of Shan Household Production Decisions," 447–458; Durrenberger, "Chayanov's Economic Analysis in Anthropology," 133–48. Durrenberger and Tannenbaum, "A Reassessment of Chayanov and His Recent Critics," 48–63; Lewis "Domestic Labor Intensity and the Incorporation of Malian Peasant Farmers into Localized Descent Groups," 53–73; Smith, "Chayanov, Sahlins, and the Labor-Consumer Balance," 477–48; and several major critiques of the model (Hunt "Chayanov's Model of Peasant Household Resource Allocation and its Relevance to Mbere Division, Eastern Kenya," 59–86; Minge-Kalman, "On the Theory and Measurement of Domestic Labor Intensity," 273–84; Patnaik, "Neo-Populism and Marxism: The Chayanovian View of the Agrarian Question and its Fundamental Fallacy," 375–420.

8. Mara de los Angeles Crummett, "Class, Household Structure, and the Peasantry: An Empirical Approach," 363–79.

9. Park collected the production data (copied) by hand from the rural tax office in Essaouira. The Census material was published: Royaume du Maroc., Direction de la Statistique. Population rurale 1971. Région du Tensift. Royaume du Maroc., Direction de la Statistique. Situation Demographique Régionale au Maroc, 1988.

10. Several scholars have discussed some of these issues including intensification vs extensification. cf. Wanda, "On the theory and measurement of domestic labor intensity," 273–84; Hunt, "Chayanov's Model of Peasant Household Resource Allocation and its Relevance to Mbere Division, Eastern Kenya," 59–86; Lewis, "Domestic Labor Intensity and the Incorporation of Malian Peasant Farmers into Localized Descent Groups," 53–73.

11. Chayanov in his *Theory of the Peasant Economy* put considerable emphasis on the worker/consumer ratio which, along with other factors, was intended to directly impact the levels of drudgery acceptable to the workers of the household—the more mouths to feed per productive member the more the incentive to work long hours. In an agricultural society even fairly small children have agricultural tasks and so most household members contribute both labor and needs to the household. Moreover, when small children or unproductive adults only contribute needs, others, according to Chayanov, work harder. Thus, even without knowing the demographic profile or worker consumer ratio at the household level one would, following Chayanov, expect that on average larger households would expand production relative to smaller households. Given the impossibility of collecting all the data needed for a full Chayanovian analysis for 62,000 households, this seems a relatively defensible simplification that benefits from averaging the demographics over a very large number of households.

12. Tannenbaum, "The Misuse of Chayanov: 'Chayanov's Rule' and Empiricist Bias in Anthropology," 927–42.

13. Tannenbaum, "The Misuse of Chayanov: 'Chayanov's Rule' and Empiricist Bias in Anthropology."
14. Pascon, "Comparaison de Quelques Informations Statistiques."
15. Harrison,"Chayanov and the Economics of the Russian Peasantry," 389–417.
16. Harrison "The Peasant Mode of Production in the Work of A.V. Chayanov."

Chapter 7

Ethnicity and Social Capital in 1970s Sefrou

"Geertz is like a very fine baker. He takes a little bit of data and he kneads it and kneads it and then he kneads it some more. Then he rolls it and rolls it out until it is exceedingly thin. When you hold up his work by the corners you discover that it is transparent and you can see right through it."[1]

SOCIAL CAPITAL

Social capital, as Coleman notes, "inheres in the structure of relations between actors and among actors."[2] We have illustrated the financial significance of social capital in various ways in the earlier chapters but due to the absence of high quality quantitative data our argument so far has been qualitative in nature. In this chapter we use a data set for urban shops in the city of Sefrou, Morocco, to estimate the significance of social capital in an urban market. As the high quality of this data allows us to do a proper mathematical analysis, here we address various aspects of social capital that we feel are relevant for many other cases in a more analytical way. Of the two prevailing theories of social capital, those by Bourdieu and Putnam, this chapter fits more into the active social networking perspective advocated by Bourdieu while the last chapter focused on long enduring institutions such as norms, institutionalized trust, and established networks that Putnam suggests are fundamental components of social capital.

When anthropologists think of social capital they intuitively understand it as the networks available to people for empowering or enhancing their activities, projects, life goals, or more generally, their opportunity sets. Network analysis illustrates nodes and their relative importance quite well but by itself provides only the crudest tools to assess the comparative value of social capital. In this chapter, we elaborate a complementary approach aimed at assessing the overall importance of social capital within urban professions rather than its importance to particular people. While the data used are from the twentieth century we imagine that, were the data available, this sort of evidence for the importance of social capital would differ only marginally throughout the Near East over millennia as our earlier chapters have suggested.

In Morocco, and much of the Near East urban shops have traditionally been established as religious endowments (*awqaf* or *ahbas*) whose occupancy costs are intended to provide continuing sources of income. These costs have been divided into two portions, an initial large and market priced key right auctioned off to the highest bidder that establishes a leasehold or annuity over a money generating asset (a shop) and a minor continuing rent. An initial feature is that the occupant cannot pass the right on to heirs for the shop is auctioned anew each time an occupant dies. This serves to keep the key right at current market value and maintains the value of the endowment. Given this auction (winners are selected behind closed doors by those managing the endowment) and the inability of any occupant to pass on occupancy to an heir, we would not expect high levels of ethnic monopoly with most traditional trades. That is unless social networks regularly influence those managing the auction.

In post-independence (1956–) Morocco, such endowments have been administered as part of a national ministry to maintain the honest administration and value of each endowment. In effect, each occupant is a leaseholder, a position for which they have made a substantial investment, and a renter—although rents are often quite nominal. The lease is of indefinite duration, though it has a finite term, generates revenue like any annuity, and ends at the death or retirement of the occupant. It differs from the annuities common in Europe from the Middle Ages primarily in that it cannot be traded or inherited but like such annuities it has a finite term, even if not defined as a fixed number of years. Nevertheless, the leasehold system for commercial property endowments is, similarly, a system of credit managed by state, private, or religious institutions.

Traditionally, each trade in the market was organized under an Amin whose primary responsibility was to make the trade responsive to rules and regulations designed to promote honesty and transparency in commerce. Unlike European guilds, these trade organizations had no mandate to regulate labor, prices or quantities though Sultans did levy taxes and on occasion prohibit the export of certain products or engage in other regulations of the market.

We follow Geertz in our approach to measure the relative monopolization of different urban trades by specific ethnic groups on the, reasonable we believe, assumption that ethnic identity in a multi-ethnic situation provides some prima facie basis for differential social capital. Ethnographic intuition leads us to suspect that kinsmen may preferentially facilitate their own kin within their urban profession. We provide a relatively sophisticated mathematical analysis of a published data set to elucidate how much this seems to be the case and in which trades this influence on the institutional system of leaseholds is most important, that is, in which trades ethnicity is least randomly distributed.

SOCIAL CAPITAL AND STUDIES OF MARKETS IN MOROCCAN TOWNS

Markets have long been fora where credit and capital combine to facilitate many interests, public and hidden.[3] In this chapter, we examine the urban market (the *sūq*) in 1970s Sefrou, a medium sized town in central Morocco which was extensively studied by Clifford Geertz, Hildred Geertz, and Lawrence Rosen.[4] This study is a classic in the field and published an important set of data that lends itself to further analysis. It is worth noting that Sefrou, like a number of other Moroccan towns, had a large Jewish community before Morocco's independence who mostly emigrated before the study began and so many shops were filled by new occupants no more than a couple of decades before the Geertz *et al* study began. The time frame of the study is particularly conducive to the analysis we intend for two reasons: because the market had not yet been seriously inundated with modern standardized commodities and influenced by a proliferation of suburban shops. Thus, many traditional trades were still common, while this is less the case in recent times, and the recentness of the Jewish emigration is an indication of how quickly market constraints can be implemented. This chapter develops a methodology for unearthing hidden interests in the control of information and access to annuity like investment opportunities within the endowment system. We will see that the political nature of the link (the degree of constraint) has been distinctly more significant for some trades in the Moroccan *sūq* than for others.

Modern social science might be seen as having an obsession with power. This may have more than a little to do with the rise of technological means of domination that are unsurpassed in history and something to do with a perceived need to identify with the oppressed. Broadly speaking, one major focus has been on hegemony, defined as the ability to dominate people through ideological means rather than through recourse to brute force. The failure of communist countries to eradicate a whole series of antithetical beliefs supports the contention that power, conceived as hegemonic or not, has limitations even if they are fairly substantial in a market context. Although there are many studies of power, particularly in the field of political economy,[5] there are few which attempt to study the articulation of specific power structures with economic or political decisions within a traditional market context. Still, the general questions posed by Foucault (how is power exercised and what are its effects) have long been answered: through variants of monopoly which produce excess profit. There is a general consensus, particularly in structural Marxist and Neo-Weberian writing, that power may derive in particular social formations / societies from economic, political, or ideological sources.[6] Appadurai[7], perhaps influenced by world systems emphasis on trade in bulk goods, suggested that attention to the things exchanged rather than the form or function of the exchange would reveal the political character of the link between exchange and value.

Various scholars have suggested that the bazaar operates in a fundamentally different way than a capitalist market.[8] Geertz suggested that the key differences are:[9]

1. A great multiplicity of small-sized enterprises.
2. A very finely drawn division of labor in technical, social, and spatial terms.
3. Transactions that are mostly interpersonal.
4. Goods and services that are not homogeneous.
5. Formal signaling systems that are undeveloped.
6. The predominance of exchange skills over managerial or technical ones.
7. The undifferentiation of buying and selling.
8. The predominance of the personal (usually oral) contract as the main legal form of relationship.
9. The informal, diffuse, and weak character of overall integrative institutions: governmental controls are marginal, no true guilds, little hierarchical business organization.

Geertz suggested that these differences make the practice of information and credit management far different than in a western market. Geertz's focus on information could be made more persuasive if it did not assume so little knowledge of prices on the part of the majority of actors in the market. My own impression from two years' work in a similar-sized Moroccan town, Essaouira, is that almost everyone has, or can readily get from a friend, a good estimate of the price of any commodity they plan to purchase. This estimate would specify a narrow range within which one ought to be able to obtain the item. Most negotiation is, therefore, over small differences, but the range cannot be narrowed to a single price for commodities that are heterogenous in quality or not packaged in standardized quantities. Inventories made on the death of a shop owner invariably list and appraise every item in the shop. Since this is done so that the property can be precisely divided among heirs, precision is important, yet there is no evidence of regular quarrels over the appraisals. This would suggest that, once quality and quantity are evident, consensus over value is readily obtainable. In a negotiation it is, however, generally more difficult to compare two commodities in different shops along a set of qualitative or variable quantitative criteria. The margin shaved off for a regular client may, thus when intensive search is practiced, be more than enough to discourage serious comparative shopping.

In 1990, Fanselow[10] developed the idea that the key difference to a consumer is the lack of homogeneity in the quality of goods. This provides an opportunity for sellers to manipulate prices via manipulation of quantities and the quality of goods sold. He suggests, contra Geertz, that a critical component of this is the superior bargaining position of the seller in such a situation, because while the goods being sold are hard to evaluate the money paid by the buyer is far less uncertain. Fanselow argued that not all goods exchanged in the bazaar are equally heterogenous and that Geertz errs in not separating out the commodities that do have a high degree of standardization from those that provide significant advantages to the seller due to their lack of homogeneity.[11] Fanselow in fact suggests that many of the characteristics of transactions in the bazaar, which appear irrational from a neoclassical perspective, are directly tied to the properties of the goods being transacted.

The introduction in recent years of more standardized commodities, often with brand names, shifts the buyers' ideal activity away from a pattern of intensive search, developing a personal relationship with sellers, to a pattern of extensive search, in which the buyers canvass widely and makes decisions based on known differences between the quality of brands and available prices. From the sellers' perspective, the strategy shifts as the situation changes from one in which knowledge is disproportionately on the sellers' side and buyers depend on developing ties to a seller to one in which sellers must view other sellers as direct competitors on a daily basis.

In the former situation, one might expect a much greater incentive for collusion among sellers since there is less direct competition between sellers. If members of a kin-group control a trade, this is advantageous and does not lead to conflict since the focus is on controlling information vis-à-vis the buyers and extracting a high price from them rather than competing directly with other members of the trade. As the traditional situation transforms and standardized commodities prevail, a single breach in the oligopoly would tend to force members into competition with each other because buyers would engage in extensive searches rather than intensive ones. Thus in practice, the rewards to partial oligopolistic control of a trade might diminish where the commodities traded were more homogeneous.

Our analysis will allow us to look at all these issues. The reason we have reanalyzed his data set is that Geertz's original attempt is one of the few notable efforts, in anthropology, to study the articulation of power structures and economic practice in a Muslim *sūq* (bazaar). Geertz makes a serious and admirable attempt to provide a way of measuring the link between ethnicity and domination of particular trades in the Sefrou market. His analysis is based on a subtle analysis of the market as a system in which access to information and credit comprise two critical constraints which help distinguish the bazaar economy from a typical capitalist market. Ethnicity (a narrow version is well defined in Morocco under the rubric of *nisba*) becomes a dominant focus for networks which themselves control access to basic resources such as membership in a trade, information about supply and demand, and credit.

The focus in this chapter will be Geertz's proposed measure of "compactness" or the degree to which a given trade is dominated by people from a limited subset of these ethnic affiliations. We will argue that there are serious inadequacies in the proposed measure and that the formula used is not up to the task assigned it. Instead, we will first modestly improve Geertz' formula and then propose a radically different measure that, due to its focus on probability, does a better job indicating which particular trades most constrain access along ethnic lines or, put another way, least appear to allow free access to the profession for all ethnic groups. The concluding discussion will use the results of the analysis to evaluate the market expression of various sources of power in 1970s Sefrewi society. It is worth noting that as the introduction of standardized commodities increased since the 1970s, this particular data set is particularly appropriate for our analysis even though it reflects a post-independence situation following a major outmigration of Jewish merchants in the 1960s—and their replacement by locals from the region.[12]

Structure of the Moroccan *Sūq*

Geertz suggests that the bazaar (*sūq*) lacks a collective organization and organizes itself along two axes: the division of labor and ethnic identity. The former defines the division of people into specific professions or trades while the latter is the basis for personal identity and provides the basis for networks that control the market to a significant degree. He suggests:[13]

> The development of these two classifications to extraordinary levels of differentiation, together with their partial but quite real interfusion, provides the bazaar with both map and mold, an image of its form that is also a matrix for its formation.

The flow of information about commodities and people provide the basis for an unending set of negotiations and transactions where enormous concern is paid to the quality of the information and moral evaluation of the transaction. Geertz emphasizes the role of particular terminology in this evaluation process and suggests the terminology illustrates the importance of the control of information in the market. There are positive and negative terms whose commonality is frequency of usage in the market and relevance to transactional decisions. Associated Arabic vocabulary often share a root such that connotations developed for one word easily spill over to a related one. Thus while, in English, book, library, office, secretary, and to write are not etymologically related, in Arabic the corresponding terms, *kitāb*, *maktab*, *maktaba*, *kātib*, and *kataba* all share the root k-t-b. The term *'arafa*, to know, gives rise to the term *ma'rūf*, prevailing opinion or normal and fair, which is found in the common refrain, wa-hadi *ma'rūf* (is this fair). Similarly, the verb *'aqala*, to have intelligence or be endowed with reason, is linked to the term *ma'qūl*, reasonable or just, found in the omnipresent phrases *ma shi' ma'qūl*, it is not fair, or *wakhkha ma'qūl*, yes it is fair or reasonable.

Other key terms for evaluating information, what might be said to involve the truth or falsity of a claim, similarly have no connotation of absolute truth. Rather, Moroccan terms refer primarily to the quality of a relationship not an abstract standard. Thus *sadaqa*, friendship, is important, as is *tasdīq*, faith, or *sihha*, health, as applied to a transaction or a contractual relationship or the market in general. Instead of referring to an abstract of "perfect health," discussion in the market refers to normalcy, reasonableness, tradition (*'urf*) and so is intrinsically relative and relational not abstract and singular. False information, *kadhab* (lies), or *bātil* (worthless vacuous statements), are ever-present worries because success in the market requires information management, not free flowing information; yet the Quran forbids lying and social etiquette forbids face-to-face insults.

The result is a strong incentive to distort information in some form with a resulting high value put on being able to sift information for accurate and timely clues. Conversely, networks based on ethnic identity and patron-client ties provide the organizational ability to profitably control access to both information and professional membership. Information management, provision of credit, and control of professional membership are the means by which domination in the market are achieved. One critical component of information management, in Geertz's model, is the non-standardized quality and measures of the commodities traded. This characteristic makes comparative shopping difficult and leads people to focus on "intensive search"—developing personal relationships with a seller, rather than "extensive search"—in which a buyer optimizes returns by comparing prices between various sellers for a given quality and quantity of the desired commodity.[14]

Ethnicity as a Relative and Nuanced Identity

Sefrou is a small Moroccan town not far south of Fez whose inhabitants come primarily from the surrounding rural area or from Fez and Meknes, major nearby urban centers. In Arabic, the term *nisba* refers to kinship, the related *nasab* refers to lineage and in Morocco identity is regularly provided by an adjective (*nisba*) ending in long "i" such as Maghribi, from Morocco, or Sefrewi, from Sefrou. While an individual can choose an identity as a Moroccan, a person from a particular city, tribe, sublineage or smaller subdivision, the nominal link is kinship or ethnicity in the sense of tribal ties, though many *nisba* refer to places rather than specific lineages. Despite the relative nature of the term, a given context will generally determine the most useful identity an individual can claim.[15] Within a city, identity as a Moroccan or as someone from the city would have minimal value in most relationships. Similarly, if the goal is to gain access to information or employment a given individual may have no valid claims that will usefully distinguish him from other aspirants. Thus, in a given context such as membership in professions within a given city, the operant ethnic identities will be easily ascertainable, unambiguous, and mutually exclusive.

In Sefrou a full list of *nisba* include sixty-six relative terms (many of which aggregate others at lower/more narrow levels) of which a representative set might be the following:[16] Adluni (member of a prominent Sefrou family), Alawi (member of a family with claims to sherif status—descendants of the prophet), Bhaluli (from a nearby rural area), Buhadiwi (from a fraction of the Ait Yusi confederation), Fassi (from Fez), Jebli (from the rural / mountainous area), Meghrawi (an old Sefrou family name), Robini (a Sefrou Jewish family), Susi (Berber from the Sus), Tobali (a Sefrou Jewish family), Yazghi (from a nearby rural community), Zaikumi (from a nearby Berber village), and Zgani (from a nearby Berber village). As this list suggests, the operant ethnic identities can vary from membership in a locally prominent extended family to membership in a fraction of a large Berber confederation. Rosen[17] has made a rather persuasive case for the contextual negotiation of ethnic identity in Sefrou. Geertz[18] however notes that in 80 percent of the trades four *nisba* account for more than three-quarters of the occupants. This fact and the relative nature of ethnicity (its overlapping character at the level of the *nisba* defined by Geertz) suggest that a significantly smaller set of non-overlapping terms (in this case ten) would adequately cover the ethnicities relevant to access to all the major trades.

In the 1970s there were 1,013 shops involved in the traditional professions,[19] there are clearly not enough members in some of the most narrowly defined *nisba* to fill more than a fraction of total spots—if one counts only those currently in trade. Nevertheless, conceptually the filling of spots (shops) within a trade might be better viewed as a problem in probability where replacement occurs. That is to say, the market can support only a small number of shops relative to the number of people who would like to fill those spots. The selection of a person from one *nisba* is not likely to significantly decrease the availability of another person from that *nisba*. In particular, most *nisba* (at least of the wider mutually exclusive variety of interest here) have their roots in, for practical purposes, an inexhaustible source for new members within the rural area or extended family ties elsewhere in Morocco. The important constraint is how many shops the market can profitably support, not the availability of personnel to fill them.

MEASURES OF ETHNIC DOMINATION IN PROFESSIONS

Geertz devises a compactness index[20] intended to measure the concentration of traditional trades in the hands of specific *nisba*. The basic idea in the measure is to calculate average deviations from expected levels of *nisba* representation for each trade and then rank the trades from greatest average deviation to lowest. Those trades with the greatest deviation would thus have the greatest compactness (control by fewest *nisba*) or the greatest concentration of the trade in the hands of the fewest *nisba*.[21] The measure requires most prominently a decision about how to calculate expected levels, for without this the calculation of an average deviation would be impossible. Geertz decides to define the expected level as the total number in the trade (e.g., how many bakers the town supports) divided by the number of *nisba* in the trade itself. This definition is by no means persuasive, but seems to be based on reservations about the suitability of the material to statistical treatment.[22]

Thus, Geertz devises the following formula summing average deviations from a mean calculated as the total (100 percent) divided by the number of *nisba* represented:

For all *nisba* in a given trade or profession,

$$\frac{\sum |(\text{Expected percentage of people belongining to } nisba - \text{Real percentage})|}{\text{number of } nisba \text{ in the trade}}.$$

Geertz's formula calculates the average deviations from expected value for members of the trade belonging to each *nisba* , where expected value is 100 percent divided by the number of actual *nisba* in the given trade, provides a ranking of the traditional professions. This ranking is claimed to reflect the degree to which given *nisba* have proportionally more or fewer than expected members in the trade. Geertz defines ten *nisba* that together include well over 99 percent of shop owners. His ranking, in order of most compact by Geertz's formula, and using the distributions shown, would be as follows:

There are two obvious problems with this formula and its resultant statistically counter-intuitive ranking beyond that the ranking also makes no ethnographic sense:

Table 7.1 Results of Geertz's Formula Recalculated

	(n,k):(Distribution)=>Compactness
RANK TRADE	(# in Trade, distribution in compactness) = compactness as deviation from *nisba* equality for *nisba* in trade
1. Blacksmith	(15,2): (1,14) => 43.333
2. Carpenter	(18,3): (1,1,16) => 37.037
3. Weaver	(22,4): (1,1,1,19) => 30.681818
4. Butcher	(22,5): (1,1,2,2,16) => 21.0909
5. Mason	(31,5): (2,2,2,3,22) => 20.387
6. Silk	(22,6): (1,1,1,1,5,13) => 16.1616
7. Hardware	(10,5): (1,1,1,1,6) => 16
8. Prepared food	(15,5); (1,1,2,2,9) => 16
9. Coffee shop	(29,6): (1,1,1,4,4,18) => 15.1341
10. Cloth	(35,9): (1,1,1,1,1,1,1,1,27) => 14.6737
11. Baker	(19,7): (1,1,1,1,2,2,11) => 12.4597
12. Tinsmith	(10,4): (1,2,2,5) => 12.5
13. Miller	(12,7): (1,1,1,1,1,1,6) => 10.2041
14. Tobacconist	(16,7): (1,1,1,1,2,2,8,) => 10.2041
15. Barber	(42,10): (1,1,1,1,1,1,2,5,5,24) => 10.19
16. Wool and hides	(11,5): (1,1,2,2,5) => 10.1818
17. Odds-and-ends seller	(17,8): (1,1,1,1,3,3,3,4) => 6.61765
18. Wheat/bean trader	(13,9): (1,1,1,1,1,2,2,2,2,) => 3.79867

Source: Recalculated and sorted from Geertz et al. *Meaning and Order in Moroccan Society*, Table 3, 146.

1. There is no justification for basing the calculation of the expected number of members in each *nisba* only on the *nisba* actually in the trade, it is important that those *nisba* which might appear, but do not, also count.
2. The formula does not include any statistic to reflect the size of each profession, it is more significant statistically that most members of a large profession are from a limited number of *nisba* than if the same proportions are found in a trade with only a few members. We will consider this point in a later section but the basic issue is that deviation from a mean does not recognize how many objects deviate from the mean.

Point 1 implies that any calculation should compare given membership in *nisba* with the proportion expected in a trade from all *nisba* (defined in a mutually exclusive way). If we take the eighteen trades above, showing high to low compactness, in Geertz's terms, we find a maximum of ten *nisba* represented. The data set does not provide specific information on which *nisba* are represented in which proportions in each trade. It is quite likely that the total number of *nisba* represented exceeds ten, but for the purposes of a theoretical discussion, we can assume the same ten *nisba* are involved.

A more sophisticated way to estimate the relative degree of monopoly in trades that might seem appropriate would be to use an entropy based measure such as a biodiversity index. This would measure the deviation from randomness by assuming that all trades should have an equal representation of each ethnicity (*nisba*) and deviations from such a distribution represent forces that act to skew the random distribution into the current distribution. Conceptually, this is similar to measuring the biodiversity in a particular eco-niche where the niche becomes the profession. Since such a measure produces an index number per trade, the trades could be directly compared. A well-known example of such an index is a Shannon index.

Unfortunately, a Shannon index does not satisfy Point 2 above. That is to say it does not adequately acknowledge that a given average deviation is less significant in a small trade than in a large one. Using the Shannon index we find that the distribution in the cloth trade (1, 1, 1, 1, 1, 1, 1, 1, 27), which has thirty-five merchants distributed into nine *nisba*, appears less significant than the distribution of the blacksmith trade (1, 14), which has fifteen merchants of whom all but one are in one *nisba*. Yet, mathematical intuition suggests that the odds are substantially greater against getting a distribution such as that of the cloth trade than those against getting one such as that of the blacksmith trade.

A better analysis, a purely combinatorial method, focuses on the simple statistical probability of the actual distributions. It is not at all clear that an equal distribution of these amalgamated ethnicities would be the norm in a situation devoid of structural obstacles but if some reason could be adduced for why this might be the case the Shannon index might be the way to go. For the moment it may be worth remembering a few of the reasons why we might not want to assume an equal distribution would be ideally random:

- the populations of the different ethnicities are not equal;
- the proximity of the *nisba* populations to the market may be different or constrain access;
- the traditions of some ethnicities may include one activity, for example, pastoralism even as others include another, for example, agriculture;
- the ties of some ethnicities to other urban areas may be far stronger and disproportionately facilitate certain types of trade; and
- we have no reason to be particularly interested in an equal distribution and a focus on such a distribution will prevent a more pure statistical analysis.

In biology, a Shannon index is usually used either to point out the greater diversity of different areas or to compare diversity over time within a specific area. In both cases the comparison is in effect used to highlight differences which can then reasonably be explained through further investigations.

Measuring the deviation from evenness is a way to highlight topics for investigation rather than an assumption that were it not for some constraint all plants would be equal in their numerical ability to propagate. Ecologists in fact do not classify all species as equally prolific. In the market, we cannot assume an indifferent preference for profession or for maintenance in a chosen profession and there are few reasons to assume an equal distribution of all ethnicities would represent pure randomness. The method proposed below does not require the assumption of any particular distribution as a norm for comparison.

Using mathematical reasoning similar to that we might use for estimating the probability of a hand in poker we can compare the probability of the current distributions of *nisba* in the various professions to the total possible set of distributions.[23] To devise a strictly probabilistic measure of differential probability, we could begin by regarding the actual distributions as one way of allocating the available positions in each trade or profession to particular groups. Then one could compare the possible ways of arriving at the actual distribution with the total possible ways of allocating the spots in the profession to a given number of ethnic groups. In this case, we wish to compare each actual distribution of *nisba* among the shops in the trade with total number of ways the ten *nisba* could have been allocated to the "n" shops.

The formula for counting the ways of distributing "n" shops to "k" ethnic groups in specific quantities r1, r2, r3...rk (the actual ethnographically found distribution) is given by the Multinomial Coefficient (MC) for "n" things (shops) allocated in "k" quantities to each *nisba*:

$$\frac{n!}{r1!r2!r3!\cdots rk!}$$

We want, however, a ratio of the MC for the actual distribution of spots in a profession (assuming the market supports just that many bakers, butchers, etc.) divided by the total ways of allocating that number of spots to "k" or fewer groups, providing an estimate of the likelihood of the actual distribution being the result of chance. Here we are filling the "n" shops with one of the "k" (ten) *nisba*—multiple shops might be filled with someone from the same *nisba*.

The simplest way to calculate the total possibilities is to imagine that we had a ten-sided die that we rolled to see which *nisba* got each of the "n" shops. This would give us ten choices per shop or a total of 10^n possible distributions.

Thus we need to divide our MC result by our figure for the total possibilities in each case. This formula, although it produces small probabilities, since all eighteen cases are far from random, treats each distribution properly and generates an accurate ranking of probabilities (some of which are much less likely than others):

$$\frac{\text{MC of Actual Distribution}}{\text{Total possible distributions}} = 10^n$$

This formulation does not directly measure distance from an even distribution nor does it assume that any distribution is random. Nevertheless, the calculation of all possible distributions (disregarding order) will find more distributions that are near the central point than those that are not. Other things being equal, extreme distributions will have low probability but extreme distributions in large professions will have even lower probability than in smaller professions, as statistical intuition should suggest. In our case, this formula, assumes a "k" of ten *nisba* in each case (as categorized by Geertz) but "n" varies by case as there are different numbers of positions available in each profession. This model produces the following ranking reflecting the probability of a given distribution being due to chance for each of the traditional professions.

Table 7.2 *Nisba* Ranking Using Multinomial Coefficient.

Rank.Trade	Number in Trade: Number of nisba	Actual Distribution ethnicities across nisba	P(D) | n, k
1. Cloth	35:9	1, 1, 1, 1, 1, 1, 1, 1, 27	9.48964 * 10^–24
2. Mason	31:5	2, 2, 2, 3, 22	3.0482 * 10^–20
3. Barber	42:10	1, 1, 1, 1, 1, 1, 2, 5, 5, 24	7.86285 * 10^–20
4. Weaver	22:4	1, 1, 1 , 19	9.24 * 10^–19
5. Coffee shop	29:6	1, 1, 1, 4, 4, 18	2.39759 * 10^–17
6. Carpenter	18:3	1, 1, 16	3.06 * 10^–16
7. Butcher	22:5	1, 1, 2, 2, 16	1.34303 * 10^–15
8. Blacksmith	15:2	1, 14	1.5 * 10^–14
9. Silk	22:5	1, 1, 1, 5, 13	1.5042 * 10^–13
10. Baker	19:7	1, 1, 1, 1, 2, 2, 11	7.61867 * 10^–11
11. Prepared food	15:5	1, 1, 2, 2, 9	9.009 * 10^–10
12. Tobacconist	16:7	1, 1, 1, 1, 2, 2, 8	1.2973 * 10^–8
13. Hardware	10:5	1, 1, 1, 1, 6	5.04 * 10^–7
14. Miller	12:7	1, 1, 1, 1, 1, 1, 6	6.6528 * 10^–7
15. Odds-and-end seller	17:8	1, 1, 1, 1, 3, 3, 3, 4	6.86125 * 10^–7
16. Tinsmith	10:4	1, 2, 2, 5	7.56 * 10^–7
17. Wool and hides	11:5	1, 1, 2, 2, 5	8.316 * 10^–7
18. Wheat/bean trader	13:9	1, 1, 1, 1, 1, 2, 2, 2, 2	3.89189 * 10^–5

Table created by Thomas K. Park.

This formula provides a radically different ranking than Geertz's formula and one that better supports statistical intuition and confirms ethnographic intuitions. Cloth merchants, the most elite of these professions, end up not only at the top, but well above any other profession. Blacksmiths slip from first place to eighth place. Perhaps most notably from a statistical point of view, all the small professions, even if relatively unevenly distributed between *nisba*, do not appear to represent as unlikely a random outcome as is the case for unevenly distributed large professions. The greater the size of a profession the more significant a narrowing of possibilities becomes from a probabilistic perspective. One of the most dramatic changes in ranking is that of barber (1, 1, 1, 1, 1, 1, 2, 5, 5, 24) which goes from fifteenth using Geertz's original formula to third in the new ranking. Thus, despite having representatives from all ten *nisba*, the profession's large size and extremely high skew toward one *nisba* that includes twenty-four of the forty-two barbers makes the outcome highly improbable, as a purely random outcome. Overall, the ranking clearly confirms statistical intuition, less likely outcomes being ranked as such.

GENERAL APPLICABILITY OF THIS PROBABILITY-BASED METRIC

A division of shop owners into a large number of fairly narrowly defined *nisba* provides an opportunity for inferring constraints to membership of particular professions. A measure of the likelihood of finding a particular distribution across groups provides a way of ascertaining the relative amount of constraint to membership. In some cases these constraints might be due to one or more groups' privileged control of resources, in another case it might be due to other groups having generally better options and in some cases it may represent constraints to exit from a particular life option. Extremely improbable outcomes, on the assumption of purely random selection, should delineate significant contours to the societal power structure. These contours, to the extent they do not confirm the obvious, merit further historical and sociological investigation.

Geertz's ranking which placed cloth merchants well down in the ranking and way below blacksmiths and butchers was intriguing for this reason alone but it did not stand up to further analysis. His appendix[24] provides a series of general figures for all professions in Sefrou which gives the profession for almost 4000 individuals divided into eight mutually exclusive ethnic groups. The professions are listed as high-status, medium-status, and low-status, and the ethnic affiliations range from Sefrou-born Arabic speakers to Jewish. There are substantial memberships in each group.

Table 7.3 Ethnicity and Professions in Sefrou.

	Sefraoui Arabic	Rural Arabic	Rural Berber	Fassi Arabic	Urban Berber	Urban Arabic	Bhalil	Jews	Total
High Status									
Prof. Administrator	7	2	1	2	1	0	0	2	15
Large-scale commerce	8	1	4	0	0	2	0	5	20
Large-scale farmer	2	0	0	0	0	0	0	0	2
White-collar employee	110	75	21	42	17	38	10	96	409
Medium-scale commerce	10	2	2	0	1	0	0	8	23
Medium- and small-scale farmers	122	52	48	2	10	2	4	5	245
Police, military	30	81	61	20	21	32	5	2	252
Medium Status									
Petty commerce	190	92	63	9	17	17	10	153	551
Modern skilled indep. worker	14	3	6	2	1	0	0	7	33
Master craftsman, traditional	194	72	33	13	7	8	16	100	443
Low status									
Commercial worker	61	33	18	1	1	2	4	71	191
Modern skilled worker	70	43	28	6	5	13	6	12	183
Traditional skilled worker	346	134	51	18	7	21	34	130	741
Service occupations	90	94	33	5	7	20	18	39	306
Farm laborer and manual laborer	143	146	98	1	18	15	44	4	469
Total	1397	830	467	121	113	170	151	634	3883

Source: Geertz et al. *Meaning and Order*, 438–42, selected data.

These figures can be similarly plugged into the model defined above, to estimate the probability that a given distribution is the result of chance. The assumption is that none are purely chance outcomes but some are far less chance outcomes than others. It should be kept in mind that the formula calculates the chance of precisely the actual distribution. This is very small in the general case because there are many possibilities. The actual figures suggest, however, that there are significant and consistent differences between professions. Ranks are, as in the earlier examples, from greatest indication of ethnic oligopoly to least.

The size of the data set and the general level of the skew would allow one to make a rough ranking. Yet this is far from adequate, the formula clarifies the order in many cases and makes the general picture much more obvious. It is not apparent before the analysis that the high status occupations, generally, end up with low rankings, implying that the distributions in these professions are less ethnically skewed than in others. One explanation, though I will offer another in the Discussion section, is that access to education, the *sine qua non* of most of these occupations, is somewhat more widely available than other resources, such as land, credit, or usable connections. In contrast, the most unlikely ethnic distribution, from a probability perspective, is the traditional skilled worker category. Here, Sefrou-born Arabic speakers, rural-born Arabic speakers, and Jews dominate. The odds are exceedingly slim that they do so by chance. Petty commerce, the main focus of C. Geertz's attention, ranks second in order of improbability or skew. Here, Sefrou-born Arabic speakers and Jews predominate with significant numbers of rural-born Arabic and Berber speakers as well. The third, most-skewed category, farm laborer and other manual laborers, differs primarily in the absence of Jews and the greater role of rural-born Arabic and Berber speakers. The fourth, most-skewed category, traditional master craftsmen once again has a large number of Jews and a predominance of Sefrou-born Arabic speakers.

The four most-skewed professions are also the professions with the four highest memberships. The following ranks, however, indicate that size of membership is not a determining factor. The next largest profession, white-collar employee, with 409 members, is ranked eighth overall and clearly exhibits, despite its size, a much more even distribution among the eight ethnic groups. While traditional trades (skilled workers [one] and petty commerce [two]) are highly skewed, modern trades (such as modern skilled worker, employed or independent), rank in the low to moderate range (ten and eleven, respectively). Commercial workers and service occupations, where training and education is less significant, rank six and seven, at the top of the moderately skewed range.

Table 7.4 Professions and Probabalistic Ranking.

	Number in Profession	Rank by probability	$P(D) \mid n, k_{small}$ = high rank
High Status			
Prof. Administrator	15	14	$9.21784 * 10^{-7}$
Large-scale commerce	20	13	$9.08619 * 10^{-9}$
Large-scale farmer	2	15	$1.5625E-02$
White-collar employee	409	8	$4.28895 * 10^{-52}$
Medium-scale commerce	23	12	$7.48309 * 10^{-11}$
Medium- and small-scale farmers	245	5	$4.61323 * 10^{-84}$
Police, military	252	9	$8.80552 * 10^{-44}$
Medium Status			
Petty commerce	551	2	$2.20526 * 10^{-117}$
Modern skilled indep. worker	33	11	$3.60881 * 10^{-12}$
Master craftsman, traditional	443	4	$2.37566 * 10^{-110}$
Low status			
Commercial worker	191	6	$5.19158 * 10^{-59}$
Modern skilled worker	183	10	$1.60527 * 10^{-38}$
Traditional skilled worker	741	1	$2.85867 * 10^{-185}$
Service occupations	306	7	$4.00422 * 10^{-55}$
Farm laborer and manual laborer	469	3	$8.38476 * 10^{-113}$
Total	3883		

In sum, the formula provides a clear indication that the most significant constraints to entry (or perhaps exit) are in the traditional trades and that status of the trade is not a significant proxy for degree of constraint. Within the traditional sector, as C. Geertz's data suggest, the most prestigious trade (cloth) is also the most-skewed in its membership, but in the context of all professions, modern or traditional, there is a clear contrast with the latter as a group exhibiting the most-skewed membership. Middle-level professions, in terms of skew, such as police (nine), medium- and small-scale farmers (five), white-collar employees (eight), commercial workers (six), and service occupations (seven) span the status range from high to low.

The calculated improbability that a given distribution is the outcome of a pure random process depends in part on the size of the data set. Thus, although there are two large-scale farmers, and both are Sefrou-born Arabic speakers, the data set is simply too small to argue, despite the relatively high probability of a purely random result, that there is no ethnic skewing in this occupation. In contrast, large trades will tend to produce lower probabilities than smaller professions, indicative of a high degree of non-random skewing. This result will reflect the greater degree of statistical confidence a larger data set provides, but it does not imply that a smaller data set could not in reality be fully monopolized, complete with rules of exclusion, by a subset of ethnic groups. This statistic should, therefore, be taken primarily as an initial diagnostic device; humans are not random particles.

DISCUSSION

If we examine the final ranking derived for C. Geertz's shop occupancy data on traditional trades in Sefrou from the perspective of the commodities transacted, we find that they confirm Fanselow's suggestions that heterogeneity of the commodity is critical to the rationality of the bazaar transactions. The ranking of the trades, cloth, masons, barbers, weavers, coffee shop, carpenters, butchers, blacksmith, silk, baker, prepared food, tobacconist, hardware, millers, odds-and-ends sellers, tinsmith, wool hides, and wheat/bean traders, very clearly exhibit a general order going from trade in heterogenous products to trade in more standardized products.

Spooner and Reddy[25] provide brilliant discussions of the ambiguities involved in evaluating oriental carpets and cloth which have relevance to many other areas. While the coffee shop trade is the most prominent exception to the rule, its relatively high rank is undoubtedly due to the high cost of entry, in terms of capital investment, credit and control of capital as well as the possibilities for monopolization of ideal locations by a few people. The top trades (cloth, masons, barbers, and weavers) are unquestionably dealing in commodities that are less standardized than the lowest-ranked trades (hardware, millers, odds and ends, tinsmith, wool hides, and wheat/bean traders).

There are in fact standardized measures that are legally enforced, for sales of flour, wheat, and beans. Although these historically varied from place to place they were uniform in a given place and have long since been standardized in Moroccan towns. Hardware, odds and ends, and tinsmiths generally deal in standardized modern commodities. In the contrasting case of the barber trade, what may be critical is not the enormous variety in terms of service provided or price charged, but rather the importance of the personal relationship established between client and barber and hence the inapplicability of extensive search in the trade. Because client loyalty is high in the barber profession, what might seem a standardized product is not so considered and barbers are not in such direct competition with each other and can therefore easily derive significant advantages from collusion.

As we have suggested, the data provided in the Geertz et al. Appendix (Table 4 and raw data of Table 5) is also susceptible to a similar analysis.

The high ranking of traditional trades relative to modern ones confirms the far greater heterogeneity of goods traded in the traditional sector compared to services, labor, and goods involved in the modern sector. This is perhaps best highlighted by the disparity in ranking between modern skilled workers (eleven) and traditional skilled workers (one) or medium-scale commerce (twelve) and petty commerce (two). The role of personal relationships, heterogeneity of measures (since clients regularly buy minute quantities), and extension of credit in petty commerce preclude extensive searches and direct competition between sellers in a way not found in the larger-scale businesses who now transact a great variety of name brand commodities in standardized quantities.

Even when a tiny store sells a name-brand item, such as Tide, they generally do not sell it in the producer quantity. Instead the client asks for enough for a single wash and is measured out a seller-determined quantity. Credit, clientship, and poverty preclude most clients from engaging in extensive search for a better deal elsewhere.

In the microcosm of Sefrou several sources of power are evident. Most obviously, this analysis points to the opportunities provided ethnic groups through control of professions dealing in non-standardized products sold in the *sūq* where access to shops is obtained in a traditional fashion. The articulation between oligopolistic power based on ethnic identity and the structure of the market is to a significant degree based on a distinction between non-standardized commodities and newer commodities more susceptible of standardization. At the same time, the more traditional economic bases for power, access to capital and land (urban and rural), are clearly also significant. Since the ratio proposed measures probability, the high rank (five in Table 5) of medium- and small-scale farmers or the high rank of coffee shops (five in Table 3) must be taken as more significant than the low rank of large-scale farmers (fifteen in Table 5) which had a population of only two.

It should be stressed that any statistic will behave similarly, it is entirely possible that with a larger sample of large-scale landownership an extremely strong skew toward a small number of ethnic groups would emerge. The data examined, however, do not themselves establish a particularly strong trend. Access to education, a potential source of symbolic power is organized at the national level and so is not easily controlled by any ethnic group but its relevance as a source of power in Morocco is indisputable, even if the current analysis is not designed to measure it. Educated Moroccans, as a group, have distinctly more power than uneducated ones in numerous arenas.

In conclusion, the measure of probability proposed provides a consistent way of measuring the degree to which a given commodity market is cornered by a non-random subset of merchants. As such it helps to delineate the structure of hidden interest in this market. These interests affect access to investment opportunities, credit, and market position.

Real estate dealers talk of "location, location, location" and, in Moroccan urban centers, the control of real estate has traditionally been in the hands of the professions. As we have noted, traditionally, the "key right" to a shop was auctioned and provided the buyer with a life interest in an income generating asset and his(her) heir with no transmissible right to that key right. Yet the existence of distributions that are highly skewed by ethnicity suggests some preferences influence the auction even if bids remain in the range suitable to management. In most cases, of private endowments (run by a family) the property itself over time become owned by a mosque and, as with most conservative institutions, mosques were highly unlikely to sell a key right to those that other members of the profession did not approve. After obtaining Independence from France, Morocco quickly set up a government ministry to supervise management of all religious endowments (*awqaf*).

Our measures indicate that the role of power in the economy is quite heterogenous. Some trades are far more susceptible to oligopolistic control. The strong confirmation of Fanselow's emphasis on the importance of the distinction between standardized and non-standardized commodities supports Appadurai's more general suggestion that analytical attention to commodities, as well as financial instruments, may help establish the way value is linked to politics.

Our evidence of the hidden interests in the status quo and the indication that trades requiring modern education are more open to all ethnic backgrounds has added some detail to standard assumptions that there are institutionalized constraints on social mobility. Bourdieu's claims that social capital is significantly tied to other forms of capital seem to be confirmed in this case. The likelihood that ethnic networks are used both to secure positions and to raise the significant amounts of credit necessary to purchase a key right (providing leasehold or annuity on an income generating asset) seems to be the most probable explanation for the data collected by Geertz et al. In this and many other areas, finance in the Islamic world has long paralleled that in Europe and given rise to the still valuable ethical perspectives we examined in our first two chapters as well as in *The Roots of Western Finance*.

NOTES

1. This is a summary of the response one of Geertz's key informants for the Sefrou work gave Park (in Arabic) in an interview in 1980 in response to the question of what he thought of Geertz as an ethnographer. The informant was a long time employee and officer in the Moroccan secret police service. We too admire Geertz'

work and try to reanalyze it, to knead it just a little more in this chapter in order to better see the world the original presentation still slightly obscures.

2. Coleman, "Social capital in the creation of human capital," 95–120.

3. The economics profession has long written about market networks, e.g. Rees. "Labour Economics: Effects of more Knowledge—Information Networks in Labour Markets," or Stiglitz, "Information in the Labour Market." Nevertheless, their analyses have largely focused on the developed world and shown little concern with the assessment of the relative degree of constraint in less developed markets.

4. Geertz, Geertz, and Rosen, *Meaning and Order in Moroccan Society*. Tables 1, 2, include raw data. Table 3, also includes raw data as well as an analysis of the data, (see Geertz "Sūq: The Bazaar Economy in Sefrou," chapter 2). Table 4 in the appendix includes raw data (extracted from tables on pages 438–42 which are analyzed in Table 5.

5. e.g. Foucault "Omnes et singulatim," and Lukes, *Power A Radical View*, Roseberry "Political Economy," 161–85, Wolf, "Distinguished Lecture: Facing Power—Old Insights, New Questions," 586–96.

6. Gellner *Plough, Sword and Book*, Godelier *Horizon, Trajets Marxistes En anthropologie*, Mann, *The Sources of Social Power*.

7. Appadurai, *The Social Life of Things*.

8. Alexander and Alexander, "Striking a Bargain in Javanese Markets," 42–68; Mintz, "Standards of Value and Units of Measure in the Fond-des-Nègres Market Place, Haiti," 23–38; Mintz, "Pratik: A Hawaiian Personal Economic Relationship;" Rosen, "Social Identity and Points of Attachment: Approaches to Social Organization; Rosen, *Bargaining for Reality: The Construction of Social Relations in a Muslim Community*.

9. Geertz. "Sūq: The Bazaar Economy in Sefrou," 214–215.

10. Fanselow, "The Bazaar Economy or How Bizarre is the Bazaar Really?" 250–65.

11. Ibid., 261. See also, Akerlof, "The Market for 'lemons,'" 488–500.

12. There are practical reasons for not trying to incorporate the proportion of each *nisba* within a larger population into our calculations. In the real world, many constraints other than population size inhibit people from wanting to join a given profession and most of these will be unknown to the ethnographer. Thus, one group may have better opportunities in agriculture, better ties in alternative professions, or a longer tradition in emigration to France such that some local options do not have equal appeal. To assume there was competition from members of each group in direct proportion to their population (however delimited) is surely unrealistic. Instead, given the levels of unemployment or underemployment in Moroccan urban areas, it may be quite realistic to assume that there is a ready over supply of similarly qualified people from most of the less narrowly defined *nisba* who would like to avail themselves of an opportunity to join the great majority of trades, or at least the more important and profitable ones. It would even be hard to make a persuasive argument that the particular numbers of people represented in the market at a given point in time accurately represent the proportions of people potentially supplied to the market from a larger area. Without this assumption, the proportions of people belonging to given

ethnic groups found in a census cannot reasonably be used as a basis. These theoretical concerns are in our case complemented by a complete lack of comparable *nisba* definitions in the census—should we have no theoretical misgivings. It seems much more persuasive to assume that each group in the market represents merely the tip of an iceberg, comprising people who would participate given the chance.

13. Geertz, *Meaning and Order in Moroccan Society,* 150.

14. Ibid., 224.

15. Rosen, *Bargaining for Reality. The Construction of Social Relations in a Muslim Community.*

16. Geertz et al 1979: 140 ff.

17. Rosen, *Bargaining for Reality. The Construction of Social Relations in a Muslim Community.*

18. Geertz, *Meaning and Order in Moroccan Society,* 145. The ten *nisba* included in Geertz's compactness index were: Fassi, Alawi, Sussi, Annonceur, Bhaluli, L-Wata, Jew, Jebli, Qlawi, and Yazghi, Geertz, Chapter 2, Table 5, p. 148.

19. Ibid., 141

20. Ibid., 146.

21. Geertz's formula, the numbers provided for n and k and algebra have been used to reconstruct the distributions shown in Table 7.1 and used to calculate Table 7.2. Unfortunately, Geertz's data do not provide the *nisba* identities for his actual calculation for numbers of *nisba* in each profession.

22. Ibid., 147.

23. Those unfamiliar with combinatorial theory might consult a standard text such as Cohen. *Basic Techniques of combinatorial Theory* or appropriate chapters in a text such as Grossman. *Discrete Mathematics. An Introduction to Concepts, Methods, and Applications.*

24. Geertz, *Meaning and Order in Moroccan Society,* 438–42.

25. Spooner, "Weavers and dealers: the authenticity of an oriental carpet." and Reddy. "The structure of a cultural crisis: thinking about cloth in France before and after the Revolution."

Chapter 8

Problematizing Modern Consumer Credit

This chapter explores the roots of modern consumer credit in its decidedly imperfect manifestations. In a perfect credit market, there is a single interest rate and everyone can borrow or lend as much as they want at that rate.[1] We noted in chapter 3, that the bourse in Antwerp began to facilitate credit evaluations for merchants in the early 1600s, but it is only more recently that institutions for construction of quantified credit ratings have become widespread. Although we do not pretend to follow its evolution in detail, we argue that what we call modern consumer credit, to individuals and corporations, contrasts significantly with the way credit operated in the capitalist world during the nineteenth century. We suggest that consumer credit, in contrast to earlier forms, is now increasingly impersonal, yet paradoxically it is so thoroughly dependent on rating agencies that presentation of self has become critical both to individuals and corporations.

MODERN CONSUMERS

A capitalist economy turns out to be more complex than Marx envisaged, and not well delineated by some Marxist models. Simple under-consumptionist models; for example, industrial productivity depends directly on the short-term consumer standard of living for its sales with inevitable consequences for stability, have long been known to misrepresent capitalist reality. Such models neglect, among other things, the financial sector's contributions, cost savings resulting from innovation or substitution, and the general impacts of relative currency valuations. The relationships between consumption, aggregate income, and savings in a capitalist economy are still debated, and we need not examine this issue here. Clearly credit institutions or industries do benefit from a vibrant consumption sector and credit, by enlarging purchasing power through long-term financing, can significantly benefit both individuals and institutions. We will focus on the historical development of consumer finance, though we extend this to include financing corporations when they borrow to pay their wage bills.

Consumption levels are sometimes seen as synonymous with levels of affluence, and from an environmental point of view this seems obvious, though technically insurance can substitute for short-term decreases in production.[2] Our concern in this chapter is with decisions related to consumer borrowing not consumption levels *per se*. Viewing the corporation also as a consumer, some corporate financing (e.g., to cover the wage bill) could be seen as consumption related, but corporate decision criteria mostly involve a focus on longer-term productive profits. The distinction between near- and long-term advantage may be seen as a matter of well-being versus relations of advantage.[3] For simplicity, in this chapter, consumer credit will be credit constrained by near-term financing, rather than longer-term future expected rates of return. We may view this as credit where the lender has the borrower by the short hairs. This largely became the realm of credit cards and bank loans to consumers. This distinction is both somewhat arbitrary and obviously difficult to distinguish historically, but it has long since not simply coincided with lending to address urgent livelihood needs.

In the late eighteenth and early nineteenth century, an emergent industrial capitalism profoundly reorganized the lives of working peoples, and propelled a wave of colonial expansion and globalization. Although moneyed-classes dominated the circulation of modern forms of credit, credit for long remained embedded in and dependent on social relations. As capitalism came to dominate the means of production, the ability of households to control, much less own, productive resources was severely curtailed. Rapid urbanization was among the most significant trends accompanying the development of a capitalist economy. Between 1500 and 1750, the proportion of the English population engaged in agriculture declined from 74 to 45 percent. In Britain during the second[4] half of the eighteenth century, landlords stopped giving tenants either copyhold tenure (inheritable tenancy based on historical entry in a manorial register) or beneficial long-term leases, and countless peasants were dispossessed.[5] Smallholders also lost their farmstead to debt,[6] so by 1800 only 35.5 percent of the population was engaged in agriculture.[7]

NINETEENTH-CENTURY LONDON

As precarious as peasant livelihoods were, those of the urban poor were even more so. Engels, describing the living-conditions in Bethnal Green in London's most extensive working-class district in 1845, noted that in an area less than 400 yards square, there were some 1,400 houses, occupied by 2,795 families, or about 12,000 persons. An analogous area in Queens, N.Y. today because of vertical expansion has approximately twelve times as many.

In 1861 Mayhew[8] wrote four volumes describing London's poor: street vendors, day-laborers, rag pickers, rat catchers, tinkers, and hundreds of similar jobs, all typified by low, variable, and irregular earnings. He noted,

> In this overcrowding it is nothing usual to find a man, his wife, four or five children, and sometimes both grandparents, all in one single room of ten to twelve square feet, where they eat, sleep, and work ... . Not one father of a family in ten in the whole neighborhood has other clothing than his working suit, and that is as bad and tattered as possible, many, indeed, have no other covering for the night than these rags, and no bed, save a sack of straw and shavings.[8]

Even the pay of wage-workers seldom covered more than a couple of weeks, and often only that day. All households were vulnerable to shifts in composition intrinsic to family life cycles that affected skills, earnings, and spending commitments. Because households had few assets, they were governed by a rapid turnover logic. Income was spent almost immediately to meet daily necessities.[9]

This household logic has a myriad of implications. Where peasants could make ends meet by working-harder, consuming less, they usually had some stores to fall-back on. Working classes depend upon the sale of labor, no matter how much labor might be thrown on the market, working harder is contingent on the availability of work, which leaves consuming less as the only backup. Consumption has its own logic. For example, rent generally must be paid up front. Wages, by contrast, as Marx notes in Volume I of *Capital*, are usually paid after labor has been expended.[10] Because workers cannot afford to advance their labor on credit to their employers for very long, pay periods need to be short: daily, weekly, or biweekly but seldom longer.

A similar logic governs rents: the longer the period the harder it is for households to make the rent. Whether payments are made before or after consumption matters a great deal in household management. To meet an emergency, households could raise significant sums if they could borrow small amounts from lots of family and friends, thereby spreading the burden as well as obligations of repayment over a large group.[11] Such forms of personal credit are fairly fragile, and rest on trust built in face-to-face social relations, summed up in one's reputation. Because these sources are limited, especially for cash, they could not always be counted upon. When cash could not be earned or borrowed, the only alternative was to sell or pawn personal possessions. The poor, however, often had little to pawn other than their clothes or bedding. Engels provides us vivid descriptions of this kind of destitution.[12]

CREDIT AND PETTY COMMERCE

In nineteenth-century London, vast numbers of the poor made their living in petty trade. Buying and selling, everything from matches, fresh produce, wilted vegetables or half-rotten meat, to rags and bones, used clothing, household wares, and patent medicines. Mayhew estimates, not more than one-fourth of goods traded were the property of the sellers. [13] Much of this trade depended upon a variety of forms of credit. It should be noted that most of the nineteenth century was deflationary as this squeezed profits on sales and stimulated the search for other sources of profit.[14]

One source of money, particularly needed in petty commerce to purchase stock, was from moneylenders. In England during this period the legal rate of interest on loans was five percent per annum, moneylenders typically charged twenty percent per week, without compounding, the interest would amount to 1,040 percent per annum, consequently, most loans were short term.[15] As a rule, such loans required no security deposit, as long as a moneylender could satisfy himself that the borrower was whom he represented himself to be, and creditworthy. If a borrower defaulted, moneylenders almost never had recourse to the law. They would simply let the other members of their fraternity know, and the borrower would have a difficult time ever getting another loan. Because borrowers knew this, as Mayhew notes, "not once in twenty times was the money lender exposed to any loss by the nonpayment of his usurious interest."[16] Mayhew gives us a picture of such transactions from the borrower's perspective.

> If I want to borrow in a hurry ... as I may hear of a good bargain, I run to my neighbor L—'s and he first says he hasn't 20s. to lend, and his wife's by, and she says she hasn't 2s in her pocket, and so I can't be accommodated. Then he says if I must borrow the money, he'll have to pawn his watch—or to borrow it of Mr. — (an innkeeper) who would charge a deal of interest, for he wasn't paid all he lend two months back, and 1s would be expected to be spent in drink—though L— don't drink—or he must try his sister would trust him, but she was sick and wanted all her money—or perhaps his barrow merchant would lend him 10s., if he'd undertake to return 15s. at night; and it ends by my thinking I've done pretty well if I can get 1£ for 5s interest for a day's use of it.[17]

Because such credit was rooted in social ties and trust, the social costs of default could be painful. Personal credit long continued to depend upon continuing exchanges, gift giving, or being a good customer.[18] Much of the theatrics of English life during the nineteenth century was created around obtaining loans, being forced to repay debts or beg for more time. And, all classes both as borrowers or lenders played in this drama. Often, bar owners would lend money to good customers, at perhaps half the interest charged by moneylenders; and occasionally without interest charges. The catch was that the borrower had to be a good customer who drank a lot of beer.[19]

Aside from cash, credit took other forms as well. Many vendors sold borrowed merchandise, others rented pushcarts, donkey carts, baskets, even weights, and measures. Rent here is simply another name for interest on a loan. Mayhew describes the transaction of renting a pushcart or barrow. The rate was 3d a day during the winter, and 4d a day during the summer. A barrow to put this in perspective could be purchased new for 2 pounds. Thus at 3d a day one could buy 2.28 barrows a year; at 4d, 3.04 barrows. Despite, rents equivalent to 228 and 304 percent interest per annum, barrow lenders did a thriving business simply because so many street peddlers were so poor that they could not scrape enough capital together to buy their own carts—and so had to rent them. Like moneylenders, the barrow lender required no security, no deposit, but simply had to satisfy himself that the borrower was who he claimed to be—when not regularly paid he would send someone, or go himself, to carry away the barrow. Advancing merchandise on credit to a vendor was another common practice. Frequently young men unable to buy goods on their own account would work "on half profits." The lender advancing goods in hope of expanding his business, might say to any poor fellow willing to work on those terms, "these goods are worth so much, if you sell them at this price, the profit on them will be this; and yo can keep half of it." The catch is that when the goods are sold the lender must be paid the stipulated amount, whether any profit is realized.[20]

Poor families bought basic items in tiny quantities, but did so very frequently, making several dozen local shopping trips a week.[21] More expensive purchases, like cheap meat, fruit, and vegetables, were usually bought late on Saturday evening where markets were closing and unsold items in poor condition were discounted or discarded by traders.[22] Because credit was such a present part of so many transactions, and interest rates so dear, the prices paid by the poor for cheap goods regularly included interest. The small retailers to turn a profit had to buy inferior quality goods—the wilted vegetables, adulterated goods, factory seconds, used clothes, and second hand goods—and had to be willing to often sell these on credit. As Engels observed, "the poor ... to whom a couple of farthings are important ... cannot inquire too closely into ... quality."[23] They were not only forced to buy inferior goods, but were often cheated as well by dealers who used false weights and measures.[24]

Working-class credit took two basic forms: (1) crisis credit from friends, family, coworkers, neighbors, grocers, doctors, and moneylenders to see a household through a shortfall; (2) credit for on-time purchases of durable or semi-durable goods.[25] With precarious livelihoods, and so many living on the edge, debt collection was often problematic. While local grocers and merchants could stop advancing credit, and put the word out, making it difficult for the debtor to obtain further credit, many lenders—family, friends, and neighbors—were often not much better off than borrowers, and demands for payment could become unpleasant.

DEBT COLLECTION

In England, imprisonment for debt can be traced to statutes enacted in the thirteenth century which gave creditors the power to have delinquent debtors arrested to guarantee their presence in court. While this law did not give the creditor rights to the debtor's assets, the threat of imprison gave the creditor a powerful weapon. Unless debtors[26] posted bail (which required offering assets equal to the debt as security or finding someone to act as a guarantor for the debt) they had to deal with a uniform system of small claims courts in England that made it easy to recover debts. Small claims of less than £20 (raised to £50 in 1850) could be heard in 500 county courts, within fifty-nine county court circuits. Johnson notes that in 1865, these small claims courts issued 430,000 judgments, of these 70 percent were for sums of 40s. or less, and a further twenty percent were for sums of between £2 and £5.[27] Creditors merely had to file a complaint with the court's registrar. A summons was then served. If the debtor failed to appear in court, then a warrant to seize possessions or for imprisonment was issued.

Until the Debtors Act of 1869 abolished imprisonment for debt, debtors could be imprisoned until they satisfied their creditors. Even after 1869 if debtors had the means to pay but refused to do so, they could be held in contempt of court and incarcerated for up to six weeks. Once a case came to court, Johnson notes that 1–2 percent were decided in the debtor's favor.[28] Worse, debtors not only faced imprisonment, but on top of what they owed to the creditor, they also had to pay court fees. Besides court fees, the plaintiff could claim his court costs, which could add a third or more to the sum owed.[29]

The debtor's nightmare did not end there. Debtor's prisons were profit-making enterprises. Inmates had to pay for their food and lodging, as well as various fees for "services." The position of debtors in prison was slightly different from than that of felons. In theory the idea was to confine debtors, not to punish them. Debtors were segregated from the rest of the prison inmates; however, the squalid living conditions of these prisons were notorious. How well one faired in prison was tinged by class, debtors with a little money, could procure better rooms, and even could buy some freedoms. Some prisons allowed inmates to conduct business and receive visitors. The Fleet and King's Bench Prisons even allowed inmates to live a short distance outside the prison provided they compensated the keeper for loss of his earnings. Of necessity, whenever possible prisoners carried on business or earned money making handicrafts. Prisoners in the Farringdon Street Prison begged alms from passers-by from a grille in the wall. However, those unable to earn money, or without friends and family who could help provide necessities, often died in prison because of the terrible living conditions.

While the threat of imprisonment gave creditors a powerful weapon, how effective it was in debt recovery is doubtful. Given the multiple costs—time, money, and self-esteem—it is unlikely debtors willingly defaulted on the debts or willfully refused to pay if they had the means to do so. Imprisoning debtors hardly increased the creditor's chances of repayment,[30] and clearly made it harder for debtors to earn money.

CHARITY, CREDIT, AND THE STATE

As the old feudal order was transformed into capitalist one, several groups came into conflict. The landed gentry and old merchant classes who enjoyed monopolies and special licenses, and privileges—whom we may label conservatives—were opposed by the rising capitalists or liberals. Liberals, aware that the state's protective role could be abused, wanted its powers to be severely circumscribed. They sought to end the granting of royal monopolies to favored groups. They sought equality before the law. They demanded personal liberties: freedom of people to move from place to place or from job to job, freedom to buy and sell, borrow, lend, accumulate, and use their property as they saw fit.[31] The moral ideal underlying capitalism (offered by liberals like David Hume, Adam Smith, Edmund Burke, Immanuel Kant, Montesquieu, Tocqueville, J.S. Mill, and Acton) was that "human relations should, as far as possible, be based on free mutual consent instead of force or command."[32] In this view, which emphasized rule by law not men, government had two primary functions: to uphold justice and prevent abuse; and to provide essential services to be paid for by taxes with the consent of the governed. The corner stone of this liberal stance was that individuals ought to be held morally responsible in all circumstances.

One area where ancient and capitalist regimes have clashed is over the role the state should play in the provision of charity. The state had, since Tudor Times, enacted poor laws to provide funds for the relief of those unable to work: the lame, the crippled, the blind as well as young orphans, or those too old or ill to work. These funds came from taxes on property. As the numbers of indigent grew during the Industrial Revolution, there was increasing pressure to distinguish the deserving poor from able-bodied workers. This led to the persecution of paupers and beggars, often placed in houses of correction.

Symptomatic of this pressure was the passage in 1723 of Knatchbull's Act requiring any person who wanted to receive poor relief to enter a workhouse, and work in exchange for relief. By 1750 some 600 parish workhouses had been built. In the 1780s, the number of poor seeking relief rose rapidly because of high food prices, low wages, and the effects of enclosures. Liberals argued that relief to the poor undermined the position of independent laborers, and that poor laws were the cause of poverty.[33]

CREDIT AND WORKING CLASS ORGANIZATIONS

Consideration of the alternatives to simple implementation of the Poor Law provides a useful insight into the problematic and naive ways eighteenth century scholars tried to deal with numbers and derive implications therefrom. The Amendment Act of 1834 transformed Poor Law workhouses into little more than prisons, on the theory that doing so would make them less attractive than what the poor might expect outside. Yet, during the nineteenth century while these repressive institutions were evolving, there was also a rapid proliferation of voluntary associations of one sort or another that, while reflecting Victorian values of thrift, personal responsibility, and mutual aid, offered members financial assistance and credit. Associations took various forms: rotating credit associations, savings clubs, burial clubs, benefit clubs, box clubs, building societies, dividing societies, friendly societies, ancient orders, church and chapel associations, cooperatives, trade unions, and penny banks. These were alternatives to the exploitative terms of moneylenders, but also represented an alternative to the state's repressive institutions.

Voluntary associations typically had a declared purpose, a minimal set of rules, and some means of joining or becoming a member, but none of the prescriptive power of the state for enforcement. Rotating credit associations, known as *menages*, or slate[34] clubs, were among the simplest, and most prevalent associations. Rotating credit associations rested upon relations of trust with friends, kin, neighbors, coworkers, members of a congregation, social club, or trade union. In their common form members would put in a specified amount each week, and take turns receiving the collected pot, the turn being decided by lot. Depending on where in the cycle one's turn came, the pot looked more like credit or more like savings. Savings, it should be remembered, when entrusted to others is a loan to them. Many of these savings clubs were organized for particular purposes—often to buy a commodity that otherwise, they could not afford—blankets, a goose, etc.[35]

During the nineteenth century, dividing societies and friendly societies evolved to become the most important providers of social welfare in Britain. These societies were self-governing mutual-aid associations founded by manual workers to provide against hard times. Members contributed sums weekly for stipulated benefits, typically for medical expenses or sick pay during an illness that left them unable to work. Mayhew describes a dividing society organized among paper-workers who sold various kinds of tracts:

> The Benefit Society of Patterers ... "sprung up accidental" as it was expressed to me. A few paper-workers were conversing ... and one ... suggested a benefit club ... It was established [and had 40 to 50 members] ... The subscription was 2d a week, and meetings of the members were held once a week. Each member, not an officer, paid 1/2d for admission to the fund, and could introduce a visitor, who also paid 1/2d. No charge was made for use of the club-room (in a public house) ... Every one using bad language was fined 1/2d, and on second offense was ejected, and sometimes, if the misbehavior was gross, on the first ... [The purpose for the society was to provide financial assistance when members were sick.] The assistance has 5s. weekly to sick members, who were not in arrears in the subscriptions. If the man had a family to support, a gathering was made for him, in addition to his weekly allowance ... There was no allowance for the burial of a member, but a gathering took place, and perhaps a raffle, to raise funds for a wake (sometimes) and an interment.[36]

Dividing societies differed from friendly societies primarily in the length of member investments. In dividing societies, funds were accumulated for no longer than a year. At year's end, any funds left would be divided among the members, often with some ceremony before Christmas. Each society was completely autonomous. Some societies[37] had no written rules; others had elaborate rule books, but one of their strongest attractions was their self-governing character.[38] Often meeting in a local tavern or public house, most of these societies began as local clubs, holding their common fund in a wooden chest or strongbox. However, some of these during the nineteenth century evolved into national federations with hundreds of thousands of members and carefully managed investments.[39]

The historical rise of dividing societies and friendly societies is particularly interesting, as it speaks to class interests and dynamics. Although friendly societies were established as early as the sixteenth century "Incorporation of Carters in Scotland" concurrent with the Industrial Revolution, their rapid expansion began in the eighteenth century. "By 1801 an authoritative study by Sir Frederic Eden estimated that there were about 7,200 societies with around 648,000 adult male members out of a total population of about nine million."[40] While such societies were working class organizations, the governing classes, motivated by the rising costs of poor relief had made sporadic attempts to impose friendly societies on particular groups of workers. Between 1757 and 1770, coal heavers working on the River Thames were forced to contribute to a friendly society organized and administered by the

City of London. In 1792 shippers and keelmen working in the coal trades on the River Wear were compelled to join a friendly society.[41]

In the wake of the French Revolution and Napoleonic Wars the attitude of governing classes toward such societies was mixed.[42] While friendly societies reduced both the numbers of poor and the cost of providing relief, self-governing organization of the poor, raised fears that such societies were a threat to the social order. Legislation was enacted (the Seditious Meetings Acts of 1795 and 1817, the Unlawful Societies Act of 1799, and the Combination Acts of 1799–1800) that cast a shadow of illegality over these societies until 1846. In 1834, the "Tolpuddle Martyrs" were sentenced to seven years transportation for establishing the "Friendly Society of Agricultural Labourers," a part trade union concerned to maintain the wages and part friendly society, creating a fund members could call on in times of sickness, accident, or other hardship.[43]

Up to 1834, justices of the peace were required to satisfy themselves that the rules of a society were "fit and proper" and "in conformity with law"; and, that two actuaries skilled in calculation had approved a society's tables of contributions and benefits. The Friendly Societies Act of 1834 removed these restrictions. In its stead, a centralized system of registration was instituted. It simply required a government barrister (later the Registrar) to be satisfied that the society's rules conformed to the law, effectively allowing friendly societies to engage in any activity not otherwise illegal. The 1846 Friendly Societies Act finally declared that the Seditious Meetings Act did not apply to friendly societies.[44]

In 1834 the Poor Laws were amended to make relief available to able-bodied workers and their families only within workhouses. By 1840 government per capita expenditures on relief had fallen by 45 percent and there was a sharp rise in friendly society membership. Where in the early 1830s, membership in friendly societies probably totaled 600,000 members or 16 percent of adult males, by 1850 conservative estimates suggest that some two million men or about 40 percent of adult males belonged to friendly societies.[45] In 1870 a Crusade against outrelief, further limited the relief available outside workhouses and spurred further growth in friendly society membership. The Royal Commission on Friendly Societies (1870–1874) estimated membership at about four million. A recent estimate puts it at between 3 and 3.5 million. In sum, after 1834 the responses of the working class to government policies were the cornerstone of the major shifts in their coping strategies.[46]

This meant that somewhat less than half of working-class households had savings accounts or were members of friendly societies that paid sickness benefits. Not just skilled workers were involved. Dock workers had their own societies, large numbers of lowly paid railway workers could be found in major friendly societies, and the members of Ancient Order of Foresters were mostly unskilled laborers.[47] It is probable that steady work was the key to membership, that workers lacking regular employment could not save any money or afford the premiums charged by friendly societies, even if they offered significant benefits. Around the turn of the nineteenth century, Charles Booth and Seebohm Rowntree showed that there were additional[48] holes in the public-private safety net:[49] living in poverty were large numbers of elderly, sick, and underemployed, with little or no savings, who did not belong to friendly societies or trade unions. Either out of shame or fear of the workhouse, this segment of the population also refused to apply for poor relief.[50]

SAVINGS BANKS

While no mainstream banker in the early nineteenth century would have lent to England's poor, it was clear that while working men may not have much per household, as a class they represented significant sums. In 1810, a Scottish clergyman, Rev. Henry Duncan (1774–1846), established a savings bank for his parishioners, inspiring a savings bank movement that spread to England. In 1817, to encourage working-class savings, Parliament passed a savings bank act that established Trustee Savings Banks. Under the Act, each bank was to be supervised by an honorary Board of Trustees. Surplus, beyond that required for its operations, was to be deposited with the National Debt Commissioners in a Fund for the Savings Banks at the Bank of England.

This legislation was a phenomenal success. Almost immediately, savings banks sprang up all across the British Isles. By 1818, there were 465 such banks. By 1847, small deposits in Trustee Saving Banks amounted to than £30 million in savings. Despite the impressive sums deposited in Trustee Savings Banks, they were so plagued by fraud and mismanagement that between 1818 and 1844, seven further Acts were required to regulate them.[51]

In the 1850s, C.W. Sikes, a banker in West Yorkshire, established a number of penny banks connected to Mechanic Institutes in Huddersfield. These inspired Colonel Edward Ackroyd in 1859 to open the Yorkshire Penny Bank, which was to become the most successful of the penny banks, accumulating £100,000 by 1865, more than a £1 million by 1884, and £12.5 million by 1900. In 1859, Sikes wrote to William Gladstone, then the Chancellor of the Exchequer, to propose a national system of postal savings banks that would place banks within an hour's walk of everyone in Great Britain. Gladstone quickly saw that it had the potential of placing huge sums of cheap money at the government's disposal, and was, moreover, consistent with his Liberal ideology of reforms to provide citizens equal opportunities while emphasizing individual responsibility. In 1861, the Post Office Savings Bank was created. In 1864, Gladstone persuaded the House of Commons to pass a Government Annuities Act that allowed Post Offices to offer cheap annuities.[52]

The promotion of savings banks by Liberals was intended to reduce the expenditures on relief for the poor by promoting self-help.[53] By 1870, relief was half of its 1830 level, and annual expenditures on relief were less than a third of working class deposits in savings banks. Trustee Savings Banks and Post Office Savings Banks proved to be enormously popular. By 1870, almost 25 percent of working class households had savings accounts, and by 1913 this number was nearly two-thirds of such households.[54]

CONSUMER CREDIT VIA INSTALLMENT SELLING

One of the first steps toward modern consumer credit was installment sales, scheduled partial payments made until goods are fully paid. In the mid-nineteenth century, it was the sale of sewing machines that really popularized this form of credit. While sewing machines were being mass-produced, purchasing a sewing machine that cost between $50 and $150 was beyond the means of most individuals. While manufacturers found a ready market for their machines in the garment industry, they understood that millions of families were their largest potential market. Edward Clark of the Singer Sewing Machine Company proposed to rent them, and apply the rental fee toward the purchase price.[55]

The underlying idea of lease-purchase allowed qualified buyers easy terms, such as Singer's dollar down and a dollar a week, yet the underlying lease-purchase contract gave Singer legal standing to repossess the unit in the event of non-payment.[56] In 1904, the Spiegel Company took this idea even further. Establishing a mail order department that advertised, "We Trust People—Everywhere," it extended credit nationwide. While the catalog promised customers "all the time you need to pay," this generally meant a year. What they didn't advertise was that credit charges of 5.2 percent were hidden in their prices, higher than elsewhere. Within two years, the mail order department was doing twice the business of its retail stores.[57]

Installment sales became big business with the advent of the automobile industry. Even mass production could not lower the price enough for the mass market. Initially, car manufacturers expected dealers to make a deposit on order, and pay cash on delivery. Dealers could not afford to extend credit to manufacturers and consumers. Banks would lend capital at interest to dealers to purchase stock, but financing consumer auto loans was, initially, out of the question. Such loans violated every canon of traditional banking practices: consumption loans did not automatically produce profit, repayment schedules were too long, and because cars depreciate the security they offered was dubious.

In 1913, sales finance companies were created to solve this problem. These acted as intermediaries between banks, dealers, and their customers. They could borrow from banks and give qualified customers access to credit. In 1915 the Guarantee Security Company devised a model of finance that became standard in the industry. The company not only provided auto loans through dealers, but also lent dealers the capital needed to buy vehicles from factories at wholesale prices. Guarantee Security Company also helped established the practice of "floor planning" which allowed dealers to display automobiles in showrooms even when the vehicles belonged to the finance company.[58]

THE CREDIT BUREAU: TRUST AND ENFORCEMENT

Extending credit to strangers required a series of innovations. The obvious issues are not simply how to decide who to trust and how far; but also what to do if they default. This begins with assessing risk. Because of jurisdictional issues, differences in state laws, crowded dockets, long delays, it was often not worth the expenses involved to take a debtor to court, and even if one did, there was no guarantee of loan recovery. The evolution of modern states, as Scott has argued, has required increasing legibility, and has driven bureaucracies to gather information on their citizens. To sort the creditworthy from the untrustworthy has forced the private sector to engage in an analogous intelligence effort.[59] Modern consumer credit was made possible by the development of credit reporting systems, and collection and repossession agencies.

Currently, there are three major U.S. consumer credit agencies Trans Union, Equifax, and Experion that either own or have contracts with the more than a thousand local and region credit bureaus in the United States. These big three maintain enormous databases on over 200 million Americans. They gather data from thousands of sources, retailers, credit card companies, financial institutions, and companies of all sizes, each month on how people pay and use their accounts; and supplement this information with public records of bankruptcies, tax liens, monetary judgments, delinquent child support payments, etc. This massive project of assembling individual credit histories is not simply surveillance it is, like Foucault's metaphor of the Panopticon based on the architecture of Bentham's ideal prison, also an instrument of discipline.[60]

The two billion credit reports generated each year determine whether credit is extended and govern its rates and terms. In the United States in the

1830s, the first credit reporting firms was formed. Lewis Tappen (1788–1873), a silk merchant in New York, founded one of the earliest of these. He began keeping files on customers to assess their character and credit-worthiness. Soon, other merchants were turning to him for advice. In 1841, Tappen turned this into a business: Tappen's Mercantile Agency. By 1851, the company—which was eventually, to become Dun & Bradstreet—had established an elaborate system of branch offices with 2,000 full-time local correspondents who gathered, codified, and processed information about tens of thousands of firms.

Beginning in 1850s the firm published a "Reference Book" that offered fairly systematic and comparable information about firms and rating their credit-worthiness. By 1859, their reference volumes rated 20,268 companies. This number grew to nearly 1.3 million by 1900.[61] Reports by early credit agencies went well beyond financial assets; they tried to assess the moral character of businessmen. Aside from an individual's capital resources and business skills and experience ("capacity"), the agencies sought to discover whether individuals were honest or dishonest, punctual, or tardy with payments, thrifty or extravagant, energetic or slothful, and focused or unfocused. Agencies inquired about a borrower's vices but restricted this inquiry to drinking and gambling. Agencies wanted to know, too, about a borrower's age and marital status. All these traits had one thing in common: they tended to affect a borrower's liquidity and perceived willingness to pay their debts in a timely manner.[62]

DEVELOPMENT OF RISK BASED CONSUMER LOANS

Credit bureaus provided the lender a valuable tool to decide who was a good risk, but also a tangible threat that aided in collection. Failures to pay debts could ruin one's credit standing. Because a bad credit report would follow a person no matter where they moved to in the country, making this threat was both more credible and cost-effective than the courts.[63] This system was not without serious drawbacks. No standards about fairness or accuracy existed. Competitors to Dun & Bradstreet pushed their way into the market in the 1870s and 1880s, offering reports at cut rate prices, with little regard to reliability. In 1906, an international trade association, Associated Credit Bureaus, Inc. was founded to allow members to share fraud prevention and risk management products and provided collection services, but also to set standards, and lobbied state and federal governments to support those standards.[64]

Despite Associated Credit Bureaus Inc. the protection of consumer's rights took nearly a century to come into being; and, was linked to the development of civil rights. Even in the 1960s, consumers still had no rights to inspect their credit reports; which, besides financial data also contained comments about lifestyle such as sexual orientation or drinking habits. If we use Douglas' ideas about "Purity and Danger," we see hiding beneath the language of moral character are the class values and racial prejudices of white elites who construct anyone that may be different from themselves as suspect, dangerous, and risky.[65]

During the civil rights movements of the 1960s, it became increasingly obvious that the criteria and language of credit reports institutionalized patterns of discrimination. So, in 1970 Congress enacted the Fair Credit Reporting Act (FCRA) that defined the categories of information that credit bureaus could and could not use, and gave consumers the right to see their reports. While the act permitted bureaus to gather information about current and former address, marital status, age, social security number, employment history, and information from public records, such as judgments or bankruptcies, it specifically forbade them from gathering any information about race, religious preferences, medical history, personal life style, personal background, political affiliations, or criminal record.

While the FCRA (which has been amended several times, most notably in 1993 and 2003) attempts to balance benefits credit bureaus provide to the market against consumer privacy and concerns about accuracy, it does so in a peculiar way.[66] While it gives consumers the right to review their credit reports, it also places burdens of correcting inaccuracies on them. It also predictably limits the credit bureau's liability. While it enjoins credit bureaus not to provide erroneous data knowingly, unless falsehoods are entered with malicious and willful intent to injure a consumer, inaccuracies in themselves are not a violation of the act. So while FCRA provides mechanisms to allow consumers to correct their reports, it also prevents them from suing credit bureaus, or credit reports users, or information providers for defamation, invasion of privacy, or negligence.[67] The FCRA also contains provisions that prevent "states from enacting legislation affecting such aspects of credit reporting."[68]

The FCRA, however, did force credit bureaus to devise, more defensible, and seemingly more objective algorithms that weight factors to produce a score that predicts default rates.[69] The lower the score in these formulae the greater the risk. These scores as Gandy[70] and Lyon[71] argue, permit panoptic sorting and triaging of consumers to decide who is worthy of credit, and how they are to be treated. In this process, information, and actions that were once embedded in personal relations, become a matter of quantifiable probability and risk. Credit becomes a matter of actuarial risk, based on the economic behavior of consumers sorted into groups by these scores. While seemingly objective, scores must still be created and interpreted, and the credit and terms that consumers may be offered will vary accordingly.

Credit reporting, distilled into individual credit scores, needs to be understood as part and parcel of wider processes of abstraction and discretization within capital.[72] Just as houses are abstracted by legal description and mortgage details, credit scores abstract economic behavior generally. Analogously wages, individually or as corporate wage bills, represent discretized labor as a factor of production that can be calculated separately from actual people. Where once personal reputation and credit were embedded in social relations, processes of abstraction and discretization have reduced social relations to credit scores, thereby creating fungible value, a disembodied form of social capital.[73]

Bourdieu and Wacquant define social capital as "the sum of the resources, actual or virtual, that accrue to an individual or a group by virtue of possessing a durable network of more or less institutionalized relationships of mutual acquaintance and recognition."[74] Their explanation of how social capital could be appropriated or converted into economic capital leaves something out. By the discretization of social relations what credit scores do is effectively privatize and institutionalize social information to create a form of social capital that can be appropriated, and from which others can derive profits. In sum, value in social capital today is about reliable information that can be more easily appropriated by others; it is through such processes of discretization that social capital is now subsumed by capital.

CREDIT CARDS

Although the evolution of credit reporting, along with computers, made the modern credit card industry possible, its roots go back to at least the early 1900s, when retail stores began issuing charge cards to their better customers. These were little more than an extension of carrying customers on their books, something retailers had long done. Such loyalty cards were good only at their own stores, but oil companies soon picked up on the value of "courtesy cards." In 1924, they began to issue gas credit cards, which could be used at the company's stations all across the country.

In the late 1940s, retailers began experimenting[75] with revolving lines of credit that allowed customers to carry a balance as long as they did not exceed their credit limit, and made a minimum monthly payment. In 1948, several New York department stores banded together to issue a charge plate that could be used in all their stores. While these credit charges were cleared through a central agency, they did not have the same intent as modern credit cards. Retailers who participated did so primarily to aid sales and promote customer loyalty.

The issuing of charge cards was not a profit making enterprise in and of itself.[76] The first card to be set up as a business itself was Diners' Club. In 1950, Diners' Club began issuing cards to consumers to use at twenty-seven restaurants in New York City, then Los Angeles. Soon, the company was seeking to enroll hotels and retail stores all across the country. Unlike earlier special purpose cards, Diners' Club was the first general purpose charge card that multiple merchants beyond a local geographic area would accept as payment.[77] In 1958, American Express got into the card business, introducing its green card. Such cards were extremely profitable, participating merchants paid a service charge on each sale, and cardholders paid an annual fee for the privilege of having the card.[78]

Banks soon realized that credit cards could be a real moneymaker. In 1951, the Franklin National Bank of Long Island introduced the first bank credit card. Quickly emulated, by 1953 local banks across the country offered sixty plans. Most of these local programs lacked the economies of scale to be successful, so more than half soon failed. In 1958, Chase Manhattan and Bank of America entered the field.[79] The initial challenge they faced was how to persuade merchants to sign up, especially as they charged hefty service fees. Bank of America's approach was to initially issue cards to its 60,000 customers in Fresno demonstrating to local retailers that they had enough consumers to make participation worthwhile. Chase Manhattan invited consumers to apply for cards and screened them.

To convince merchants to accept their cards, they offered to waive a $25 registration fee. Although Diners' Club, American Express, and various banks offered general purpose cards, each card issuer set up essentially a closed ecosystem populated by specific consumers and retailers, with themselves at the center. These closed systems were problematic, and only marginally successful. Merchants were reluctant to sign up with several issuing banks; and, consumers found cards with little acceptance or geographic coverage unattractive.[80]

The solution was the evolution of open systems. In 1966 Bank of America set up the Bank America Service Corporation to franchise to banks across the nation its Bank Americard (later to become Visa). About the same time, competing banks set up the Interbank Card Association, which later became MasterCard. These open-system associations require banks to cooperate. When a merchant charges a card, the amount and cardholder's details are sent to the merchant's bank, which if it is not the issuer, forwards it to the issuing bank, which then either approves or declines the transaction.[81]

The impact of the evolution of credit cards is readily apparent in Federal Reserve statistics on consumer debt. In 1928 The Federal Reserve began amassing data on consumer debt. In 1928, consumer debt reached $6.5 billion. It rose to $7.7 billion in 1929, and 6.9 billion in 1930. Debt rose smoothly until 1958 when it totaled $45 billion. Then, suddenly, the trend line rose more rapidly reaching $94.9 billion in 1965. By 1988 consumer debt reached $666 billion, which meant that the average American household owned approximately $7,400 for consumer purchases.[82]

One implication of the rapid rises in consumer debt is that banks competing for this market rapidly saturated the good credit risks, and were forced to move toward the base of the consumer pyramid: from the wealthy, to the middle-class, to the poor. Despite the 1862 Homestead Act facilitating ownership of property by single, widowed or divorced women it was not until 1974, that the Equal Credit Opportunity Act was passed in the United States which for the first time allowed single, widowed, or divorced women to apply for credit without a male co-signer. This is approximately 4,000 years later than women acquired such rights in Ancient Egypt or Ancient Mesopotamia[83] and in the case of United States this concession was probably motivated by a search for gain rather than for justice. Banks understood, because service fees generate small profits on every transaction, more cardholders meant greater potential earnings. In chasing larger segments of the market, banks had to rethink their terms. The original vision of Diners' Club and American Express was that consumer credit was short term, and accounts were paid in full at the end of the month. When Chase Manhattan introduced its card in 1958, the terms would allow the payment of a charge to be spread over five months, with a one percent interest charged on the unpaid balance. To attract the less-than-well-off consumer, banks discovered that the terms had to be different.

Consumers were willing to pay higher interest rates, as long as the minimum payment was smaller. Smaller minimums require longer terms of repayment. Long-term, high interest loans are, of course, more profitable for banks. They discovered that because credit affords consumers greater flexibility in handling their finances, cardholders were willing to pay annual fees, late fees, and even higher interest rates, all of which made credit even more profitable.[84] Usury laws stood in the way of greater profits in many states, preventing card issuers from charging higher interest rates. Each time market interest rates on corporate bonds and Treasury bills rose sharply; banks' profits on credit cards dropped. In the late 1970s and early 1980s, during the period of stagflation, this problem was particularly vexing.

With Reagan's election in 1980, there was a sharp neoliberal turn in fiscal policy toward deregulation. In 1978, Supreme Court's decision (*Marquette National*[85] *Bank v. First of Omaha Service Corporation*) held that interest rates regardless of where cardholders reside are governed by the laws of the state where the loan is made. This decision opened new opportunities to card companies as it permitted them to incorporate and run their credit card operations from states that gave them the best deal. One such place was South

Dakota, which had recently struck usury laws from their books. In the early 1980s, card companies rushed in. No longer constrained by usury limits, they could target the risky bottom of the pyramid as never before. Now students graduating high school, even before they have jobs, are routinely offered credit cards.

The deregulation of credit card rates was part of a broader pattern of neoliberal deregulation across many industries. Banking was deregulated in dramatic ways: during the 1980s and early 1990s. The neoliberal arguments that held sway at the time had it that regulations create inefficiencies and hamper the competitiveness of US banks that cost them market share both domestically and internationally. Proponents framed the choice starkly, either deregulate now, or there will be nothing left to regulate. Between 1987 and 1999 restrictions on bank underwriting activities, branch banking, consolidation limits, separation of commercial and investment banking, and conflict-of-interest rules that created "firewalls" between banks and their nonbank affiliates were relaxed.[85] While it can be argued that deregulation made US banks more competitive, and profitable, it also opened the doors to a darker side, predatory lending, and turned what used to be the sin of usury into the virtue of profit.

While credit card companies must disclose the annual percentage rate (APR), they generally try to conceal the actual costs to the consumer of the money they lend. As the APR depends both on the prime rate of interest established by the Federal Reserve Board and the consumer's credit score, it is subjected to change. A cardholder that pays charges off each month may not pay any interest. But, suppose he or she pays 7.9 percent APR and owes $1000 and pays the loan off in five years, it will cost $214 in interest fees. This same loan at 18.9 percent APR paid off in five years would cost an additional $535 in interest; and, at 29.9 percent APR, it would cost an additional $937 in interest. In a desperate case scenario, this $1000 loan at 29.9 percent, if one were to pay it out in standard payments over twenty years, principle and interest would amount to $4995. Should the borrower opt for minimum payments the situation would be much worse because sums would compound into stupendous sums.

Paying high prices for money quickly escalates problems when funds are already in short enough supply to make paying high interest rates even remotely attractive. The system therefore discriminates heavily against the poor and matters are aggravated by Madison Avenue efforts to inculcate "needs." Deregulation also gave birth to a new industry; the pay-day loan and check cashing companies, whose presence has changed the landscape of poor and not so poor neighborhoods. A similar predatory profile is seen in the mortgage market, where a wide range of practices have evolved in deregulated markets. We examine this in the next chapter on the 2008 credit crisis.

CONCLUSION: INSTABILITY AND AN ETHICAL VOID

This chapter has provided the consumer credit background for the 2008 crisis examined in detail in the next and final chapter. We have shown how the subprime lending industry came to be built like a house of cards from which clever people sought to extract maximal profits. By 2007, the consequence led to the bankruptcy of Countrywide, and a mounting wave of foreclosures that caused more than 100 subprime mortgage lending companies to fail. As the underlying value of the mortgage assets fell, the market for mortgage backed securities collapsed as well because mortgage companies had passed their rights to mortgage payments on to third-party investors via mortgage backed securities and collateralized debt obligations.

The damage affected investors not just in those markets, but people who never invested in them. House values fell as countless foreclosed properties flooded the market, draining away equity, which in turn threatened community property tax revenues and everything they financed. While many blame this debacle on the lack of Federal oversight (which is itself a consequence of neoliberal deregulation), more insight is gained by viewing it as a part of wider processes by which predatory policies oriented toward elite short-term profits regularly reallocate wealth.

NOTES

1. World Bank, *World Development Report* 2006, *Equity and Development*, 89.
2. Stern et al., *Environmentally Significant Consumption*.
3. The terms come from Sen's *Commodities and Capabilities*.
4. Weisdorf, "From Domestic Manufacture to Industrial Revolution: Long-Run Growth and Agricultural Development," 270.
5. Duchesne and Hilton, "The Peasant Road to 'Capitalism' in England," 143–44.
6. Holderness, "Credit in English Rural Society before the Nineteenth Century, with Special Reference to the Period 1650–1720," 98.
7. Weisdorf, "From Domestic Manufacture to Industrial Revolution: Long-Run Growth and Agricultural Development," 270.
8. Mayhew, *London Labor and the London Poor*, vols 1–4.
9. Engels, *The Condition of the Working-Class in England*, 69.
10. Heyman, "The Organizational Logic of Capitalist Consumption on the Mexico-United States Border," 175–238.
11. Marx, *Capital*, vol. I, Part Six.
12. Shipton, "Two East African Systems of Land Rights," 85.
13. Engels, *The Condition of the Working-Class in England*, 70.
14. Mayhew, *London Labor and the London Poor*, vol. 1, 29.
15. Hobsbawm, *The Age of Capital*, 35.

16. Mayhew, *London Labor and the London Poor,* vol. 1, 29–33.
17. Ibid., 31.
18. Ibid., 30–31.
19. Finn, *The Character of Credit.*
20. Mayhew, 1968, vol. 1, p. 31.
21. Ibid., 33.
22. Benson, *The Rise of Consumer Society in Britain.*
23. Glennie, "Consumption, Consumerism, and Urban Form: Historical Perspectives," 932.
24. Engels, *The Condition of the Working-Class in England,* 110.
25. Ibid.
26. Johnson, "Small Debts and Economic Distress in England and Wales," 69.
27. Innes, "The King's Bench Prison in the Later Eighteenth Century: Law, Authority and Order in a London Debtors' Prison," 253.
28. Johnson, "Small Debts and Economic Distress in England and Wales," 68.
29. Ibid., 67.
30. Ibid., 70–71.
31. Ibid., 71.
32. Green, *Reinventing Civil Society: The Rediscovery of Welfare without Politics,* 9–10.
33. Ibid., 11.
34. Poovey, *A History of the Modern Fact,* 307ff.
35. Morris, "Urban Associations in England and Scotland, 1750–1914: The Formation of the Middle Class or the Formation of a Civil Society?" 139–40.
36. Ardener, "The Comparative Study of Rotating Credit Associations," 201–29.
37. Mayhew, *London Labor and the London Poor,* vol. 1, 242.
38. Gilbert, "The Decay of Nineteenth Century British Provident Institutions and the Coming of Old Age Pensions in Great Britain," 550–63.
39. Green, *Reinventing Civil Society: The Rediscovery of Welfare without Politics,* 26–27.
40. Ibid., 25.
41. Ibid., 26.
42. Ibid., 42.
43. Riots and radicalization of urban proletariat were common in midcentury, (Hobsbawm, *The Age of Capital,* 22).
44. Green, *Reinventing Civil Society: The Rediscovery of Welfare without Politics,* 73.
45. Ibid., 74–75.
46. Boyer, "Insecurity, Safety Nets, and Self-help in Victorian Britain," 59–61.
47. Ibid., 68, 47.
48. Green, *Reinventing Civil Society: The Rediscovery of Welfare without Politics,* 54–55.
49. Booth, "The Inaugural Address of Charles Booth, Esq., President of the Royal Statistical Society. Session 1892–93. Delivered 15th November, 1892," 521–57; Mayhew, *Life and Labour of the People in London, vol. 2;* Booth, *The Aged Poor in England and Wales.*

50. Rowntree, *Poverty: A Study of Town Life.*
51. Boyer, "Insecurity, Safety Nets, and Self-help in Victorian Britain," 26–27.
52. Ibid., 14.
53. Davies, "A History of Money," 334–38.
54. The liberal motives in promoting savings banks for the poor may be reasonably seen as the antecedents to the modern microcredit movement which neoliberal ideologies similarly motivate. See Greenberg, "Microfinance, Law, and Development: A Case Study in Mali," 135–62.
55. Johnson, *Saving and Spending: The Working-Class Economy in Britain,* 91–92; Boyer, "Insecurity, Safety Nets, and Self-help in Victorian Britain," 22–27.
56. Calder, *Financing the American Dream,* 164.
57. Ibid., 164–65.
58. Ibid., 173–75.
59. Ibid., 185–89.
60. Scott, *Seeing Like a State.*
61. Foucault, *Discipline and Punish.*
62. Rowena. *A Culture of Credit: Embedding Trust and Transparency in American Business,* 6.
63. Ibid., 7.
64. Greif, "Commitment, Coercion, and Markets: The Nature and Dynamics of Institutions Supporting Exchange," 738.
65. Madison, "The Evolution of Commercial Credit Reporting Agencies in Nineteenth-Century America," 184–85.
66. Douglas, *Purity and Danger.*
67. Hunt, "A Century of Consumer Credit Reporting in America."
68. Ibid., 51.
69. Ibid., 31.
70. Avery et al., "Overview of Consumer Data and Credit Reporting."
71. Gandy, *The Panoptic Sort: A Political Economy of Personal Information.*
72. Lyon, *Theorizing Surveillance.*
73. Greenberg and Heyman, "Neoliberal Capital and the Mobility Approach in Anthropology."
74. Bourdieu, "The Forms of Capital."
75. Bourdieu and Wacquant, *An Invitation to Reflexive Sociology,* 119.
76. Sienkiewicz, "Credit Cards and Payment Efficiency," 1–13.
77. Wolters, "Carry Your Credit in Your Pocket: The Early History of the Credit Card at Bank of America and Chase Manhattan," 320.
78. Sienkiewicz, "Credit Cards and Payment Efficiency," 3.
79. Wolters, "Carry Your Credit in Your Pocket: The Early History of the Credit Card at Bank of America and Chase Manhattan," 321–322.
80. Ibid., 322–324.
81. Sienkiewicz, 2001, 3.
82. Sienkiewicz, "Credit Cards and Payment Efficiency," 4–5.
83. Calder, *Financing the American Dream,* 10.

84. See Park and Greenberg, *Roots of Western Finance*, Chapters 1 & 3.
85. Kahr, "The Secret History of the Credit Card."
86. For a detailed discussion of Neoliberalism See Greenberg, et al., "Theorizing Neoliberalism," 33–50.
87. Calomiris, *U.S. Bank Deregulation in Historical Perspective*, xi–xv.

Chapter 9

An Anthropology of the 2008 Credit Crisis

John A. Paulson, billionaire and hedge fund manager of Paulson & Company, in an interview noted, "Bankruptcy investing is also a very attractive area. ... the economy went into recession after Lehman Brothers failed ... we bought Extended Stay, a 50% discount ... did some management changes, some restructuring ... . So we put in $1.5 billion in 2010, and now that $1.5 billion is worth $6 billion."[1]

Unlike for Paulson, for many the subprime mortgage crisis that began in 2007, unfolded like a bad vampire movie with a script that drained the lifeblood of millions of innocent victims; many of whom lost their homes, and saw their pensions, stocks, securities, and other investments lose value. Unfortunately, most of the standard economic explanations of this credit crisis seem content with skating over the surface of the problem.

In this chapter, we argue that the roots of the 2008 credit crises include deep systemic disorders, the erosion of ethics, and the dissipation of concerns about transparency in financial matters. We evaluate standard economic explanations, in light of the historical record discussed in earlier chapters, the human costs of the crisis, and the logic of justice in lending.

AN OVERVIEW OF THE MORTGAGE CRISIS

The short-term plot of this horror movie is well known though we suggest that the plot is but the tip of the iceberg. The epicenter of the crisis started in the mortgage markets where banks and mortgage brokers discovered they could make money by lending to the large pool of high risk home buyers with low credit ratings, the so-called subprime market. Realizing the potential profits to be made in this pool of potential buyers, they created new kinds of mortgages and packaged them in obtuse mortgage backed securities whose real risks were almost impossible to discern.

They issued adjustable rate mortgages (ARMs) with artificially low, teaser interest rates that would adjust after a number of years to a profitable percentage above the Fed's prime rate, the rate at which banks borrow money. Another common instrument was a mortgage with low payments for a fixed number of years, after which a large balloon payment would come due. Buyers steered into such loans were led to believe that when these rates adjusted, or balloon payments came due, they could refinance their loan or use their equity to get into a better home. House prices after all were on the rise. While NIJA loans (to those with no income, jobs, or assets) have gotten the most press, because commission rates were higher on such subprime loans—high incentives also drove brokers to push many better-qualified buyers into these types of mortgages.

Banks and mortgage companies knew perfectly well the risks involved in lending to the subprime segment of the population but believed that such risks were calculable. Even if a buyer defaulted, the collateral for the loan, the house, could always be sold to another buyer. To offset the risks of default and foreclosure, net interest rates were higher on such loans. Taking a statistical approach to risk, banks bundled thousands of mortgages together into new financial products—mortgage-backed securities (MBSs) and collateralized debt obligations (CDOs).

A MBS represents a claim on the cash flow from monthly payments from a set of mortgages. By bundling mortgages together into securities, this both artfully blended and disguised the inherent risks, and offered banks an attractive way of turning debts into salable assets. To make these securities attractive to investors, banks began slicing their riskiest MBS into CDO slices, called "tranches" (to Anglophones the French seemed more sophisticated than the English "slices") of varying quality.[2]

The top-tier of CDOs, which contained the cash flows from the least risky mortgages qualified for AAA ratings, but also paid the least interest. For a fee these could be insured against default through credit default swaps (CDS). The next tier qualified for BBB ratings and offered higher interest rates, but also greater risk of defaults that would reduce the flow of payments. The bottom tier of unrated toxic assets carried high risk but offered investors such as hedge funds high returns in the short term.

Following the dot-com bubble and the terrorist attacks of 9/11, the Federal Reserve lowered interest rates to one percent, and continued to hold interest rates low into mid-2004, so the demand for asset securities was high. MBSs and CDOs offered better returns than U.S. treasury bills and could also be used as collateral.[3] Wall Street as well as investors around the world quickly bought them up. "Banks earned large fees securitizing mortgages, selling them to capital markets and servicing them after they were sold."[4] The sale of such securities allowed lenders to make a profit and to recoup their capital, so they could make more loans; and, importantly, move the riskier loans off their books.[5] This strategy of "originate and distribute" thus generated commissions and fees for those originating mortgages, and cunningly transferred default risks to buyers of "securities."

The illusion of security these financial instruments provided created an enormous market for them, and they quickly spread across the financial system—from investment banks, savings, and loans, mortgage companies, investment houses, pension funds, insurance companies, to other institutional and individual investors. With cheap credit readily available throughout the financial system, banks and investment firms borrowed heavily to leverage deals, and gorged on short-term profits accessible through these assets.

Leveraging allowed investment banks, and other entities to use a small amount of their own capital (cash or assets) to borrow much larger amounts needed to buy mortgages, which once sold or transformed into securities could provide the funds needed not just to payoff these loans, but to reap high profits. By the time the subprime crises hit in 2007 the pool of mortgage based assets stood at about $7.5 trillion, of which some $5 trillion had been securitized by government sponsored enterprises or agencies, while the remaining $2.5 trillion had been securitized by private sector firms.[6]

A chink in this leveraged borrowing was that it carried its own inherent risks from exposure. Prior to the financial melt-down, for example, "Morgan Stanley and Lehman Brothers had leverage (assets to shareholders' equity) of 33-to-1, while Merrill Lynch had leverage of 28-to-1 ... [and] a broad range of both commercial and investment banks had significant leverage, including Barclays Bank (61-to-1), Deutsche Bank (53-to-1), UBS (47-to-1), Fortis (33-to-1), Lehman Brothers (31-to-1), Goldman Sachs (26-to-1) and Bank of America (11-to-1)."[7] Seeking to manage risks, institutions attempted to hedge their exposure by buying credit default swaps (CDSs)—basically a derivative contract invented by J.P. Morgan Chase in 1997. CDSs function like insurance and pay off if insured securities default. Complicating matters, however, there was a market for CDSs, which allowed investors to bet against the solvency of a corporation for speculative purposes. In this CDS market, buyers need not own the underlying security, nor even face a potential loss to participate.

To draw an analogy, unlike buying car insurance, anyone can buy these derivatives—and like betting on the ponies—be paid if this security defaults. Like insurance the annual premium paid for CDS protection depends on risk, a small percentage of its face value. Risk changes through time, so investors in the CDS market look at the percentage spread between rates, measured in points—where one percent equals hundred points—and speculate on the changes in CDS spreads of individual companies or indexes, such as the North American CDX or the European iTraxx.

Between 1998 and 2008, the size of the CDS market increased "100 fold ... as banks, hedge funds, insurance companies, and other investors used such contracts to protect against losses or speculate on debt they didn't own."[8] Because there is no central market for CDSs and they are traded over the counter (OTC), it is hard to be sure of the size of the market, but subsequent estimates put it at between $33 and $47 trillion dollars. Regardless of which figure one chooses for 2008, the CDS market dwarfed both the $18.5 trillion in U.S. stock market and $4.5 trillion in the U.S. Treasury bond market.[9]

From 2005–2006, as the Federal Reserve began to raise the prime interest rate, the subprime mortgage crisis began to unfold. Facing rising interest and payments on their adjustable rate loans, and finding refinancing difficult, people began to default on their loans, and foreclosure rates rose dramatically. Hoping to avoid foreclosure, many more people put their homes up for sale causing home prices to drop. As they did, many homeowners found they owed more on their property than it was worth—and walked away from their mortgages. "By October 2008, an estimated 10 million homes in the United States had a mortgage balance higher than the value of the house."[10] As the subprime epidemic spread, foreclosures and sinking property values created a vicious cycle that led to more foreclosures and deflation of property values.

As default and foreclosure rates rose, the cash flows into MBSs and CDOs declined, and their value fell. As their value dropped, investors who had used MBSs and CDOs as collateral to leveraged speculation found themselves facing "margin calls" from their brokers, and had to scramble to provide either additional money or securities, or default and lose their investment.[11] Moreover, the complex way that mortgages had been bundled, and then sliced and diced into securities made it impossible to determine how many "toxic" assets such securities might contain, and this uncertainty caused their value to plummet. "The spread of 'toxic' assets soon threatened the capitalization and liquidity of a broad range of financial institutions around the world."[12]

The falling value of MBSs and CDOs triggered payment obligations by CDS sellers that made it difficult for the holders of mortgage based financial assets to sell or even value them. Greatly exacerbating the problem was the vast use of leverage throughout the financial system. Hedge funds had leveraged to borrow huge sums from banks. Simultaneously banks were using strategic investment vehicles (SIVs) to borrow from the short-term commercial paper market and take overnight interbank loans to purchase long-term MBSs, and so too had a great deal of "off-balance sheet" risk exposure, which came home to roost when credit markets seized up.[13]

Like a string of fat men tied together on a tight rope, the crisis spread to a list of firms—which read like an alphabet soup of fortune 500 companies—from mortgage companies, to banks, and credit unions, to insurance companies, to brokerage houses, to investment firms and hedge funds, threatening to bring down not just financial firms but also the auto industry and even retail companies. The credit crisis was not limited to Wall Street or Main Street. It was global. In an age of integrated markets, toxic securities had spread their poison around the world, and tight credit, and illiquid markets threatened economies around the world.

THE BLAME GAME

Mad and hurt, many have looked for villains to blame in this crisis as in others. There is, as usual, no shortage of possible culprits. In 2009, Time Magazine[14] published a list of the usual suspects. Among mortgage companies, they singled out Angelo Mozilio the co-founder of Countrywide and IndyMac as well as Ian McCarthy, the CEO of Beaser Homes, for predatory lending practices. Bankers naturally are on the list. Marion and Herb Sandler, owners of World Bank, are blamed for inventing the adjustable-rate mortgage (ARM) in the early 1980s. Time included Sandy Weill, founder of Citibank, for his role in lobbying to change Glass-Steagall, the depression era legislation that separated commercial banks from Wall Street, and limited the investment risks banks could take, and for also building a bank that became too big to fail, and hence has received massive bailout moneys from the government. The Royal Bank of Scotland's Fred Goodwin was on the list for similar reasons. Wall Street firms featured prominently. Lew Ranieri of the Salomon Brothers made the list of culprits for his invention in the 1970s of mortgage backed securities.

Those associated with MBSs and CDOs, like Sam O'Neal who got Merrill Lynch deeply involved in these securities were on the list. At Bear Stearns, CEO James Cayne is blamed for investing its highly leveraged hedge funds in MBSs, which then collapsed mid-2007. Richard Fuld, CEO of Lehman, was blamed for steering his firm into the subprime mortgage business, for making such loans, and for bankrolling other lenders who made them. John Devaney who as a hedge fund manager helped make it profitable for lenders to sell-off questionable loans, was also listed. AGI's Joe Cassano, is listed for involving his firm in massive issuance of CDSs that was at the heart of AGI's problems, and that required taxpayers to come to the rescue. Just as blamed was Kathleen Corbet, CEO of Standard & Poor's, whose agency gave even some of the riskiest CDOs AAA ratings. This list of notorious Wall Street personalities wouldn't be complete without Bernie Madoff's Ponzi scheme, the biggest financial fraud in history—pulled off because regulator's were negligent, and banks and hedge funds failed to do due diligence.

Since none of this could have happened without regulatory failure, Time's list includes: Christopher Cox, Chairman of the Securities and Exchange commission; Franklin Raines, the CEO of Fannie Mae who bending to a political push to boost home ownership led the company into subprime lending and big investments in MBSs. A large share of the blame was reserved for Alan Greenspan who as Chairman of the Federal Reserve championed deregulation, because he firmly believed in the ability of markets to be self-regulating, and helped stimulate the housing bubble by maintaining very low interest rates. Hank Paulson, as Treasury Secretary, under President Bush, presided over the unfolding crisis, and was blamed for failing to act sooner.

Politicians also were blamed. Republican Senator Phil Gramm, as chairman of the Senate's Banking Committee from 1995 through 2000, was blamed for the key role he played in the 1999 repeal of the Glass-Steagall Act, as well for his insertion of a key provision in the 2000 Commodity Futures Modernization Act exempting CDSs from the regulatory oversight of the Commodity Futures Trading Commission.

On the theory that the buck stops here, both President Clinton and President Bush were on the list. Clinton was on it for his support for the repeal of Glass-Steagall and for signing the Commodity Futures Modernization Act, as well as the Community Reinvestment Act that put pressure on banks to lend in low-income areas. Bush was singled out for his embrace of deregulation, for his pushing federal oversight agencies into easing off controls over banks and mortgage brokers, and for blocking the regulation of mutual and hedge funds.

Others on the list included; David Oddsson, Iceland's prime minister for his role in that country's financial meltdown; Wen Jiabao was guilty as a proxy for the Chinese government's manipulation of exchange rates for its currency to stimulate exports, allowing China to amass huge reserves of U.S. currency and to supply the United States with vast amounts of cheap credit. Burton Jablin, at Scripps Networks owner of lifestyle channels was blamed for programming that glamorized real estate as investment. David Lereah, the chief economist for the National Association of Realtors, was likewise chastened for his rosy forecasts that championed real estate as an infallible investment. Lastly, *Time* blamed American consumers for forty years of using credit to live beyond their means.

MORE PLAUSIBLE EXPLANATIONS

Blaming naive or greedy individuals, while it may satisfy some deep-seated need to hold someone accountable, is not particularly persuasive. Most of the "so-called" culprits were involved with only some particular aspect of the problem, so while they may share some measure of blame, their actions cannot provide a sufficient account for a financial disaster of this magnitude. The finger pointing dissipates social concern by providing simple to understand explanations. Underlying these sorts of explanations is the neoclassical economic view of markets as trending naturally towards equilibrium through the inputs of individuals. Within this framework, bubbles and manias, build when "irrational exuberance" overcomes normal good sense (wise greed). When investors come to their senses, the bubble bursts, and market corrections restore equilibrium.[15]

From this fundamentalist point of view, markets are inherently efficient and self-regulating, and it is undue governmental interference in them that causes their problems. An alternative view harking back at least to Hobbes, but most strongly associated with the English economist John Maynard Keynes's *General Theory Of Employment, Interest And Money* written in 1936, holds that markets are fundamentally unstable, and so need to be regulated.[16] In this view, bubbles and manias must be explained by poor oversight. Marxists also weigh in; like the Keynesians, they see markets as unstable, but locate the causes of instability in basic contradictions within capital, instead of in markets themselves.

Complexity science offers yet another view of financial systems that emphasizes the importance of non-linear dynamics, where small events can induce large-scale changes in systems, and cause bifurcation of paths of development.[17] Its proponents suggest complexity science offers new insights into puzzles in economics, such as persistent cycles, interruptive crises, market resilience, social movements, and organizational diversity, without any particular ideological narrative.[18] As examined in earlier chapters, the issues of justice in lending including just profit, liability, risk, and returns to labor and capital addressed by both Muslims and Christians for millennia also suggest any number of neglected concerns in the standard model.

Neoliberal market fundamentalism starts with an equilibrium model that offers the efficient market hypothesis. It holds that market prices and resource allocations are optimized as markets tend toward equilibrium. If this is even approximately true, neoliberals argue, then market forces must be given free rein, and it follows that any interference with them will push the system toward less optimal states. The most persuasive version of this theory argues that markets are at best efficiently inefficient; inefficient enough for experts to make profits but efficient enough for prices to reflect approximate near-term value.[19] The most obvious problem with this view is that "value" should be problematized in terms of the distribution of income, the long term impact on the environment and other medium and long-term factors so claims of social optima being reflected in prices would be unpersuasive even if, from the perspective reflected by the current distribution of income, prices were efficiently inefficient.[20]

In 1929, investors following a laissez-faire approach became overextended, so when the crash occurred and the economy began to contract, debt became an almost insuperable burden, further depressing the economy as forced liquidations drove down asset prices. In his 1936 book, Keynes attacked the idea of efficient markets, and described detailed mechanisms that cause economies to become stuck in depressed states, far from the optimum predicted by equilibrium models. As economies contract, Keynes argued a "paradox of thrift" may develop in which consumers respond to losses in income by becoming increasingly thrifty; unfortunately, this in turn causes more businesses to fail, and more people to be laid off. Keynes argued persuasively that the way out of such debt traps, was to increase government spending, even if this meant deficit spending, and he told governments that in these circumstances even reckless spending was better than none.[21] Such spending he argued would boost profits, encourage more borrowing that would generate more profits, and expand the economy. In 1938, the New York Stock Exchange revealed a fifteen point program to upgrade protection for public investors in response to the blame for the great depression generally attributed to speculators that is depicted in Figure 9.1.

Beginning in the 1960s, Hyman Minsky[22] wrote a series of papers that offered a financial instability hypothesis that extended Keynesian arguments to its logical conclusions. Minsky proposed that boom and bust cycles are endogenous to financial markets: in good times when corporate cash flow generates revenues over and above what is needed to pay off debt, a speculative euphoria gives rise to a paradox of gluttony, leading to increased borrowing, increased investment, higher employment, rising consumer confidence, higher profits, and a willingness to borrow more money. This creates a positive feedback cycle till the bubble bursts, and the urge for thrift sends the economy spiraling downwards. It has been noted that both trends are "linked to the same credit creation processes that drive asset market instability."[23]

The key contrasts between market equilibrium and non-equilibrium models, has to do with the assumptions they make. Classical equilibrium models make a long list of assumptions about optimal this and optimal that. Non-equilibrium theorists begin by asking what set of "realistic" assumptions are needed to describe the "actual" behavior of markets.[24] The differences between these two approaches can be seen in how they explain what moves market prices. Equilibrium models posit that markets move naturally toward equilibrium, and remain there unless disturbed by some external force or event. Non-equilibrium models, by contrast, see markets as having their own internal forces and dynamics.[25] More to the point, these dynamics are closely linked to credit, debt financing, and the pricing of financial instruments tied to

Figure 9.1 The Cathedrals of Wall Street, Florine Stettheimer, 1939. Oil on canvas. *Source*: Gift of Ettie Stettheimer, 1953 to the Metropolitan Museum of Art, accession number 53.24.2. http://www.metmuseum.org/art/collection/search/488733

market accounting practices instead of to consumer assessments of the value of the underlying assets.[26]

Among the standard claims of the non-equilibrium view of markets is that markets need to be regulated, and that government has an important role to play in providing a level playing field, defining fair competition, and maintaining market stability. From this perspective, the key guilty parties on the Time's list would be those who pushed deregulation, they included: Senator Phil Gram, Sandy Weill, Christopher Cox, President George W. Bush, President Bill Clinton, and though not on the Time's list surely President Ronald Reagan and Prime Minister Margret Thatcher.

The starting point for Marxist analyses of crises is the relationship between capital and labor. For capitalists to earn a profit, their workers must not only produce commodities worth their wage, but a surplus for their employers. As capitalists compete with one another to sell commodities, and try to undercut their competition, their profit margins thin. To defend their profit margins, they both force laborers to work harder to produce more and pay them less. They may also try to replace labor with machines or find cheaper labor elsewhere. The problem, Marxists have argued, is who will buy the commodities produced. To the degree wages paid to labor are cut, so too is labor's ability to purchase commodities. Because capital's capacity to produce commodities is greater than society's capacity to consume them, capital regularly experiences crises of accumulation. In these crises, unsold commodities glut the market and capital finds it harder and harder to find profitable uses of its accumulated capital. Critics have called this the underconsumptionist flaw in Marxist analysis which dogmatically ignores the role of credit and growth.

Since Marxist analysis predicts that mounting crises will cause the eventual collapse of capital, the latter's continuing resilience and expansion require explanation. Marxist efforts to account for its persistence have focused on spatial and temporal fixes to crises of accumulation. In 1913, Rosa Luxemberg[27] hypothesized that the survival of capitalism depends upon its continual incorporation of non-capitalist regions into itself. Extending this logic, David Harvey[28] posits that capitalism overcomes these crises through either spatial or temporal fixes in which credit may figure prominently. Such fixes include finding new markets or appropriating new resources through what he terms processes of "accumulation by dispossession," essential strategies to take resources from others—land from American Indians, for example. Accumulation by dispossession, however, can also happen within developed capitalist societies by engineering massive transfers of assets between classes. The 2008 subprime disaster and subsequent credit crises, one could argue, are prime examples.

Marx argued, in Capital, that credit plays an important role in capitalist circulation and accumulation. In the cycle M->C->M' capitalists invest money, M, to produce commodities, C, but instead of waiting until they sell to earn M' to cover their initial outlay, they can continue production by borrowing money against expected revenues, or they can also extend C to merchants on credit rather than paying for warehousing. When credit tightens, commodity flows also become sluggish. Following this logic, credit functions as a temporal fix in two ways. Since the speed of M->C->M' defines the profit cycle within capital, the faster the turnover, the greater the rate of accumulation. Credit increases the efficiency of transactions by shortening this cycle. The other type of temporal fix displaces problems in time by taking surplus capital, and lending it against future returns.

From a Marxist point of view, the current credit crisis is simply a symptom of the unstable dynamics internal to capitalist logic. And regarding whom to blame, the entire list is just a starting point, for Marxists would not stop there. They would blame all capitalists, and would see the wealth destroyed in the credit crisis as part of a massive exercise in accumulation by dispossession, as part of creative destruction that is concentrating wealth into new hands.

While parts of this analysis at least seem reasonable; given the logic of capital, there are some basic problems with this explanation. Haunting it is an underlying grand narrative, a holdover from Hegel, a dialectic in which contradictions drive the transformation of society teleologically. Much like nineteenth-century neoclassical models, the logic of capitalism defines a bounded system, that while expanding and dynamic, continues to have an over determined quality even applying to its spatiotemporal fixes. In this narrative, one of the least persuasive claims is that growth and credit simply cannot combine to eliminate the inevitability of crisis. Many feel that the greater problem is that capitalism ignores the real cost of externalities and is damaging the planet and people—not that it cannot continue to do so because of internal and purely economic contradictions.

Complexity theory examines the general properties and dynamics of self-reproducing systems, and would seem to have something to offer to the analysis of crises. The origins of complexity theory may be found in General Systems Theory[29] (GST) and cybernetics. GST attempted to describe open systems, but influenced by biological models, tended to see them as bounded, and as containing subsystems, feedback loops, and hierarchies of control. The serious problems noted with older systems theories (e.g., neofunctionalism and undefined system/environment boundaries) have been overcome by contemporary approaches. At their best such approaches focus on systems as composed of parts, surrounded by an environment that acts on the system, a recognition that bonds and relations among system components or components of the environment are critical just as is a focus on mechanisms that make or allow the system to behave in particular ways. Agency need not be confined to individuals but can also usefully be attributed to "powerful particulars" such as corporations or states.[30] Modern approaches also differ from earlier theories by recognizing that processes of change are dynamic and involve non-linear, complex adaptive systems that interact with one another and co-evolve within changing fitness landscapes that their interactions help to shape.[31]

What complexity theory offers over other economic approaches is new tools of analysis, a more dynamic understanding of the processes by which systems emerge, reproduce themselves, change, or are transformed; as well as a better understanding of system/environment boundaries. Boundaries have been rethought. It is not just that systems have other systems as their environment, but that the boundaries themselves are seen to be dynamic, changeable, permeable, overlapping, and intersecting.[32]

While coevolution of complex adaptive systems may explain gradual change, crises involve sudden precipitous change. Two concepts have been developed that are useful to understandings of sudden change: paths of development and nonlinear effects. Paths of development focus on identifying critical turning points that cause paths to bifurcate. Taken from chaos theory, the principal of nonlinear effects underlines the notion that small changes may have large effects on unstable systems. Much like a boulder rolling down hill, while initially it may not take much force to shift its path, once it gathers momentum, its path is increasingly locked in. The non-linear effects pose a major challenge to neoclassical assumptions of decreasing returns (e.g., to capital or labor), maximization, and equilibriums. In complex systems there may be multiple and distinct equilibrium points and this notion helps to problematize any claim that capitalist or market economies naturally seek a single optimum—though given the inequality in the distribution of income, and the greater similarity of a market to an aristocracy than to a democracy, claims of the market producing social optima have long been muted.

An adequate concept of causality requires a model of reality that is realistic and this in a complex world must include both emergent properties and agency in all its forms from individual greed, societal decisions related to justice in economic policy, and the implementation of the agenda of powerful particulars (e.g., corporations, banks, agencies, and governments). What complexity theory does best is to point out that the 2008 financial crisis was long in the making and reflects social capital, institutional arrangements, and the near-term agency of economic actors.

The 2008 financial crisis in some ways is the story of a perfect storm to which multiple systemic problems contributed: the complex architecture of financial markets, regulatory failure, imperfect information, strategies of risk management, and globalization to list but a few. Among basic problems, contributing to this crisis is the complexity of financial markets themselves. The problem is not simply one of the number and variety of institutional players, and the complex relations among them, but that this complexity gives rise to local, state, federal, and industry rules and laws, as well as a Byzantine set of regulators generating myriad motivations for concealment or lack of transparency. Globalization, which has increased the integration of financial markets around the world, has only contributed to this complexity.

This institutional complexity has a series of implications that are worth noting. To begin with, the classical definition of markets as places where buyers and sellers meet, and as arenas subject to regulation, does not map well on to actual economies. Trade takes place through multiple channels, only some of which are within formal, regulated spheres. Like icebergs, because only those portions that show above water may be regulated, the unseen portions may contain titanic risks. Structured financial products such as MBSs, CDOs, and CDSs would seem to be cases in point.

Such icebergs floating through financial systems pose an enormous problem. The securitization process, bundling and slicing of mortgages, creates instruments of such complexity that it has often proved impossible even for "powerful particulars" to determine the value of the underlying assets. Because these largely unregulated securities are inherently opaque they cannot be traded in competitive markets, but must be sold "over the counter" by originating institutions.[33]

Banks, hedge funds, private equity funds, brokerage houses, however, have found that it is more profitable to trade such securities through private networks or internal networks where, because prices are unpublished, they can maintain high profit margins.[34] Such channels facilitate secretive transactions. Many trades that formerly happened on the floors of public exchanges have shifted to private platforms.

This creates "dark pools of liquidity" where orders may be executed without either public display or price paid being disclosed.[35] The anonymity and secrecy that trade through private platforms offers are very attractive to large traders and money managers who do not want to expose their trading strategies. The profitability of such platforms has influenced many companies "such as UBS, Goldman Sachs, and Credit Suisse to direct as much as 12 percent of U.S. stock trades away from the exchanges to their own internal systems."[36] The "dark pools of liquidity" within these private networks, with their undisclosed practices, prices, and holdings have profound implications for markets.

Modern markets violate classical assumptions of perfect knowledge and perfect competition. This lack of transparency "makes it difficult for market participants to "interpret" markets, heightens uncertainty, and increases financial network risk."[37] These private and internal channels also challenge existing regulatory frameworks, and make it difficult for regulators to recognize and manage network risks.[38]

Neoliberal deregulation and globalization have made these financial seas even more uncertain. In the early 1980s, neoliberal market fundamentalism gained a political base with the elections of British Prime Minister Margaret Thatcher (1979), and U.S. president Ronald Reagan (1980). Opposed to Keynesian economics, right wing conservatives brought into play the Chicago School message preached by Milton Friedman that markets were self-correcting and so regulating them was misguided and ideally governments should focus on regulating currency and the Fed. Almost immediately, deregulation became the order of the day.

Rejecting conventional wisdom that unless financial markets are tightly regulated they are prone to systemic crises that require substantial bailouts, conservatives enthusiastically began to dismantle the regulatory frameworks put in place in response to a series of financial crises that culminated in the 1929 crash. Savings and Loans and other thrift institutions were among the first financial institutions to be deregulated. Deregulation gave Savings and Loans carte blanche to wheel and deal in mortgages, commercial property, stocks, junk bonds, and even issue credit cards.[39]

By 1986 these institutions were in trouble. "In all, nearly five hundred S&Ls collapsed or were forced to close down; roughly the same numbers were merged out of existence under the auspices of the Resolution Trust Corporation set up by congress to clear up the mess."[40] Ultimately, the Savings and Loans mess required a bailout that cost taxpayers over $200 billion.[41] The Saving and Loans fiasco did not lessen the right-wing commitment to deregulation. The 1933 Glass-Steagall Act, that separated commercial and investment banking activities and put tight controls on their activities, had long been a neoliberal target for deregulation. As neoliberalism swept both parties the elimination of Glass-Steagall in 1999 under Clinton, cleared the way for merging commercial and investment banking into giant financial conglomerates that were deemed "too big to fail."[42]

Even as deregulation was dismantling government controls over financial markets at home, the neoliberal project of globalization was giving capital increasing mobility, making it easier to evade any remaining regulation. As financial capital became free to move about, it became increasingly difficult for any nation to regulate or tax it since it could always move someplace else. This enormously strengthened its bargaining power. To attract or keep capital, governments had to be able to offer a favorable business climate, one that provided security without onerous regulations or requirements. Current regulation of the financial system is still at best weak, and its disorders are profound. Because regulation is institutionally focused, control through Byzantine agencies is piece meal, expensive, and even contradictory.

Controls that do exist do not apply to large parts of the financial order. Non-bank institutions not only escape bank regulations but self-finance not with deposits but with rapidly maturing (daily) debt thereby creating money equivalents and risk almost with impunity. With parts of the financial system lurking offshore, and easily moved elsewhere, existing regulations are easy to evade. The globalization and the increasing integration of financial markets around the world are itself a disorder: their hypercoherence means that local problems can spread everywhere.[43]

The yet to be approved Tobin tax has been suggested as a way to constrain and stabilize global flows of funds that take advantage of minute price differentials. The asymmetry of power that has put capital in a privileged position in its negotiations with nation-states is another disorder, one which often forces governments "to pay more heed to the requirements of international capital than to the aspirations of their own people."[44]

This has given rise to an emerging pattern of foxes guarding the henhouse, of capture of regulatory agencies by the industries that these agencies were meant to regulate, of industries helping write the law and rules meant to regulate them, and of standards becoming "voluntary" instead of mandated. This elite capture, in which the interests of special interest groups come to so dominate regulatory agencies that they can put their interests ahead of the nation, simply extends the old adage that "what is good for General Motors is good for the nation."[45]

Among the profound disorders, responsible for the 2008 credit crisis is the notion of calculable and manageable risk. Here the story is complex, but worth delving into in some detail. It is the account of the movement from "personal knowledge" of borrowers to "ratings" by agencies. It is a tale in which credit decisions based on scores for individuals come to substitute for traditional practices of credit that required a lender to make a qualitative judgment about loans.[46] Eventually, it became a story of new risk management strategies based on statistical calculations of pooled risk.

This transition to market valuation of credit worthiness (see chapter 3) entailed the movement from personal knowledge of borrowers to the emergence of consumer credit agencies capable of tracking 200 million Americans (chapter 8) as well as the assessment of all businesses. The large databases would not have been possible, without computers. Computers allowed credit agencies such as Trans Union, Equifax, and Experion to assemble massive amounts data on individuals from disparate sources, and companies such as FICO to create programs and algorithms to crunch these data to produce "scores" that measure credit risk.

Scores predict how likely it is that an individual or business will default on a loan. Such scores allowed card companies to set up control-by-risk regimes. The statistical concept underlying control-by-risk is seemingly simple. By classifying borrowers by their ranked FICO scores, one may treat them as a population pool, making the default rates for each class of borrowers calculable. This works for businesses as well as consumers. Calculable rates of default, allow companies to manage risk through insurance and by adjusting interest rates and terms and conditions for the credit. Control-by-risk meant both that Card companies could offer almost anyone who had a FICO score a credit card but also that they needed to similarly evaluate businesses.

In 1995, a government sponsored enterprise (GSE), the Federal Home Loan Mortgage Corporation, known as Freddie Mac, adopted FICO scores as part of its attempts to standardize mortgage underwriting practices, and moved to an automated system of screening credit risk. The use of FICO scores in mortgage underwriting made the move from control-by-screening to control-by-risk possible. Where under the control-by-screening regime, subprime loans could only be made by overruling a screener's judgment, under the control-by-risk regime, the new calculative possibilities turned subprime lending into a risk management exercise, one that used scores to create multiple options for borrowers according to their level of risk. Following Freddie, the rest of mortgage industry quickly followed suit. Control-by-risk regimes quickly spread. Standard and Poor, for example, came out with a program called "Levels" to rate securities. It was generally thought that such lending practices themselves minimized corporate risks both in investment and lending.

The problem was not that these statistical methods of risk analysis did not work well. Under normal market conditions, they worked splendidly. Standard and Poor's "Levels" program, for example, not only could rate *individual* loans but through a loan by loan analysis it could either be used to assemble a pool of assets, or rate a pool of securities.[47] Problems came when the unexpected occurred, and seemly impossible black swans appeared. Part of the problem was that the historic data used to test such algorithms lack sufficient depth and did not include crisis conditions. As well, the algorithms used in such programs were based on statistical models that made events of twenty-five standard deviations seem virtually impossible.

Yet, one of the world's largest hedge funds suffered twenty-five standard deviations events for several days in a row.[48] Such "fat tail" events, far from the mean, confirm the insights of chaos theory—that in many systems the mean for any particular period is not an unbiased estimator. Like the flapping of butterfly wings in the Amazon causing hurricanes in the Atlantic—positive feedback loops may occur that may amplify problems, so that when defaults in subprime loans passed the predicted levels, their amplifying effects soon threatening companies, securities, banks, and ultimately the financial system itself.

The concepts from complexity theory such as "paths of development" and "emergence" also seem to offer some insights into this crisis. While the need to develop large databases to rate credit applicants existed well before the computer age, computers greatly facilitated the development of this path. Arguably, as computer technology advanced, the path toward automated systems of credit application processing developed in tandem. As computers became ever more capable of handling large databases, and doing complex calculations, the path toward automation taking financial decision making out of human hands, and algorithmic driven control-by-risk regimes emerged.

Analogously, invention of the mortgage backed securities that fundamentally transformed Wall Street illustrates the dynamics of path development. In 1983, in the midst of the Savings and Loans debacle, in an attempt to help S&Ls to sell mortgages to stay solvent, Lewis Ranieri, the chief trader at Salomon Brothers, hit on the clever idea of transforming mortgages into bonds by bundling thousands of mortgages together into new asset backed securities, collateralized mortgage obligations (CMOs) that then could be sold as alternatives to traditional corporate or government bonds. What initially made these CMOs particularly attractive is that the majority of the mortgages that were bundled together had been issued by Fannie, Freddie, or Ginnie, and were backed by federal government guarantees, and so could be represented as being virtually the same as investment grade, government bonds. The market for such GSE-mortgage backed securities grew quickly, expanding from $200 million when they appeared in the 1980s to $4 trillion by 2007. As the demand for GSE-backed securities exceeded supply, securitization was applied to loans that were not-eligible for GSE-guarantees. By 2007, $2 trillion in non-guaranteed residential mortgages had been similarly securitized.[49]

What is important to note is that much like the history of credit cards where cards were initially offered to the wealthy, and entailed little risk when faced with inherent limits of GSE backing, traders went down the path of exploiting increasingly risky market segments, deluded by the notion that the risks were calculable.

A lot could not be factored into their calculations including numerous trends in the world economy. At the same time that financial capital was becoming increasingly abstract, hedged, and digital, globalization was creating the conditions for capital to become increasingly mobile. The increasing integration of global markets, reflected in the movement of trade out of face-to-face trade in the pits and on to computer screens, increasingly connected global financial markets together. While new technologies increased the speed and efficiency of trading, and increased the range of information available to traders, the faceless trade that followed movement out of the pits, deprived traders of traditional human feedback, and the ability to interpret actions of knowledgeable traders.[50] In fast moving markets, for better or worse, computers increasingly drove technical trading. The wired together emerging e-trading spaces not only facilitate global trading, but may inevitably also increase the probabilities that any crisis will spread.

GLOBALIZATION, DISCRETIZATION OF CAPITAL, AND CRISES

Recent financial trends have been enabled by an increase in the discretization of capital. This is to say that capital has become sufficiently abstract that it can be subdivided and marketed (discretized) in myriad ways not traditionally possible for the underlying assets. In historical terms, we might view this as the Italian *compagnia* on steroids. Not only are profitable investment opportunities tailored to the investor but liability and risk can also be sliced and diced to suit. This new level of abstraction both facilitates more profitable and precise investment and, equally importantly, radically increases the difficulty of estimating risk and thereby discourages transparency and makes it easier for issues of justice to be minimized or even ignored. This trend has allowed investors to view their operations as made up of separable elements, and to comparison shop on multiple dimensions.

Globalization additionally created the conditions that allowed capitalists not just to move their money around the world, but also to shift their operations (in whole or in part) to wherever the returns were most advantageous. In the United States, certain kinds of capital began to move overseas in search of cheap labor. A rust belt developed through the heartlands as heavy industries like steel moved abroad. Increasingly, manufacture of consumer goods also moved overseas, and particularly to China from the mid-1980s. At the same time that our manufacturing eroded, American standards of living became increasingly dependent on cheap imports.

Since 1980, this transformation of the U.S. economy has meant that income distributions have become increasingly unequal. For the bottom 40 percent of households incomes have remained almost flat, when measured in constant dollars corrected for inflation, and their share of the nation's aggregate income has dropped from 14.4 percent in 1980 to 12.1 percent in 2007. For the top, 40 percent incomes have risen, and for the top 5 percent spectacularly—by nearly 60 percent. These upper income brackets have increased their aggregate share of national income from 68.1 to 73.1 percent. The top five percent share has risen from 16.5 to 21.2 percent. The third quintile during this period has seen some moderate increase in household income, but their share of aggregate income has dropped from 16.8 to 14.8 percent.[51] This inequality has been bolstered by continuous campaigns to convince Americans that the rich have earned their wealth and need tax breaks more than others.

What is also evident during this period is the steadily increasing levels of household debt. Before the crisis, this debt as estimated in 1990 dollars had increased from about $25,000 in 1980 to about $70,000 in 2007 as it went from around 74 percent of annual household income to about 165 percent over the same period.[52]

By 2007, of this 165 percent of annual income, about 130 percent was mortgage and 35 percent was consumer credit. Overall, increasing percentages of disposable income went to debt service benefiting the wealthy, rising from about 10.93 percent in 1980 to 14.18 in 2007.[53] The story these numbers tell seems to be a simple one: even as incomes stagnated, and many lost ground, the easy availability of credit lured large segments of the population into increasing debt. As this debt burden increased, default rates rose.

Underlying these figures there are a couple of other tales to be told. The first story is of the forces that pushed the economy toward real estate investments. As manufacture of consumer goods shifted abroad, working- and middle-class incomes stagnated and this gradually stifled purchasing power, making cheap imports an increasing necessity. Mounting trade deficits eventually led government risk management decisions to devalue the dollar. In response, investors began to look for places to put their capital to safeguard its value.

Traditional wisdom steered investors to the stock market and to real estate. The value of stocks it was thought over the long term would grow with the economy. Real estate, likewise, was touted as a safe investment, one that built equity, and was better than paying rent, which was likened to "throwing money down a rat hole." Also, fueling the drive toward real estate investment was the American Dream Down Payment Act that President George W. Bush signed in 2003 which subsidized first time home purchases and which had as its goal adding 5.5 million new minority homeowners by the end of the decade. Under pressure from the administration "lenders were encouraged ... not to press subprime borrowers for full documentation. Fannie Mae and Freddie Mac also came under pressure from HUD to support the subprime market."[54] So, by "2005, sixty-nine percent of all U.S. households were homeowners, compared to 64 per cent ten years before."[55] The rest of the story is familiar that of rising default rates and falling financial dominos.

The second story is that of an unforeseen crisis of accumulation by dispossession. It begins with globalization, the erosion of working and middle-class purchasing power, and attempts to cope by thrift or through the use of credit. From a systemic point of view neither of these strategies was entirely satisfactory. Although thrift may help households make ends meet, reduced consumption is hardly an engine for prosperity. Credit solves present problems, and for a time fuels economic engines, but too much borrowing against future income to meet consumption needs is unsustainable. For those with capital (such as Paulson), the crisis creates fire sale conditions and bargain basement opportunities in real estate as well as in stocks, and in increased market shares as many investors go belly up.

Similar equity-stripping practices in mortgages include: folding exorbitant fees into the loan that substantially raise payments or reduce the equity remaining in the home when the loan is paid. Such predatory fees include single premium credit insurance, typically a sum equal to five years premiums, on which the buyer also pays interest for the life of the loan. Prepayment penalties are another example, commonly requiring borrowers to pay six months of interest if the loan is prepaid during the first five years. "Predatory lenders often disguise the fact their mortgages have balloon payments or adjustable rates, only to inform the borrowers of this fact after closing to convince them to get a new and "better" loan.[56] "The ultimate and tragic consequence of the wealth stripping and steering associated with predatory lending was the loss of homes, and the destruction of entire communities through high rates of foreclosure."[57]

Unfortunately, such abuse was particularly egregious in minority communities. According to the 2000 HUD/Treasury "Report of Recommendations to Curb Predatory Home Mortgage Lending" subprime loans accounted for 51 percent of home loans in black neighborhoods as compared to 9 percent in white ones.[58]

While it might be tempting to see the 2008 crisis as an exercise in accumulation by dispossession, no one seems to have "engineered" it. Clearly, too many big interests were damaged and the consequences were too profound to believe that this credit crisis was a deliberate exercise in accumulation by dispossession analogous to driving native peoples from their lands; or a political maneuver similar to Mexico's use of Land Reform to "dispossess" peasants from communal and ejido lands by first offering them titles and then cutting off credit and other subsidies, so as to force them to sell their lands.

While the 2008 crisis might not have been engineered, the "fire sale" it created functioned as a "fix" in much the same way—falling prices; eventually, clear the glut of commodities clogging markets—and provide those with capital new opportunities, further concentrating wealth. The rub is that there is no guarantee how or where these profits will be invested in a global economy, no reason to imagine it will lessen inequality in the United States or elsewhere; so a low wage recovery with continuing weakness of the economy is a real possibility.

HUMAN COSTS OF THE CRISIS AND THE LOGIC OF JUSTICE IN LENDING

A decade later most Americans still have some sense of the local costs of this crisis. It filled the news, and failed businesses and empty storefronts still stand witness. Many Americans suffered personal losses—homes, jobs, and often health insurance, or the value of properties, stocks, and pension funds.

While Americans paid a terrible cost, the suffering this crisis has caused in many parts of the developing world is truly horrific. According to the World Bank, the spreading world crisis will drive 180 to 200 million more people in developing countries into poverty on top of the over 1.5 billion who already live on less than $2 a day.[59] Africa has been among the worst hit and may serve as an example.

Even in countries that were somewhat insulated from the direct effects of the global credit crisis because of their limited integration into international capital markets, the indirect impacts on their economies have been devastating. A UNESCO report has warned that reduced growth in sub-Saharan Africa, will cost the some 390 million people living in extreme poverty, $18 billion, or $46 per person, and push millions into deeper poverty.[60] The World Bank estimates that in the near term, annually as result of this crisis, as many as 700,000 more African infants may die before reaching their first birthday.[61]

The credit crises hit African nations with a double-barreled blast—their export commodity prices fell sharply, and credit dried up. With globalization, economies of the developing countries have become increasingly dependent on exports of basic export commodities: oil, minerals, and cash crops. Because African countries depend on these exports for much of their revenue, declining prices affect not just companies and workers, but their government's few foreign reserves. As revenues have fallen, governments in several oil-producing nations have had to scale back public expenditures.

Angola's revenues, as an example, are based in large part on oil production with a 2015 estimated breakeven point of about $110 a barrel.[62] Lower oil prices impact Angola's accumulation of foreign exchange and have real impacts on the ability to maintain and improve oil infrastructure as well as on non-oil sectors, including manufacturing, construction, and services. Calculations of such break-even points are somewhat arbitrary given that they cannot reflect future loan rates, future global prices for oil industry inputs, or potential discounting on past loans.

Nevertheless, falling commodity prices after 2008 forced oil and mining companies across Africa to lay off workers. In the Democratic Republic of the Congo, 100,000 workers lost their jobs because of smelter closures, and foreign reserves so low that the country has had difficulty purchasing imported essentials such as food, fuel, and medication.[63] Adding to this gloom, migrant remittances go down in every downturn. In Kenya, for instance, remittances between January and June of 2009 were 11.4 percent lower than for the same period in 2008.[64] For households that depend on such remittances to make ends meet—diminishing revenues are an additional burden.

In this financial tsunami, because exports have fallen faster than imports, trade balances have deteriorated, forcing currency devaluations that have effectively driven up the prices of imports. Cash crops are particularly sensitive to the withering of credit. Typically, credit is necessary to production and provided by buyers in advance of the harvest.

The problems in Mali are illustrative. Mali is one of the poorest countries in the world and since the crisis has been heavily impacted by globally financed terrorist networks. Cotton, its principal agricultural export crop is grown by 1.7 million small farmers, of whom, eighty percent live in poverty.[65] In recent years, cotton production has declined. Mali had produced 600,000 tons of cotton a year, but production has fallen to half that due partly to falling world prices for cotton, and rising costs for fertilizers and pesticides, but also due to poor management of the state owned, Malian Company for the Development of Textiles, (CMDT) which monopolizes the country's cotton production.

In Mali, the CMDT helps finance cotton production through a "campaign" that offers credit to producers so they can buy fertilizers and pesticides. The CMDT was in trouble even before the crisis. Small cotton farmers, squeezed by poor prices, and high costs, increasingly defaulted on CMDT loans, leaving the company with a debt of U.S. $65 million. "Because of these debts, after the October 2007 harvest the CMDT was unable to pay many of its producers at all."[66]

Farmers complained that CDMT gouged them for pesticides and fertilizers, and were as much as six months late paying them for their cotton. Even before the 2008 crisis, many farmers were abandoning cotton. When the crisis hit, credit dried up completely, and most farmers were left with no choice but to switch to other crops that paid less, but at least did not require credit or inputs to grow. For many poor Malian farmers, whose livelihoods are already precarious, even small losses of income can have grave consequences. For them this crisis has been disastrous, threatening not just their incomes, but driving the costs of goods they need beyond their reach.

While other global processes, including the effect of climate change and wild fluctuations in energy costs, reap havoc around the globe, those processes with least similarity to the credit crisis elicit much more concern and efforts have been undertaken to counteract their most deleterious effects. The issues of justice in lending to which brilliant minds in Europe, the fertile crescent, both sides of the Mediterranean and the broader Islamic world devoted so much attention are seriously neglected in discussions of the credit crisis. There is a woeful consensus that the vast differences in return on a given transaction are not just nothing unusual but signs of brilliance to be admired.

Escaping liability for damages caused is viewed as normal for elites and criminal for the poor. Risk taking is most admired by the wealthy when someone else bears its burden. Truth in lending is less emphasized in the twenty-first century than in the twentieth with governments proposing only minimal regulations while many individuals, and most powerful particulars, exhibit a cultivated blindness to the global impacts of the financial system and view regulation with unmitigated disdain and admire attempts to circumvent it.

Recent research by Ouroussoff has shown why agency ratings were so wrong before 2008 and why many high risk institutions were rated as low risk by the agencies.[67] Interviews with major corporate executives and rating agency employees discovered that there were important and systematic reasons such discrepancies occur. An original consensus between investors and corporations had recognized that profit and risk taking are intertwined. In recent decades, rating agencies have taken a more proactive role which paradoxically has broken this consensus and contributed to the problems aggravated by deregulation. Rather than relying on historical performance data, the agencies have been scrutinizing each corporation's investment portfolio, with the aim of minimizing risk by forcing corporations to avoid risky ventures and risky financing, trying to force them to balance their remaining risk with broad portfolios of stock in other industries—thereby sewing all corporations tightly together.

In response, many corporations assigned a special vice-president to meet with the rating agencies and made sure that this VP was unaware of the corporation's more speculative / risky activities. By 2008, this meant that ratings though focused on risk, as reported to them by corporations, both ignored actual corporate risk and paradoxically came to increase risk, Further, with deregulation mesmerizing poorly educated politicians, there were no efforts to encourage outside scrutiny of risk.

It would be a mistake to imagine that the credit issues examined in the last chapter are confined to loans made to "real" people. In the modern economy, corporations and other "powerful particulars" to an increasing degree have the legal status of individuals in a variety of *fora*. In recent years, corporate profit rates have been significantly higher than the cost of money. This means it pays to borrow money to pay a corporate wage bill instead of using company profits to pay wages. This may seem paradoxical, but it works quite simply: a million dollars of profits reinvested by the corporation might in a year net, conservatively, 1.05 to 1.1 million dollars. In contrast, borrowing a million dollars at an annual rate of 2–3 percent and making twenty-four payments a year will cost at most 1.013 million dollars implying a profit of at least $470 thousand by borrowing to pay wages even if the entire sum were borrowed at the beginning of the year. In reality, corporations borrow for their wage bill in many smaller increments, since wages are often paid on a two-week basis: meaning in simple terms that they owe interest each year on closer to their annual wage bill borrowed for half a year.

The significant benefits of borrowing to cover employee wages are optimized if a corporation has a high credit rating and borrows at low rates. Credit agencies meet regularly with corporations to assess their rating and, as noted, are concerned both about returns on investment and the riskiness of corporate investments. This dual concern set up the 2008 financial meltdown under the Bush administration. Deregulation of banks allowed them to lend with few federal obligations to minimize the risks their portfolios involved. Consequently, the federal government and other "powerful particulars" such as banks relied almost exclusively on credit agency ratings, derived directly from corporate deception, rather than doing their own assessments. As the crisis of 2008 developed, credit suddenly became scarce and borrowing to pay wage bills became almost impossible even for corporations that were otherwise in good financial condition.

PROBLEMATIZING GREED: FROM MORTAL SIN TO CARDINAL VIRTUE

While finger pointing is tempting, placing blame on individuals may not be particularly useful. To some degree, however, our collective dismissal of justice in lending and adoration of greed seem to blame. A wide variety of societies in the past have applied diverse principles of justice to finance. The credit crisis we have argued is perhaps better understood as an emergent phenomenon but one heavily influenced by a long neglect of financial justice. At its deepest levels, it reflects complex underlying dynamics within capitalism that periodically unhinge markets and produce crises both of productivity and of justice. To argue, that market confidence can remain when vast numbers of victims are regularly created is naive.

Several trends within capitalism seem particularly problematic in this regard. Driven by the neoliberal project of free trade, globalization aimed at creating secure conditions for capital investment and capital mobility, and in the process it has made financial systems around the world more coherent and markets more consistently transparent to powerful particulars. It has also made financial systems more subject to power differentials and more vulnerable to contagion. Integral to these processes was a trend toward discretization of capital advancing its increasing pseudo calculability, abstraction, and opaqueness to most observers including virtually all politicians.

Both the abstract financial instruments and the strategies based on calculations of risk turned out to be deeply flawed, they obfuscated real levels of risk and used the subsequent lack of regulatory transparency to repeal or minimize the few rules that promoted justice in lending or investment. The growing complexity of linkages among markets also had profound implications for regulation—the primary legacy of classic thought on financial justice. Under assault from market fundamentalists, not only were regulatory controls removed, but the growing private spheres of exchange and the subrosa economy hid ever greater portions of the market and the risks inherent in it from scrutiny. Regulation was made even more problematic by the transfer of regulatory control from governments to international organizations staffed by unelected representatives of the very powerful particulars to be regulated.

The movement of capitalist production out of the core industrial nations in search of cheap labor and greater profits and the increasing reliance on unelected global institutions ultimately produced trade imbalances that undermined currencies even as they diminished civic influence for the great majority.[68] Both investors and the middle-class sought to protect their capital from influences beyond their control by investing in real estate. Yet, an emerging subprime market predicated on taking and hiding-risk, government subsidies to encourage first time minority buyers to purchase homes, and a Fed that held interest rates at low levels hoping to stave off a recession, created a super bubble that precipitated massive bailouts and nearly took down the U.S. financial system. While the 2008 crisis was not "engineered" it was driven by elites with new and less restrained uses for their capital.

Deregulation led to significant decreases in financial justice if we look at who ultimately bore the brunt of the economic havoc caused by elite decisions and assume elites cannot by fiat define others as increasingly less worthy. Financial crises, more generally, have had the predictable result of recoveries in employment levels lagging far behind the return to high incomes for elites.[69] They, in the longer term, also contribute to increases in inequality. These statistical regularities are a reasonable indicator of financial injustice, given that it is invariably elite actions which give rise to financial crises and elites who suffer the least from them.

The OED cites Lithgow in 1618 rendering a criticism of greed early in the Industrial Revolution: "Is hee poore, then faine hee would bee rich: And rich, what torments his great griede doth feele." Despite the other causal explanations we have considered for the 2008 crisis, the preeminent position of greed in the pantheon of financial virtues after four centuries of capitalism should be troubling. It may be salutary to compare this chapter's early citation, from an interview with Paulson, to the following Middle Kingdom Egyptian advice:[70]

To be free from every evil,
Guard against the vice of greed:
A grievous sickness without cure,
There is no treatment for it.

NOTES

1. The interview of John A. Paulson of Paulson & Co is in Pedersen *Efficiently Inefficient*, 319–20.
2. Soros, *The New Paradigm for Financial Markets*, xvii.
3. Crotty, "Structural Causes of the Global Financial Crisis: A Critical Assessment of the 'New Financial Architecture'," 50–51.
4. Ibid., 3.
5. Phillips, *Bad Money,* 97.

6. Federal Reserve. FRB, Mortgage Debt Outstanding, First Quarter, 2009.

7. Arewa, "Trading Places: Securities Regulation, Market Crisis, and Network Risk," 25.

8. Harrington and Moses, "Company Bond Risk Surges on Argentina Default Concerns."

9. Soros, *The New Paradigm for Financial Markets*, xviii–xix.

10. Arewa, "Trading Places: Securities Regulation, Market Crisis, and Network Risk," 15.

11. Schwarcz, "Complexity as a Catalyst of Market Failure: A Law and Engineering Inquiry."

12. Arewa, "Trading Places: Securities Regulation, Market Crisis, and Network Risk," 15.

13. Ferguson, *The Ascent of Money*, 273; Crotty, "Structural Causes of the Global Financial Crisis: A Critical Assessment of the 'New Financial Architecture'," 41–43.

14. *Time Magazine*, "25 People to Blame for the Financial Crisis."

15. Poon, "From New Deal Institutions to Capital Markets: Commercial Consumer Risk Scores and the Making of Subprime Mortgage Finance," 655–59.

16. Keynes, *General Theory of Employment Interest and Money*.

17. Walby, "Complexity Theory, Globalisation and Diversity," 12.

18. Chen, "Equilibrium Illusion, Economic Complexity and Evolutionary Foundation in Economic Analysis," 81.

19. Pedersen, *Efficiently Inefficient*.

20. Stiglitz, "Information in the Labour Market," 94–105.

21. Cooper, *The Origin of Financial Crises*, 79–80.

22. See Minsky, "Can 'It' Happen Again?" 101–11; Minsky, "The Financial-Instability Hypothesis: Capitalist Processes and the Behavior of the Economy," 13–38; Minsky "Financial Instability Hypothesis," 153–58.

23. Cooper, *The Origin of Financial Crises*, 119–21.

24. Crotty, "Structural Causes of the Global Financial Crisis: A Critical Assessment of the 'New Financial Architecture'," 11–12.

25. Ibid., 13–14.

26. Ibid., 105.

27. Luxemberg, *The Accumulation of Capital*.

28. Harvey, *The New Imperialism*; Harvey, *A Brief History of Neoliberalism*.

29. von Bertalanffy, *General System Theory*.

30. cf. the work of Mario Bunge discussed in Wan, *Reframing the Social. Emergentist Systemism and Social Theory*.

31. Walby, "Complexity Theory, Globalisation and Diversity," 6.

32. Portugali, "Complexity Theory as a Link Between Space and Place," 652–653.

33. Crotty, "Structural Causes of the Global Financial Crisis: A Critical Assessment of the 'New Financial Architecture'," 24–25; Arewa, "Trading Places: Securities Regulation, Market Crisis, and Network Risk," 14.

34. Crotty, "Structural Causes of the Global Financial Crisis: A Critical Assessment of the 'New Financial Architecture'," 25; Arewa "Trading Places: Securities Regulation, Market Crisis, and Network Risk," 66–67.

35. Arewa, "Trading Places: Securities Regulation, Market Crisis, and Network Risk," 65–66.
36. Ibid., 65–66.
37. Ibid., 7.
38. Ibid., 7.
39. Ferguson, *The Ascent of Money,* 254–55; Phillips 2008:41–42.
40. Ferguson, *The Ascent of Money,* 257–60.
41. U. S. General Accounting Office. "Financial Audit, Resolution Trust Corporation's 1995 and 1994, Financial Statements," 21.
42. Crotty, "Structural Causes of the Global Financial Crisis: A Critical Assessment of the 'New Financial Architecture," 8.
43. Rappaport, "Distinguished Lecture in Anthropology: The Anthropology of Trouble," 295–303; Rappaport, "Disorders of our Own: A Conclusion," 235–94.
44. Soros, *The New Paradigm for Financial Markets*, 95.
45. Rappaport, "Distinguished Lecture in Anthropology: The Anthropology of Trouble," 302.
46. Poon, "From New Deal Institutions to Capital Markets: Commercial Consumer Risk Scores and the Making of Subprime Mortgage Finance," 6–7.
47. Ibid., 25.
48. Cooper, *The Origin of Financial Crises,* 11.
49. Ferguson, *The Ascent of Money,* 257–60.
50. Zaloom, *Out of the Pits.*
51. US Census Bureau Table H-2, "Share of Aggregate Income Received by Each Fifth and Top 5 Percent of Households, All Races: 1967 to 2007." US Census Bureau "Table H-3. Mean Household Income Received by Each Fifth and Top 5 Percent All Races: 1967 to 2007."
52. Wenger, "Continuations. Household Debt, 2008."
53. Federal Reserve, "Household Debt Service and Financial Obligation Ratios."
54. Ferguson, *The Ascent of Money,* 267.
55. Ibid., 266.
56. Stein, "Qualifying the Economic Cost of Predatory Lending," 5.
57. Ibid., 11.
58. Ibid.
59. United Nations New Centre, "Financial Crisis to Deepen Extreme Poverty, Increase Child Mortality Rates."
60. United Nations New Center, "Economic Crisis Set to Drive 53 Million more People into Poverty in 2009."
61. World Bank, "Africa Likely to be Worst Hit by the Financial Crisis, April 24, 2009"
62. http://www.cnbc.com/2015/12/03/oil-prices-and-budgetsthe-opec-countries-most-at-risk.html
63. Committee of African Finance Ministers and Central Bank Governors, 2009:4.
64. Gitari Koori, "Commentary on Remittance Volumes for the Period January–June, 2009."
65. IRIN, "Mali: Fears over Privatising Cotton. Humanitarian News and Analysis."

66. Ibid.
67. Ouroussoff, *Wall Street at War. The Secret Struggle for the Global Economy.*
68. See Perkins, Radelet and Lindauer, *Economics of Development.*
69. See Figure 9.6 "Labor Shares Fall During Crises and Don't Fully Recover Afterward" in World Bank, *World Development Report,* 2005–2006.
70. Speech of Ptahhotep to his son dating to the Middle Kingdom (c. 2055–1650 BC) in Lichtheim. *Ancient Egyptian Literature. The Old and Middle Kingdoms,* 68.

Conclusion

Hidden Interests and the Development of Finance

In this book, we have examined the development of increasingly sophisticated technologies of credit and, beginning with the scholastics, also the hard intellectual struggle to reconcile the benefits of commerce with ethical obligations to the poor. The evolution of banking techniques, the financial needs of the Papacy, and the exigencies of European states provided pragmatic motivations for this effort; we saw an early example of the latter in the Iberian *Siete Partidas* of Alfonso X of Castile which abandoned the Islamic focus on transparency paired with shared risk and liability along with proportionality between inputs and profits. The scholastic labor within the church was long characterized by a parallel attention to ethical issues that stimulated financial thinking—reaching economic insights centuries ahead of later secular economists. The Atlantic slave trade we have suggested was both a massive and centuries spanning financial project and an unmitigated ethical disaster that only slowly led to ethical reform; ethical progress in finance seems to have been both critical and problematic in all periods up to the present.

The financial technologies elaborated in this book were always constrained by ethical considerations: from concerns about exploitation to societal impacts. In the Middle Ages, periodic fairs, such as the Besançon fair located between Lyon and Genoa, were the first significant financial fora in Western Europe, arising in response to problems in security, transport and constraints on economic freedom. The periodicity of the fairs initially established a standard time for a credit contract; for example, three months at a fair that met four times a year. Further innovations distinguishing capitalistic finance first appeared in Italian city states, but subsequent developments in Bruges, Lyon, Antwerp, and London were no less important.

Europe urbanized gradually under the influence of exposure to the prosperous Islamic cities in Iberia. Transport and security issues motivated newly urban merchants to develop new credit practices both to facilitate the transportation of commodities, and to make bringing goods to the fair often optional. Rather than retaining Islamic approaches to lending, one of the outcomes of the reconquest was that Christian Iberia adopted the Roman principle of fairness which considered commerce to be a form of combat; whatever buyer and seller agreed to was therefore "fair," so *caveat emptor*.

As bans on usury complicated commerce, centuries of toil by intellectuals in France and Italy and later in Salamanca were devoted to the effort to rehabilitate lending at interest. This included Buridan's introduction of the idea of subjective utility (*complacibilitas*) to moderate the thrust of *caveat emptor*. As these ideas matured, selected cities such as Florence, Genoa, Lyon, Paris, and Bruges became permanent centers for trade in both commodities and enriched versions of financial paper.

By the sixteenth century, the silting up of Bruges' access to the sea led merchants to move to Antwerp. Both Lyon and Antwerp became cities concentrating the exchange of commercial paper, with Lyon particularly devoted to this, and Antwerp with its great harbor also concentrating the actual commodity trade of Western Europe. The bourses in Bruges and subsequently in Lyon, Antwerp, and later Amsterdam and London became clearing houses for credit and early capital exchanges where credit could be raised and appraised even for massive military endeavors.

In mid-sixteenth century, Thomas Gresham, the brilliant British Royal Agent in Antwerp, managed to convince the Crown of the necessity of building up London's financial infrastructure, and so managed to wean England of its dependency on Antwerp's exchanges. In one aspect, discounting of credit instruments, British finance had long been on the cutting edge. Having had a discount market, for example, for exchequer's tallies since the late twelfth century, with the Glorious Revolution of 1688, England quickly developed the institutional matrix of banking, stock markets as well as laws and courts to enforce contracts and rationalized markets, laying the foundations for industrial capitalism.

Although hindsight is notoriously seductive, we would argue that the social dissatisfactions associated with the industrial revolutions of the seventeenth to twenty-first centuries have all been tied to the rapid neglect of ethics and of the real role of social capital (aka power) in the headlong rush for self-aggrandizement by elites. This began with the neglect of the brilliant insights of the Islamic world following the *Reconquista* and the amnesia about the best of scholastic thought following the Reformation, correct as Luther and others were in assessing church corruption. Few simple ideas, such as Weber's Protestant Ethic or the wholly European construction of modern finance, survive a close scrutiny in a sufficiently broad comparative perspective.

Few in Washington or other elite modern capitals are naive about the importance of social networking to politics or the market. We have shown that social networking is critical to even a small urban market in Morocco and that, in the form of institutions, social capital has significant long-term influences on economic behavior everywhere. We have also documented how financial forms and rules were adapted to economic needs as readily in the Ottoman or Byzantine areas as in Europe. Yet, what is a little surprising is that this commonality through time and across civilizations is so easily ignored in the public sphere and in Western-centric histories.

In modern financial analysis of both normal times and crises, quants in their algorithms include reputation, market risk, liability, and insurance, as well as individual credit worthiness, human capital in corporate networks, and commodity prices. A truly rigorous approach is only possible with modern data and computational power but attempts to assess credit worthiness have a long genealogy. Romans in the Early Republic fully understood the motivation for assessing human capital and social networks but they would have been puzzled most by the apparent criminalization of using social networks for personal gain. Partisanship was the essence of honorable behavior in the Republic while today under the influence of Weber we imagine bureaucratic impartiality to embody honorable procedure, ironically, for all except advocates in our courts.

It may be that our current version of virtue blinds us to this difference making it difficult to appreciate the true causal role of social capital in the past or present. Similarly, academic prejudice against the Near-Eastern monotheistic religions makes it difficult for many to subscribe to the notion that religious scholars might have contributed to modern finance or that they might have long since contributed ideas that could still be used to improve finance as we currently practice it. In this conclusion, we briefly reference key points from this and our earlier book[1] as illustrative material for more general theoretical conclusions.

Knowledge of the deep multicultural roots of modern finance in many societies studied by historians, archaeologists, and ethnographers is deeply important if we are ever to approach justice in lending or commerce. Even so, disciplinary boundaries and blinders have limited its advance in certain respects.

As Jack Goody notes: "The problem of the theft of history and of the social sciences also affects other humanities. In recent years, scholars have also taken steps to make their disciplines more comparative, more relevant to the rest of the world. But these measures are grossly inadequate to the task … supposing the development of human society from the Bronze age is regarded in different terms, as an ongoing elaboration of urban and mercantile culture without any sharp breaks involving categorical distinctions of the kind suggested by the use of the term "capitalist.""[2]

We have focused in this and our earlier book on the technical, social, and ethical contributions of many cultures even as we recognized, particularly in our chapter on the 2008 credit crisis, that modern economies have a number of original features as well.

UNDERSTANDING FINANCIAL HISTORY

Trust and social capital have been proxies for predictability and keys to profit yet risk levels can be positively (or negatively e.g., in oligopolistic situations) correlated with net benefits. For this reason there are few substitutes for intelligence in the pursuit of gain. Yet, when networking and financial justice are added to the mix, the problematic character of benefit maximizing can be seen to open avenues for excusing injustice and unethical behavior. Simple admonishments to treat others as you would have them treat you are readily countered by constructs of the tenor "a fool and his money are easily parted." This indeed was the basis for the recourse to *caveat emptor* first in Iberia and then across Europe. Nineteenth-century claims for the public utility of Darwinian competitive struggles favoring the fittest may have reached a peak of popularity in 2008: about 150 years after their introduction.

Yet few captains of industry actually favor a free for all, rather, even as they claim to promote the public interest, they prefer a civilized struggle in which the institutions of society take their side on every occasion. Although there are many devotees who imagine Darwin's praises of competition have a claim to being sacrosanct, a new theory of Darwinian economics has noted a different Darwinian insight; that competition over relative position promotes inefficiency rather than efficiency.[3] The antlers of male elk are inefficiently large as are the salaries of quants in the stock market. We would argue more broadly, that there are other goals than efficiency and, beyond the irrationality of relying solely on competition, ample reasons for societies to revise financial rules to promote justice in the distribution of liability, risk, and profit.

It has been said that you can't squeeze blood from a turnip yet even Karl Marx, who thought peasants were about as bright and lively as potatoes in a sack, might have disagreed.[4] One elitist version of the alternative position, put in a nutshell by H.L. Menckin, was "no one in this world ... has ever lost money by underestimating the intelligence of the great masses of the plain people."[5]

Lenders since ancient times, who have counted on making profits from poor and rich alike, may have shared Menckin's disdain, yet, intelligence, we would argue, is not the issue while productive inequalities[6] or development traps are; at least if one is to squeeze money from the rural or urban poor, or from turnips, potatoes, grain, dates, sugar cane, beets, or other crops. Financial inequalities led to high profits with disastrous consequences during the Irish potato famine of 1845–1849 and lay behind many other famines as well.[7] Such extremes are best seen as illustrating the capacity of socioeconomic infrastructure to facilitate the extraction of profits even at the worst of times.

Braudel focused attention on the reproductive cycle of capitalism by suggesting that credit (borrowing) is as fundamental to growth as profit making itself. His suggestion was that unless earnings are quickly and wisely reinvested the reproductive cycle is impeded. Since there is no automatic double coincidence of personal accumulation (savings) and real investment opportunities, those with an entrepreneurial bent have readily discovered that credit can facilitate the growth of their and others' incomes; and incidentally that of the economy itself.

The recognition that credit can be an instrument of growth, not just an instrument of wealth, undoubtedly predates the more explicit sociological discovery that it should more properly be seen as a technology of power where growth is only one possible side effect. The histories of Europe and its colonies, Western Asia, and the Mediterranean are replete with centuries during which the application of sophisticated credit instruments might best be characterized as involving serious exploitation leading to at best modest growth in the investment locale. The seventeenth to twentieth centuries, however, might oddly enough be characterized as a period in which both extremes of exploitation and economic growth can be tied to the proliferation of credit technologies.[8]

Adopting an ecological economics perspective[9] may help to clarify this extraordinary period. The Industrial Revolution may be seen as releasing a flood of investment into the ecosystem; oriented toward harvesting low entropic packages of energy and materials whose use by humanity eventually increased the standard of living and, not coincidentally, the overall wealth available for harvest by technologies of power.

This development, and the spread of public health knowledge created by intellectuals and benefiting many, casts doubt on Marx's anthropocentric insistence on a labor theory of value anchored in the labor of blue collar workers—viewed as the primary *productive* input—though one can always try to use some measure of labor to make a *moral* claim about the ideal distribution of goods and services to humans. Credit institutions facilitated the use of this initial increased accumulation for additional investment in industries; once again based on the perceived advantages of extracting "free goods" from the natural resource base. In many periods, humanity's symbolic skills contributed substantially as well.

Financiers time and again have convinced themselves and others that credit and money can be multiplied indefinitely through the "miracle of compound interest"—each overextended bubble of speculation being quickly forgotten, or deliberately banished from conversation, in a later elite generation's rush for gain. Translating what appears within society as labor, value, and profit into energy and matter admittedly obscures important details but in its simplicity it clarifies something important as well.

The immediate cause of growth is not compound interest (a cultural convention of particular importance to the distribution of wealth) but physical investment (in natural or human resources), the emergence of new possibilities and constraints as well as the intellectual productions of individuals and powerful particulars. To the extent that credit speeds up or helps to increase productive activities, it makes a short-term instrumental contribution to general human welfare—though this may be at the expense of the environment or at the expense of the health of particular sectors of society. Marx was quite wrong to think only blue-collar workers created value: his insights into the dialectical relationships between nature, the productive process and the creation of human identity were more insightful: value is a tandem creation of society and nature harnessed in one yoke.[10]

We have shown throughout the two books that whatever else credit may be, it is first a social relationship. For credit arrangements to work, the basic problem that must be resolved is how to ensure that the relationship between the parties endures, and that promises made are kept.[11] Our analysis of financial history has in no sense been intended as an adequate explanation of the course of events in any of the regions discussed. Many social and economic transformations have been deliberately ignored in our efforts to use a subset of available materials to tell our main story in as non-redundant a fashion as possible. The many conquests, the immiseration, and economic expansion that occurred in the areas studied, and that comprise the greater part of most historical accounts, have mostly suffered from benign neglect.

In the most recent millennium, European concern with potential injustice to merchants led usury to be gradually redefined by the medieval Catholic Church as limited to lending at rates of interest over and above the rate of return available through investment by the lender in normal commerce.[12] This rather sophisticated Thomistic "opportunity cost of money" model, that is hinted at by Plato, took a long time to develop and even longer to replace the Biblical and Greek prohibitions or contempt for most forms of lending.

While throughout the Middle Ages an opportunity cost of money model was impractical, both because of the unavailability of suitable statistics to establish a rate and because it relied on unqualified clergy to make that evaluation, this intellectual effort clearly helped rehabilitate the use of interest in banking and commerce. One late medieval state solution was to take a seat-of-the-breeches approach to national interest rates, which rather than make any serious attempt to calculate an opportunity cost for money, set a national rate by decree, deeming anything above it as usury.

While abstract consideration of risk were not absent in Europe, Europeans never developed quantitative criteria for evaluating credit risk nor was there a decision, as in the Islamic world, that risk had to be shared proportionally to profit: thus guaranteeing a future date amount of repayment automatically opened the door to exploitation through a failure to fully share risk. The problem with pre- and post-harvest loans of the type even Egyptians and Mesopotamians thought through so carefully did not give rise in Europe to the admirable Islamic insistence on transparent specification of inputs, profits, risk, and liability; and came to be explicitly rejected in Christian Iberia.

Our account directs historical attention to significant issues whose neglect has had sundry deleterious consequences. The modern "credit" economy has such deep roots that it might be better to speak of the factors of production as land, labor, and credit. Traditional definitions of capital tend to unidimensional perspectives that ignore its multidimensional impacts. The distinctiveness of the modern "capitalist" economy in our view is that competition has come to influence production more directly as the prices of the factors of production in some arenas more nearly represent their productive value. Our analysis of the 2008 credit crisis suggested that misunderstandings of the role of power and social capital as well as indifference to financial justice played key roles and were themselves examples of inexcusable historical ignorance.

While hierarchy as Dumont[13] suggests can have cultural bases as well, the difficulty of fooling all the people all the time makes it hard to ignore the hidden interests of hierarchy or the role of power for long. Sraffa's 1960 economic analysis[14] had the merit of pointing out that the price structure in an industrial economy can be elegantly modeled as one shaped by negotiations between major players (corporations): negotiations in which the portions distributed to the working, owning, and financing sectors represents no more than a negotiated settlement and quite demonstrably are not a technically derived precise calculation of who deserves what.

While Sraffa's model may work best for an early stage of the capitalist economy, his Gramsci inspired insight that the powerful influence the overall structure of distributions in the economy more than do the weak is less tied to a particular time and place. The importance of social networks for financial success predates the rise of modern transnational corporations and, as we have shown, brought similar advantages in earlier times and cultures.[15]

The evidence from the last 1,000 years allow us to substantiate Nell's[16] insight that while competition may have transformative impacts on production technology and on the social relations of production in any capitalist economy, such transformative effects long predate capitalist economies.

Defining institutions in terms of culturally set norms and forms of behavior, our chapters have focused on financial institutions seen through a broad cultural lens. Although we have ignored many of the cultural and political reasons a capitalist economy developed where and when it did, we have shown how even financial institutions need to be understood in a broader context as social institutions reflecting cultural values. In this sense we have followed Nell and Errouaki in advocating a methodological institutionalism.[17]

Few scholars still accept the simple mantra derived from, but not attributable to, Adam Smith, that self-serving individualism is always socially beneficial. Adam Smith thought the psychology of commerce involved sympathy (empathy) not greed. A couple centuries later Simon and Sen pointed out that altruistic behavior can be more socially beneficial than self-serving behavior and that to suggest that humans engage exclusively in self-serving behavior is to suggest they are rational fools.[18]

Yet, the evidence from history has led us to recognize the creative potential of financial inequalities to transform human societies and this justifies our reluctance to assume either that exchange implies equality or that inequality is always to be avoided. Modern understandings of causality and ontology have shaped what might be called our emergent capabilities[19] approach to studying financial institutions, social capital, ethical systems, and economic transformations. Attention to the institutionalization of differential interests, especially the hidden interests that attracted so much concern about transparency in the Islamic world, allows us to better understand the freedoms that new financial instruments confer as well as the ways in which they motivate and constrain human behavior and thereby transform institutions.

THE SOMETIMES FANTASTICAL LINKAGES BETWEEN FINANCE AND PROSPERITY

At some level, all cultural difference is fantastical in the sense of imbuing a sense of normality to somewhat arbitrary ways of behaving and an aura of power to arbitrary individuals. The unpredictable financial consequences of the Inquisition in Iberia, including the subsequent elite capture and economic stagnation in the peninsula, are a case in point. The gift of silver, derived from pillage of the Americas, turned surprisingly into an early example of the resource curse; one might almost think gifts need to be returned.

Instead, the modern market increasingly depicts sales (e.g., of fair trade coffee, endangered species tagged chocolate, and romanticized products more generally) as embodying a semiotics of the ethical suitable for addressing individual consumer guilt over the blatant inequalities of the exchange. In this way, despite vastly higher standards of living than most producers, western consumers too can be on the side of the angels. It is informative that the neoclassical economics view that exchanges are really exchanges of equal value; once subjective preferences are calculated, it is hard pressed to explain modern advertising based on guilt.

Advertising, fashion trends, inflation, unpredictability in nature and society, the imbrication of the ethical and speculation itself leaven the market and produce opportunities. Advertising and speculation regularly maintain a profitable valuation disjuncture: one reason stock analysts give for referring to stocks as being over- or under-valued and a key reason for rejecting the notion that current market price is the only measure of value needed: a point Ricardo emphasized in the early nineteenth century.[20] The notion of a disjuncture in valuation is critical because it opens the way to a more critical understanding of all technologies of power, including credit, as involving inequalities not equalities.

The pretense that commodity values are fixed at fair market price is both confused and biased yet this is regularly extended to the notion that the value of a loan (seen as a commodity like any other) is the same for both parties to a transaction. The epistemological unreasonableness of the latter proposition is easily illustrated by the recourse to quite disparate and incommensurable sets of psychological factors for the recipient of a loan (liquidity preferences, undervaluation of future goods, and the desire to own a home) and the lender (the current opportunity cost of money and the risk of non-recovery). The opportunity cost and the risk over the period of the loan are of course as unknowable as is the future interest rate and political situation.

The obliviousness to inequality in lending also goes against a more recent observation by economists that a key to development, perhaps more important than rights, is opportunity sets. Most social scientists, including economists, acknowledge that the wealthy have greater, more varied, and more useful opportunities and that these are tied to social, cultural, and economic capital. It is also clear that the very wealthy ensure themselves access to returns on investment that consistently provide higher net rates (especially after taxes) than anything available to the public.

Resistance to this view is encouraged by a nineteenth-century suspicion that introduction of differential power, with the implication that prices in exchange usually favor one party, undermines a significant assumption of both the neoclassical and Marxist economic models. This is the claim that all commodities on average trade at their real value: that average price equals value. We advocate a more nuanced view.

Many relations which analytically may be seen as credit transactions between lenders and borrowers are called many other things—rents, leases, annuities, sharecropping, or user fees. Economists, since Ricardo, have disparaged obviously unearned benefits derived from "rents" (e.g., excessive profits due to monopolies) or elite capture (e.g., large benefits made by elites from neoliberal reforms leading to sales of public utilities to cronies at fire-sale prices), but few venture so far as to evaluate transactions in general as not necessarily fair.

Recognition of the widespread nature of inequalities puts quite a different complexion on the provision of free services: rather than being strange, or even so unbelievable as to require explaining away as greed under another guise, they count merely as yet another transaction which does not involve equal valued goods. In this case, they rely on the incommensurability of both goods and aspirations and an agreement to participate in the game that creates social capital. Absolute fairness removes incentives, so we need some degree of unfairness even as most of us recognize that there are degrees of unfairness so deplorable they also remove incentive.

Although some credit arrangements need only willing partners, most agreements require the presence of forms of power to work. Power has the odd characteristic of being viewed as the most important thing by some social scientists and as utterly irrelevant by others. By power, we mean not only the ability of authorities to enforce payments or to mediate disputes, but, more broadly, the everyday processes that create the customary practices, bureaucratic procedures, and laws that are essential for certain kinds of credit. At their most basic, these are what Bourdieu called symbolic capital that is established and maintained not only through customary practices but through political processes as well. We have suggested that credit often becomes one of the instrumental technologies through which power is exercised. We might even view this as a symbiotic relationship between financial institutions and the exercise of power by governments and individuals. None of this implies that hierarchy or the exercise of power have no positive social value for they motivate much of human behavior.

The vocabulary of power has attracted such devotion that major theorists seem to have felt obliged to define it differently. We largely follow Lukes' Gramscian perspective, though we accept several ideas from Foucault, Bourdieu, Wolf, and Popper.[21] Foucault insisted that not only is power pervasive in human relations (and not intrinsically bad) but it also requires resistance in order to exist and passes into mere domination once resistance is overcome.[22] Foucault was aware of Weber's suggestion that one elucidate a causal influence by imagining what might have happened without that cause being present but perhaps Weber's failure to imagine multivariant analysis contributed to Foucault's failure to go beyond a binary and subjective understanding of power.

Bureaucracy makes sense as organized power but interactions between merchants combine both the search for profit and the exercise of power.[23] Modern models of causality recognize that minute factors can change a balance and give rise to major change. Lukes' three dimensional definition; a) direct influence (e.g., the force of logical, ideological, or ethical argumentation); b) agenda control (deciding what gets discussed or oligopolistic influence over what goods are produced at what prices); and c) hegemonic ideas influencing people's desires; acknowledges that all three might also involve various amounts of brute force. As we noted in our chapter on the 2008 credit crisis, there are also more social, emergent properties of complex systems enhanced by the clever discretization of capital. All causal factors are best seen as influencing situational propensities in particular conjunctures.

In the current admiration of economics, some doubt that any credit instruments might be deleterious to general welfare or the environment; those modern substitutes for the *summum bonum* of philosophers. Yet, many scholars recognize that credit can be destructive as well as constructive and that long-term social or ecological benefits may not be optimized by short-term profits.[24]

Important disagreements still exist over how to ensure that finance is socially beneficial. It is unlikely there will ever be a simple guide to ethical finance given the complexity of the issues involved and the unpredictability of even the near-term future as well as because competition has some merits, and so some degree of inequality is both inescapable and socially beneficial. Still, wise assessments of financial systems need to address explicitly transparency, profit, investment of time and labor, risk, and liability. Modern mortgages and consumer protection legislation have made a few small steps in this direction but they have a long way to go.

No system yet has been optimally just while providing reasonable incentives to everyone. General welfare will, nevertheless, benefit from greater elaboration of how codes of morality should imbricate with financial institutions and economic norms. Equally beneficial would be a clear recognition that transparency in finance[25] cannot be achieved without recognizing the connections between productive inequalities, or inequality of opportunity sets, and social hierarchy.

CONCEPTUALIZING CREDIT

Economists treat credit as a commodity that ideally sells at an efficient price in appropriate quantities even if they acknowledge no perfect credit market exists:

> In a perfect credit market, there is a single interest rate and everyone can borrow or lend as much as they want at that rate.[26]

In our view, not only is there not a perfect market for credit today but there has, as we have shown, never been a perfect market for credit, as so defined, since the first significant institutionalization of credit practices more than five thousand years ago. We have provided many historical reasons and specific examples, but the underlying reason for this non-existence is that credit, an instrument of power and at best a quasi-commodity, always imbricates people, powerful particulars, and societies differentially. It is likely to remain the case that different parties borrow at different rates.

We may add a page to Marx and suggest that, like the employer-employee relationship,[27] credit represents a relationship of power and, similarly, is not best characterized as commodity exchange. Thus imagining an ideal world with efficient pricing for credit is as naive as imagining hired labor receiving 100 percent of the value it creates: leaving no benefits to the employer. Clearly, this does not preclude the selling of loan contracts as commodities in the market: a change of ownership does not, itself, impact the legal force of the contract nor its many impacts. Thus a loan by the World Bank to an African country remains effectively in force, as do its ramifications, if it is assumed instead by the IMF: though a change in conditionalities would create a different loan and abolish the old. Authority and hierarchy, in or outside the market, would be little valued if they provided no source of advantage. Systems of ethics have pushed to mitigate extremes of disadvantage precisely because they have well understood such benefits and how they incentivize people.

The issue of getting the prices right, in the sense of significant correlation with productive value, is sometimes seen as a hallmark of capitalism. Non-capitalist economies do not regularly get many prices right in this sense. Yet, we are saying something different about credit. We can agree that societal instantiations of credit have varied substantially in their liberality or conservatism; in who has access and under what conditions. In this sense the role of credit has and does vary significantly in terms of how it contributes to production and influences society.

Credit involves obligations themselves tied to networks of other obligations, and implies acquiescence in systems of inequality that stimulate and organize society. Credit is a regular source of investment funds, but one with a great potential for a long-term multiplier impact both on economic prosperity and on social inequality. This is of greatest interest to us because that impact is particularly enhanced by the hierarchical forms of human organization we typically associate with the term civilization.

One of the great appeals of credit is that states, which have significant control over the use of power, can more readily lay their hands on productive collateral such as lands than on money itself, as the thousands of buried hoards over the ages so vividly attest. There are modern calls to eliminate currency because more than 80 percent of U.S. dollars circulate underground as

$100 bills and animate criminal networks. Land is something that, because it cannot run away or be hidden, is potentially easy to monitor. Modern stocks and bonds similarly rely on their digital existence to establish their utility. From the ancient world to the present any history of states would benefit from attention to credit and its collateral. We have every reason, therefore, to suspect influence meddling when states focus on income tax rather than property tax.

The reader may at this point imagine we are suggesting it suffices to point out that credit relationships are relationships of inequality not equality. Yet this is clearly insufficient for we need to focus on the multidimensional, short and long term, unequal impacts of financial instruments. We would argue that we actually need what might be called a tensor theory of credit[28] in which the tensors measure stresses (Latin *tensus*) with directional properties along multiple dimensions (e.g., evolution of financial systems, ethical and legal transformations, social hierarchy and issues of liability and risk, issues of empowerment, neocolonial relationships, and public policy). Such a conception would enable us to go beyond drawing attention to hierarchy in financial transactions and the particular advantages or disadvantages of social hierarchy.

Viewed as a force, credit recaptures the instrumental agency Sumerians long ago envisaged for it. At its most elementary, a tensor theory of credit would focus attention on the power of credit to create social bonds and the directionality of its societal impacts: in contrast, a quantity theory of credit is like a molecular theory without chemical bonds (note that the word "valence" derives from late Latin "valentia" meaning power or competence).[29] Current work in economic theory has suggested replacing the neoclassical economic focus on efficiency and equal value exchange with positional analysis that assumes plural normative criteria and a hierarchy of political economic persons rather than an imaginary array whose cells are occupied by "rational fools." We view our work as potentially contributing to this effort by centering the analysis of finance on differentials, impacts, and ethics to encourage a more nuanced structural econometrics.[30]

Turning to historical considerations, we would argue that credit initially benefitted and empowered institutions and then gradually came to add specifications to facilitate long-distance trade. Eventually credit practices moved toward the possibility of fuller specification within documents themselves and, thereby, empowered their individual bearers (lenders and, secondarily, recipients of loans) across multiple jurisdictions.

If we ask who, historically, determined loan specifications with their multidimensional implications we may envisage history as three overlapping periods in which loans have conditions established in societal and institutional matrices:

Who controls: Type and Evolution of Conditionalities

C3: Society;
No conditionalities recorded beyond basic loan amounts and names of parties, unknown oral components.
C2: Institutions and Society;
Increasingly elegant and useful, even elaborate specification; oral commitments and assumptions become less important.
C1: Individuals, Institutions, and Society;
Further elaboration of specifications, facilitated by increasing discretization in finance, adding value but decreasing elegance as time goes on due to increasingly sophisticated lending practices targeting individuals, powerful particulars, and even nations.

Elegantly packaged credit (C1, C2) established the terms between parties in a single document and earlier less elegant forms of credit (C3), though they bind parties into hierarchical webs of interdependency, seem to have relied on social forces or religious and government power to sanction obligations without attempting to specify particulars within a contract. An elegant document (C2) may rely on an extensive, common infrastructure while the less fully specified loan document (C3) may empower individuals better across multiple jurisdictions sharing religious values.

The key characteristics we would like to focus on are: a) the gradual transformations over time from forms of obligation that offer few guarantees and rely on diffuse social sanctions towards ones in which increasing numbers of particulars are specified and b) the potential for increasing empowerment of private parties, defined as those in a weak position to redefine the general rules, to engage in credit relationships. Throughout the periods we have examined, governments have continued to control some aspects of credit.

In this tripartite chronology (with C3 being most ancient and C2 and C1 having been evolving for millennia), we can distinguish three incarnations of credit showing the locus of the power to decide on the details and to impose sanctions associated with credit. Thus, long before the elaboration of detailed contracts, societies would have used peer pressure and various incentives, for example, access to prestige or recourse to religious notions, to pressure people to reciprocate loans (C3) at varied levels of advantage to the lender.

Over the course of time, institutions such as temples and governments, and then bureaucratic institutions more generally,[31] defined credit relationships in more careful ways and established sanctions (C2). The right of private parties to enforce credit (C1) contracts depended on the prior development of institutional practice and legal norms—without this a private party would be in a poor position either to enforce an obligation or to determine what details could usefully be specified in a contract. Institutional practice established such norms and legal codes as institutions were gradually elaborated such that private parties could have recourse to the law and could call on governments to impose sanctions on debtors who defaulted.

Thus we define C2 as credit in which institutions, with considerable sanctioning power (e.g., states and temples, the IMF or the World Bank), decide by specifying a number of particulars in a well-defined contractual way. Similarly, C1 would additionally involve private parties with limited power within institutionally determined rules but great contractual clarity (e.g., a Jacob Fugger, the Medici firm, a monarch or a dictator, and later every adult). Both C2 and C1 develop over time in the sense of increasing specification of particulars in increasingly elegant or useful forms and depend on ethical considerations at the societal level.

Obligations do not all have to be stipulated in a single document for credit to exist—they merely need to be socially accepted. A modern example (C2) may help introduce this idea. Loans to poor countries, when swallowed by elites, tend to incur debts for the poor (the "people" or "country" who of course sign no documents and frequently receive no benefits) and these debts have tended to be collected through structural adjustment programs trimming "fat" from already emaciated education or health budgets. Such inequalities are, broadly speaking, socially acceptable in Europe or the United States, if imposed outside these areas, but their stipulations depend on a multitude of documents, practices, and cultural attitudes that range from obtuseness to racism and indifference. Thus they are sanctioned by society (social norms) and by institutions but are not simple private party arrangements.

Economists have focused on money and this has, on occasion, led them to an asocial view of credit. Only recently have economists begun to recognize that money itself may be viewed as credit vouchers tied to an authority framework. Just how symbolic "gifts" resolve into other forms of obligation and imbricate with ethical concerns is both an empirical and a theoretical issue. While we have not tried to answer questions about the origin of modern finance in a definitive way, we follow Bachelard in encouraging an epistemological break involving both criticism of received theoretical views and an analysis of credit that is both broader and deeper than a simple focus on the origin or specifications of particular forms of credit.[32]

We have shown in this book and our previous book, *The Roots of Western Finance*, how far back in the past we can find parallels to these types of (C3–C1) credit. That financial contracts have been established for millennia is not in question, nor have the societal legal and extraordinary ethical efforts to deal with their impacts been difficult to find. We have also discussed at length the diffuseness of the groups tied together by these credit arrangements and the multiplicity of institutions and social capital actively involved in assuring the direction of financial flows in different eras.

It is worth noting that while the significance of credit in financing trade or production has been regularly acknowledged, claims that such investments are to be seen as obligations tied to religious or sacred goals have also long been present. Today as in the past, many view government regulation of finance as unjust interference in a sacred practice and react with the outrage typical of a true believer to attacks on their favorite religious principle: the right to lend, buy, or sell blessed by greed, *caveat emptor,* and the invisible hand.

The roots of such views are far deeper than many suspect. Yet, even today they are as likely to enchant the financial elite as the uneducated. Misgivings driven by the failures of the Washington Consensus solutions to global and national problems have nevertheless led many to realize that austerity and good governance are financial and policy dogma that disguise hidden interests in preserving the status quo. Our analysis suggests their limited success in improving global welfare, despite the extraordinary productivity of the modern economy, must be linked to financial obscurantism, a variety of dogma, neglect of justice, social exclusion of those outside the elite, and a general lack of moral probity.

CONCLUDING REMARKS BY WAY OF SOME ETHNOGRAPHIC REFLECTIONS ON CREDIT

We have focused on those aspects of the history of finance that best explain the current situation in the countries of some key players in global finance, but most societies studied by ethnographers lie outside that tradition. We cannot close without some attention to the majority of humanity past and present. Here we add a few remarks about this topic we have so far largely ignored; to make the point that human approaches to credit have much in common even when an inherited common cultural tradition is not a critical factor.

"Gifts make slaves, like whips make dogs," is how an Eskimo proverb conveys something of the problematic nature of gift exchange.[33] Gifts entail coercive social and moral burdens that are like manacles until one reciprocates them. Yet, even when one does reciprocate, because gift requires gift, one is never free from the social bonds created. As Mauss[34] notes about the Maori, the coercive nature of gifts can stem from their being seen as imbued with some part of the giver's spirit. The gift is not just an object, it is a pledge that stands for the giver and embodies his relationship to the recipient, so that to refuse a gift or fail to reciprocate is to reject the giver as well. In other words, because person and gift are not completely separable, just as with a loan the giver retains a lien on what he has given away, constraining the recipient to make a return.

In the anthropological literature, Mauss' discussion of the "Gift" has long been seen as an example of an early set of institutionalized behaviors or, in the Durkheimian sense,[35] a total social fact in which the significance of a unidirectional gift actually involves unpacking a set of linked social and moral practices that directly or indirectly entail return flows.[36] Mauss described the Maori / Polynesian notion that gifts were accompanied by a spiritual element ("*hau*") that in some fashion engendered reciprocity. Much has been written on this and Mauss himself was not consistent.[37] Yet, toward the end of his first chapter, Mauss noted that the biblical *zadaqa*, which came (like Arabic *sadaqa*) to mean alms, originally meant justice. The important point was that justice was not seen as an individual perception but rather as a moral or legal concept—defined by society, for Durkheim's students, and, by God or the gods, for the religious.

The Indo-European term giving rise to the term "credit" (*kred*) had a spiritual quality like that of the "*hau*" yet was as much an establishment of trust (as in "credo") as it was an institutionalization of obligation. Bourdieu thus writes of symbolic power:

> Symbolic power is a power which the person submitting to grants to the person who exercises it, a credit with which he credits him, a *fides*, an *auctoritas*, with which he entrusts him by placing his trust in him. It is a power which exists because the person who submits to it believes that it exists. *Credo*, says Benveniste, "is literally 'to place one's *kred*,' that is 'magical powers,' in a person from whom one expects protection thanks to 'believing' in him."[38]

Malinowski's famous discussion of the Kula ring, describing the continuous flow of two durable symbolic goods (shell necklaces going clockwise and shell armbands going counterclockwise) around a series of Melanesian islands, might be taken as an early illustrative example fitting both Mauss' perspective on credit and ours. Traditionally, young Trobriand trading partners involved in the Kula trade would hope to advance to more prestigious partners over time but would not do this by taking advantage of their superiors, on the contrary they would hope to get better than they gave from equals or inferiors but give more than they received to superiors in order to cultivate the relationship and eventually move up the hierarchy:[39]

> each man has an enormous number of articles passing through his hands during his lifetime, of which he enjoys the temporary possession, and which he keeps in trust for a time. This possession hardly ever makes him use the articles, and he remains under the obligation soon again to hand them on to one of his partners. But the temporary ownership allows him to draw a great deal of renown, to exhibit his article, to tell how he obtained it, and to plan to whom he is going to give it. And all this forms one of the favourite subjects of tribal conversation and gossip, in which the feats and the glory in Kula of chiefs and commoners are constantly discussed and re-discussed.[40]

These exchanges were sometimes accompanied by trade in consumables but seem primarily designed to establish relations of trust that themselves turn normal barter into part of a credit system in which exactly equal exchanges perform less well than unequal transactions. As in the establishment of credit in the United States, the establishment of a system of delayed exchange using highly valued symbolic durables also created dependencies and hierarchies of prestige that provided an infrastructure of credit in which trade in consumables was both stimulated and made more reliable—for who would jeopardize social prestige and the chances of its increase over misbehavior in the realm of trade in mere consumables, even yams, the closest thing to a Trobriand traditional currency.

A more chaotic process competing over honors is exemplified by the potlatch of the Kwakiutl, involving the disbursement of vast quantities of wealth at feasts, which first expanded after the 1830s and then declined early in the twentieth century as alternative pathways to honor available through the modern economy became more attractive:

> With the acceleration of capitalist development, capitalist accumulation in expanding markets, coupled with population loss, cumulatively subverted the structural conditions that had underwritten this earlier concentration of chiefly power. Opportunities for raiding also decreased, and "fighting with property" grew more important ... repeated epidemics reduced the number of legitimate claimants to titles and to the chiefship, and access to new sources of wealth allowed new aspirants to validate spurious claims to privileges through participation in giveaways and feasting.[41]

The potlatch illustrates the close tie between cultural practices and historical transformations that we have examined at length throughout our two books. The general link between debt, fighting, and alliance was first carefully elaborated by Edmund Leach who, writing about the Kachin of highland Burma, suggested:

> In principle any outstanding debt, no matter what its origin, is potentially a source of feud ... It is especially debts between strangers that must be settled quickly ... in contrast, debts between relatives, especially affinal relatives are not urgent matters. Indeed as between *mayu* and *dama* some debts are always left outstanding almost as a matter of principle; the debt is a kind of credit account which ensures the continuity of the relationship.[42]

There can be few who imagine that today debtors are not similarly treated with punitive terms in some cases and friendly terms in others. The point of most exchanges is that they are not equal in the short or long term: this is why they motivate in terms of desire for profit, power, or honor. They provide opportunities via ties of obligation for advancement as well as significant rewards for investments of hard work. Such exchanges can be more or less formal contracts or a series of outright gifts. Gifts, in this view, partake of and help maintain a moral universe that would not be sustained by mere simultaneous exchange of equivalents (it would have no power to generate trust). It should be no surprise that the powers that run the global economy usually view debts as an instrument for global direction and control—a service harnessed explicitly to their own self advancement.

While the Maori interpretation of gifts provides a more democratic social explanation in terms of Maori spiritual beliefs, we saw in *The Roots of Western Finance* that in the Early Republic of Rome complete social catastrophe was the fate of anyone who refused to engage in honorable financial behavior and that such behavior included the free services of the *mandatum*. Similarly, in the Islamic world refusal to perform burdensome yet unremunerated ibdā'a, or to engage in honorable financial performance more generally, would have completely ruined a merchant. The basic rule was that to be human was to respect social obligations as defined by one's society and to do otherwise was to set oneself outside of society.

Etymologically, we can contrast capital,[43] which began as an object of investment (livestock), with credit, which began as the establishment of obligation. The Ur-example of obligation was human understandings of the expectation of Mesopotamian gods that humanity would provide for them and the recognition that people were primarily empowered to be the agents of the gods. In Assyrian *naruqqu* contract terms, that by the Middle Ages had become the ubiquitous *commenda* contract, we might say the gods leased the world to humanity who did the work and received a third of the profits. A structural anthropologist might well argue that, in Sumerian times, cultural norms predisposed people to view this original contract as a just contract even when the gods and their temples took a disproportionate share of production. We hope that distance will disabuse all of us of our conviction, probably abetted by marginal analysis and poor analytical skills, that financial contracts normally involve exchange of equal value. Perhaps a realistic and ethical approach to finance will one day prevail; one that accepts a reasonable degree of hierarchy and a high degree of justice; one in which the gods, in their incarnation as the poor, receive a reasonable allocation here on earth.

NOTES

1. Park and Greenberg, *The Roots of Western Finance: Power, Ethics, and Social Capital in the Ancient World*, begins in Mesopotamia circa 4000 BC and ends with the development of classic Islamic financial ideas up to circa AD 1100. While we allude

to some of those ideas in this volume the reader should refer to our earlier volume for more details.

2. Goody, *The Theft of History,* 286.

3. Frank, *The Darwin Economy*. Darwin's examples began with the wasteful (in terms of energy) escalation of antler size among male *Cervidae* while Frank directs attention in particular to salaries on Wall Street, military budgets, and the extravagant life styles of the rich and famous which divert resources from more socially productive uses.

4. Marx in 1852 wrote that "The small-holding peasants form an enormous mass whose members live in similar conditions but without entering into manifold relations with each other. Their mode of production isolates them from one another instead of bringing them into mutual intercourse. The isolation is furthered by France's poor means of communication and the poverty of the peasants. Their field of production, the small holding, permits no division of labor in its cultivation, no application of science, and therefore no multifariousness of development, no diversity of talent, and no wealth of social relationships. Each individual peasant family is almost self-sufficient, directly produces most of its consumer needs, and thus acquires its means of life more through an exchange with nature than in intercourse with society. A small holding, the peasant and his family; besides it another small holding, another peasant and another family. A few score of these constitute a village, and a few score villages constitute a department. Thus the great mass of the French nation is formed by the simple addition of homonymous magnitudes, much as potatoes in a sack form a sack of potatoes." Marx, *The Eighteenth Brumaire of Louis Bonaparte*, Section VII.

5. Much quoted, the source is Mencken, "Notes on Journalism," *Chicago Tribune*, September 19, 1926.

6. Donham. *History, Power, Ideology.*

7. Sen, *Poverty and Famines.*

8. A brilliant article has recently mapped out the seriously different consequences of the institutions established by colonial powers: Acemoglu, Johnson and Robinson, "*The Colonial Origins of Comparative Developme*nt," 1369–1401.

9. This perspective introduces a significant role for thermodynamics, environmentally specific causality, and resource quality (in terms of thermodynamics, for example, oil is both depletable and is a low entropy source of energy which when consumed inevitably produces high entropy pollution implying both that increased consumption may encounter shortfalls in the general category of low entropy energy sources and cause, via pollution, costs that inevitably will have to be incorporated into economic calculations), cf Common and Stagl, *Ecological Economics* or Hahnel, *Green Economics,* as well as a vast literature on this subject.

10. Mészáros, *Marx's Theory of Alienation,* Chapter III. The Conceptual Structure of Marx's Theory of Alienation.

11. Firth and Yamey, *Capital, Savings and Credit in Peasant Societies*, 29–31.

12. Schumpeter, *History of Economic Analysis*, 103.

13. Dumont, *Homo Hierarchicus,* argued that cultures can have overarching hierarchical oppositions built into them. Parkin, *Louis Dumont and hierarchical opposition,* summarizes the argument of many of Dumont's publications that such oppositions

shape perceptions and behavior and contrast dramatically with the sorts of individualistic traditions developed in Europe as developed in Lukes, *Individualism.*

14. Sraffa, *Production of commodities by means of commodities,* leaves little role for the "sovereign consumer" and gives a large role to corporate negotiation in determining the price structure. This argument does a good job in describing a fairly early stage of industrial capitalism but it has not been extended to cover many subsequent changes. Nell's *The General Theory of transformational growth* provides a more sophisticated model that can accommodate recent transformations without granting a major role to a neoclassical (Edgeworth type) consumer demand and producer supply derived equilibrium in prices.

15. It is, for example, the overall conclusion of Spufford, *Power and Profit,* that the structure of the medieval economy was primarily shaped by the opportunities arising to satisfy the needs of the elites; in addition to demographic and other factors such as the continual trade imbalances between Europe and the Near East or secondary imbalances in flows of species to Russia (for furs) or England (for wool). The role of power in the ancient world, including Ancient Egypt and Ur III Mesopotamia is discussed in Gibson and Biggs, eds *The Organization of Power,* which, in line with our financial analysis, focuses on institutions rather than individuals. Our discussion of the Early Republic and of dynastic Egypt suggests that both perspectives are relevant in the ancient world.

16. Nell, *The General Theory of Transformational Growth.*

17. Nell and Errouaki, *Rational Econometric Man.*

18. Simon, "Altruism and Economics," 156–61; Sen, "Rational Fools," 317–44.

19. Our minor quibble with the Nussbaum and Sen capabilities approach is its lack of a dynamic dimension and we follow a large numbers of scholars in recognizing the importance of emergence in social systems. Wan, *Reframing the Social,* provides a valuable review of the literature with a focus on the early contributions of Mario Bunge.

20. As Dobb so elegantly pointed out long ago, *Theories of value and distribution since Adam Smith,* the only strong arguments for denying the utility of a distinction between price and value are ideological. Marx liked to talk of "averages" but, as many analysts now view prices as fundamentally chaotic, the concept of a price average, over any particular period, as representative of a functional tendency is as unpersuasive as that average is an unbiased estimator of future trends.

21. Lukes, *Power A Radical View*; Bourdieu, *Language and Symbolic Power*; Swartz, *Culture & Power. The Sociology of Pierre Bourdieu*; and Popper, *A World of Propensities* make a strong case for understanding causality as influencing situational propensities. In such a model, power (to influence) is intrinsically non-deterministic (no simple cause is sufficient to determine an outcome).

22. Foucault, *Dits et Ecrits,* vol. II, 580, claims his analyses are historical fictions whose value may yet be considerable both in terms of illuminating the past and suggesting positions in the present. Although Foucault's emphasis on techniques of the self (*du soi*) places him squarely in the methodological individualistic camp he is also what might be called a methodological dyadist—insisting that power involves two parties and can profitably be analyzed as such. There are two types of problems with

this stance. In the first place, it is a simplistic approach to reality. The second issue is that there are several good reasons for thinking it is methodologically irrational to take this position. Even in chemistry the order of combination of ingredients is critical and the notion that in the social sciences you could profitably take elements two at a time (Noah notwithstanding) is less than persuasive. More significantly, any conjunctural model allowing for emergent systemic properties would not allocate causality to discrete dyadic factors. Multiple factor causality and emergent system properties are here to stay.

23. Power in these senses has been the subject of excellent historical works discussed in various chapters e.g., Gibson and Biggs, *The Organization of Power,* and Spufford, *Power and Profit.*

24. There are many critiques of the financial policies and results of World Bank and IMF lending including, Farmer, *Pathologies of Power*; Caufield, *Masters of Illusion*; Blustein, *Misadventures of the Most Favored Nations*, and Gray, *False Dawn.*

25. Scholars have imagined two versions of transparency we might designate Freirean and Foucauldian. The former would deal with transparency about relations of power as viewed by the powerless and the latter would target clarity in surveillance of the governed. Justice in finance may require a balance between these two as well as a measure of interpersonal transparency in financial dealings, these are all areas with which Islamic finance has traditionally been concerned though modern Islamic banking neglects the first.

26. The World Bank, *World Development Report 2006. Equity and Development,* 89.

27. Although we agree with Marx on this humanistic ideal, Bauman, *Consuming Life*, 9 notes that in the 1990s employers in Silicon valley coined the term "zero drag" to define the ideal employee as a commodity without attachments, intellectual or other, who could be endlessly repurposed or relocated as their employer desired. These days the young have unconsciously assimilated these ideals into their notions of an optimal vita. Ironically, this scenario approximates Marx's *German Ideology* vision (Volume I, Part 1. Private Property and Communism) for producers' flexible activities under communism—except for the marionette strings.

28. Tensors deal with quantities that are invariant under translations in coordinate systems, e.g., temperature at a point or the length of a vector, and originate with the idea that forces provide stresses (Latin: *tensus*) to areas: thus a force applied at a 90 degree angle to a metal causes tensile stress while one applied at a more acute angle causes both tensile and shear stress. An appropriate scalar can be seen as a tensor of rank zero and similarly a vector can be seen as a tensor of rank one. Loans (whose amounts are invariant scalars as required) could profitably be viewed in a comparable way: forces that stress individuals, groups, and nations. Tensors can cope with multiple influences and though generally easy to imagine (construct), interactions between tensors are often mathematically hard to resolve as complexities grow with the rank of the tensor.

29. More simply, we might imagine credit as flows within a network, and our task as similar to that of a theoretical ecologist mapping trophic flows between compartments of an ecosystem and their long term potential consequences. The mathematics

for this has been satisfactorily developed by Ulanowicz, *Ecology, The Ascendant Perspective* and provides a way to measure changes in constraint (or hierarchies) within a system as well as basic measures of resilience or network health. For economic prosperity the net return and flow of investment is critical but would depends a lot on the character of the network and its resilience in the face of historical conjunctures.

30. Brown, Söderbaum and Dereniowska, *Positional Analysis for Sustainable Development,* and Nell and Errouaki, *Rational Econometric Man.*

31. We rely on the Weberian notion of bureaucracy because bureaucratic institutions, such as temples, governments or even (later) banks acquired a legitimacy not available to private parties and had the means to sanction their decisions. This is not to say that their claims of a just administration of credit stand up to close scrutiny but we do argue that historically they first experimented with the elaboration of credit contracts and successfully made claims to legitimately administer and regulate credit.

32. Bourdieu, Chamboredon and Passeron, *The Craft of Sociology.* Emphasize the difficulties of stepping back from received theoretical positions and the ineluctable connection between "data" and "theory." Bachelard in *Rationalisme Appliqué* (idem., 87–90) cautions against taking "empirical facts" as such rather than recognizing that they are intimately connected to assumed theoretical positions.

33. Sahlins, *Tribesmen,* 87–88.

34. Mauss, "Essai sur le don. Forme et raison de l'échange dans les sociétés archaïques" has been translated and reprinted in English many times under the title of The Gift.

35. Durkheim in *Les règles de la méthode sociologique* argued that social facts are institutionalized to the extent that they shape behavior.

36. Mauss, *Essai sur le don,* 13ff.

37. As many have noted, Mauss vacillated between psychological arguments and structural ones with the latter undoubtedly predominating.

38. Bourdieu, *Language & Symbolic Power,* 192 (citing Beneveniste, *Indo-European Language and Society,* 99).

39. Malinowski, *Argonauts of the Western Pacific.*

40. Ibid., 94.

41. Wolf, *Envisioning Power,* 128.

42. Leech, *Political Systems of Highland Burma,* 153.

43. The OED suggests it is derived from a root meaning "head" that gave rise both to the French word for cattle, cheptal, by the twelfth century and our modern economic term at least by 1611.

References

Abu-Lughod, Janet L. *Before European Hegemony: The World System 1250–1350.* Oxford, Oxford University Press, 1989.

Abulafia, David. *The Great Sea. A Human History of the Mediterranean.* Oxford: Oxford University Press, 2011. Chapters 3–5 of Part Three.

Acemoglu, Daron, and Simon Johnson and James A. Robinson. "The Colonial Origins of Comparative Development: An Empirical Investigation." *The American Economic Review* 91 (2001): 1369–1401.

Akerlof, G. A. "The Market for 'lemons': Quality Uncertainty and the Market Mechanism." *Quarterly Journal of Economics* 84 (1970): 488–500.

Alexander, J. and Alexander P. "Striking a Bargain in Javanese Markets." *Man* (N.S.), 22 (1987): 42–68.

Appadurai, Arjun (ed). *The Social Life of things.* Cambridge: Cambridge University Press, 1986.

Aquinas, Thomas. "Summa Theologica," in *The History of Economic Thought, A Reader,* 2nd edn., ed. Steven G. Medema and Warren J. Samuel. London: Routledge, 2003, 21–37.

Ardener, S. "The Comparative Study of Rotating Credit Associations." *Journal of the Royal Anthropological Institute of Great Britain and Ireland* 94 (1964): 201–29.

Arewa, Olufunmilayo. "Trading Places: Securities Regulation, Market Crisis, and Network Risk." Northwestern Law & Econ Research Paper No. 09–01; Northwestern Public Law Research Paper No. 09–01, 2009 (Accessed June 2, 2015). ssrn.com—abstract=1324951.

Avery, Robert B. et al. "Overview of Consumer Data and Credit Reporting." *Federal Reserve Bulletin* 89 (2003): 47–73.

Bachelard, Gaston. *Rationalisme Appliqué,* in Bourdieu, Pierre, Jean-Claude Chamboredon and Jean Claude Passeron, *The Craft of Sociology. Epistemological Preliminaries*, trans. Richard Nice, ed. Beate Kraise. New York: Walter deGruyter, 1991, 87–90.

Baer, Yitzhak. *A History of the Jews in Christian Spain, vol. 1, From the Age of Reconquest to the 14th Century*, trans. from the Hebrew by Louis Schoffman. Skokie, IL. Varda Books, 2001.

Ballard, Michel. "A Christian Mediterranean: 1000–1500," in *The Mediterranean in History*, ed. David Abulafia. Los Angeles: The John Paul Getty Museum, 2003.

Baptiste, Victor N. "Bartolomé de las Casas and Thomas More's Utopia: Connections and Similarities." *Labyrinthos* 1990.

Barron Baskin, Jonathon and Paul J. Miranti, Jr. *A History of Corporate Finance*. Cambridge: Cambridge University Press, 1997.

Bauman, Zygmunt. *Consuming Life*. Malden, MA: Polity Press, 2007.

Bautier, Robert-Henri. *The Economic Development of Medieval Europe*. Harcourt Brace, New York: Jovanovich, 1971.

Benson, J. *The Rise of Consumer Society in Britain 1880–1980*. Harlow: Longman, 1994.

Beneveniste, E. *Indo-European Language and Society*, trans. E. Palmer. London: Faber, 1973.

Biddick, Kathleen. "People and Things: Power in Early English Development." *Comparative Studies in Society and History* 32 (1990): 3–23.

Blair, John. "The Anglo-Saxon Period," in *The Oxford History of Great Britain*, ed. Kenneth O. Morgan. Oxford: Oxford University Press, 1996, 60–119.

Blaut, James M. "Colonialism and the Rise of Capitalism." *Science & Society* 53 (1989): 260–96.

Blustein, Paul. *Misadventures of the Most Favored Nations. Clashing Egos, Inflated Ambitions, and the Great Shambles of the World Trade System*. Philadelphia: Perseus Book Group, 2009.

Boissonnade, P. *Life and Work in Medieval Europe. The Evolution of Medieval Economy from the Fifth to the Fifteenth Century*. New York: Harper Torchbooks, 1964. [Originally published in 1927].

Booth, Charles. "The Inaugural Address of Charles Booth, Esq., President of the Royal Statistical Society. Session 1892–93. Delivered 15th November, 1892." *Journal of the Royal Statistical Society* 55 (1893): 521–57.

———. *The Aged Poor in England and Wales*. London: Macmillan, 1894.

Borah, Woodrow W. and Sherburne F. Cook. *The Indian Population of Central Mexico, 1531–1610*. Berkeley: University of California Press, 1960.

Bourdieu, Pierre. "The Forms of Capital," in *Handbook of Theory and Research for the Sociology of Education*, ed. J. Richardson. New York, Greenwood, 1986, 241–258.

———. *Language & Symbolic Power*. Cambridge, MA: Harvard University Press, 1991.

Bourdieu, Pierre, Jean-Claude Chamboredon and Jean Claude Passeron. *The Craft of Sociology. Epistemological Preliminaries*. New York: Walter deGruyter, 1991.

Bourdieu, Pierre and Loic J. D. Wacquant. *An Invitation to Reflexive Sociology*. Chicago: University of Chicago Press, 1992.

Boyer, George R. "Insecurity, Safety Nets, and Self-help in Victorian Britain," in *Human Capital and Institutions: A Long Run View*, ed. Frank Lewis and Kenneth Sokoloff. Cambridge: Cambridge University Press, 2009, 46–92.

Braudel, Fernand *Civilisations matérielle, Economie et Capitalism XVe–XVIIIe Siècle, Les Structures du Quotidien, Tome* 1. Paris: Armand Colin, 1979.
———. *Civilisations matérielle, économie et capitalisme, XVe–XVIII, Les Jeux de l'Echange, Tome* 2. Paris: Armand Colin, 1979.
———. *Civilisations matérielle, Economie et Capitalism XVe –XVIIIe Siècle, Tome* 3. *Le Temps du Monde.* Paris: Armand Colin, 1979.
———. *La Méditerranée et le monde méditerranéen à l'époque de Philippe II. Tomes* I–III. Paris: Armand Colin, 1990.
Brenner, Robert. "The Origins of Capitalist Development: A Critique of Neo-Smithian Marxism." *New Left Review* 1 (1977): 30–75.
———. "Agrarian Class Structure and Economic Development in Pre-Industrial Europe," in *The Brenner Debate: Agrarian Class Structure and Economic Development. in Pre-Industrial Europe*, ed. T.H. Aston and C.H.E. Philpin, Cambridge: Cambridge: Cambridge University Press, 1987, 10–63.
Brezis, Elise S. "Foreign Capital Flows in the Century of Britain's Industrial Revolution: New Estimates, Controlled Conjectures." *Economic History Review*, XLVIII (1995): 46–67.
Brown, Judy, Peter Söderbaum, and Małgorzata Dereniowska. *Positional Analysis for Sustainable Development: Reconsidering Policy, Economics and Accounting.* London: Routledge, 2017.
Broz, J. Lawrence and Richard S. Grossman. "Paying for Privilege: The Political Economy of Bank of England Charters, 1694–1844." *Explorations in Economic History* 41 (2003): 48–72.
Bruscoli, Francesco Guidi. *Papal Banking in Renaissance Rome. Benvenuto Olivieri and Paul III, 1534–1549.* Aldershot: Ashgate Publishing, 2007.
Burns, S.J. and I. Robert. *Las Siete Partidas,* vol. 4, trans., Samuel Parsons Scott. Philadelphia: University of Pennsylvania, 2001.
Cajetan, Thomas. *On Exchange and Usury*, trans. Patrick T. Brannan. Grand Rapids: CPL Academic, 2014.
Calder, Lendol. *Financing the American Dream: A Cultural History of Consumer Credit.* Princeton: Princeton University Press, 1999.
Calomiris, Charles W. *U.S. Bank Deregulation in Historical Perspective.* Cambridge: Cambridge University Press, 2000.
Caufield, Catherine. *Masters of Illusion. The World Bank and the Poverty of Nations.* New York: Henry Hold & Co., 1996.
Cannadine, David. "The Empire Strikes Back." *Past and Present* 147 (1995): 180–94.
Cantor, Norman F. (ed). *The Enclyopedia of the Middle Ages.* New York: Viking, 1999.
Carrier, James G. and Daniel Millers, eds. *Virtualism: A New Political Economy.* Oxford, UK: Berg, 1998.
Carruthers, B.G. "Rules, Institutions, and North's Institutionalism: State and Market in Early Modern England." *European Management Review* 4 (2007): 40–53.
Carruthers, Bruce. G. *Politics and Markets in the English Financial Revolution.* Princeton: Princeton University Press, 1996.
Chafuen, Alejandro A. *Faith and Liberty. The Economic Thought of the Late Scholastics.* New York: Lexington books, 2003.

Chapman, S.D. "Financial Restraints on the Growth of Firms in the Cotton Industry 1790–1850." *The Economic History Review*, New Series, vol. 32 (1979): 50–69.

Chayanov, A. V. *The Theory of the Peasant Economy* [Original Russian publication, 1925], ed. D. Thorner, B. Kerblay, and R. E. F. Smith, Madison: University of Madison Press.

Chen, Ping. "Equilibrium Illusion, Economic Complexity and Evolutionary Foundation in Economic Analysis." *Evolutionary and Institutional Economics Review* 5 (2008): 81–127.

Chown, John F. A. *History of Money from 800 A.D.* London and New York: Routledge. 1994.

Cohen, D.I.A. *Basic Techniques of combinatorial Theory*. New York: John Wiley & Sons, 1978.

Coleman, J. "Social Capital in the Creation of Human Capital." *American Journal of Sociology* 94 (1988): (Supplement), 95–120.

Collins, Roger. *Early Medieval Spain. Unity in Diversity, 400–1000.* New York: St. Martin's Press, 1983.

Common, Michael and Sigrid Stagl. *Ecological Economics. An Introduction.* Cambridge: Cambridge University Press, 2005.

Committee of African Finance Ministers and Central Bank Governors, 2009.

Constable, Olivia Remie (ed). *Medieval Iberia: Readings from Christian, Muslim, and Jewish Sources.* Philadelphia: University of Pennsylvania Press, 2011.

Constable, Olivia Remie. *Trade and Traders in Muslim Spain: The Commercial Realignment of the Iberian Peninsula 900–1500 [Originally published in 1994].* Cambridge: Cambridge University Press, 1996.

Constant, Benjamin. *Constant Political Writings,* ed. Biancamaria Fontana. Cambridge: Cambridge University Press, 1988.

Cooper, George. *The Origin of Financial Crises: Central Banks, Credit Bubbles, and the Efficient Market Fallacy.* New York: Vintage, 2008.

Crosby, Alfred W. *The Measure of Reality: Quantification in Western Society 1250–1600.* Cambridge, University of Cambridge Press, 1977.

Crotty, James. "Structural Causes of the Global Financial Crisis: A Critical Assessment of the 'New Financial Architecture'" Political Economy Research Institute. University of Massachusetts, Amherst. Working Paper Series: Number 180, Septemper, 2008, 50–51.

Crow, John A. Spain: *The Root and the Flower: An Interpretation of Spain and the Spanish People* [Originally published 1963]. Berkeley: University of California Press, 1985.

Crummett, Maria de los Angeles. "Class, Household Structure, and the Peasantry: An Empirical Approach." *The Journal of Peasant Studies* 14 (1987): 363–79.

Carruthers, B.G., *City of Capital: Politics and Markets in the English Financial Revolution.* Princeton University Press, Princeton, 1996.

———. "Rules, Institutions, and North's Institutionalism: State and Market in Early Modern England." *European Management Review* 4 (2007), 40–53.

Curtin, Philip D. *The Atlantic Slave Trade. A Census.* Madison: The University of Wisconsin Press, 1969.

———. *Economic Change in Precolonial Africa*. Madison: University of Wisconsin Press, 1975.

———. *Cross-Cultural Trade in World History*. Cambridge: Cambridge University Press, 1984.

Davidson, Basil. *The African Slave Trade*. New York: Little, Brown and Company, 1980 [Originally published in 1961].

Davies, Glyn. 1994. *A History of Money: From Ancient Times to the Present Day*. Cardiff: University of Wales Press.

Davies, Kenneth Gordon. *The Royal African Company*. London: Routledge/Thoemmes Press: 1999.

Davis, Mike. *Planet of Slums*. London & New York: Verso, 2006.

de la Cruz, Felipe. *Tratado Unico de Intereses, Sobre si se Puede Llevar Dinero por Prestallo*. Madrid: Francisco Marinez, 1637.

de Bertier de Sauvigny, Guillaume. *History of France*, trans. from French David H. Pinkney. Arlington Heights: Forum Press, 1983.

de Ridder-Symoens, Hilde (ed). "A History of the University in Europe." *Universities in the Middle Ages*, vol. I. Cambridge University Press, 1992, 240–43.

De Roover Raymond. *The Medici Bank: Its Organization, Management, Operations, and Decline*. New York: New York University Press, 1948.

———. *Money, Banking and Credit in Mediaeval Bruges - Italian Merchant Bankers, Lombards and Money Changers - A Study in the Origins of Banking*. London; New York : Routledge/Thoemmes Press, 1999a.

———. *The Rise and Decline of the Medici Bank 1397–1494*. Washington, DC: Beard Books, 1999b.

De Soto, Hernando. *The Mystery of Capital: Why Capitalism Triumphs in the West and Fails Everywhere Else*. New York: Basic Books, 2000.

Dickson, P. *The Financial Revolution in England*. New York: St. Martin's Press, 1967.

Dobb, Maurice. *Theories of Value and Distribution Since Adam Smith. Ideology and Economic Theory*. Cambridge: Cambridge University Press, 1973.

Donham, Donald L. *History, Power, Ideology. Central Issues in Marxism and Anthropology*. Cambridge: Cambridge University Press, 1990.

Douglas, Mary. *Purity and Danger*. New York: Routledge, 2002 [Originally published in 1966].

Dow, George Francis. *Slave Ships & Slaving*. Toronto: Coles Publishing, 1980 [Originally published in 1927].

Duchesne, Ricardo. "Remarx on the Origins of Capital." *Rethinking Marxism* 14 (2002), 129–37.

Duchesne, Ricardo and Rodney Hilton "The Peasant Road to 'Capitalism' in England." *The Journal of Peasant Studies* 30 (2003): 129–45.

Dumont, Louis. *Homo Hierarchicus. The Caste System and Its Implications*. Chicago: University of Chicago Press, 1970.

Durkheim, Emile. *Les règles de la méthode sociologique*. Paris: Presses Universitaires de France, 1975 [Originally published 1937].

Durrenberger, E. Paul. "An Analysis of Shan Household Production Decisions." *Journal of Anthropological Research* 5(1979): 447–58.

———. "Chayanov and Marx." *Peasant Studies* 9 (1982): 119–29.
———. "Chayanov's Economic Analysis in Anthropology." *Journal of Anthropological Research* 36 (1980): 133–48.
Durrenberger, E. Paul and Nicola Tannenbaum. "A Reassessment of Chayanov and His Recent Critics." *Peasant Studies* 8 (1979): 48–63.
Ehrenberg, Richard. *Capital and Finance in the Age of the Renaissance. A Study of the Fuggers, and Their Connections*. New York: Harcourt, Brace & Company, 2012.
Engels, Fredrick. *The Condition of the Working-Class in England*, 1st edn. Moscow: Progress Publishers, 1973.
Ennew, Judith, Paul Hirst and Keith Tribe. "'Peasantry' as an Economic Category." *The Journal of Peasant Studies* 4 (1977): 295–322.
Erdoes, Richard, *AD 1000: Living on the Brink of Apocalypse*. New York: Harper and Row, 1988.
Farmer, Paul. *Pathologies of Power. Health, Human Rights, and the New War on the Poor*. Berkeley: University of California Press, 2003.
Fanselow, Frank S. "The Bazaar Economy or How Bizarre Is the Bazaar Really?" (N.S.) *Man* 25 (1990): 250–65.
Federal Reserve. "FRB: Mortgage Debt Outstanding, First Quarter, 2009." Board of Governors of the Federal Reserve System Report, 2009. federalreserve.gov/econresdata/releases/mortoutstand/mortoutstand20090331.htm (Accessed June 2, 2015).
Federal Reserve. "Household Debt Service and Financial Obligation Ratios." December 10, 2007. http://www.federalreserve.gov/releases/housedebt/ (Accessed June 2, 2015).
Ferguson, Niall. *The Ascent of Money: A Financial History of the World*. New York: Penguin, 2008.
Ferns, H.S. "The Baring Crisis Revisited." *Journal of Latin American Studies* 24 (1992): 241–73.
Finn, Margot C. *The Character of Credit: Personal Debt in English Culture 1740–1914*. Cambridge: Cambridge University Press, 2003.
Firth, Raymond and B.S. Yamey. *Capital, Savings and Credit in Peasant Societies: Studies from Asia, Oceania, the Caribbean and Middle America*. Chicago: Aldine Publishing Company, 1964.
Flood, Robert P. and Peter M. Garber. *Speculative Bubbles, Speculative Attacks, and Policy Switching*. Cambridge, MA: The MIT Press, 1994.
Fossier, Robert (ed). *The Cambridge Illustrated History of the Middle Ages II*. Cambridge: Cambridge University Press, 1997.
Fossier, Robert (ed.). "The Beginning of European Expansion," Chapter 6, in *The Cambridge Illustrated History of the Middle Ages II*. Cambridge: Cambridge University Press, 1997.
Fossier, Robert (ed.). "The Leap Forward," Chapter 7, in *The Cambridge Illustrated History of the Middle Ages II*. Cambridge: Cambridge University Press, 1997.
Foucault, Michel. *Discipline and Punish: The Birth of the Prison*. New York: Vintage Books, 1979.
———. "Omnes et singulatim," in *The Tanner Lectures in Human Values*, vol. 2, ed. S.M. McMurrin. London: Cambridge University Press, 1981.

———. *Dits et Ecrits, 1976–88,* vol. II. Paris: Editions Gallimard, 2001.

Frank, Andre Gunder. *Dependent Accumulation and Underdevelopment.* London: Macmillan, 1978.

Frank, Robert H. *The Darwin Economy. Liberty, Competition, and the Common Good.* Princeton: Princeton University Press, 2011.

Gallagher, John and Ronald Robinson. "The Imperialism of Trade." *The Economic History Review,* New Series, 6 (1953): 1–15.

Gandy, Oscar H., Jr. *The Panoptic Sort: A Political Economy of Personal Information.* Boulder, CO: Westview Press, 1993.

Garcia Diaz, Jesus. "El Fenomeno del mercado en la obra legislativa de Alfonso X," *El Sabio HID* 38 (2011): 111–40.

Geertz, Clifford. "Suq: The Bazaar Economy in Sefrou," in *Meaning and Order in Moroccan Society: Three Essays in Cultural Analysis,* eds. Clifford Geertz, Hildred Geertz, and Lawrence Rosen. Cambridge: Cambridge University Press, 1979.

Geertz, Clifford, Hildred Geertz, and Lawrence Rosen. *Meaning and Order in Moroccan Society: Three Essays in Cultural Analysis.* Cambridge: Cambridge University Press, 1979.

Gelderblom, Oscar and Joost Jonker. "Completing a Financial Revolution: The Finance of the Dutch East India Trade and the Rise of the Amsterdam Capital Market, 1595–1612." *The Journal of Economic History* 63 (2004): 641–72.

Gellner, Ernest. *Plough, Sword and Book.* Chicago: The University of Chicago Press, 1988.

Gerli, Michael E. *Medieval Iberia: An Encyclopedia.* New York: Routlege, 2003, 240–246

Gibson, McGuire and Robert D. Biggs (eds.). *The Organization of Power: Aspects of Bureaucracy in the Ancient Near East.* Chicago: The Oriental Institute of the University of Chicago, 1991.

Gies, Frances and Joseph Gies. *Life in a Medieval Village.* New York: Harper and Row, 1991.

Gilbert, Bentley B. "The Decay of Nineteenth Century British Provident Institutions and the Coming of Old Age Pensions in Great Britain." *Economic History Review* 17 (1965): 550–63.

Gillingham, J. "The Early Middle Ages," in *The Oxford History of Great Britain,* ed. Kenneth O. Morgan. Oxford: Oxford University Press, 1996.

Gitari Koori, Charles. Commentary on Remittance Volumes for the Period January–June. Central Bank of Keyna, 2009. http://www.centralbank.go.ke/forex/Diaspora_Remit.aspx

Glennie, Paul. "Consumption, Consumerism, and Urban Form: Historical Perspectives." *Urban Studies* 5 (1998): 927–95.

Godelier, Maurice. *Horizon, Trajets Marxistes En Anthropologie.* Paris: Maspero, 1973.

Goitein, S. D. *A Mediterranean Society: The Jewish Communities of the World as Portrayed in the Documents of the Cairo Geniza,* vol. 1: *Economic Foundations.* Berkeley: University of California Press, 1967.

Goldthwaite, Richard, A. *The Economy of Renaissance Florence.* Baltimore: The Johns Hopkins University Press, 2009.

Goody, Jack. *The Theft of History.* Cambridge: Cambridge University Press, 2006.
Gotas, Demetrios. "The Byzantine Law of Interest," in *The Economic History of Byzantium, 1096–1100,* vol. 3, ed. Angeliki E. Laiou. Washington: Dumbarton Oaks, 2007, 1095–1104.
Gonzalez Zymla, Herbert. *Año 929 El Califato de Cordoba.* Madrid: Ediciones de Laberinto, 2011.
Graeber, David. *Debt: The First 5000 Years.* Brooklyn, NY: Melville House. 2011.
Gray, John. *False Dawn.* New York: The New Press, 1998.
Green, David. G. "Reinventing Civil Society: The Rediscovery of Welfare without Politics. Civets, London." *Choice in Welfare* 17 (1993), 9–10.
Greenberg, James B. "Microfinance, Law, and Development: A Case Study in Mali." *Arizona Journal of International and Comparative Law* 30 (2013): 135–162.
———. "Medio Milenio de Credito entre los Mixes de Oaxaca." *Cuadernos del Sur* 10 (2004): 31–50.
———. "Capital, Ritual, and the Boundaries of Closed Corporate Communities," in *Articulating Hidden Histories: Exploring the Influence of Eric R. Wolf*, ed. Rayna Rapp and Jane Schneider. Berkeley: University of California Press, 1995, 67–81.
Greenberg, James B. and Josiah McC Heyman. "Neoliberal Capital and the Mobility Approach in Anthropology," in *Neoliberalism and Commodity Production in Mexico*, ed. Thomas Weaver et al, Boulder. University of Colorado Press, 2012, 241–68.
Greenberg, James B. et al. "Theorizing Neoliberalism," in *Neoliberalism and Commodity Production in Mexico*, ed. Thomas Weaver, et al. University of California Press, 2012, 1–32.
Greif, Avner. *Institutions and the Path to the Modern Economy: Lessons from Medieval Trade.* Cambridge: Cambridge University Press, 2006 (Kindle).
———. "Commitment, Coercion, and Markets: The Nature and Dynamics of Institutions Supporting Exchange," in *Handbook of New Institutional Economics*, ed. Claude Menard and Mary M. Shirley. Heidelberg: Springer-Verlag, 2005, 727–786.
Grossman, Jerrold W. *Discrete Mathematics. An Introduction to Concepts, Methods, and Applications.* London: Macmillan Publishers, 1990.
Guillen, Pierre. *L'Allemagne et le Maroc.* Paris: Presses Universitaires Françaises, 1967.
Gutas, Demitros. *Greek Thought, Arabic Culture. The Graeco-Arabic Translation Movement in Baghdad and Early Abbasid Society (2nd–4th 8th–10th centuries).* New York: Routledge, 1998.
Guyer, Jane I. "Currency Interface and Its Dynamics," in *Money Matters: Instablity, Values and Social Payments in Modern History of West Africa*, ed. Jane I. Guyer. London: James Currey, Ltd., 1995, 1–34.
Hahnel, Robin. *Green Economics. Confronting the Ecological Crisis.* Armonk, NY: M.E. Sharpe, 2001.
Harrison, Mark. "Chayanov and the Economics of the Russian Peasantry." *The Journal of Peasant Studies* 2 (1975): 389–417.
———. "Chayanov and the Marxists." *The Journal of Peasant Studies* 7 (1979): 86–100.
———. "The Peasant Mode of Production in the Work of A.V.Chayanov." *The Journal of Peasant Studies* 4 (1977): 323–36.

Harvey, David. *A Brief History of Neoliberalism.* Oxford: Oxford University Press, 2005.

———. *The New Imperialism.* Oxford: Oxford University Press, 2003.

Heyman, Josiah McC. "The Organizational Logic of Capitalist Consumption on the Mexico-United States Border." *Research in Economic Anthropology* 15 (1994): 175–238.

Hicks, Sir John. *A Theory of Economic History.* Oxford: Oxford University Press, 1969.

Hilton, Rodney. *Bond Men Made Free: Medieval Peasant Movements and the English Rising of 1381.* London: C. C. Dyer, 2003 [Originally published 1973].

Ho, Karen. "Situating Global Capitalism: A View from Wall Street Investment Banks." *Cultural Anthropology* 20 (2005): 68–96.

Hobbs, Thomas. *Leviathan.* Seattle: Pacific Publishing Studio, 2011 [Originally published 1651].

Hobsbawm, Eric. *The Age of Capital.* New York: Vintage Books, 1996 [Originally published 1975].

Hodgett, Gerald A. J. *A Social and Economic History of Medieval Europe.* New York: Harper Torchbooks, 1974.

Holderness, B. A. "Credit in English Rural Society before the Nineteenth Century, with Special Reference to the Period 1650–1720." *The Agricultural History Review* 24 (1976): 97–109.

Hollister, C. Warren. *Anglo-Norman Political Culture and the Twelfth-century Renaissance.* Rochester and Suffolk: Boydell and Brewer Ltd., 1995.

Hornborg, Alf. *The Power of the Machine: Global Inequalities of Economy, Technology, and Environment.* Walnut Creek, CA: Alta Mira, 2002.

Hoppit, Julian. "The Myths of the South Sea Bubble." *Royal Historical Society* 12 (2002): 141–65.

Thomas, Hugh *The Slave Trade.* New York: Simon and Schuster, 1997.

Humes, David. *Hume's Political Discourses.* Kindle Edition, 2012 [Originally published 1752].

Hunt, Diane. "Chayanov's Model of Peasant Household Resource Allocation and Its Relevance to Mbere Division, Eastern Kenya." *Journal of Development Studies* 15 (1978): 59–86.

Hunt, Robert M. "A Century of Consumer Credit Reporting in America." Working Papers Research Department, Working Paper No. 05-13. Philadelphia: Federal Reserve Bank of Philadelphia, 2005. http://philadelphiafed.org/research-and-data/publications/working-papers/2005/wp05-13.pdf (Accessed May 25, 2015).

Inalcik, Halil. *An Economic and Social History of the Ottoman Empire, 1300–1914.* Cambridge: Cambridge Univeristy Press, 1994.

Ingham, Geoffrey. "Capitalism, Money, and Banking: A Critique of Recent Historical Sociology." *British Journal of Sociology* 50 (1999): 76–96.

Inikori, Joseph E. and Stanley L. Engerman (eds.). *The Atlantic Slave Trade. Effects on Economies, Societies, and Peoples in Africa, the Americas, and Europe.* Durham: Duke University Press, 1992.

Innes, Joanna. "The King's Bench Prison in the Later Eighteenth Century: Law, Authority and Order in a London Debtors' Prison," in *An Ungovernable People:*

The English and Their Law in the Seventeenth and Eighteenth Centuries, ed. John Brewer and John Styles. London: Hutchinson, 1980.

IRIN. "Mali: Fears over Privatising Cotton. Humanitarian News and Analysis," UN office for the Coordination of Humanitarian Affairs, Report August 15, 2009. http: www.irinnews.org-report.aspx (Accessed June 2, 2015).

Isreal, Jonathan I. *Dutch Primacy in World Trade 1586–1740.* Oxford: Oxford University Press, 1989.

Jacks, Philip and William Caferro. *The Spinelli of Florence. Fortunes of a Renaissance Merchant Family.* University Park: The Pennsylvania State University Press, 2001.

Jardine, Lisa. *Worldly Goods: A New History of the Renaissance.* New York: W.W, Norton and Company, 1998.

Johnson, Paul. *Saving and Spending: The Working-Class Economy in Britain 1870– 1939.* Oxford: Clarendon Press. George Boyer, 2009.

Johnson, Paul. "Small Debts and Economic Distress in England and Wales, 1857– 1913." *The Economic History Review*, New Series, 46 (1993): 65–87.

Jones, Geoffrey. *British Multinational Banking, 1830–1990.* Oxford: Oxford University Press, 1993.

Kahr, Andrew. "The Secret History of the Credit Card." *Frontline Interview. PBS*, 2004. http://www.pbs.org/wgbh/pages/frontline/shows/credit/interviews/kahr.html (Accessed May 25, 2015).

Kent, Dale. *Cosimo De' Medici and the Florentine Renaissance.* New Haven: Yale University Press, 2006.

Keynes, John. *General Theory of Employment Interest and Money.* New York, Harcourt, Brace, 1936.

Kindleberger, Charles P. *A Financial History of Western Europe*, 2nd edn. Oxford: Oxford University Press, 1993.

Klein, Matin. *Slavery and Colonial Rule in French West Africa.* Cambridge: Cambridge University Press, 1998.

Kula, Witold. *An Economic Theory of the Feudal System: Towards a Model of the Polish Economy 1500–1800.* Atlantic Highlands, NJ: Humanities, 1976.

Lakoff, George and Rafael L. Nuñez. *Where Mathematics Comes From: How the Embodied Mind Brings Mathematics into Being.* New York: Basic Books, 2000.

Laider, David. "Rules, Discretion, and Financial Crisis in Classical and Neoclassical Monetary Economics." *Economic Issues* 7 (2002), Part 2, 11–33.

Laiou, Angeliki E. and Cécile Morrison. *The Byzantine Economy.* Cambridge: Cambridge University Press, 2007.

Laiou, Angeliki E. "Political History: An Outline," in *The Economic History of Byzantium*, vol. 1, ed. Angeliki E. Laiou. Washington: Dumbarton Oaks, 2007, 9–28.

———. "Economic and Noneconomic Exchange," in *The Economic History of Byzantium*, vol. 2, ed. Angeliki E. Laiou. Washington: Dumbarton Oaks, 2007, 681–96.

Largardere, Vicente. *Mi'Yar D'al-Wansarisi Histoire et Société en Occident Musulman au Moyen Age.* Madrid: Consejo Superior de Investigations Cientificas, 1995.

Law, Robin. "Cowries, Gold and Dollars: Exchange Rate Instablity and Domestic Price Inflation in Dahomeny in the Eighteenth and Nineteenth Centuries," in *Money*

Matters: Instablity, Values and Social Payments in Modern History of West Africa, ed. Jane I. Guyer. London: James Currey, Ltd., 1995, 53–74.
Leech, Edmund. *Political Systems of Highland Burma*. Boston: Beacon Press, 1954.
Lessio, Leonard. *De Iustitia et Iure* (Antwerp, 1626), bk. 2 chap. 20, 3–19.
Lewis, David Levering. *God's Crucible: Islam in the Making of Europe, 570–1215*. New York and London: Norton, 2002.
Lewis, John Van D. "Domestic Labor Intensity and the Incorporation of Malian Peasant Farmers into Localized Descent Groups." *American Ethnologist* 8 (1981): 53–73.
Lichtheim, Miriam. *Ancient Egyptian Literature*, vol. 1. *The Old and Middle Kingdoms*. Berkeley: University of California Press, 2006.
Locke, John. *Two Treatises of Government*, ed. Peter Laslett. Cambridge: Cambridge University Press, 1988 [Originally published 1689].
Lomax, Derek WIlliam. *The Reconquest of Spain*. New York: Prentice Hall Press, 1978.
Lopez, Robert S. *The Commercial Revolution of the Middle Ages, 950–1350*. Cambridge: Cambridge University Press, 1976.
Lopez, Robert S. and Irving W. Raymond (trans.). *Medieval Trade in the Mediterranean World. Illustrative Documents*. New York: Columbia University Press, 2001.
Lukes, Steven. *Individualism*. Oxford: Oxford University Press, 1973.
———. *Power a Radical View*, 2nd edn. London: Palgrave Macmillan, 2005.
Luxemberg, Rosa. *The Accumulation of Capital*. New York: Monthly Review Press, 1968 [Originally published 1913].
Lyon, David. *Theorizing Surveillance. The Panopticon and Beyond*. Oxford: Taylor & Francis, 2006.
MacKay, Angus. *Spain in the Middle Ages. From Frontier to Empire 1000–1500*. New York: St. Martin's Press.
Madison, James H. "The Evolution of Commercial Credit Reporting Agencies in Nineteenth-Century America." *The Business History Review* 47 (1974): 164–86.
Malinowski, Bronislaw. *Argonauts of the Western Pacific*. New York: E.F. Dutton & Co., Inc., 1953 [Originally published 1922].
Mann, Michael. *The Sources of Social Power*. Cambridge: Cambridge University Press 1986.
Mann, Michael E. et al. "Global Signatures and Dynamical Origins of the Little Ice Age and Medieval Climate Anomaly." *Science* 326 (2009): 1256–260.
Manning, Patrick. "The Slave Trade: The formal Demography of a Global System." *Social Science History* 14 (1990): 255–79.
Maridaki-Karatza, Olga. "Legal Aspects of the Financing of Trade," in *The Economic History of Byzantium*, vol. 3, ed. Angeliki E. Laiou. Washington: Dumbarton Oaks, 2007, 1105–1120.
Márquez Villanueva, Francisco. "La escuela de traductores de Toledo." *Lingua Tholetana* (2006): 23–34.
Martin, John E. *Feudalism to Capitalism: Peasant and Landlord in English Agrarian Development*. New York and London: Palgrave-Macmillan, 1983.
Marx, Karl. *Capital*, vol. 1, trans. Ben Fowkes. New York: Penguin, 1976.
———. *Capital*, vol. 2, trans. Ben Fowkes. New York: Penguin, 1976.
———. *Capital*, vol. 3, trans. Ben Fowkes. New York: Penguin, 1976.

———. *The Eighteenth Brumaire of Louis Bonaparte (1852)*. Rockville, MD: Serenity Publishers, 2009.

———. *The German Ideology*. Marx-Engels Archive (1846). marxists.org.

Mauss, Marcel. "Essai sur le don. Forme et raison de l'échange dans les sociétés archaïques." *Années sociologiques, 1923–4*. Edition électronique de 17 février 2002.

Mayhew, Henry. *London Labor and the London Poor*, vols. 1–4. Toronto: Dover, 1968 [Originally published 1861].

Meillassoux, Claude. *The Anthropology of Slavery. The Womb of Iron and Gold*, trans. Alide Dasnois. Chicago: University of Chicago Press, 1991 [Original French edition, 1986].

Mencken, H. L "Notes on Journalism." *Chicago Tribune* [September 19, 1926].

Menocal, Maria Rosa. *The Ornament of the World: How Muslims, Jews, and Christians Created a Culture of Tolerance in Medieval Spain*. New York: Little, Brown and Company, 2002.

Meszáros, István. *Marx's Theory of Alienation*. London: Merlin Press, 1970.

Miers, Suzanne and Igor Kopytoff. *Slavery in Africa. Historical and Anthropological Perspectives*. Madison: University of Wisconsin Press, 1977.

Minge-Kalman, Wanda. "On the Theory and Measurement of Domestic Labor Intensity." *American Ethnologist* 4 (1977): 273–84.

Minsky, Hyman. "Financial Instability Hypothesis," in *Elgar Companion to Radical Political Economy,* ed. P. Arestis and M. Sawyer. Cheltenham Glos: Edward Elgar Publications, Ltd., 1994, 153–58.

Minsky, Hyman. "The Financial-instability Hypothesis: Capitalist Processes and the Behavior of the Economy," in *Financial Crisis, Theory, History and Policy,* ed. C.P. Kindleberger & J.-P. Laffargue. New York, Cambridge University Press, 1982, 13–38.

Minsky, Hyman. "Can 'It' Happen Again?" in *Banking and Monetary,* ed. D. Carson. Homewood Illinois: R.D. Irwin, 1963, 101–11.

Mintz, Sidney. "Pratik: A Hawaiian Personal Economic Relationship," in *Proceedings of the American Ethnological Society*. Seattle: University of Washington Press, 1967.

———. "Standards of Value and Units of Measure in the Fond–des–Nègres Market Place, Haiti." *Journal of the Royal Anthropological Institute* 91 (1961): 23–38.

———. *Sweetness and Power: The Place of Sugar in Modern History*. New York: Penguin Books, 1985.

Montesquieu, Charles-Louis. *The Spirit of the Laws*. The Internet Archive [Original French in 1777].

Morrill, John. "The Stuarts," in *The Oxford History of Great Britain,* ed. Kenneth O. Morgan. Oxford: Oxford University Press, 1996, 327–98.

Morris, R. J. "Urban Associations in England and Scotland, 1750–1914: The Formation of the Middle Class or the Formation of a Civil Society?" in *Civil Society, Associations, and Urban Places: Class, Nation, and Culture in Nineteenth Century Europe,* eds., Graeme Morton, Boudien de Vries, and R.J. Morris. Hampshire, England: Ashgate Publishing Ltd., 2006.

Moses, Abigail and Shannon D. Harrington. "Company Bond Risk Surges on Argentina Default Concerns." *Bloomberg* (October 23, 2008). http://thisbluemarble.com/archive/index.php/t-3743.html (Accessed June 28, 2016).

Neal, Larry. *The Rise of Financial Capitalism: International Capital Markets in the Age of Reason.* Cambridge: Cambridge University Press, 1990.

Neale, Walter C. *Monies in Societies.* Corte Madera, CA: Chandler & Sharp Publishers Inc., 1976.

Nell, Edward J. *The General Theory of Transformational Growth.* Cambridge: Cambridge University Press, 1998.

Nell, Edward J. and Karim Errouaki. *Rational Econometric Man. Transforming Structural Econometrics.* Northampton, MA: Edward Elgar, 2013.

Netanyahu, Benjamin. *The Origins of the Inquisition in Fifteenth Century Spain.* New York, Random House, 1995.

Noin, Daniel. *La Population Rurale du Maroc.* Paris: Presses Universitaires de France, 1970.

North, Douglass C. and Barry R. Weingast. "Constitutions and Commitment: The Evolution of Institutional Governing Public Choice in Seventeenth-Century England." *The Journal of Economic History* 49 (1989): 803–32.

O'Callaghan, Joseph F. *A History of Medieval Spain.* Ithaca: Cornell University Press, 2013 (Kindle) [Originally published 1975].

O'Fahey, R.S. "Slavery and Society in Dar Fur," in *Slaves and Slavery in Muslim Africa*, vol. 2, ed. John R. Willis. London: Frank Cass, 1985.

Oikonomidas, Nikolas. "The role of the Byzantine State in the Economy," in *The Economic History of Byzantium*, vol. 3, ed. Angeliki E. Laiou. Washington: Dumbarton Oaks, 2007, 973–1058.

Olegario, Rowena. *A Culture of Credit: Embedding Trust and Transparency in American Business.* Boston: Harvard University Press, 2006.

Ouroussoff, Alexandra. *Wall Street at War. The Secret Struggle for the Global Economy.* Malden, MA: Polity Press, 2010.

Palmer, Colin A. *The First Passage: Blacks in the Americas 1502–1617.* Oxford: Oxford University Press, 1995.

Pamuk, evket. *A Monetary History of the Ottoman Empire.* Cambridge: Cambridge University Press, 2000.

Papagianni, Eleutheria. "Byzantine Legislation on Economic Activity Relative to Social Class." *The Economic History of Byzantium*, vol. 3, ed., Angeliki E. Laiou. Washington: Dumbarton Oaks, 2007, 1083–1093.

Papal bull of Boniface VII, *Unam Sanctam*, November 23, 1302.

Papal bull of Clemente V, *Ad Providam,* March 22, 1312.

Park, Thomas K. Administration and the Economy. Ph.D. thesis (Anthropology and History), University of Wisconsin–Madison, 1983.

Park, Thomas K. and James B. Greenberg. *The Roots of Western Finance: Power, Ethics, and Social Capital in the Ancient World.* Lanham, MD: Lexington Books, 2017.

Parkin, Robert. *Louis Dumont and Hierarchical Opposition.* New York: Bergbahn Books, 2003.

Pascon, Paul (ed.). "Comparaison de quelques informations statistiques sur les exploitations agricoles en haute Chaouia," in *Etudes Rurales*. Rabat: SMER, 1980, 49–57.
Patnaik, Utsa, "Neo-Populism and Marxism: The Chayanovian View of the Agrarian Question and its Fundamental Fallacy." *The Journal of Peasant Studies* 6 (1979): 375–420.
Paulson, John A. of Paulson & Co Interview in Lasse Heje Pedersen. *Efficiently Inefficient. How Smart Money Invests and Market Prices are Determined*. Princeton: Princeton University Press, 2015, 319–20.
Pedersen, Lasse Heje. *Efficiently Inefficient. How Smart Money Invests and Market Prices are Determined*. Princeton: Princeton University Press, 2015.
Pérez-Mallaina, Pablo E. *Spain's Men of the Sea: Daily Life on the Indies Fleets in the Sixteenth Century*, trans. Carla Rahn Phillips. Baltimore: Johns Hopkins University Press, 1998.
Pérez, Joseph. *Los Judíos España*. Madrid: Poligona Igarsa, 2005.
Perkins, Dwight H., Steven Radelet and David L. Lindauer. *Economics of Development*, 6th edn. New York: W.W. Norton & Company, 2006.
Pertev, Rashid. "A New Model for Sharecropping and Peasant Holdings." *The Journal of Peasant Studies* 14 (1986): 27–49.
Peters, Edward. "Henry II of Cyprus, Rex inutilis: A Footnote to Decameron 1.9." *Speculum* 72 (1997): 763–75.
Phillips, William D., Jr. and Carla Rahn Phillips. *A Concise History of Spain*. Cambridge: Cambridge University Press, 2013 (Kindle) [Originally published 2010].
Phillips, Kevin. *Bad Money: Reckless Finance, Failed Politics, and the Global Crisis of American Capitalism*. New York: Viking, 2008.
Pirenne, Henri. *Medieval Cities: The Origins and Revival of Trade*. Princeton: Princeton University Press, 1969.
Pollard, Sydney. "Fixed Capital in the Industrial Revolution in Britain." *The Journal of Economic History* 24 (1964): 299–314.
Poon, Martha. "From New Deal Institutions to Capital Markets: Commercial Consumer Risk Scores and the Making of Subprime Mortgage Finance." *Accounting, Organization, and Society* 34 (2009): 654–74.
Poovey, Mary. *A History of the Modern Fact: Problems of Knowledge in the Sciences of Wealth and Society*. Chicago: University of Chicago Press, 1998.
Popper, Karl. *A World of Propensities*. Bristol: Thoemmes, 1995.
Portugal, Juval. "Complexity Theory as a Link Between Space and Place." *Environment and Planning* 38 (2006): 647–64.
Pounds, N. J. G. *An Economic History of Medieval Europe*. New York: Longman, 1974.
Power, Eileen. *The Wool Trade in English Medieval History*. Oxford: Oxford University Press, 1955 [Originally published in 1942].
Rappaport, Roy A. "Distinguished Lecture in Anthropology: The Anthropology of Trouble." *American Anthropologist* 95(1993): 295–303.

———. "Disorders of our Own: A Conclusion," in *Diagnosing America: Anthropology and Public Engagement,* ed. Shepard Forman. Ann Arbor: University of Michigan Press,1995, 235–94.

Real Academia Española. *Libre Judiciorum. Fuero Juzgo o Libro de los Jueces contjado con los mas antiguos y preciosos codices.* La Real Academia Española. Madrid, Ibarra, J. Impresor de Camara de S.M., 1815.

Reddy, W. "The Structure of a Cultural Crisis: Thinking about Cloth in France before and after the Revolution," in *The Social Life of Things,* ed. Arjun Appadurai. Cambridge: Cambridge University Press, 1986.

Rees. A. "Labour Economics: Effects of more Knowledge—Information Networks in Labour Markets." *American Economic Review* 56 (1966): 559–66.

Reynolds, Susan. *Fiefs and Vassals. The Medieval Evidence Reinterpreted.* Oxford: Clarendon Press, 1994.

Ricardo, David. *Principles of Political Economy and Taxation.* London: John Murray, Albermarle Street, 1817.

Rodriguez Oromendia, Ainhoa et al. "Historia, definicion y legislacion de las ferias comerciales." *Anuario Jurídico y Económico Escurialense* XLVI (2013): 449–66.

Roseberry, William. "Political Economy." *Annual Review of Anthropology* 17 (1988): 161–85.

———. "Anthropology, History, and Modes of Production," in *Anthropology and Histories: Essays in Culture, History, and Political Economy.* New Brunswick, NJ: Rutgers University press, 1989, 145–174.

Rosen, Lawrence. "Social Identity and Points of Attachment: Approaches to Social Organization," in *Meaning and Order in Moroccan Society. Three Essays in Cultural Analysis*, eds., Geertz et al. Cambridge: Cambridge University Press, 1979.

Rosen, Lawrence. *Bargaining for Reality: The Construction of Social Relations in a Muslim Community.* Chicago: The University of Chicago Press, 1984.

Rostow, Walt W. *The Stages of Economic Growth: A Non-Communist Manifesto.* London: Cambridge University Press, 1971 [Originally published 1960].

Rothbard, Murray N. *Economic Thought Before Adam Smith.* Auburn, Alabama: Ludwig Von Mises Institute, 1995.

Rotman, Youval . *Byzantine Slavery and the Mediterranean World*, trans. Jane Marie Todd. Cambridge: Harvard University Press, 2009 [Original French 2004].

Rousseau, Jean-Jacques. *The Social Contract.* Oxford: Oxford University Press, 2008 [Originally published 1762].

Rout Jr., Leslie B. *The African Experience in Spanish America: 1502 to the Present.* Cambridge: Cambridge University Press, 1976.

Rowntree, B. S. *Poverty: A Study of Town Life.* London: MacMillan, 1901.

Royaume du Maroc. Direction de la Statistique. Population rurale, Region du Tensift, 1973.

Royaume du Maroc. Direction de la Statistique, Situation Demographique Regionale au Maroc, 1988.

Rubin, Jared. "Institutions, The Rise of Commerce and the Persistence of Laws: Interest Restrictions in Islam and Christianity." *The Economic Journal*, 121 (2011): 1310–39.

Ruf, Urs Peter *Ending Slavery. Hierarchy, Dependency and Gender in Central Mauritania*. Bielefeld: Rutgers Transaction Press, 1999.

Sahlins, Marshall. *Tribesmen*. New York: Prentice-Hall, Inc., 1968.

Schumpeter, Joseph A. *History of Economic Analysis*. New York: Oxford University Press, 1974 [Originally published 1954].

Schwarcz, Steven I. "Complexity as a Catalyst of Market Failure: A Law and Engineering Inquiry." Stanley A. Star Professor of Law & Business, Duke University School of Law, 2008. http://works.bepress.com/steven_schwarcz/10/ (Accessed June 2, 2015).

Scott, James. *Seeing Like a State: How Certain Schemes to Improve the Human Condition Have Failed*. New Haven: Yale University Press, 1998.

Searing, James F. *West African Slavery and Atlantic Commerce. The Senegal River Valley, 1700–1860*. Cambridge: Cambridge University Press, 1993.

Sen, Amartya. *Poverty and Famines. An Essay on Entitlement and Deprivation*. Oxford: Clarendon Press, 1961.

———. "Rational Fools: A Critique of the Behavioral Foundations of Economic Theory." *Philosophy and Public Affairs* 6 (1977), 317–44.

———.*Commodities and Capabilities*. Oxford: Oxford University Press, 1999.

Shafaeddin, Mehdi. How did Developed Countries Industrialize? The History of Trade and Industrial Policy: The Cases of Great Britain and the USA. Macroeconomic and Development Policies, GDS, United Nations Conference on Trade and Development (UNCTAD), Palais des Nations, CH-1211 Geneva 10, Switzerland, Discussion Papers, No. 139, 1998.

Shipton, Parker. "Two East African Systems of Land Rights." M.A. Thesis. University of Oxford, 1979, 85.

Sienkiewicz, Stan. "Credit Cards and Payment Efficiency. Payment Card Center." Discussion Paper. Philadelphia: Federal Reserve Bank of Philadelphia, 2001, 1–13.

Simon. Herbert A. "Altruism and Economics." *The American Economic Review* 83 (1993), 156–61.

Smart, Alan. "Local Capitalisms: Situated Social Support for Capitalist Production in China." Department of Geography, Occasional Papers. Hong Kong: Chinese University, 1995.

Smith, Adam. *The Wealth of Nations*. New York: Random House, 2000 [Originally published 1776].

Smith, A.E., "Chayanov, Sahlins, and the Labor-Consumer Balance." *Journal of Anthropological Research* 35 (1979): 477–80.

Smith, C.F. "The Early History of the London Stock Exchange." *The American Economic Review*, 19 (1929): 206–16.

Smith, Mark B. *A History of the Global Stock Market from Ancient Rome to Silicon Valley*. Chicago: Chicago University Press, 2003.

Sornette, Didier. *Why Stock Markets Crash: Critical Events in Complex Financial Systems*. Princeton, NJ: Princeton University Press, 2002.

Soros, George. *The New Paradigm for Financial Markets: The Credit Crisis of 2008 and What It Means*. New York: Public Affairs Books, 2008, xvii.

Spooner, Brian. "Weavers and Dealers: The Authenticity of an Oriental Carpet," in *The Social Life of Things,* ed. A. Appaduri. Cambridge: Cambridge University Press, 1986, 195–236.

Spufford, Peter. *Power and Profit. The Merchant in Medieval Europe.* New York: Thames and Hudson, 2002.

Sraffa, Piero. *Production of Commodities by Means of Commodities. Prelude to a Critique of Economic Theory.* Cambridge: Cambridge University Press, 1960.

Stein, Eric "Qualifying the Economic Cost of Predatory Lending." A Report from the Coalition for Responsible Lending, July 25, 2001. http://www.responsiblelending.org/mortgage-lending/research-analysis/the-economic-cost-of-predatory-lending-2001.PDF (Retrieved May 25, 2015).

Steinmetz, Greg. *The Richest Man Who Ever Lived. The Life and Times of Jacob Fugger.* New York: Simon and Schuster, 2015.

Stern, Paul C. et al. *Environmentally Significant Consumption.* Washington: National Academy Press, 1997.

Stiglitz, G.J. "Information in the Labour Market." *Journal of Political Economy* 70(5), (1962): 94–105.

———. "The Economics of Information and Knowledge," in *The Economics of Information and Knowledge,* ed. D.M. Lamberton. Harmondsworth: Penguin, 1971.

Swartz, David. *Culture & Power. The Sociology of Pierre Bourdieu.* Chicago, University of Chicago Press, 1997.

Tannenbaum, Nicola. "The Misuse of Chayanov: 'Chayanov's Rule' and Empiricist Bias in Anthropology," *American Anthropologist* 86 (1984): 927–42.

Thorner, Daniel, Basile Kerblay, and R.E.F.Smith, eds. *Chayanov on The Theory of Peasant Economy.* Homewood: The American Economic Association, 1966.

Thorton, John. *Africa and Africans in the making of the Atlantic World, 1400–1680.* Cambridge: Cambridge University Press, 1992.

Tilly, Charles. *Coercion, Capital, and European States: AD 990–1992.* Malden, MA: Blackwell Publishers Inc., 1990.

Time Magazine. "25 People to Blame for the Financial Crisis." February 12, 2009. http://www.time.com/time/specials/packages/completelist/0,29569,1877351,00.html (Accessed June 2, 2015).

U. S. General Accounting Office. "Financial Audit, Resolution Trust Corporation's 1995 and 1994, Financial Statements." Report to Congress: July, GAO/AIMD–96–123, 1996:21.

U.S. Census Bureau. "Table H-2. Share of Aggregate Income Received by Each Fifth and Top 5 Percent of Households, All Races: 1967 to 2007." *Current Population Survey, Annual Social and Economic Supplements,* 2008a. http://www.census.gov/hhes/www/income/data/inequality/tableb2.html (Accessed June 2 2015).

U.S. Census Bureau. "Table H–3. Mean Household Income Received by Each Fifth and Top 5 Percent All Races: 1967 to 2007." *Current Population Survey, Annual Social and Economic Supplements,* 2008b. http://www.census.gov/hhes/www/income/data/historical/household/ (Accessed June 2, 2015).

Udovitch, Abraham. *Partnership and profit in medieval Islam.* Princeton: Princeton University Press, 1970 [Also Kindle Edition, 2011].

Ulanowicz, Robert, E. *Ecology, The Ascendant Perspective.* New York: Columbia University Press, 1997.
United Nations News Centre. "Economic Crisis Set to Drive 53 Million more People into Poverty in 2009"—World Bank. February 13, 2009. http://www.un.org/apps/news/story.asp?NewsID=29897&Cr=financial&Cr1=crisis. (Accessed June 2, 2015).
United Nations News Centre. "Financial Crisis to Deepen Extreme Poverty, Increase Child Mortality Rates"—UN Report, March 3, 2009. http://www.un.org/apps/news/story.asp?NewsID=30070&Cr=Financial+crisis&Cr1 (Accessed June 2, 2015).
Vansina, Jan. *Kingdoms of the Savanna.* Madison: University of Wisconsin Press, 1966.
Veinstein, Gilles. "Les marchands étrangers dans l'empire Ottoman (XVI–XVIIIe siècles) Questions de Prix." in *Merchants in the Ottoman Empire,* ed. Suraiya Faroqhi and Giles Veinstein. Leuven: Peeters, 2007.
Verboven, Koenraad. *The Economy of Friends. Economic Aspects of Amicitia and Patronage in the Late Republic.* Buxelles: Editions Latomus, 2002.
Von Bertalanffy, Ludwig. *General System Theory.* New York: George Braziller, 1968.
Walby, Sylvia. "Complexity Theory, Globalisation and Diversity." Paper presented to conference of the British Sociological Association, University of York, April 2003.
Wallerstein, Imannuel. *The Modern World System I: Capitalist Agriculture and the origins of the European World-Economy in the Sixteenth Century.* New York: Academic Press, 1974.
Wan, Poe Yu-Ze. *Reframing the Social. Emergentist Systemism and Social Theory.* Farnham: Ashgate Publishing, 2011.
Weatherford, J. M. *The History of Money: From Sandstone to Cyberspace.* New York: Three Rivers Press, 1997.
Weber, Max. *Economy and Society,* 2 Volumes, ed. G. Roth and C. Wittich. Berkeley: University of California Press, 1978 [Originally published 1921–1922].
Wenger, Albert. "Continuations. Household Debt, 2008." continuations.com/post/56990289/household-debt (Accessed June 2, 2015).
Weisdorf, Jacob Louis. "From Domestic Manufacture to Industrial Revolution: Long-Run Growth and Agricultural Development." *Oxford Economic Papers* 58 (2006): 264–287.
Willcox, WIlliam and Walter Arnstein.*The Age of Aristocracy 1688–1830 (History of England),* vol. 3. Boston: Houghton Mifflin Company, 2000.
Williams, Eric. *Capitalism and Slavery.* Chapel Hill: The University of North Carolina Press, 1994 [Originally published 1944].
Wolf, Eric R. *Europe and The Peoples Without History.* Berkeley: University of California Press, 1982.
———. "Distinguished Lecture: Facing Power—Old Insights, New Questions." *American Anthropologist* 92 (1990): 586–96.
———. *Envisioning Power. Ideologies of Dominance and Crisis.* Berkeley: University of California Press, 1999.

World Bank, *World Development Report 2006. Equity and Development.* Oxford: Oxford University Press, 2005.

"World Bank, Africa "Likely to be Worst Hit by the Financial Crisis," April 24, 2009. web.worldbank.org/WBSITE/EXTERNAL/COUNTRIES/AFRICAEXT/0,,contentMDK:22154832~menuPK:258649~pagePK:2865106~piPK:2865128~theSitePK:258644,00.html (Accessed June 2, 2015).

———. *World Development Report,* 2005–2006.

Wolters, Teun. "Carry Your Credit in Your Pocket: The Early History of the Credit Card at Bank of America and Chase Manhattan." *Enterprise and Society: The International Journal of Business History* 1(2000): 315–54.

Wood, Charles T. (ed.). *Philip the Fair and Boniface VIII: State vs Papacy.* New York, Holt, Rinehart and Winston, 1967.

Wood, Ellen Meiksins. *The Origins of Capitalism: A Longer View.* London and New York: Verso, 1999.

Woodfine, Philip. "Debtors, Prisons, and Petitions in Eighteenth Century England." *Eighteen-Century Life* 30 (2006): 1–31.

Wordie, J. "The Chronology of English Enclosure, 1500–1914." *The Economic History Review*, Second Series, XXXVI (1983), No. 4.

World Bank. *World Development Report 2006. Equity and Development.* Washington, DC: World Bank Group and Oxford: Oxford University Press, 2005.

World Bank, "Africa Likely to Be Worst Hit by the Financial Crisis, April 24, 2009," http://web.worldbank.org/WBSITE/EXTERNAL/COUNTRIES/AFRICAEXT/0,,contentMDK:22154832~menuPK:258649~pagePK:2865106~piPK:2865128~theSitePK:258644,00.html (Accessed June 2, 2015).

Zaloom, Caitlan. *Out of the Pits: Traders and Technology from Chicago to London.* Chicago: University of Chicago Press, 2006.

Index

2008 financial crisis, 213–40. *See also* key figures in 2008 financial crisis

accounting (accounts): xi–xiii, 21, 51n28, 62, 65–70, 72, 74, 76–77, 79n20, 89, 91, 94, 129, 198, 200–1, 206, 221; abacus, 92; actuarial, 203; assessments, viii, ix, 59, 86, 147, 159, 221, 227, 235, 251; bookkeeping, xii, 62, 65–67; contadores, 44; Domesday Book, 86–87; double entry, 65–66; drawer and drawee, 68; financing trade, 126–27; geld, 86–87, 109n23; Geniza, 51n28; hisāb, 79; hiyal (financial tricks in the Islamic world), 9; imbalances, 236, 261n15; innovation(s), ix–x, 1–*2*, 9, 11–12, 19, 57, 64–66, 74, 83, 189, 201, 241; junk bonds, 226; leverage, 74–75, 215–17; liquidity, *14*, 20, 73, 83, 99, 202, 216, 225, 249; margins, 4–5, 12, 117–18, 222, 225; memoranda tally, 92; mutuum, *15*, 20; notaries, 68–69, 151; off-balance sheet, 216; overdrafts, 62; overextended, 220, 246; oversight, 208, 218–19; penalties for late payment, 16, 33; redemption, 41; scritta, 62; scutage, 91; tallies (tally), 72, 78, 91–94, 242

accounting treatises: La Pratica della mercatura, 66; Summa de arithmetica, geometrica, proportioni e proportionalità, 66

affidavit, 91

agricultural strategies, 145–65

ahbas. *See* waqf

Albrecht of Mainz, 89

almojarife mayor, 44

alum, 65, 76

anti-semitism, 45, 47; anti-jewish decrees, 46; blood libel, 46, 54n109; expulsion, 39, 48, 63; Laws of Catalina, 47; pogroms, 39, 41, 46–47

asentista, 138

asiento, 99, 119, 133, 138. *See also* permits to trade in slaves

assignments, 73; of customs 63; tallies of, 92–93

associations and clubs: ancient orders, 196, 198; benefit clubs, 196–97; benefit society, 197; Benefit Society of Patterers, 197; building societies, 196; burial clubs, 196;

285

286 · Index

church and chapel associations, 196; cooperatives, 155, 196, dividing societies, 196–97; Elks, 132; friendly societies, xiv, 196–99; hanses, 84; Kawanis, 132; koinonia (informal association); Leopard society, 132; Masons, 132; mutual-aid associations, 196; Rotarians, 132; rotating credit associations (*menages* or slate clubs), 196, 209n36; savings clubs, 196; trade unions, 196, 198–99; voluntary associations xiv
Atlantic slave trade, 115–44
awqaf. *See* waqf

banking: Bank of America, 205, 210nn77, 79, 215; Bank Americard (Visa), 205; Bank of Barcelona, 65; Bank of England, 64, 95, 97–99, 104, 111n60, 139, 199; Bank of St. George, 65; Barclays Bank, 215; Barings Brothers, 102–4, 112n92; Brown Shipley, 102; Castillian banking, 72; Chase Manhattan, 205–6, 210nn77, 79; Citibank, 217; correspondent banks, 102–3; Deutsche Bank, 158, 215; German Postal Service, 158; Hope & Company, 104, 112n92; Hospitallers, 60–62; House Egibi, 62; House of Morgan, 104, 215; Interbank, 205, 216; Jacob Fugger, 65, 255; J. P. Morgan Chase, 215; merchant bankers, 60, 62, 69–70, 72–77, 79, 100, 102–4, 112n78; Morgans, 102, 104, 215; Morgan Stanley, 215; multinational banks, 80n51, 103–4, 112nn79, 88, 94, 96, 113n97; National Bank of Long Island, 205; private banking houses (private banks), xi, 41, 63–64, 101–2, 135; quasi-banks, 101; Raphaels, 102; Royal Bank of Scotland, 217; Savings and Loans, 215, 226; S&L debacle, 228; Schroders, 102; Seligmans, 102; Templars, 36, 51n51, 60–62; UBS (Universal Bank in Switzerland), 225; Warburgs, 102; World Bank, 208n1, 217, 232–33, 239n1, 240n69; 252, 255, 262n26. *See also* Italian merchant bankers
Bardi. *See* Italian merchant bankers
barons, 86, 88–89, 91, 108n13
bazaar, 170–72, 184, 187n4, 187n9, 187n10
Benveniste, 257
Bethnal Green, 190
Booth, Charles, 199, 209n49
boundaries, xvi, 223
brokers, xv, 128–32, 134, 213–14, 216–18, 225: Afro-Lozano, 130; pawn 44; power 38. *See also* Italian merchant bankers
Brüe, André, 115
Byzantine. *See* history

Caids, 155, 157–58
capitulations, xiii
Casa de Contracción, 125
Cavazzi, Gio Antonio, 115
caveat emptor, x, 41, 48, 242, 244, 256
change: bifurcation, 219; critical turning points, 224; gradual change, 224; nonlinear, 224; paths of development, 219, 224, 228; precipitous change 224. *See also* complexity
Chicago economics, 225
cities and towns: Alcala, 52n64; Alexandria, 29; Almeria, 29; Amalfi, 2; Amsterdam, 111, 135–36, 242; Antwerp, ix–x, 20, 59, 78n3, 127, 189, 241–42; Athens, vii, xi; Augsburg,

65, 89; Avignon, 75; Axim, 122; Babylon, 62; Baghdad, 29–30, 50n7; Barcelona, 42, 65, 69; Berar, 103; Bologna, 108; Bombay, 72; Bresse, 125; Bruges, 70–71, 79n20, 80n28, 30, 241–42; Burgos, 47; Cambria, 52; Carmona, 47; Ceuta, 122; Constantinople, 4–5, 29, 60, 73; Córdoba, x, 27–30, 35, 37, 47, 50nn6,13,17; Covadonga, 35; Cuenca, 47; Damascus, 29; Ecija, 47; Elmina, 122, 136; Essaouira, 146–49, 153, 155–56, 158, 161, 164n9; Fès, 172–75; Florence, 2, *15*, 63–64, 67–69, 72, 74, 77, 79nn12, 20, 26, 80n32–33, 35–37, 40–41, 47–48, 54, 81n67, 242; Geneva, 71; Genoa genoese, genovese), 2, 41–42, 64–65, 69, 72, 74–75, 120, 125, 127, 241–42; Gibraltar, 42; Granada, 37, 42; Hong Kong, 103; Huddersfield, 199; Istanbul, 9–10; Izmir, xiii; Jaén, 37, 47; Jerusalem, 37, 60; Kowloon, 103; Lagos, 103, 122; Lisbon, 29, 122; Lleida, 52; Logroño, 47; London, 63, 72, 78, 83, 88, 93–94, 97–98, 101–4, 107, 110n36, 112nn78, 92, 190–92, 198, 208nn8, 14, 209n16–18, 20–21, 37, 49, 241–42; Lucca, 63–64; Lyon, ix–x, 59, 71–72, 74, 78n3, 203, 210n72, 241–42; Macerata, 52; Madrid, 47, 72, 125; Malaga, 29, 35, 147, 158; Marseilles, 42; Meknes, 173; Montpelier, 52; Murcia, 52; Naples, 52, 63; Navarre, 32; 52n63; New York, 136, 202, 204–5, 220; Northampton, 52n64; Old Calabar, 132; Oxford, 52n64; Padua, 52n64; Palencia, 52n64; Parma, 72, 81n63; Pera, 10; Pisa, 2, 69; Rheims, 71; Rome, 75–77, 81nn60, 63–65, 111nn53–54, 59, 62, 112n85, 259; Salamanca, xi, 11, 18–20, 26n51, 49, 52n64, 242; Sefrou, xiv, 167, 169, 172–75, 180, *181*, 182, *183*, 184–85, 186n1, 187n9; Sevilla, 29, 37, 42, 47; Shama, 136; Siena, 52n64, 64; Smolensk, 71; Tabriz, 9; Toghou, 116; Toledo, 29, 31, 35–36, 39, 52n61, 52n64; Tortosa, 29; Toulouse, 52n64; Ubeda, 47; Valladolid, 52n64; Valencia, 29, 37, 52n64, 69; Venice venitian, 26n48, 60, 64, 69, 72–74; Vienna, 116; Washington, 243, 256; Winchester, 89; Wittenberg, 89; Zaragoza, 29, 37. *See also* places

class, x, xv, 24n17, 29, 49, 50n6, 85, 95–96, 98, 111n69, 145–47, 154, 161–63, 164n8, 190–200, 203, 206, 208nn9, 13, 24, 35, 210n55, 222, 231, 237; gentry, 85, 195; merchant class, 85, 98, 195; working class, 190–91, 193, 196–200, 208nn9, 13, 209n24, 210n55. *See also* social structure

clients, 62–63, 67, 77, 155, 171, 173, 184–85

climate change, 234

Columbus, Christopher, 123

commerce, 21, 241, 243, 246: Early European, 65, 70, 73; Feudal, 83–84, 89–90; global commerce, ix; Iberian, 27, 32–33, 37–41, 43–44, 242; interreligious, 22; North African, 168, *181*, 182, *183*, 185, 192; psychology of, 248–49, sea commerce, 41. *See also* Atlantic slave trade

commodities, xiii, xv, 4, 10–12, 15, 18, 21–22, 29, 31–33, 42, 49, 57, 66–67, 69–70, 73, 105, 107, 119, 128–29, 134, 157, 170, 196, 232–33, 242–43, 261n14; commodity chain, 117, 124;

commodity futures, 218; credit as not a commodity, 251–53; credit as quasi commodity, 94–96, 252; labor power as, 118, 262; Marx's usage, xviii8, 221–22; money as 12, 19, 100; standardized, 169, 171–73, 184–86; trading at true value, 249–50; true commodity, xviii8
communes 147
complexity: complex adaptive systems, 223–24; fitness landscapes, 223; institutional complexity, 224; nonlinear analysis, 224; powerful particulars, 224–25, 234–36, 246, 252, 254. *See also* theoretical arguments
computer trading, 229
concessions, 4, 46, 63, 129
conservative views, 11, 19–20, 25n32, 49, 158, 225–26
consumers, xiii–iv, 4, 16, 90, 123, 164n11, 218, 220–21, 230–31, consumer borrowing, 190; consumer credit, 96, 140, 189–212, 210n67, 227, 230, 238n15, 239n46, 251; consumer debt, 205–6, consumer finance, 190; consumer guilt, 248–49, consumption loans, 11, 20, 23, 43–44, 46, 140, 190–91, 200, 208n10, 231; potatoes in a sack, 260n4, sovereign consumer, 261n14
corporations (companies): British Royal African (not Africa) Company, 118; Chamber of Insurance, 135; Dutch East India Company, (Dutch East Indies Company), 111n52, 117, 135; Dutch West India Company, 135–36, 138; General Motors, 227; Malian Company for the Development of Textiles (CMDT), 234; Merchant Adventures, 84; merchant guilds, 43, 84; merchant trading companies, 41; New East India Company, 98–99; parastatal charter companies, 135; Royal Adventurers into Africa, 137; Royal African Company (RAC), 137, 139, 143n83; Singer Sewing Machine Company, 200; South Sea Company, 98–99, 111nn64–65, 138–39; Spiegel Company, 200; Staplers, 84; Tappen's Mercantile Agency, 202
corvée labor, 157
Cosimo de Medici, 77. *See also* Italian merchant banks
cottars 87, 109n20
Council of the Indies, 138
courts, xii–xiii, 29–30, 33, 43, 101, 194: Consular courts, xiii, 157; enforcement, vii, 33, 46, 87,95, 100; 201–2, 242; excommunication, 47; foreclosure, 208, 214, 216, 232. *See also* law
credit: abstract forms of credit, 95; annuities, xi, xiv, 7, *15*, 19, 21, 23, 41, 57, 64, 95, 97, 98–100, 168–69, 186, 200, 249; bailouts, 217, 225–26, 237; bill of exchange, 41, 63, 65–73, 94, 97, 101–2, 110n42, 134–35, 140; bonds, 95, 99–100, 102–4, 206, 229, 253; bottomry loans, 41; bourse, 9, 20, 69, 71, 189, 242; census, 19, 21; conditions on credit, 8, 227, 231, 236, 252–53; conditionalities, 252, 254; creditor, xvi, 5–6, 59, 64, 92, 194–95; Credo, 257; credit bureau, xiv, 201–3; credit crisis, 207, 213, 217, 222–23, 227, 232–34, 236, 244, 247, 251; credit histories, 201; credit-money, 95, 98; credit report, 201–4, 210nn65, 67, 70; credit worthy, ix, 21, 59,

64, 68, 102, 155, 192, 201–2, 227, 243; Danegeld, 86, 109n23; debtor, xiv, xvi, 55n113, 91–92, 94, 194, 201; defaults, 10, 41, 63, 192, 195, 201, 203, 214–16, 227–28, 231, 234, 255; deposits, *14*, 15, 20, 41, 51n28, 61–65, 67, 69, 71, 74–77, 81n59, 104, 192–93, 199–200, 226; discount market, 91, 94, 242; forced loan, 41, 45, 59, 96; guarantee, 5, *14–15*, 16, 40–41, 44, 67, 73, 97, 104, 194, 201, 229, 247, 254; hassa çiflik, 8–9; havale (aval), 9; ibdā'a, 259; inland bill 96, 102; junk bonds, 226; justice in lending, vii–viii, 10, 213, 219, 232–36, 243; kred, 257; lease, 6, *16*, 20, 126,168; lease-purchase, 200; leasehold, xiv, 7, 168, 186; lenders, 5, 10, 15, 61, 97, 192–94, 215, 217, 231, 244, 249, 253; letters of credit, 9, 39, 95, 100, 118, 127; lien, 256; negotiability, 95, 110n42; negotiable instrument, 69, 73, 93; personal credit, 95, 191–92; pledge, 9, *14*, 15–16, 23, 256; potlatch, 258; promissory notes, 97–98, 101–2; prebends, 8; primordial contract, 7; pronoia, 6, 8; public debt, 77, 95, 97, 99; shop token, 101; short-term, 101–2, 104; suftaca, 10; tamlik, 8; tapu, 7; timar, 8; tontines, 97; transitive credit arrangements in early banking, 67; treasury bill, 206, 214; working class credit, 193. See also credit agencies; credit cards; credit innovations; credit indexing; ethical motivations in finance; interest; liability; partnership; risk

credit agencies; CRCA (crédit rural crédit agricole), 155, 161–62; credit ratings, xv, 189, 213–14, 217, 227, 234–35; Equifax, 201, 227; Experion, 201, 227; Standard and Poor's, 217, 228; Trans Union, 201, 227

credit cards, xiv, 190, 201, 204–7, 210nn76–77, 79–82, 211n85; charge plate, 204; courtesy card, 204; general purpose card, 205; green card, 205; gas credit card, 204, Interbank Card Association, 205; loyalty cards, 204; MasterCard, 205; minimum monthly payment, 204; revolving line, 204

credit innovations: AAA rating, 214, 217; ARM (adjustable rate mortage), 214, 216–17, 232; BBB rating, 214; balloon payment, 214, 232; calculability, 236; CDMT (Malian Company for the Development of Textiles), 234; CDO (collateralized debt obligations), 208, 214, 216–17, 225; CDS (credit default swaps), 214–18, 225; CMO (collateralized mortgage obligations), 229; commercial paper, 216, 242; commission, 77–78, 102–3, 214–15; junk bonds, 226; MBS (MBSs) (mortgage backed securities), 208, 214, 216–18, 225, 228; NIJA loans (to those with no income, jobs or assets), 214; prime rate, 207, 214; redeemable securities, 41; SIV (strategic investment vehicles), 216; subprime, 100, 208, 216; teaser interest rates, 214; top-tier, 214; toxic assets, 214, 216; toxic securities, 217; tranches, 214. See also credit, ethical motivations in finance, Scholastic financial ideas

credit indexing: CDX (credit default swap index), 216; iTRAXX, 216 crimes, 132; criminals, 203, 234, 243, 253; culprits, 217, 219; illegality, 22, 34, 198; imprisonment, 127, 133, 194–95; impunity, 226; Panopticon, 201 Ponzi schemes, 217; prisoners, 194; prisons, xiv, 108, 196

Crusade against outrelief, 198

cultural categories: Aboriginal, 123; Afro-Lozano, 130; Anglo-Saxon, 85–86, 109n17; Aro 131–32; Asante, 131; Assyrian, 259; Austro-German, 156–58; Bambara, 116; Berber, 35, 148, 174, *181*, 182; British, 59, 72, 80n51, 83, 94, 102–4, 112nn74, 79, 88–90,94,96, 113n97, 116, 118–19, 135, 138, 156, 199, 209n38, 225, 242; Chinese (China), 29, 113n106, 127, 218, 230; Danes (Denmark), 85–86, 88, 109nn16,23, 135; Dutch (Holland, Netherlands), 97, 99, 102, 110n42, 111n52, 112nn74,78,92, 117, 135–38, 143n77; English (England), xii, xiv, 60, 62–66, 70, 78, 78n1, 83–90, 94–95, 97–101, 104–6, 108n11, 109n16, 110nn29, 36, 40, 42, 111nn51, 55, 58, 60–61, 69, 73, 121, 135–39, 142n43, 173, 190, 192, 194, 199, 208nn5, 9, 13, 209nn, 24–26, 28, 35, 29; Eskimo, 256; ethnicity (ethnic), xiv, 7, 9, 22, 29, 48, 131, 168–69, 172–75, 177–79; *179,* 180, *181*, 182–86, 188n12; European, viii–xi, xiii, 2–3, 10–12, 16, 18, 21, 23, 24n14, 28, 42, 49, 53n66, 57, 60, 70, 78, 90, 108n6, 115–19, 121–24, 128–35, 137, 139–41, 141n12, 142n66, 156, 168, 216, 241–42, 246–47, 257, 263n38, Flemish, 63, 69, 125, 127; French, xiv, 61, 67, 71, 85, 92, 103, 112, 112n92, 115–16, 137–39, 1141nn9,15, 156, 158–59, 198, 214, 260, 263n43; Galacia, 32; Germans, xvi, 19, 41, 53n68, 65–66, 84, 104, 125, 147, *150*, 155–158, 160–161, *162*, 163n1; Hansards, 84; Hispano-Romans, 53n68; (sp)/ Efik/(Ifik sp), 132; Ibibio, 132; Indian (Native Americans), 123, 142n36, 222; Indian (India), 72, 127; Indo-European, 257, 263n38; Italian, xi, 1–2, 10, *15,* 19, 42, 51n51, 57, 60–66, 68–70, 72–76, 79n20, 80n54, 85, 90, 112n78, 115, 125–27, 230, 241; Jahaanke, 131; Japanese, ix, 127; Julaa, 131; Kachin, 258; kingdom of the Kongo, 116; Kwakiutl, 258; Latin, 37; Lombards, 61–62, 64; Maghribi, 42, 174; Maori, 256–257, 259; Mozarabs (Muzarabs), 30, 39; Norman, 83, 85–86, 108n9, 109n15, 110n37; Moors (Mudejars), 38–39, 121–122; Persian, 10; Polisario, 142n23; Polynesian, 257; Portuguese, 122–23, 127–29, 133–36, 138–39; Roman, vii, x, 3, 5, 13, 20, 23, 29, 31, 39–40, 43, 48–49, 50n16, 52n63, 53nn68,89, 66, 68, 75–76, 78, 87–88, 163, 242–243; Sereer, 116; Spanish, 35, 43, 45–46, 70, 72, 98, 102, 119, 123–25, 133–34, 136–39, 141n17, 142nn28, 30, 39–40, 143nn68, 80, 85–86, 144n88; Wolof, 116

currencies, 4–5, 9–10, 19, 45, 59–62, 66–69, 71, 79n25, 88, 93–94, 98, 101–102, 134–35, 140, 141n11, 189, 218, 225, 233, 237, 252, 258 (money); akçe, 9; coinage, xiii, 37, 39, 52n63, 88–90, 129; coins, 35, 45, 52n63, 62, 66–68, 87–90, 92, 101, 129, 134;

Index 291

constant dollars, 230; cowries, 129; currency debasement, 9, 59–62, 67, 71, 88, 94 currency devaluation, 233; dollars, 104, 107, 143n56, 200, 205–7, 213, 215–16, 226, 229–35, 252–53; ducat, 60; écu,71; escudos,134; ghost currency, 66–67, 79n25; groat, 69; marks, 61; medium of exchange, 66; mints, 31, 39, 52n63, 59–60, 63, 67, 88–91, 94, 109n23; nomisma, 5; pence, 92, 193; pennies, 109n23; pesos, 138–39; pounds, 63, 69, 92, 97–99, 104, 109n14, 137–39, 159, 192–94, 199; reales, 134; shillings, 92, 192, 194; solidus, 66–67; specie, 41. *See also* money of account
custom revenues, 9, 17, 63, 89, 108n14, 122, 133

dar al-islam, 21–22
databases, 201, 227–28
da Castro, Giovanni, 65
Da Vinci, Leonardo, 79n21
de' Bardi, Bartolomeo, 68
de Batarnay, Ymbert, 74
de Freitas, Lançarote, 122
de las Casas, Bartolomé, 123, 142
de Recalde, Juan López, 125
debt: delinquent debtor, 194; negotiable debt, 94; repossession, 201; wives' debts, 91
debt collection, xiv, 193–95; Apostolic collectors, 76; expropriation, 145; poor house, xiv debtor's prison, xiv, 127, 194–95, 209n27; seizure, 91; tax collector, 44 tax farmer 4, 6–7, 30, 44–45, 47, 76. *See also* Sheriff
destitution, 191
disease, 121, 123–24, 127, 138; epidemics, 216, 258; malaria, 133; plague, 41, 47; smallpox, 133; yellow fever, 133

discretization: abstraction, xii–xiii, 17, 87, 94–95, 100, 105–7, 110n4, 204, 229–30, 236, 247; calculability, xiii, 106, 214, 227, 229, 236; capital mobility, xi, 95, 106–7, 236; digital, 229, 253; dimensionless, 95; separable element 106, 230. *See also.* theoretical arguments
Divina proportione, 79n21
dowry, 16

ecology, 148, 161, 178, 245, 251, 260n9, 262n29
economic concepts: accumulation (Akkumuliert), x, xvi, 38, 46, 57–58, 103, 118, 141, 222–23, 231–33, 238n27, 245, 258; aggregate income 189, 230, 239n51; asset(s), xii, 3, 5, 8, 20, 65–66; audit, 91, 239n41; bankruptcy, 20, 63,104, 208, 213; bubbles, xv, 78, 98–100, 102, 111nn63–65,67, 138–39, 214, 218–20, 237, 246; cash flow, 107, 214, 216, 220; caveat emptor, x, 41, 48, 242, 244, 256; comparative advantage, 105–6, 161; competition, viii–ix, xi, 24, 40–42, 45–45, 49, 124, 132, 134–35, 137–38, 140, 171, 184–85, 187n,12, 221–22, 225, 244, 247, 251; compound interest, 75, 192, 207, 246; consumption, 11, 20, 23, 37, 43–44, 46, 88, 140–41, 189–90, 200, 208nn2,10, 209n23, 231, 260n9; costs, x–xi, xiii, 10, *14*, 18, 33, 44, 54n92, 59, 63, 65, 76–77, 88, 100–1, 104, 106–7, 110n43, 121, 124, 130, 133, 135, 137, 139, 149, 159, 168, 184, 189, 192, 194–95, 197–98, 200, 202, 207, 213, 223, 226, 232–35, 239nn56–58, 246–47, 249, 260n9, 262n20; Darwinian economics, 244; dead capital, 105; deregulation,

206–8, 211n87, 218, 221, 225–26, 235, 237; derivative, 43, 215; disbursements, 31, 74, 258; dispossession, 38, 101, 103, 222–23, 231–32; distribution (including statistical) 23, 77, 108, 146, 156, 175, *176,* 177–80, 182–83, 186, 188n21, 219–20, 224, 230, 244–47, 261n20; dividends, 76; dynamics, xiii, 38, 52n55, 117, 120, 141n11, 142n20, 160, 197, 210n64, 219–20, 222–23, 228, 236, 261n19; earnings, 5, 16, 29, 31, 34, 74, 126, 191, 195, 206, 245; efficiency, xvin6, 118, 210nn76, 78, 82, 222, 229, 244, 253; endowment(s), 8–10, 161, 168–69, 186; enterprises, xiii, 3, 22, 41, 71, 77, 98–99, 101, 106, 123, 125–26, 136–37, 140, 155, 170, 194, 205, 215, 227; e-trading, 229; equity (stock), 215, 225; expenditures (admirable), 16, 60, 65, 92, 198, 200, 233; export, 32, 107, 115, 137, 158, 161, 168, 218, 233; Export Processing Zones (EPZ), 107; financial capital, 107, 111n63, 112n95, 226, 229; firms, xi, xiii, 1, 6, 8, 18–19, 29, 32, 43, 47, 49, 57, 64, 68–72, 80n51, 90, 102, 136, 156–59, *162,* 202, 215–17, 255; fungibility of profit, 204; futures, xiii, 107, 130, 218; growth, x, xv, 18, 39, 59, 80n51, 84, 90, 98, 100, 107, 112n74, 120, 159, 208nn4,7, 222–23, 233, 245–46, 261n16; income, *14,* 47, 65, 74, 108n14, 145, 153, 155, 163, 168, 186, 189, 191, 214, 218–20, 224, 230–31, 234, 237, 239n51, 245, 253; inefficiency, 244; inequality, 57, 76, 107, 162, 224, 230, 232, 237, 248, 241, 245, 247; inventory, 133, 103,

invest(ment), vii, x–xiv, 3, 5–6, 12, 17, 19–20, 22–23, 44, 49, 51n34, 58, 63–64, 66–67, 74–76, 78, 90, 95, 101, 103–7, 112n74, 118, 124, 136, 140, 147, *150,* 155, 157–61, *162,* 168–69, 184, 186, 197, 207–8, 213, 215–18, 220, 222, 226, 228–32, 235–37, 245–46, 249, 251–52, 256, 259, 262n29; investors, x, 3, 5–6, *14, 15,* 25n42, 41, 57, 74–75, 90, 99, 107, 208, 214–16, 219–20, 230–31, 237; joint stock, xii, 57, 97–100, 102–3; laissez-faire, 103, 220; labor theory of value, 245; liberal market, 49, 219, 225; multiplier, 252; opportunity cost, x, *14,* 18, 54n92, 246–47, 249; OTC (over the counter) stocks, 216, 225; poverty, 185, 196, 199, 210n50, 232–33, 239nn59–60, 260nn4,7; price, viii–ix, xiii–xiv, 2, 4, 6, 9–12, *13,* 16–19, 22–23, 26n49, 32–33, 40, 45, 51n28, 57–59, 65–66, 73, 87, 99–100, 106, 115, 118–19, 123, 125, 128–32, 134, 139–40, 143n56, 149, 159, 168, 170–71, 173, 184, 193, 196, 200–2, 207, 214, 216, 219–20, 225–26, 232–34, 239, 243, 247, 249–52, 261nn14,19; profits, viii, x, xiii–xiv, 1–7, 10, 12, *13–14,* 15–21, 23, 26n56, 34, 41–42, 46, 49, 51n34,42, 53n70, 58, 63–67, 69–71, 73–76, 81n59, 89, 93, 96, 98, 100–1, 117–18, 122, 124–29, 132–33, 137, 139–41, 149, 157, 170, 173, 175, 187n12, 190, 192–94, 200, 204–8, 213–15, 217, 219–22, 225, 230, 232, 235–36, 241, 244–47, 249–251, 258–59, 261nn15, 22, 262nn23, 28; property, 2, 7, *14,* 38, 40, 44–45, 60–62, 67, 83, 89, 91, 96, 100–1, 105, 108, 132, 134, 139, 145,

155, 157–59, 168, 170, 186, 192, 195, 206, 208, 216, 226, 256, 258, 262n27; productive, viii, xi, xiii, xvn2, 4, 7–8, 43, 46, 49, 58, 65, 106, 116, 118–19, 140, 146, 164n11, 190, 244–47, 251–52, 260n3; purchases, 4, 7, 35, 44, 58, 68, 70, 73, 89, 97, 99, 104, 115, 125, 128–30, 139, 157, 161–62, 170, 186, 192–93, 200, 206, 216, 222, 231, 237; purchasing power parity (PPP), 19, 35; real estate, 9, 18, 135, 157–58, 186, 231, 237; remittances, 160, 233; rents, 28, 44, 64, 80n54, 85, 87, 93, 101, 108n14, 109n15, 109nn15,20, 116, 168, 191, 193, 200, 231, 249; repayment, 9, 16, 59, 69, 132, 156, 191, 195, 200, 206, 247; resource curse, 248; resources, 4, 26n45, 37, 39, 41, 58–59, 67, 77, 115, 140, 160, 164n7, 172, 180, 182, 190, 202, 204, 219, 222, 245–46, 260n3; revenue, xi, 4, 7–9; 23, 26n45, 30–31, 47, 57, 59–61, 63–64, 71, 74, 76–77, 87, 89, 92, 94, 96, 108n14, 124, 135, 160, 168, 208, 220, 222, 223; scale, x, xii, xv, 3, 6, 21, 28, 57, 78, 84, 90, 95, 98, 106–8, 135, 137, 140, 148, 156, *181, 183,* 185, 205, 219, 233; sale (sellers, selling, resale, resold), xi–xiii, 4, 7, 9, *13,* 16, 26n49, 33–35, 40–44, 46, 64, 66, 68–70, 72–73, 84, 89–90, 93–95, 97, 99–100, 102, 104, 115–16, 118–19, 122, 124–25, 128–29, 131–34, 136, 138, 157, 170–71, 173, *176, 179,* 184–86, 189, 191–193, 195, 197, 200–1, 204–5, 214–17, 222, 224–25, 228–29, 231–32, 242, 248, 250, 252; savings, xiv, 102, 112n74, 189, 196, 198–200; Tobin tax, 226.

See also economists, Keynesian economics, markets
economic myths: equilibrium model, 219–20, 261, 268; fair competition, 221; fair credit, 203; fair interest, 41; fair price, 32, 173, 249; fair profit; fair trade, 248; fair transactions, 250; fair wage, 59, 191, 196, 198, 204, 221–22, 232; financial unimportance of inequality, viii, xv, 105, 244–46, 249–51, 255; just price, 4, 10–13, 16–19, 22–23, 26n49, 40. *See also* Marxism, metaphors, power
economists: Daron Acemoglu, Simon Johnson and James A. Robinson, 145, 163n1, 263n8; A. V. Chayanov, xiv, 145–49, 151–52, 154–56; 160–63, *162,* 163nn2–4, 164nn6–7, 10–12, 165nn13, 15–16; Michael Common and Sigrid Stagl, 260n9; Hernando de Soto, 105, 113nn100–1; Maurice Dobb, 261n20; Edgeworth, 261n14; Fredrick Engels, 190–91, 193, 208nn9, 13, 209nn24–25; Robert H. Frank, 260n3; Milton Friedman, 225; Alan Greenspan, 218; Andre Gunder Frank, 141n11, Robin Hahnel, 260n9; David Harvey, 52n57, 222, 238n28; Sir John Hicks, 26n45, 78n2; John Maynard Keynes, xv, 219–20, 225, 238n16; Rosa Luxemberg, 222, 238n27; Karl Marx, viii, xiv–xv; xvn2, xvin8, 94, 105, 110n43, 111n69, 118, 146, 163nn3–4, 164nn6–7, 170, 187n6, 189, 191, 208n11, 219, 221–23, 244–46, 249, 252, 260nn4, 10, 261n20, 262n27; Hyman Minsky, 220, 228n22; Edward J. Nell, 247, 261nn14, 16; Edward J. Nell and Karim

Errouaki, 248, 261n17, 263n30; David Ricardo, 96, 105–6, 113n99, 249; Walt W. Rostow, 112n74; Joseph A. Schumpeter, x, xvin7, 1, 23, 24n1, 25nn32, 34, 39, 79nn18, 22, 260n12; Amartya Sen, 206n3, 248, 260n7; 261nn18–19; Adam Smith, 25nn31–32, 34, 37, 42–44, 26nn46–47,52–54,57, 55n124, 96–97, 105–6, 111nn53–54, 59, 62, 85, 113n98, 118–19, 195, 248, 261n20; Piero Sraffa, 247, 261n14

ecosystem, 245, 262n29; economic ecosystem, 205

educational institutions: libraries, 29; universities, xi, 11, 18–19, 29, 39, 52n64

enlightenment, 96

epistemology, 249

ethical motivations in finance: altruistic behavior, 248, 261n18; benevolence (beneuolentia), vii; benignitas, vii; carentia pecuniae, *14*, 20; charis, vii; chreia, 4; complacibilitas, *14*, 17, 242; damnum emergens, *13*, 15, 18, 20, 54n92; dignitas, vii; ēthikē, vii; equity, xiii, 34, 41, 65, 74, 262n26; fides, vii; gluttony, 220; guilt, 248–249; gratia, vii; greed, ix, 100, 219, 224, 236–37, 249–50, 258; hau, 257; honesty, 32–33, 61, 168, 202; honor, vii–viii, 40, 258; hope, 26n50, 59, 73, 91, 193, 257; hypothetical gain, 54n92; injustice, ix, 10, 19, 21–23, 49, 76, 237, 244, 246; justice, vii–viii, 4, 6–7, 10–11, 19, 21–23, 40, 59, 76, 96, 213, 219, 224, 230, 232–37, 243–44, 247, 256, 259; lucrum cessans, *14*, 15, 18–20; liberalitas, vii; oath, 46; officium amicitiae, 20; philia, vii; Protestant ethic, 242; poena conventionalis, *13*, 16; publicum (not publicam) utilitatem, *13*, 15–16; propter periculum, *13*, 15–16; reciprocity, 257; reputation, 21, 23, 32–33, 40, 43, 60, 191, 204, 243; responsibility, *14*, 73, 76, 91, 97, 168, 196, 199; self-serving behavior, 107, 248; stipendium laboris, 15; trust, vii–viii, xv, *13*, 21, 23, 32–33, 43, 49, 62–63, 68, 77–78, 89, 94, 126, 130–32, 167, 191–92, 196, 201–2, 210n62, 244, 257–59; turpe lucrum, 12, *13*, virtuositas, *14*, 17. *See also* transparency

European perspectives, viii, x, 11, 16, 108n1, 247

exchange, ix, 9–10, 15, 17, 19, 25n34, 41, 62–63, 66–73, 123, 129, 135, 233; bill of exchange, 65, 68–73, 94, 97, 102, 110, 134, 140; delayed exchange, 258; dry exchange, 75, fictitious exchange, 80; Exchange Commision, 218, institutionalized exchanges, 220, 236, 242, simultaneous exchange, 259

factors of production, viii, xii, 57, 100, 105, 221, 247, 252–53, 259

fairs: Besançon, ix, 71–72, 241; Brabant, 68; Champagne, ix; Lyon, ix, 71, 241; Piacenza, 72, 81

families, 8, 33, 63, 65, 77, 86, 91, 101–3, 132, 148, 174–75, 186, 191, 193–95, 197, 260n4; orphans, 5, 195

famine, 7, 16–17

farmers, 148, 155, 160, *162*, *181*, *183*, 185, 233–34; tax farmers, 6–7, 30, 44–45, 47, 76

fashion, 249

feudal. *See* history, historians (Braudel, Goitein, Greif, Kula, Pirenne, Reynolds), obligations

financial crisis: Barings crisis of 1890, 102–4, 112n92, 113n97; credit crisis of 2008, xiv, 213, 217, 222–23, 227, 232–34, 236, 244, 247, 251; dot-com bubble, 214; South Sea Bubble of 1720, 98–99, 111n63–64, 138–39; subprime mortgage market crisis of 2007, xv, 213–18, 222, 228, 231–32, 237, 238n15, 239n46
financial edicts and studies, ; Comentario resolutoio de usuras, 19; De justitia et jure, 19; The Dialogue of the Exchequer, 110n36; Domesday Book, 86–87; Fuero Real, 41; Report of Recommendations to Curb Predatory Mortgage Lending, 232. See also government regulation, Papal bulls
financial expertise, ix, xi, 44, 49, 62–63, 73–74, 85, 102, 129; corporate deception, 235; corporate financing, 190; financial justice, 236–37, 244, 247. See also accounting; banking; credit; credit innovations; Italian merchant banks; financial institutions and corporations; gambling and speculation; government finances; government regulators; money lenders; mortgage; risk; Scholastic financial ideas; taxation
financial institutions and corporations: American Express, 205–6; AGI (American International Group), 217; Associated Credit Bureaus, Inc., 202; Bank America Service Corporation, 205; Bear Stearns, 217; Beaser Homes, 217; Commodity Futures Trading Commission, 218; Countrywide, 208, 217; Credit Suisse, 225; Diners Club, 205–6; Dun and Bradstreet, 202; Exchequer, 90–94, 110nn36,38, 199, 242; Fannie Mae, 218, 231; Federal Reserve (Fed), 205, 207, 214, 216, 218, 225, 237, 238n6, 239n53; Fortis, 215; Freddie Mac (Federal Home Loan Mortgage Corporation), 227, 231; Fortune 500 companies, 216; FICO (Fair, Isaac and Company), 227; Guarantee Security Company, 201; Goldman Sachs, 215, 225; Hambros, 104, hedge funds, 213–14, 216–18, 225, 228; IndyMac, 217; IMF (International Monetary Fund), 252, 255, 262n24; Lehman Brothers, 213, 215; Lloyd's of London, 98; MasterCard, 205; Merrill Lynch, 215, 217; Securities and Exchange Commission, 218; Salomon Brothers, 217, 229; Scripps Networks, 218; Depositary of the Apostolic chamber, 76–77; acceptance house, 95, 102; brokerage house, 217, 225, Government National Mortgage Association (Ginnie), 229; insurance company, 44, 57, 75, 95, 98, 100, 135, 139–40, 190, 215–17, 227, 232, 243; investment firm, 215, 217; Monte della Fede, 77, 97; Montes pietatis, 76; stock market, 95, 97–100, 102–3, 107, 111n53, 111n59, 111nn62–63,65–66, 112n85, 118, 135, 137, 139–40, 147, 192, 200, 213, 216, 220, 225–26, 231–32, 235, 242, 244, 249, 253
financial restrictions, *13*, 29, 32, 39–40, 54n96, 97, 198, 207
financial revolution, 97–98, 111n51–52
FitzNeal, Bishop Richard, 110
Frescobaldi. See Italian merchant bankers
fuero, 43, 45, 52
funds, 17, 104, 197–99; hedge funds, 213, 217

gambling and speculation, xv, 19, 34–35, 41, 78, 98–100, 102, 111n64, 202, 214, 216, 218–20, 237, 246, 249; South Sea Bubble, 98–100, 138–40
games, 45, 128, 140, 217–18, 250
Gorrevod, Lorenzo de, 125
gente nuova ("new men"), 77
Gerard of Cremona, 79n17
gifts, 4, 7, *14*, 17, 20, 23, 24n6, 47, 60–61, 74–75, 84, 90, 128, 130, 192, *221*, 248, 255–57, 259, 263n34; make slaves, 256
Gladstone, William, 199–200
globalization, xi, 78, 102–4, 107, 190, 224–26, 229–31, 236
Glorious Revolution of 1688, 95, 97–98, 242
governance, viii, xiv, 29, 40, 77, 108, 256
government finances: indirect taxes, 76; tariff, 26n45, 30, 105, 107, 119; toll, 30, 32; levies, 86–87; minting fee, 31; subsidy, 76, 139, 147, 231–32. *See also* taxation
government regulation (Acts): Amendment Act of 1834, 196; American Dream Down Payment Act, 231; Bubble Act, 99, 102; Combination Acts of 1799-1800, 198; Commodity Futures Modernization Act of 2000, 218; Community Reinvestment Act, 218; Congress of Vienna 1815, 116; Debtors Act of 1869, 194; Domesday Book, 86–87; ejido, 232; FCRA (Fair Credit Reporting Act), 203; gabelles (qabala), 76; Glass-Steagall Act, 217–18, 226; Government Annuities Act, 200; GSE (government sponsored enterprise), 215, 227, 229; hass, 8; hass-i hümayun, 8; hassa çiflik, 8–9; hidage, 86; hides, 86–87, 109n16; HUD (Housing and Urban Development), 231–32; Justinian code, 5; Knatchbull's Act, 196; Lex Rhodia, 24n12; licencia program, 136; licenses, 136; New Laws of the Indies, 123; Poor Law, 101, 195–96, 198; Promissory Notes Act, 97, pronoia (tax exempt benefice), 6, 8; rakaba (dominium eminens), 8; regulatory failure, xv, 218, 224; Resolution Trust Corporation, 226, 239n41; Royal Charter, 52, 98–99, 102; Savings Bank Act, 199; Securities and Exchange Commission, 218; Seditious Meetings Acts of 1795 and 1817, 198; Siete Partidas, 40, 43, 53n67, 241; Supreme court decision, 206; Tonnage Act, 97; Treaty of Alcaçovas, 123, 125; Triennial Subsidy of 1543, 76; Unlawful Societies Act of 1799, 198; US Congress, 203, 226. *See also* law, Lex Rhodia; taxes
government regulators: US Senate Banking Committee, 218; US Treasury, 214, 216, 218, 232
Gresham, Thomas, 242
Guellouli, Caid, 158
guns and horses, 115

hajib, 30
Hapsburg monarchy, xvin3, 72, 136
Hastings, Battle of, 85
heads of state: Aethelred, 109nn19,23; Archduke Sigismund, 65; Athelstan, 88, 109n23; Alfonso I of Aragon, 60; Alfonso X (King of Castile and León), 40, 43, 241; Alfonso XI, (King of Castile and León), 46–47; Almanzor, 50n6; Anne (Queen), 139; Basil I, 5; Napoleon Bonaparte, 103–4; George W. Bush, 218, 221, 231, 235; Charlemagne, 52n63;

Index 297

Charles I (of Spain), 124–25, 128; Charles II (of England), 90; Charles II (of Spain), 138; Bill Clinton, 218, 221, 226; Cnut, 109n16; Constantine, 5; Damel, 115; Doges of Venice, 60; Edgar, Edward, 109n23; Edward I, 62–63, 89, 108n14; Edward II, 63; Edward III, 63; Edward VI, 90; Eodred, 106n16; Elizabeth I, 90; George I, 139; Harold II, 85, 108n10; Henry I, 88–89, 91, 108n14; Henry II, 61, 88, 90–92, 101; Henry II, (of Cyprus), 108n12; Henry the Navigator, 122; Henry VIII, 89; Jaime I of Aragon, 46, 52n63, 55n113; James II (of England), 97; John, 89; Louis XI, 71; Louis XIV, 97, 138; David Oddsson, 218; Philip IV, the Fair, 61–62, 79n8; Philip I (France), 108n9; Philip II of Spain, 72, 125, 136, 138; Philip IV of Spain, 136, 138–39; Ronald Reagan, 206, 221, 225; Richard the Lion-Heart, 89; Roger (Norman Count of Sicily), 2; Sancho el Mayor, 52n63; Saladin, 37; Stephen not Steven sp, 60; Margaret Thatcher, 221, 225; William the Conqueror, 85–86, 108n11; William III (of Orange), 97; William II, 88; Wen Jiabao, 218

heterogeneity: commodity, 184–85; county level, 163; legal, 108n1

hidden interests, xii, 40, 44, 69, 85, 93, 162–63, 169, 186, 225, 247–50, 256. *See also* transparency

historians: Fernand Braudel, viii, xvn2, xvin6, 27, 49n3, 69, 72, 79n25, 80nn29, 34, 42–43, 49–50, 84, 108n5, 120, 141nn3, 11, 19, 143nn71–73, 245; Philip D. Curtin, 50n4, 119, 141nn14–16, 142n34, 143n54, 57–62, 73; Glyn Davies, 52nn53, 63, 79n21, 80n54 109nn23, 26, 110nn28, 32, 35, 39, 111nn55–56, 112nn74–75, 80, 85, 91, 93, 113n97, 144nn88, 90–93, 210n53; S. D. Goitein, 33, 50n21, 51nn35, 41; Anver Greif, 51nn28, 37–39, 210n64; Pierre Guillen, 163n1; Dale Kent, 79n20, 81n66; Matin Klein, 141n15; Witold Kula, 109n22; Suzanne Miers and Igor Kopytoff, 142n20; Henri Pirenne, 27, 49n1, 52n54, 53n81; Susan Reynolds, 24n3, 108nn1–2; Murray N. Rothbard, 25nn31–32, 34, 37, 42–43, 26nn46, 52–53, 57, 55n124; Peter Spufford, 261n15, 262n23

history; Abbasid, 30, 50n7; Almohad, 37, 42, 50n13; Almoravid, 35–37; anachronistic, 11–12, 26n57; ancient, viii–ix, xii, 20–21; Bronze age 243; Byzantine Empire, ix, 1–12, *13*, 14, 16, 22, 24nnb4–5, 10–13, 16, 17, 19–20, 29–30, 52n63, 60, 73–74, 120–121, 142n24, 224, 226, 243; Carolingian Empire, 108n9; conjoncture, vii; Ecclesiastical, 45; Eurocentric, ix; feudal, xii, 17, 27, 28, 44–46, 49, 58–59, 62, 64, 78n2, 83–85, 88–89, 96, 100, 108n1, 109n22, 110n29, 111n69, 195; French revolution, 112n81, 198; Greco-Roman period, 3; Komnenian period, 6; Islamic, vii, x–xi, xiii–xiv, 7, 9–12, 16, 19–23, 25n42, 27–31, 33–34, 36–41, 44, 48–49, 50nn18, 51n34, 52n63, 53n70, 62, 66, 75, 79n17, 81n59, 90, 110n42, 116, 120–21, 129–31, 186, 234, 241–42, 247–48, 259, 259n1, 262n25; Medieval, xii, 3–4, 11–12, 18, 21, 24nn3, 15, 25n42; 26n56, 39,

298 Index

41, 48–49, 49n1, 50nn6, 11, 14, 17, 19, 51nn, 24, 33, 42, 52nn52, 54–56, 58–60, 63, 53nn68, 74–76, 78–81, 54nn92–93, 98, 101, 105, 107, 55nb120, 122, 57, 60, 62, 64, 69, 71, 75, 77, 78nn1–2, 79nn11, 14, 80nn45, 52, 83–85, 89, 101, 108nn1, 3, 8, 111nn71–72, 120, 246, 261n15; Napoleonic Wars, 102–4, 198; Ottoman, ix, xiii, 1, 3–4, 7–11, 16, 22, 24, 25nn23–30, 65, 243; Protectorate (Morocco), xiv, 155–58; Reconquista (reconquest), x–xi, 27–28, 35, *36*, 37–39, 42, 44–46, 49, 52nn52, 63, 53n71, 121, 242; Reformation, x, 78, 89–90, 242; Renaissance, 64, 77, 78n3, 79nn12–13, 20, 26, 80nn32, 35–37, 41, 48 81nn60, 63, 66–67, 90, 110n37; Slave trade, xiii, 115–126, 128, 130, 132–40, 141nn15, 18, 142nn20, 22, 29, 31, 37–38, 44, 48–50, 143nn52, 55, 64–66, 69–70, 75, 83, 144nn87–89, 93–94, 241; Umayyads, 30, 50n7; Visigoths 31, 53nn68,71
homogeneity in quality of goods, 171
Hospitallers. *See* banking
household(s): cift hane, 8; family life cycle, 191; rapid turnover logic, 191
homeowners, 216, 231
houses, 50n6, 191, 204; acceptance, 95, 100; appropriation of, 38, 45, 62; banking, 62–64, 101–4, 112n78; brokerage, 217, 225; clearing, 242; collateral, 10; discount, 93; equity, 208, 214–15, 225, 231; exchange, 123; investment, 215; mercantile, 134; of correction, 195; poor, xiv,
human rights, 107
humanistic ideal, 262n27

Hundreds (wapentakes), 86–87
hypercoherence, 226
hypotheses, 149, 153, 159–61, 219–20; Instability Hypothesis, 238n22

ideology, 169–70, 219, 251, 261n20; German, 262n27, hegemonic ideas, 251; laissez-faire, 103; liberal, 199; neoliberal, 107; zero drag, 262n27. *See also* Marxism, neoliberalism
Immatriculation Foncière, 151
immorality, 12
imports, 4, 115, 124–25, 230–31, 233
incentive, xii–xiii; 3–4, 17, 22, 87, 118, 126, 163n3, 164n11, 171, 173, 214, 250, 251, 254
Indian Ocean, 42
indices: biodiversity index, 177; compactness index, 175, 188n18; Shannon index, 177
indigo, 134
Industrial Revolution, 57, 78, 98, 100–3, 112nn74,76, 115, 195, 197, 208nn3,7, 237, 242, 245
industry, 28, 42, 44, 57, 80n51, 106, 121, 200, 207, 217, 224, 233; captains of, 244; credit, 201, 204; mortgage, 208, 228
information, ix, xii, xv, 32, 69, 71, 84, 87, 106–7, 152, 169–74, 176, 187n3, 201–4, 210n71, 229; imperfect information, xv, 224
infrastructure, x, xii, 61, 63, 84, 233, 242, 245, 254, 258
inheritance (heir(s)), 4, 59, 101, 108n14, 118, 132, 155, 168, 170
inquisition, 39, 48, 55n123, 62, 248. *See also* power
insights (retrospective), viii, x, 23, 37, 196, 208, 244, 247
insolvency, 91
instability, xv, 208, 219–20, 238n22
installment sales, 200

institutional analysis, 247–48, 260n8, 261n15
institutionalizing: constraints, 186; credit, xiv, 61, 94–95, 98, 100, 105, 135, 189, 201, 203, 252; inequalities, viii, 244, 248, 250; repression, 196; risk, 225–26, 234; social capital, 145, 167, 204, 257; taxes, 92; trust, 167
insurance, 44, 57, 75, 95, 98, 100, 135, 139–40, 190, 215–17, 227, 231–32, 243
intellectuals, xi, 1, 15–16, 22–23, 49, 78, 241–42, 245–46, 262n27
intensification, 145, 154, 159–60, 162, 164n10
interest: above zero, 1; APR, 207; centesimae usurae, 5; concealed, hidden, or veiled xi, 9, 33, 44, 85, 93, 97; 146, 162–63, 169, 186, 200, 247–48, 253, 256; compound, 49, 207, 246; disguised, 44, 69, 75; donativo, 77–78; hekatostiaios tokos, 5; installments, xiv, 91, 200–1; normalization, 75–78; per annum, 10, 43, 74, 77, 192–93; prime rate, 207, 214; simple, 75, 192; tokos, 5; variable, 75. *See also* usury
investors, 3, 5–6, *14–15*, 57, 66, 74–75, 90, 99, 107, 208, 214–16, 219, 220, 230–31, 234, 237
Irish potato famine, 245
irrigation, 31, 145, *149–50*, 155, 160
Italian merchant bankers, 62–68: Bardi, 63–64, 68, 112n78; Frescobaldi, 63–64; Medici, 64–66, 68, 70, 74, 76–77, 79n19,20, 112n78, 253; Peruzzi, 63–64, 112n78; Riccardi of Lucca, 63; Spinelli, 79n20, 80n47
ivory, 121–22, 129

Junta de Negros, 138

key figures in 2008 financial crisis: James Cayne, 217; Joe Cassano, 217; Kathleen Christopher Corbet, 217; Christopher Cox, 218, 221; John Devaney, 217; Richard Fuld, 217; Fred Goodwin, 217; Phil Gramm, 218; Burton Jablin, 218; Wen Jiabao, 218; David Lereah, 218; Bernie Madoff, 217; Hank Paulson, 218; John A. Paulson, 231, 237; Franklin Raines, 218, 228; Lewis Ranieri, 217; Sandy Weill, 217, 228; *See also* financial institutions and corporations, credit agencies
Keynesian economics, xv, 219–20, 225, debt trap, 220; deficit spending, 220; financial instability hypothesis, 220, 238n22; paradox of thrift, 220; paradox of gluttony, 220; positive feedback cycle, 220
khazin al-mal, 31
kharaj lands, 7
Khwarizmi, 79
klasmatic lands, 4, 9
knowledge, x, 39, 43, 66, 74, 86, 102, 110n36, 126, 170–71, 187n3, 229, 243, 245; perfect, 225; personal, 227
Kula ring, 257; prestige 90, 254, 258

labor: costs, 159; xiii, discretized, 204; division of, 170, 172, *181*, 182, *183*, 185, 191, 199, 241, 260n4; domestic, 116, 119; impoverishment and market instability, xv, 230, 236, 240n69; labores, *14*, 18; labor theory of value, 245; male, 8; onerousness of, 149; plus risk and liability, 251; productivity, 146–47, 149, 151, 164n7, 219, 222, 224; supply, 58–59, 65, 87, 96, 100–1, 106–7, 109, 118, 157, 252; *vs.*

money, 3; viewed as energy, 246. *See also* factors of production, Marxism, Scholastic ideas, slavery
laborers, 20, 182, 191, 196, 222. *See also* workers
lançados, 129
landlords, 106, 131–32, 159, *162*, 190
landowner, *150*, 154–55, 159, 185
language, 39, 116, 197, 203, 261n21
latifundia, 31
laws: American Dream Down Payment Act, 231; Bubble Act, 99, 102; Byzantine law, 5, 24n10; Canon, *13,* 30, 43, 50n18, 53n71; codes, 5, *13,* 37, 40, 43, 251; Combination Acts, 198; commercial law, xi–xii, 43–44, 48, 90, 100; Commodity futures Modernization Act, 218; Community Reinvestment Act, 218; Corpus Juris Civilis, *13*; customary law, 50n18, 53n68; Danelaw, 109; enclosure laws, 111n69, 196; Fair Credit Reporting Act (FCRA), 203; Germanic law, 53n68; Glass-Steagall Act, 217–18, 226; Government Annuities Act, 200; Homestead Act, 206; injunctions, 130; Islamic law, 21–22, 40, 44, 48, 51n43; Jewish law, 40, 48; jurists, 10, *13*, 21, 30, 33–34, ;41, 50n18; Knatchbull's Act, 196; legislation, 24n17, 77, 97, 198–99, 203, 217, 251; literalist jurists, 21; Promissory Notes Act, 97; property law, 2, 100–1, 132, 195, 206; Roman law, x, 5, *13,* 20, 39–40, 48–49, 53nn68,89; rule of law, 96–97; savings bank act, 199; secular law, 40; Seditious Meetings Act, 198; Theodosian Code, *13*; Tonnage Act, 97; Unlawful Societies Act, 198; Visigothic law, 40; writs, 91–92. *See also* courts, Lex Rhodia
legitimacy, *14*, 16, 21, 263
Lex Rhodia (Rhodian Sea law), 5, 24n12, 73. *See also* government regulation
Liber Iudiciorum, 40
liberals, 195–96, 200
liability, vii–viii, x, 3, 5, 7, *14*, 16, 22–23, 35, 41, 49, 73–74, 76, 104, 203, 219, 230, 234, 241, 243–44, 247, 251, 253
liberty, 25n32, 96, 195
literacy, 2, 33, 37, 39, 44, 53n68
livelihood, 33, 190, 193, 234
logic: of feudal society, xii, 49, 96; of household production, 160, 191; justice in lending, 213, 232–36; of capitalism, xiii, 27, 38, 208n10, 222–23; of trade, 46, 49, 124, 131, 138; of tributary state, 30
lords, 41, 44, 63, 71, 85, 87, 100–1, 139
Louvre, 61
loyalty, 45, 88, 184, 204
Luther, Martin, 89, 242

Malet, Robert, 87
manillas, 127
manors, 37, 61, 86–87, 109n21; manorial register, 190
maps: major centers of financial innovation 2; Reconquest of Iberia, 36; Italian States c. 1599 AD, 58; Flows of Slaves out of Africa, 117; Degree of confirmation for model by commune and centre urbain, 153; mapping trophic flows, 262n29
markets, xiii–xv, 31–33, 37, 42, 46, 69, 73–74, 95, 99–100, 103, 106–7, 111nn63, 65–66, 118–19, 124–25, 128–29, 137, 169, 187nn3, 8, 193, 207–208, 210n64, 213, 215–22, 224–26, 229, 232–33, 236, 237n2, 238nn9,

15, 239nn44,46, 242, 258; bond market, 216; competitive market, 87, 225; commodity market, 185; credit market, 59, 216, 251; financial market, xv, 95, 98–99, 107, 220, 224–26, 229, 237n2, 238n9, 239n44; global market, 106, 229; illiquid market, 217; instability, xv, 219–20, 238n22; integrated market, 217; local market, 102, 156; mania, 99, 139, 219; market conditions, 64, 129, 219, 228; market confidence, 236; market correction, 219; market fundamentalism, 219, 225; market mortgage, xv, 207, 213; market participation, 145, 154, 156, 160, 225; market price, 4, 6, 19, 134, 219–20, 249; market resilience, 219; market segment, 229; self-regulating, 218–19; market share, 207, 231; stock market, 95, 98, 100, 111nn53,59,62–63,65–66, 112n85, 139, 216, 231, 242, 244, 259. *See also* economic concepts
marriage, 38–39, 45, 54n107, 91, 97
Marxism: accumulation by dispossession, 32, 103, 222–23, 231–232; capitalist circulation, 113n106, 222; capitalist production, 236, crisis of accumulation, 222, 231; factors of production, viii–ix, xii, xvi, 27, 57–58, 107, 204, 231, 247; labor-power, 110n43, 118, 140; labor theory of value, 245; means of production, 100, 118, 140, 190; mode of production, 46, 100, 164n6, 165n16, 260n4; relations of production, 83, 85, 247; underconsumption, 222; spatial-temporal fixes, 222–23
al-Masudi, 29
Mayhew, Henry, 191–93, 197
el Mayor, Sancho, 52n63

mayu and dama, 258
means of production, 100, 118, 140, 190, 247, 261n14
measures, 32, 147, 154, 193; of commodities, 67, 173; of ethnic domination, 175–80, 184–86, of resilience, 263n29. *See also* currencies
Medici. *See* Italian merchant bankers
medio general, 72; Medio Milenio de Credito, xvin6
Melissenos, Nikophoros, 6
Menckin, H. L., 244
mercantilism, xiii, 46, 140
merchants: Jewish, 45–47, 49, 51n28, 61n28, 63, 172; mobile, 37, 69, 71; normative practices, xiii, 1, 3–5, 16–18, 22, 26n49, 32–33, 35, 41–43, 46, 62–63, 67, 73–4, 90, 118, 121–22, 125, 127, 132, 134, 157, 205, 242, 246; reputation, 68, 85; state revenues and, 59. *See also* accounting; banking; corporations; credit; monte; trade
metals: copper, 31, 84, 101; gold, 8, *28*, 31–32, 35, 59–61, 66–67, 71–72, 76, 92, 110n43, 121–23, 129, 134, 143n56; iron, 31, 84; lead, 31; mercury, 31; silver, 31, 35, 45, 61, 65–67, 76, 89, 92, 101, 109n23, 110n43, 134, 138, 248
metaphors: invisible hand, 97, 256; the market, xii, 11, 19, 22, 27, 75, 96–97, 99, 103, 149, 187n11, 202–3, 206, 208, 216, 222, 224, 229, 236, 243, 249, 252; Main Street, 217; nine blind men and the elephant, 163; Panopticon, 108, 201; speculative bubbles, xv, 78, 98–100, 102, 138–40, 214, 218–20, 237, 246; Wall Street, 214, 217, *221*, 228, 240n67, 260n3
mevat (empty) lands, 9
middlemen, 128–34

migration, 159–60, 162
military, 6, 8–9, 17, 30, 35, 38, 42, 45, 61, 88, 91, 109n20, 119–20, 131, 141n9, *181*, *183*, 242, 260n3
mills, 8, 31, 87, 123
minorities, 7
miri lands, 7–8
misunderstandings, viii–xiv, 247
models: Chayanovian, 146–47, 151–55, 160–64; classical, xv; complexity, 224; conjunctural, 262n22; equilibrium, 220; Geertz, 173; Marxist, 189, 249–50; neoclassical, 223; non-equilibrium 220–21, non-linear, 219; opportunity cost, 246; sales financing, 201; social capital, 167–88; Sraffan, 247; statistical, 228; transformational growth, 261n14. *See also* economic concepts, Keynesian economics, metaphors
money of account, 66–67, 71
money lenders. 42, 46, 49, 55n113, 62, 131, 192–93, 196; predatory fees, 231; single premium credit insurance, 231
monte, 57, 64, 76–77; della Fede, 77; del Paschi di Siena, 64;
mortgage xiii, xv, 18, 44, 95, 100, 105, 204, 207–8, 213–18, 225–29, 231–32, 238nn6, 15, 239n46, 251
Mozilio, Angelo, 217
Mtougi, Caid, 158
mukhalat, 157
multicultural perspective, vii, ix, 243
multinomial coefficient (MC), 178, *179*

natural resources, 58
natural rights, 96
natural science, 29
National Association of Realtors, 218
negotiation over price, 170–71, 261n14
neighborhoods, 29, 191, 207, 232
neoliberalism, 105, 107, 206–11, 219, 225–26, 236, 238n28, 250;

Chicago School, 225; efficient market hypothesis, 219. *See also* economic concepts, theoretical arguments,
networks, viii–ix, xii–xiv, 32, 43, 63–64, 67–68, 77–78, 84–85, 100, 102–3, 110n42, 127, 130–31, 167–68, 172–73, 186, 187n3, 188n15, 191–92, 204, 218, 225, 233, 238nn7, 10, 12, 33–34, 239n35, 243–44, 247, 252–53, 262–63; commercial network, 84–85, 127; financial network, xi, 225, network analysis, 167; network risk, 225, 238nn7, 12, 33–34, 239n35; private network, 225; social network, viii–ix, xii, 68, 167–68, 243, 247; trade network, 68, 130, 131
nisba, 172, 174–80, 187n12

O'Neal, Sam, 217
obligations: borrower, 63, 191, 235, 252, 254–56; CDOs, 208, 214, 216, 229; civil, 11, 80n54; contractual, 17, 22; feudal, 58–59, 78n2, 86–87, 93–96, 100; friendly, *14*, 20; religious, 8; slave, 120; state, 121. *See also* gifts
OED, 237, 263n43
oligopoly, 171, 182, 185–86, 244, 251
Olivieri family, 77
on-farm equilibrium, 146–47, 161
ontology, 248
opaqueness, 100, 233
oppositions, hierarchical, 260n13
oracles, 132
Ottoman. *See* history
oversight, 208, 218–19
ownership, 2, *15*, 20, 65, 159, 185, 218, 252, 257

Pacioli, Friar Luca, 66, 79n21
Papacy, 61, 75–77, 85, 241; Curia, 68, 75; excommunication, 47

Index

Papal Councils: Ecumenical, 43; Lateran, 43, 54n107, 75, 81n61; of Coyanza, 54; of Nicaea, *13*, 43
Papal encyclicals and Papal bulls, 37, 60–62, 79nn7,9, 123: Ad providam , 62; Unum sanctam, 61; Vix pervenit, 76, 81n62;
paper: currency, 60; financial, 67, 69, 72, 100, 242
paradox: of gluttony, 220; of thrift, 220
Parliament, 63, 90, 97, 99, 103, 116, 139, 199
partnership, xiii, 3, 5–6, 9, *14–15*, 17, 32, 34, 39, 41, 44, 51n34, 73–74, 101, 103, 127; chreokoinonia, 3, 5; collegantia, 5; commenda, 3, 5–6, 9, 24n14, 25n42, 32, 39, 53n70, 131, 259; compagnia, 3, *14–15*, 17, 21, 24n16, 57, 73–75, 90, 230; fuori del corpo della compagnia, 74; hetaireia (formal partnership), 5; mandatum, 259; naruqqu contract, 259; societas, 3, *14*, 20, 44, 73
pastoralism, 12, 177
Paulson, Hank, 216
Paulson, John, 213, 231, 237
peasants, 46, 87, 101, 109n20, 146, 148, 151, 161, 163, 190–91, 195, 232, 244, 260n4
peddlers, 32, 193
peers of the realm, 99
Pegolotti, F. B., 66
pensions, 209n38, 213
Pérez, Joseph, 50n13
peripheralization of slum dwellers, 106
permits for trading in slaves, 124–25, 133, 137. *See also* asiento
Peruzzi. *See* Italian merchant bankers
pesticides, 234
philosophers: Aristotle (Aristotelian), 4, 10, 12, *13*, 15; Gaston Bachelard, 255, 263n32; Jeremy Bentham, 108, 201; Mario Bunge, 238n30, 261; Benjamin Constant, 257; Michel Foucault, 170, 187n5, 201, 210n61, 250, 261n22; Georg Hegel, 223; Thomas Hobbes, 96, 219; David Hume, 96, 110n47, 195; Immanuel Kant, 195; John Locke, 96, 110n46; Maimonides, 33; John Stuart Mill, (J. S. Mill) 195; Charles-Louis Montesquieu, 96, 110n48, 195; Martha Nussbaum, 261n19; Plato, 10, 12, *13*, 246; Karl Popper, 250, 261n21; Robert Putnam, 167; Jean-Jacques Rousseau, 96, 10n50
Phocaea alum mines, 65
places: Aragon, 37, 52n63; Africa, xiii,11, 29, 71, 84, 115–16, *117*, 118–25, 127–37, 139–41, 141nn2,6,14–18; 142nn20,23,26,28,30,34,37–42,51, 143nn52–54, 57–62, 64–66, 68, 73–74, 76, 80, 82, 85–86, 144n88, 208n12, 232–33, 239n61, 63, 252; Agora, xi, 5, 23; Ait Daoud, 148; al-Andalus (Andalus, Andalusia), 11, 27–28, 30–32, 34, 36–37, 39, 42, 48–49, 50n7, 51nn28, 44; Algarve coast, 122; Algeria, 51n44, 142n43; Alps, 84; Amazon, 228; America, 201, 210n65; Anatolia, 65; Angola, 136, 233; Anti-Atlas, 158; Argentina, 104, 233n8; Asia, 71, 84, 245; Asturia, 35; Australia, 103; Bahia, 136; Balearic Islands, 37; Balkans, 103; Basutoland, 103; Baltic Sea, 84; Benin, 122,128; Britain, 100–1, 103–4, 106, 112n74,76, 118–19, 135, 137–39, 156, 190, 196, 199, 209nn22, 46, 210nn51, 554; Brazil, 107, 123,135–37; Burma, 258, 263n42; Calabar, 132; Caliphate of Córdoba, 28, 30, 35, 50n13; Cambria, 52; Caribbean, 65, 136–37; Castile, 32, 44, 47,

241; Castile-León, 35, 37, 40, 47, 52n63, 54n100; Catalonia, 41, 52n63; Catholic europe, 29, 37, 40, 44, 48; Central America, 102; Congo (Kongo), 115–16, 233; Coymans, 138; Crete, 42; Dahomey, 128; Dakota, 207; Dar Fur, 116, 141n8; Denmark, 85, 135; Ebro valley, 31; Egypt, 206, 237, 240n70; England, xii, 60, 62–65, 70, 78, 83–89, 95, 97–99, 101, 104–6, 108n11, 109n16, 110nn36,42 111nn51, 55, 58, 60–61, 127, 135, 139, 192, 194, 199, 208nn5, 9, 13 209nn24–26, 28, 35, 49, 242, 261n15; Europe, viii–xii, xvin6, 1, *2*, 3, 7, 10–12, 15–16, 22, 25n42, 26n45, 27–29, 31–32, 35–40, 42, 44, 48–49, 50nn9, 12, 20, 52nn56, 63–64, 53n75,78, 54n92–93,109, 55n115, 57–61, 63–66, 70–72, 75–76, 78, 79nn11, 14, 17, 80nn43, 45, 83–84, 87–90, 94–96, 103–4, 108nn1, 3, 8, 110nn29, 32; 111nn68–69, 112nn78,92, 115, 118, 120–21, 125, 127, 129, 132, 134, 140, 141n12, 143nn33, 37, 144nn52, 63–64, 78, 81, 168, 186, 234, 241–45, 247, 255, 261nn13,15; Fernando Po, 122; Flanders, 61, 71–72, 127; France 46, 60–64, 68, 71, 79n8, 80n54, 84–85, 104, 108n9, 112n81, 127, 135–36, 186, 187n12, 188n25, 242, 260n4; Galicia, 32; Germany (allemagne), 65, 84–85, 102, 112n78, 127, 135, 156, 158, 163n1; Gibraltar, 42; Gold Coast, 103, 136; Greece, (Greek), vii, 3; Greenland, 71; Grigualand, 103; Guinea, 71, 122, 125; Guyenne, 61; Haha, 148, *150*, 151, 155, 159; Henchane, 154; Hispanola, 123; Holland, (Netherlands), 102, 110n42, 112n74,92, 112n78, 135–36; Holy Land, 37, 60–61; Iberia, (Iberian), viii, x–xi, 11, 18, 27–28, 31, 34–38, 42–45, 48–49, 52nn59, 63, 72, 120–21, 241–42, 244, 247–48; Ibiza, 42; Iceland, 218; Ida ou Gourd, 148, 155; Ida ou Zemzem (Zezmem), *150,* 159; India, 72, 120; Indies, (East) 117; (West) 102–3, 123; Indonesia, 135; Italy, x–xi, 3, 7, 9, 17–19, 24n16, 41, 57–58, 60, 64–65, 70, 73, 76–77, 83–84, 95, 110n42, 112n78, 135, 142, 242; Ireland, 127; Kenya, 164nn7, 10, 233; Korimat, 148, *150*; Labuan, 103; Latin America, 102–4; Levant, 31, 84; Lebanon, 42; Majorca, 42; Mali, 116, 164nn7,10, 210, 233–34, 239n65; Mauritania, 122, 142n23; Mediterranean, viii–x, 1–3, 9, 11, 21 24nn2, 14–15, 27–28, 31–33, 39, 41–42, 50n21, 51nn28, 35, 41, 61, 63, 65, 80n52, 84, 120, 142n24, 234, 245; Mercia, 86, 109n18; Mesopotamia, vii, 206, 247, 259, 259n1, 261; Mexico, 102–103, 107, 142n36, 208n10, 232; Middle East, x, 27; Minorca, 42; Morocco, xiii–xiv, 37, 42, 142, 145–46, *149*, 153, 156–59, 161–62, 163n1, 167–69, 172, 174–75, 185–86, 243; Mozambique, 136; Natal, 103; Near East, xi, *2*, 29, 168, 243, 261; Neknafa, 148, *150*, 155, 158; New World, xii, 116, 124–25, 133–34, 136; New Zealand, 103; Normandy, 85, 108n9; Oaxaca, 112n84; Papal State, 21, 64, 76–77; Pernambaco, 136; Piraeus, 5, 23; Portugal, 19, 32, 37, 79n10, 105, 119, 122–25, 134, 136, 238n32; Prussia, 104; Punjab, 103; Pyrennees, 32;

Red Sea, 116; River Loire, 84; River Wear, 198; Russia, 104, 148, 151, 160, 164n6, 165n15, 261n15; São Tomé, 122; Sahara, 116, 120, 122, 233; Sahel, 116, 131; Scandinavia, 85, 109n16; Scotland, 88, 135, 197, 209n35, 217; Shiadma, 148, *150*, 151, 155, 159; Siberia, 146; Sicily, 2, 42, 61; Sind, 103; Senegal, 122; Senegambia, 115–16, 121, 131; Smimou, 148, *150*, 155; Somalia, 120; South Dakota, 207; Sierra Leone, 103; Sous, 158; South America, 98, 136; Spain, xi, 3, 11, 18, 22, *28*, 39–40, 44–45, 48, 50nn6, 11, 14, 17, 19, 21 51nn22–26, 29–34,36,40,49, 52nn52, 58, 60, 63, 53nn68, 70, 76, 83–88, 54nn97–112, 55n116–23, 60, 70, 72, 79nn10,17, 99, 102, 119, 123–25, 134–36, 138–39, 142nn21, 45–47, 143n67; Sweden, 127, 135; Sudan, 116; Taftech, *149, 150*, 151–54, 163; Talmest, *150*, 153, 158; Tamanar, 148; Thessalonike, 6; Transvaal, 103; Trobriand, 257–58; Tunisia, 42; Tyrol, 65; Vatican, ix, xi, xvin5; Wales, 63, 101, 209nn26, 49; West Africa, 116, 120–22, 137, 141nn2, 4–5, 15, 142nn23, 26; Yorkshire, 199. *See also* cities and towns, cultural categories

plantations, 65, 117, 123, 134

politics, 27, 38, 46, 95, 119–20, 141n13, 186, 243, ; geopolitics, 60–62, 156–57; of debasement, 67

pollution, 260n9

Popes, 41, 75; Benedict IX, 62; Benedict XIV, 76, 81n62; Boniface VIII, 61–62, 79n6, 277; Clement V, 62, 75–76, 277; Clement VI, 75; Clement VII, 76; Gregory VII, 25n36, 54n107; Leo VI, the Wise, 5; Leo X, 76; Paul III, 76; Pius II, 123; *See also* Papal councils; Papal encyclicals; Papal bulls

portfolios: of consumers, xiv; of stock, 235. *See also* credit agencies

ports, 2, 9, 32, 42, 70, 124, 133–34, 136–37, 139, 156

poverty, 185, 196, 199, 232–32, 260n4; annona, 4; Knatchbull's Act, 196; microcredit, 210n54; the poor, xiv, 4, 10, 43, 47, 50n6, 60, 64, 76, 87, 105, 107, 132, 161–62, 190–93, 200, 206–7, 233–34, 237, 241, 244–45, 255; the Poor Laws, 101, 195; poor relief, vii, 31, 195–99

power: absolutist ideologies, 59, 96; abuse, 6–7, 59, 96, 195, 232, 259; access, x, 33, 95, 98, 101, 107, 119, 125, 146, 163, 169, 172–74, 177, 182, 185, 249, 252, 254, 258; Lord Acton, 195; advantage (near and long term), 190, 208n3; agency (to have…), 121, 223–24, 253; alliance, 38, 52n58, 88, 106, 156, 258; asymmetry of power, 226; boycotts, 132; bribery, 99; collusion, 64, 171, 184–185, 201; conquest, x–xi, 28, 31, 35, *36*, 37–39, 42, 44–46, 49, 52nn52,63 53n71, 61, 84, 88, 108n9, 121, 123, 242, 246; consensus, 12, 16, 18, 20, 50n18, 171, 234–35, 256; debtor's prisons, xiv, 194; elite(s), 4, 8–9, 24n6, 58–59, 64, 90, 107–8, 109n20, 161, 180, 203, 208, 227, 234, 237, 242–43, 246, 248, 250, 255–56, 261n15; empowerment, xv, 253–54; enslave(ment), 115–16, 123, 132, 141n6, exploitation, vii, 12, 77, 85, 90, 161, 241, 245, 247; force (enforcement), xii, xv, 5, 30, 33, 39, 41, 45–48, 59, 84–85, 87, 91, 95–96, 99–100, 118, 130, 132, 134, 140, 184,

192, 196, 242, 250–52, 254, 262n28; freedom, 96, 195, 241, 248; gate-keeping, 128; hegemony, 42, 53n66, 135, 138, 169; hidden interests, 9, 33, 93, 146, 162–63, 169, 186, 247–48, 256; hierarchy(ies) (hierarchical), xii, 32, 85–86, 120, 142n23, 170, 223, 247, 250–54, 257–59, 260n13, 262n29; immiseration, 246; Inquisition, 39, 48, 52n60, 54nn99–100, 55nn117,121,123, 62, 248; invasion, 83, 85, 108, 109n23; middle passage, 118–19, 133, 143n66; monopolies, xi, 17, 26n45, 31, 96, 98, 102, 118–19, 122–25, 135–38, 140, 168, 170, 177, 184, 195, 250; non-deterministic, 261n21; partiality, 48; patronage, 41, 44–45, 49, 77, 84, 108n14, 125, 173; pillage, 115, 248; pogroms, 39, 46–47; predatory lending, xiv, 207, 217, 232, 239n56; preemptive right, 15; preference, *14*, 18–19, 23, 116, 178, 186, 249; prejudice, 203, 243, 254; pressure, 46–47, 71, 73, 90–91, 99, 152, 195–96, 218, 231; privilege, xii, 30, 41, 45–46, 63, 84, 88, 98, 111n60, 140, 180, 195, 205, 226, 258; prominence, 71, 85; racism, 255; rapine, 115; sanction, xii, 85, 130, 132, 254–55, 263; status, xiii, 5, 21, 46–47, 85, 101, 107, 142n23, 157–59, 174, 180, *181, 182, 183*, 186, 235, 256; technologies of power, 85, 88–89, 245, 249; transparency (Freirean and Foucauldian), 48–49, 108, 168, 210n62, 213, 224–25, 230, 236, 262n25; tributary mode of production, 46. *See also* class; slavery; social structure; theoretical arguments

premiums, *14*, 15, 18, 69, 75, 77, 199, 215, 231

Prester John, 122

private party market regulation, 6, 23–24, 168, 207–8, 213–37; communis aestimation (estimates of the market community), *13*, 16; guilds, 41, 43, 70, 84, 168, 170; Hanseatic League, 41, 71, 84; hanses (associations), 84; monopolies, xi, 26n45, 31, 57–58, 76, 84, 96, 122, 135, 139–40, 195, 250; predatory lending, xiv, 207–8, 217, 232, 239n56

professions: commercial workers, *181, 182, 183;* farmers, 148, 155, 160, *162*, 164n7, 164n10, *181, 183*, 185, 233–34, 262n24; modern trades, 182; petty commerce, *181*, 182, *183*, 192; police, *181, 183*, 186n1; skilled workers, *181*, 182, *183*, 185, 198; service occupations, *181*, 182, *183;* trades (tradesmen), xiv, 92, 168–69, 172, 174–77, 182–86, 187n12, 198, 225; white-collar, *181, 183*. *See also* investors, livelihood, labor, workers

profit: excess, 12, 117–18, 125, 170, 192, 206, 208, 213, 215, 225, 245, 250; famine and, 16–17; just profits, 2, 219; justification of, *13–14*, 15–16, 18–19, 21, 23, 34, 51, 53n70, 58, 76, 98; liability and risk, vii–viii, x, xiv, 20, 41, 49, 75, 81n59, 235, 241, 244, 247; lower for the rich, 10, 261n15; regulation of profit margins, 4–5, 10. *See also* interest, investors, power

prohibitions, 2, 246. *See also* usury

protégé, 158–59

proverbs, 116

qualitative analysis, 18, 146, 167, 171, 227

quants, 243–44

Quran, 28, 30, 173

Radhaniya, 120
receipts, 33, 91–93
records, 50, 65–68, 77, 79n20, 81n63, 86–87, 89, 91–93, 108n1, 109n20, 119, 131, 146, 151; public records 201, 203
reeve, 86, 109n19
religious (religion, spiritual), 29, 32, 39–40, 89, 96, 243, 257, 259; Benedictines, 60; bida'at (heresy), 9; Catholic, x, 1, 4, 29, 37, 40, 43–44, 48, 63, 75, 80n54, 89, 136, 246, 259; Christ, 121–122; Christian, ix–x, 2–3, 9, 11–12, *13*, 18, 21–22, 24n14, 27, 29–40, 42–49, 50n13, 51n28, 52nn58,63, 53nn68,71, 54nn96–97,102,104,106–7,109,111–12, 55n116, 60–63, 71, 89–90, 121, 123, 219, 242, 247; conversos, 48; crusades, xi, 3, 28, 35–38, 60–61, 63, 198; dar al-harb, 21–22; dhimmi, 29, 48, 50n13; diaspora, 125–26, 131; divine order, x, 96; dogma, 222, 256; ecclesiastical, 45; encyclicals, 81nn61–62; faith, vii, 25nn32–34,38; 26nn48,51,54, 29, 34, 43, 89, 108, 148, 173; God, vii, 12, 29, 50nn9,12, 73, 90, 96; heresy, 62; ijma, 30, 50n18; indulgences, 89; infidels, 60, 132; Islam 21, 26, 29, 50nn9,12, 51nn42–43, 54n104, 116, 122; Jesuit, 19; Jewish, xiii, 11–12, 27, 30, 32–34, 36, 39–49, 50n13, 51n28, 55n113, 62–63, 120, 169, 172, 174, 180; judaic, 21; judíos, 50n13; Jews, x, 3, 7, 9, 12, 21–22, 27, 29–30, 32, 34, 37–40, 42–49, 50n13, 51n28; 53n71, 54nn97,102–4,106–7,109,111–12, 55nn113,116,118–19, 61–63, 79n10, 104, 121, *181,* 182, 188n18; Judaic tradition, 11; Judeo-Christian tradition, vii, xi; monasteries, 4, 6; mosques, 29–31, 186; Mozarab Christians, 38; Mudejars, 38–29; Muslims, x, 3, 7, 12, 21–23, 27, 29–31, 33–35, 37–40, 42–43, 47–49, 52n58, 53n71, 55n122, 71, 121–22, 219; Muzarab/Mozarab, 30, 38–39; orthodox, 9–10; pilgrimages, 60; pious foundations, 10; Psalms, *13*; priest, 29; prophet(s), xvn2, 50n18, 174; Protestant; rabbi, 29; responsa, 34, 50n18, 51n44; Sabbath, 22; sacred, viii, 60, 132, 256; sacrosanct, 244; sadaqa, 173, 257; schism, 11, 121; sin, 12; temples, 21, 60, 254–55, 259, 263n31; ulema, 29; zadaqa, 257; zakat, 31. *See also* Papacy, Papal councils, Papal encyclicals and bulls, Scholastics
repartimento documents, 52n59
repayment, 9, 16, 59, 69, 96, 132, 156, 191, 206, 247; deferred, 33, 91; prepayment, 7, 44, 231
resilience, 219, 222, 263n29
resistance, 11, 22–23, 31, 101, 133, 249–50
rewards, 22, 41, 46, 49, 171, 259
Reynal, Pedro Gomez, 125
Richard of Middleton, 11
Richeleau, Duc de, 103
Ridolfi, Lorenzo di Antonio, 80
rights, human, 52n59, 86, 96, 107, 120, 203, 206; and capabilities, 249; divine right, 97, 140
risk, 22; actuarial risk, 203; automated systems, 227–28; concealment, xv; control-by-risk screening, 227–28; fat tail, 228; historical performance, 235; Levels program, 228; rating agency, 189, 234–35 minimizing risk, 235; risk management, 224, 227, 231; risky ventures, 103, 235; statistical methods 228

rivers: Loire, 84; Niger, 122, 131; Rhine, 84; Rhone, 84; Tagus; Thames, 197
Roots of Western Finance, vii, 12, 50n18, 53n70, 54n91, 186, 255, 277
Rothschild, 102, 104

sahib al-mazalim, 32
sailors, xiii, 124, 126–27, 129
saqaliba (slaves of Slavic origin in Iberia), 120
savings and loans (S&L): finance companies, xiv, 201; friendly society, xiv, 196–99; installment savings, xiv; Mechanic Institute, 199; National Debt Commissioners, 199; penny bank, xiv, 196, 199; postal saving, xiv, 199; Post Office Savings Bank, 199–200; savings bank, xiv, 199–200, 210n54; Trustee Savings Bank, 199–200; Yorkshire Penny Bank, 199
scapegoats, 49, 62, 89
scholars. *See* economists; philosophers; Scholastics; social scientists
scholastics as reactionary opponents of progress, 49
Scholastics: St. Antonine, 1, 11, *14*, 18, 23, 26; Thomas Aquinas, 11–18, 54n92, 80n54; San Bernadino, *14*, 18; Gabriel Biel, *15*; Alexander Bonini, *13–14*; Jean Buridan, *13–14*, 16–17, 242; Cardinal Cajetan, *13*, 16, 19, 25–26; Giles of Lessine, *13*; Hostiensis, *14*, 25n36; Huguccio, *13*, *15*, 20; Leonard Lessius, *14*, 20; Michael of Ephesus, 4, 15; Luis de Molina, 11, *14*, 18–19, 25n38; Domingo de Bañez de Mondragon, *14*, 19; Martin de Azpilcueta Navarrus, 14, 18–19, 25n38; Pierre de Jean Olivi, *14*, 17; Richard of Middleton, 11; Duns Scotus, 10; Domingo de Soto, 19, 25–26; Conrad Summenhart, *14–15*, 18
Scholastic financial ideas: cambium et recambium, 26n50, 68–69; carentia pecuniae (absence of money), *14*, 20; census, *15*, 19, 21; Comentario resolutoio de usuras, 19; commodatum, *15*, 20; communis aestimatio (estimates of the market community), *13*, 16; commutative justice, 11, 23; compagnia, 2, *14*, *15*, 17, 21, 24n16, 51, 73–75, 90, 230; complacibilitas, *14*, 17, 242; damnum emergens, *13*, 15, 18, 20, 54n92; distributive justice, 11, 23; industria (merchant diligence), *14*, 18; intent, *14*, 19, 23, 26n50, 203; just price, 4, 10–12, *13*, 16–19, 22–23, 40; labores, *14*, 18; stipendium laboris, 15; laesio enormis, *13*, 16; licit exchange, *14*, 17; loco pignoris, *14*, 15; lucrum cessans, *14*, 15, 18–20; mutuum, *15*, 20; mercatores romanum curiam sequentes, 75; pecunia non parit pecuniam, 10, *13*; pericula, *14*, 18; poena conventionalis, *13*, 16; propter periculum, *13*, 15–16; publicum utilitatem public good, *13*, 16, 26n48; raritas, *14*, 17; solicitudo, *14*, 18; Summa Theologica, 54n92; time preference, 14, 18–19, 23; trifold basis for value, 17–18; turpe lucrum, 12, *13*; undervaluation of future goods, 18, 249; virtuositas (utility), *14*, 17. *See also* credit, ethical motivations in finance
scrivener, 101, 126
Seas: Mediterranean, 2, 24n2, 28, 32, 41–42, 84, 234; North, 84; Red, 116

secular, ix–x, 11, 40, 45, 48, 61, 77–78, 90, 96, 108n1, 241
securities, 41, 98, 100, 107, 138–39, 208, 213–18, 225, 228–29
security, 38, 41, 63, 73, 92, 105–6, 130–31, 158, 192–94, 201, 203, 215, 226, 241
Seebohm Rowntree, 199
semsar, 157
serfs, 86–87, 109n21
serial monogamy, 142n23
Shannon diversity, 177. *See also* indices
shares, 34, 57, 64, 95, 99–100, 107, 126–27, 138–39, 157, 231, 249n69; sharecropping, 31, 159, 164n6, 249; shareholders, 215
sheriff, 87, 90–91, 93, 109n19
shire-reeve, 109n19. *See also* reeve, sheriff
Sidi Musa, 158
Siete Partidas. *See* government regulation
Sikes, C.W., 199
silk, 29, 31, 71, 84, 127, *176*, *179*, 184, 202
simulation, 44; triple contract, 44
slavery, 115–44; male vs. female, 116, 120–21, 128, 142n23; white, 120; The Slave's Lot, 116
social capital, iii, viii–ix, xiv, 21, 32–33, 43, 74, 77–78, 84, 105, 124–25, 167–69, 186, 187n2, 204, 224, 242–44, 247–48, 250, 255, 259n1; amicitia, 20, 78
social contract, 96, 110n50
social scientists: Arjun Appadurai, 170, 186, 187n7; Zygmunt Bauman, 262n27; Jeremy Bentham, 108, 201; Pierre Bourdieu, 167, 186, 204, 210nn74–75, 250, 257, 261n21, 263nn32,38; Charles Darwin, 244, 260n3; Alexis de Tocqueville, 195; Donald Donham, 260n6; Louis Dumont, 247, 260n13; Emile Durkheim, 257, 263n35; Clifford Geertz, xiv, 167–75, *176*, 176, 179–80, *181*, 182–84, 186, 186n1, 187nn4, 9, 188nn13–14,16,18–22, 24; Jack Goody, viii, xvin3, 243, 260n2; Antonio Gramsci (Gramscian), 247, 250; Edmund Leach, 258; Steven Lukes, 187n5, 250–51, 260n13, 261n21; Bronislaw Malinowski, 257, 263nn39–40; Marcel Mauss, 256–57, 263nn34, 36–37; Charles-Louis Montesquieu, 96, 110n48, 195, 257; Alexandra Ouroussoff, 234, 240n67; Robert Parkin, 260n13; William Roseberry, xvin6; 111n70, 187n5; Lawrence Rosen, 169, 174, 187nn4, 8 188nn15, 17; Robert Ulanowicz, 263; Poe Yu-Ze Wan, 238n30, 261n19; Loïc Wacquant, 204; Max Weber, viii, 27, 49n3, 170, 242–43, 250, 263n31; Eric Wolf, xvin6, 50n20, 55n15, 100, 111n68, 141n12, 142nn33, 37, 143nn52, 63–64, 78–79, 81, 187n5, 250, 263n41
social structure, 129, 142n23, 146, 198; hierarchy, xii, 32, 86, 142n23, 247, 250–53, 259;
societas. *See* partnerships
sokeman, 109
sorcery, 132
South Sea Bubble. *See* gambling and speculation
Spinelli *See* Italian merchant bankers
state offices: governor, 30, 50n7, 64,125; Vizier, 8, 30 *See* debt collection
Sultan, 9, 157–58, 168
Sultanate of Dar Fur, 116
summum bonum, 251
surveillance, 108, 201, 210n72, 262n25
Sumerian, 253, 259
sunna, 30, 50n18
sūq, 167–88

surplus and savings banks, 199
surplus-value, xv, 221
symbolism, xiii, 29, 95, 100, 106–7, 185, 245, 250, 255, 257–58, 261n20

ta'ifas, 35–36, 38
tallies (tally). *See* accounting
Tappen, Lewis, 202
tasdīq (faith), 173
taxes, 4, 6–8, 10, 17, 26n45, 30, 38, 44–45, 47, 59, 60, 63, 65, 76, 84, 86–87, 91–93, 96–97, 101, 126, 147–48, 155, 157, 168, 195, 249; khazin al-mal, 31; levy, 86–87; Tobin tax, 226
techniques of the self, 261n22
teleological argument, 223
Templars. *See* banking
tenants, 31, 86–88, 91, 101, 108n13, 109n21, 190; tenants in chief, 86–88, 91, 108
tensors, 12, 19, 23, 253; vector 262n28. *See also* theoretical arguments
tenure, 83, 86, 100, 101, 109n15, 148, 156, 158, 160; copyhold tenure, 190; inheritable tenancy, 190; private property, 262n27
Teruel, 45. *See also* fuero
theoretical arguments: abstraction, xii–xiii, 95, 105–8, 204, 230, 236; austerity, 256; bureaucracy, 250, 263; chaos theory, 224, 228; Chayanovian analysis, xiv, 159–65; combinatorial analysis, 177–188; competition, viii, xi, 24, 132, 171, 184–85, 187n12, 221–22, 225, 244, 247, 251; contextual pentad for finance, vii; cybernetics, 223; debasement, 9, 59, 60, 67, 71, 88, 94; demand, xi, 15, 17, 64, 121, 123, 129, 134–35, 138, 172, 214, 229, 261n14; development, ; distribution, 23, 77, 146, 156, 175–80, 182–83, 186, 188n21, 219–20, 230, 244, 246–47, 261n20; entropy, 177, 260n9; equilibrium, xv, 146–47, 161, 219–21, 224, 238, 261n14; externalities, 223; General Systems Theory (GTS), 223; marginal analysis, 106, 259; modernity, 100; neoclassical economics, 118, 161, 171, 219, 223–24, 249, 253, 261n14; neofunctionalism, 223; Neo-Weberian, 170; postmodernism, xvi; propensities, 251, 261n21; redirection of financial analysis toward a focus on inequalities, viii, 244, 248, 250; thermodynamics, 260n9; transformational growth, 261n14; under-consumptionist theory, 189; undervaluation of future goods (discounting), 18, 249; World System, 141n11, 170. *See also* complexity; discretization; economic concepts; economists; indices; interest; Marxism; neoliberalism; philosophers; power; Scholastic financial ideas; social scientists; tensors
Thomas à Becket, 61
timar, 8
Time Magazine, 217
tiraz, 31
tithes, xi, 61, 75
Tolpuddle Martyrs, 198
trade: administered trade, 32, 96–97, 119, 133, 135; assortment trading, 129–30; Atlantic slave trade, 115–44; Japanese, 127; maritime, ix, xi–xii, 2, 6, 24n12, 32–33, 35, 41–42, 57, 60–61, 71, 73, 75, 84, 97, 99, 119, 122, 124–29, 131, 133–34, 136–39, 141n6, 143n66, 198; trade routes, 32, 42, 53n82, 60, 131, trans-Saharan slave trade, 120, 142n20; triangular trade, xiii

Index

transaction vii, x, xii, 3–4, 6, 10, 32–35, 40, 44, 46, 50n18, 62–63, 65–69, 71–73, 77, 85, 87, 93, 96, 101, 103, 127, 135, 159, 170–73, 184, 192–92, 206, 222, 225, 249–50, 253, 258;
tranches. *See* credit innovations
transparency, vii–viii, x, 6, 22–23, 32–35, 40, 44, 48–49, 50n18, 108, 168, 213, 225, 230, 236, 241, 251; Freirean and Foucauldian, 262n25. *See also* ethical motivations in finance
treasuries, 30–31, 45, 47, 61, 76, 81n63 91, 99, 103, 135, 206, 214, 216, 218, 232
Treaties: of Alcaçovas, 123, 125; of St. Clair sur Epte, 108n9; of Utrecht, 98; of Versailles, 156
tribute, 28, 38, 46, 87, 96, 109n23
trope of unjust African rulers, 115–16

Umar Tal, 116
urbanism, viii, x, xiv, 10, 27, 35–36, 57, 70–71, 77, 84, 145, 148, 167–88, 190, 241–43, 245
'urf, 173
usufruct, 6, 8–9, *15*, 20, 44
usury, vii, 1, 6, 10–15, *14*, 17–25, 26n50, 33–34, 40, 43–47, 49, 55n113, 62–63, 68–71, 74–76, 78, 80n54, 89–90, 93, 130, 192, 206–7, 242, 246–47; opprobrium on, 54n91; politics of, 46. *See also* interest

vakf. *See* waqf
valentia, 253
vapnatak. *See* wapentake
vassals, 24n1, 86, 88, 108n1, 116
Victorian, 196, 209n46, 210n55
villains, 86–87, 109n20, 217
vouchers, 235

wapentake. *See* hundreds
waqf, xiv, 8, 168, 186
wars, 21, 37–38; civil, 88–89; corporate, 99, 240n67; between England and Spain, 99, 139; Hundred Years, 63; against Islam, 122; Second Dutch, 137; with French, 138; against Louis XIV, 97; with Spain and Portugal, 136; with Sicily, 61; WWI, 156; WWII, 107
warfare, xi, 36, 38, 41, 88, 96, 130, 132, 137
women, xii, 46, 88, 91, 116, 129, 139, 142n23, 191–92, 206
workers, 100, 164n11; blue collar, 193, 195–99, 221, 233, 245; commerce, 183, 185; skilled, 182–83; wage, 191
workhouses, 196, 198
worship, 29, 62, 256

ziamets, 8
Zwifach Buchhalten, 66

About the Authors

James B. Greenberg is professor of anthropology, and a senior research anthropologist in the School of Anthropology at the University of Arizona. He received his PhD from the University of Michigan in 1978. His areas of expertise lie in economic anthropology, political ecology, globalization, and law and development. His books include *The Roots of Western Finance*, with Thomas K. Park, (Lexington Books, 2017); *Neoliberalism and Commodity Production in Mexico* (University of Colorado Press, 2012); *Reimagining Political Ecology* (Duke University Press, 2006); *Blood Ties: Life and Violence in Rural Mexico* (University of Arizona Press, 1990); and *Santiago's Sword: Chatino Peasant Religion and Economics* (University of California Press, 1982).

Thomas K. Park has taught in the School of Anthropology at the University of Arizona since 1986. He received a joint PhD in anthropology and comparative world history from the University of Wisconsin–Madison in 1983, an MA in agricultural economics in 1982, and a BA with Joint First Class Honors in anthropology and philosophy from McGill University in 1974. He has worked extensively in North Africa and across sub-Saharan Africa on urban and rural development. In 2017, he also published (with James B. Greenberg) *The Roots of Western Finance: Power, Ethics, and Social Capital in the Ancient World*, which examines financial history between 4000 BC and the twelfth century AD from a multicultural perspective.